TURKISH DYNAMICS

THE MIDDLE EAST IN FOCUS

The Middle East has become simultaneously the world's most controversial, crisis-ridden, and yet least-understood region. Taking new perspectives on the area that has undergone the most dramatic changes, the Middle East in Focus series, edited by Barry Rubin, seeks to bring the best, most accurate expertise to bear for understanding the area's countries, issues, and problems. The resulting books are designed to be balanced, accurate, and comprehensive compendiums of both facts and analysis presented clearly for both experts and the general reader.

Series Editor: Barry Rubin

Director, Global Research International Affairs (GLORIA)
Center Editor, *Middle East Review of International Affairs* (MERIA)
Journal Editor, *Turkish Studies*

Turkish Dynamics: Bridge Across Troubled Lands
By Ersin Kalaycıoğlu

Eternal Iran: Continuity and Chaos
By Patrick Clawson and Michael Rubin

Turkish Dynamics

Bridge Across Troubled Lands

Ersin Kalaycıoğlu

First published in 2005 by
PALGRAVE MACMILLAN™
175 Fifth Avenue, New York, N.Y. 10010 and
Houndmills, Basingstoke, Hampshire, England RG21 6XS
Companies and representatives throughout the world.

PALGRAVE MACMILLAN is the global academic imprint of the Palgrave Macmillan division of St. Martin's Press, LLC and of Palgrave Macmillan Ltd. Macmillan® is a registered trademark in the United States, United Kingdom and other countries. Palgrave is a registered trademark in the European Union and other countries.

ISBN 1–4039–6279–0
ISBN 1–4039–6280–4 (pbk.)

Library of Congress Cataloging-in-Publication Data

Kalaycıoğlu, Ersin.
    Turkish dynamics : bridge across troubled lands / Ersin Kalaycıoğlu.
      p. cm.—(Middle East in focus series)
    Includes bibliographical references and index.
    ISBN 1–4039–6279–0—ISBN 1–4039–6280–4 (pbk.)
    1. Turkey—Politics and government—20th century. 2. Turkey—History—20th century. I. Title. II. Series.

DR576.K35 2005
956.1′02—dc22   2005045955

A catalogue record for this book is available from the British Library.

Design by Newgen Imaging Systems (P) Ltd., Chennai, India.

First edition: November 2005

10 9 8 7 6 5 4 3 2 1

Printed in the United States of America.

To Sema, Öykü, and Petek

CONTENTS

Acknowledgments

I have been working on this book since the summer of 2002, which more or less coincided with the start of my work at Sabanci University, Faculty of Arts and Social Sciences, Istanbul, Turkey. I have finished the first draft of the book while I was still employed at Sabanci University, where I had the assistance of Mustafa Oğuz, Rita Koryan, and Egemen Özalp. My collaborations with professors Üstün Ergüder, Ali Çarkoğlu, Korel Göymen, and Ahmet Evin, all of Sabanci University have also contributed to my work. I would also like to take this opportunity to thank Professor Barry Rubin for his critique and help in the publication of this text. I would also like to acknowledge the efforts of Dr. David Pervin of Palgrave, who was although at times painstakingly slow, made valuable criticisms on the draft of this book.

I would also like to thank Hilmi Çelik, the Librarian of Sabanci University, and Ersen Kavaklıoğlu of the Sabanci University for their assistance in compiling the data and for the multimedia services they kindly provided. I am grateful for the research infrastructure and assistance that the Sabanci University provided for such work to be completed.

My wife Sema and daughters Öykü and Petek have been of great help with their encouragements and patience with the long hours I put in the composition of the manuscript.

I would also like to acknowledge the secretarial assistance provided by Ipek Dübüş of Işık University for the final edition and composition of this manuscript.

List of Figures, Tables, and Maps

Figures

Tables

Maps

PREFACE

The story of Turkey is one of the most remarkable histories of development and change in all of modern times. What can now be called the first act in that drama is well-known. After the Ottoman Empire collapsed during World War I and much of the country was occupied by foreign forces, a great leader arose to reinvent the country in modern and nationalist terms.

Kemal Atatürk created a republic, replacing the centuries'-old Ottoman monarchy. He invoked Western civilization as the country's role model and joining Europe as its long-term goal. Multiparty democracy was the short-term objective. The new leader pushed Islam out of public life, extolling secularism. He reformed the Turkish language to move it toward Western tongues and away from Arabic and Persian. Women were given equal rights. Economic development, led by the state itself, became a driving priority. Turks were redefined as an old nation which encompassed all the people of Anatolia and none outside. Territorial expansionism or even an attempt to regain lost Ottoman territory was rejected in favor of a policy of peace.

Atatürk fought for these objectives during the remainder of his life, which ended in 1938, and his successor, Ismet Inonu, carried on the task until 1950. Yet afterward, when the political hegemony of the party Atatürk established was successfully challenged, the Atatürk era continued, even up to the end of the twentieth century.

This book describes this process in detail, with a keen analysis and a balanced perspective. Few are as qualified to do so as is Ersin Kalaycıoğlu, who I regard as the best chronicler of Turkish politics. But there are also two newer, far more original, tasks that this book tackles.

The first of those are the consequences of the Atatürk era's success. True, Turkey suffered many problems in the decades after Atatürk established the republic. There were many foreign policy challenges, all successfully met. Turkey avoided entanglement in World War II until the very end, a path its leaders saw as the only way to avoid German or Soviet domination. It entered into an alliance with the Western democracies to protect itself in the Cold War period. Decades of friction with Greece were weathered without resort to war. The currents of the perilous Middle East were managed. And by the century's end, Turkey was on course to full—albeit still distant—membership in the European Union.

In economic terms, the country's development was nothing short of spectacular. Using a rich base of agricultural and other resources, Turkey made progress on every front, transforming itself into an industrial state while still retaining a high agricultural productivity. There were certainly setbacks and economic depressions along the way, and Turkey did not catch up to Europe. But the gaps were closed considerably and the country made a bigger leap than virtually any other non-Western state outside of Japan.

The social and political fronts were more persistently troublesome. The highly centralized and bureaucratic structure of the republic, necessary at an earlier point, became burdensome. Corruption proved hard to root out. A wide gap opened within the country between the prosperous center and the poorer, less advanced periphery (notably in the east). This neglect and identity issues led to the rise of a massive Kurdish problem which sparked a war that Turkey eventually won though with heavy losses.

There were thus more and less developed areas, democracy combined with a bureaucracy and government that limited citizens' rights and civil society, incipient ethnic conflicts, and other such problems.

But this was only part of the problem in the political sphere. Instability arose also from the weakness of party structures, leadership, and constitutional frameworks. Finding an electoral majority was a difficult task, with governments being built on constantly shifting coalitions. At times, extremists of left and right fought in the streets. As a result, the military—which saw itself as the guardian of Atatürkist virtues—repeatedly had to intervene. Yet if the system's problem was the sporadic coups, its strength was that each one returned the country to a democratic system.

By the end of the twentieth century, the Atatürkist system had achieved most of its objectives. Would Turks continue to accept it as the only framework in which the country could live, as the very definition of their society and identity? In the early 1990s such a development was almost unimaginable. A decade later, by the early twenty-first century, it was undeniable.

This does not mean that Turks jettisoned all the principles and concepts of Atatürkism. But consider the fate of Atatürk's six "arrows." This was a way of summarizing the main principles of his political ideology and these ideas were enshrined in the country's 1937 constitution. They are secularism, republicanism, nationalism, populism, statism, and reformism.

Secularism had clearly eroded, partly in the face of massive immigration from the more traditional villages into the main cities. This was Islam Turkish-style, lacking the hard edge of Islamism in the Arab world and elsewhere. But whether the Turkish Islamists were genuinely more moderate or simply professed such positions because they knew that a great extremism was politically disadvantageous was a matter of dispute.

Turkey remained a largely secular country. The electoral victories of Islamic parties were due in large part to the disorganized and divided alternatives rather than a widespread desire for a religiously directed state. Still, in terms of this issue the post–Atatürkist Turkey is unrecognizable in regard to its founder's intentions.

Republicanism meant that Turkey would be a democratic state based on a multiparty system, free elections, and the rule of law. While the system has

repeatedly broken down, the armed forces—though this seems a contradiction in terms—did indeed restore a stable republic by means of temporary
military coups and altering the constitution on several occasions.

Certainly, Turkey remains a republic. Arguably, the post–Atatürk era has
gone further in realizing that ideal. For the first half-century after its establishment, Turkey was a highly paternalistic state largely dominated by a single
party. A powerful national civilian bureaucracy and armed forces also wielded
extensive power. Since then the system has steadily widened and civil
society—though still fragile—has begun to play an independent role. This
process was furthered by changes demanded as part of the price for membership
by the European Union.

Populism was a third basic principle of Atatürk, the notion that the state
was responsive to the will of the people. This idea, of course, was quite different from the way the country had been conceived and run during the centuries of the Ottoman Empire that preceded the establishment of modern
Turkey.

Yet, as noted above regarding the republican concept, the people played
only a limited role in Atatürkist Turkey. Aside from the official top–down
hierarchies was the structuring of political parties controlled very much from
the leadership. The public's role was largely to obey the central government
and establishment in Ankara rather than to debate or decide. Interest groups
have organized to lobby for their own goals and needs. Again, the trend has
been toward a further opening up of the system—arguably a greater fulfill-
ment of populism—as the provinces and nonestablishment forces say more
and have more of a say.

The fourth principal is that of nationalism, defined as a highly unitary
identity of all citizens as Turks who had great loyalty to the state. Religion
and ethnicity were to be obliterated as factors shaping identity. Like many
aspects of Atatürk's creed, this was not only an attempt to apply modern concepts but also a reaction against the fragmentation of identities which had
caused the Ottoman Empire to collapse.

Clearly, the main challenge to this notion came from the Kurds, a non-
Turkic people who inhabited the country's poorer southeastern region. A
long Kurdish rebellion led by radical separatist forces cost the country dearly
in blood and resources before being defeated. It is easy to overstate the
nature of this issue. Individuals move easily across the lines denoting "Turk"
and "Kurd."

The great majority of Kurds want to remain within Turkey and to a large
degree are assimilated into the mainstream. Still, the opening up of this issue
has undermined the traditional Atatürkist concept. Moreover, European
Union pressure has opened up the extent of Kurdish communal rights,
though tremendous pressure continues to be brought to bear against
Kurdish organizations and political groupings.

To some extent, other debates have opened regarding Turkish identity. The
Alevis, are openly distinctive, a large religious grouping which—in opposition
to an Islamism they perceive as threatening—support secularism. Interest in

the newly independent Turkic states carved from the Soviet Union as well as the turmoil in the Balkans has inspired some increased expression of the identity of those ethnic Turks who came originally from these areas as well.

The fifth of the sixth arrows, statism, has failed even more poorly. As in other countries, a high level of state activity was needed to develop the Turkish economy into a modern industrial and commercial one. But this necessary stage was also a transient one. The state began to constrain development through its inflexibility and bureaucracy. Prime Minister Turgut Ozal recognized this problem and pressed for privatization. The domination of the state continues to inhibit progress and is continually being reduced.

Finally, the sixth arrow, reformism, is a bit more vague as a concept. It basically means a willingness to bring change, breaking with the continuity prized by traditional society. Inasmuch as Turkey has accepted this as a basic principle, it is able to modernize and adapt to the modern world.

To summarize, three of the arrows—republicanism, reformism, and populism—have been further extended in the post–Atatürkist era, while another three—secularism, nationalism, and statism—have eroded in importance and application.

In international terms, the main change made by Turkey into the post–Atatürkist era is its growing importance. This is partly due to Turkey's relative stability and successful development as well as partly being due to geographical factors. From being the "sick man of Europe" in Ottoman times, Turkey is now a medium-ranked power which has surpassed virtually the entire Third World and belongs in Europe.

It has played an important role as an ally of the United States, as a factor in Middle East considerations, as a patron for the ethnic Turkic states emerging from the Soviet Union, as a significant player in trying to cope with Balkan crises, and in many other ways.

This is the dynamic country and the remarkable evolution so well represented in Ersin Kalaycioğlu's book.

—Barry Rubin, director, Global Research in
International Affairs (GLORIA) Center, and
editor of the Palgrave Middle East in Focus series

Introduction: Change and Stability

It is not hard to notice the name of Turkey being mentioned frequently in the international media and in most major daily newspapers in many parts of the world. Turkey was mentioned in the press and media in the recent years when she applied for full membership in the European Union in 1987, or when the Turkish troops took part in the Stability Force in Bosnia-Herzegovina that came to serve as a peace mission since 1996. Indeed, Turkish troops have been similarly serving in Macedonia to sustain the peace efforts there. Turkey participated in the military campaign of North Atlantic Treaty Organization (NATO) against the Yugoslav army in Kosovo in 1999. Turkey was one of the first countries to condemn the attacks of September 11, 2001 in New York City, Washington, DC. and Pennsylvania, and declare allegiance with the United States in the "war against terror." Turkey took over from Britain the command of the 5,350-strong International Security Assistance Force (ISAF) in Afghanistan on June 20, 2002 for a period of six months, and again in January 2005. Soccer fans would also recall that the Turkish national team came only third to Brazil and Germany in the World Cup finals in Japan and Korea in 2002. Indeed, whenever the Iraqi crisis recurred from 1990 until 2003 Turkey's name reappeared in the press and the media around the globe. More recently, on November 15 and November 20, 2003 four bombs exploded in the city of Istanbul, Turkey, which devastated parts of two ancient synagogues, the British Consulate and the headquarters of the HSBC bank in Turkey. More than 60 people died in those ominous attacks, hundreds were wounded, and some were crippled for life. Turkey and its main cultural and industrial metropolis Istanbul in particular, thus became the target of attacks of some al-Qaeda cells in Turkey. As a NATO member democracy with a large Muslim population, and also as a member of the Islamic Conference Organization (ICO) the Turkish involvement in peace and/or stabilization missions, and especially in the last case of its participation in the war against terror have been considered as a critical move by the United States, Britain, and their allies.

A Closer Look at the Turkish Society

World Development Report of 2005 reports the most recent population figure for Turkey for the year 2003 and as 70.7 millions, and in 1990–2003 it grew by about 1.8 percent per annum.[1] The population of the country grows by more than one million per year in the early 2000s. However, the demographers indicate that the population growth rate is following a dropping trajectory.[2] Indeed, in the 1980s average annual growth rate of the population was 2.3 percent, which dropped to 1.5 percent per annum in the 1990s.[3] Demographers project that the Turkish population growth rate will eventually drop down to 0 percent per annum by about the middle of the twenty-first century.[4] The same projections indicate that Turkey will have a population of about 84.4 million in 2020 and 88.0 million by 2025.[5] Of that population approximately 97 percent indicate some degree of affiliation with Islam. Very small numbers of Greek Orthodox, Armenian Catholic, Gregorian, Roman Catholic, Protestant, Jewish, Assyrian, Yazidi, agnostics and atheists constitute the rest of the 3 percent of the population. Ethnic composition of the country is no less mixed, yet most consider themselves as Turks (reliable surveys report that anywhere between 60 and 75 percent identify themselves as Turks), among the rest Kurds (about 12 percent of the population), Abkhaz, Chechen, Albanian, Arab, Laz, and so on emerge as other ethnic groups, which constitute the rest of the 3–5 percent of the Turkish society.

Turkey had a Gross National Income (GNI) of $473 billions in 2003[6] and the Gross National Product (GNP) of Turkey for 2004 is estimated as $273 billions,[7] which places Turkey as the twenty-second largest economy in the world, with a per capita income of about $2790 (or GNI measured at purchasing power parity (ppp) of $6690 per capita).[8] Owing to a severe financial crisis in the country the Turkish economy went through a severe meltdown in 2001, and the GNP per capita fell down to $2.190 (and GNP measured at ppp per capita fell to $6012).[9] The economy started to recover in 2002, and hence the most recent statistics indicate considerable variations in those figures for 2001, 2002, and 2003. Although the financial crisis of 2001 was an unprecedented event in the history of the Turkish Republic, the Turkish economic growth pattern has always been somewhat erratic (see figure I.1). Indeed, a closer look at figure I.1 gives the impression that the Turkish economy lurches from one crisis to another. Nevertheless, by most accounts Turkey demonstrates the characteristics of a newly industrializing country, or if we adopt the terminology and use the indicators of the World Development Report Turkey is a lower middle-income economy.[10]

Interestingly enough Turkey has been a member of the Organization for Economic Co-operation and Development (OECD) alongside with Japan, United States, Germany, Britain, France, Canada, Italy, and other postindustrial economies. Turkey has also been a member of Council of Europe since 1949 and of the NATO since 1952.

Turkey has also been seeking full membership in the European Union (EU) since its early days (1959–1963), when it was only a humble Common Market of six countries of Western Europe, established only in 1957. In 1963 Turkey established associate membership with the Common Market, which evolved into the European Economic Community (EEC), the European Community (EC), and eventually into the (EU). In 1995 Turkey established

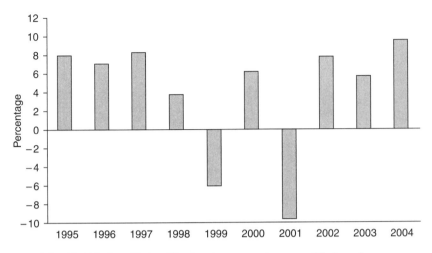

Figure I.1: Turkish Gross National Product (constant prices, annual % change)

Note: * First three quarters (nine months).

Source: TÜSIAD, *Türkiye Ekonomisi 2004* (Istanbul: TÜSIAD Publications, 2004): 15.

a Customs Union with the EU, which became operative as of January 1, 1996. In December 1999, at the Helsinki Summit of the EU, Turkey was accepted as a candidate for full membership. In the Copenhagen Summit of 2002 Turkey was given the date of "end of 2004" as the time when the EU would decide upon when and if the accession negotiations with the "candidate" Turkey will start. Indeed on December 17, 2004 the European Council has decided that accession negotiations start with Turkey as of October 3, 2005.

Turkey can now be accepted as having reached the standards of EU democracies (the Copenhagen Criteria), though it is a newly industrializing country, with a large population and an erratically performing economy. How is it then possible for such a country to develop such proximal and intimate political and economic relations with the United States, OECD, NATO, EU, and other similar countries or organizations? Why do the postindustrial states of the world seek such close and cooperative links with Turkey? The first three and the last chapters of this book will provide the background to Turkey's current role in the international arena, and thus provide answers to those and other similar questions about Turkey.

GEOGRAPHY AND HISTORY: CURSE OR BLESSING?

Turkey is situated between the Black Sea to its north, the Aegean Sea, Greece and Bulgaria to its west, the Mediterranean Sea, Cyprus, Syria and Iraq to its south, Iran to its southeast, and Georgia, Armenia, Azerbaijan (Nachcivan) to its east (see map I.1). Such a location often elicits different depictions for the political or strategic location of the country. Some pundits and scholars refer

4

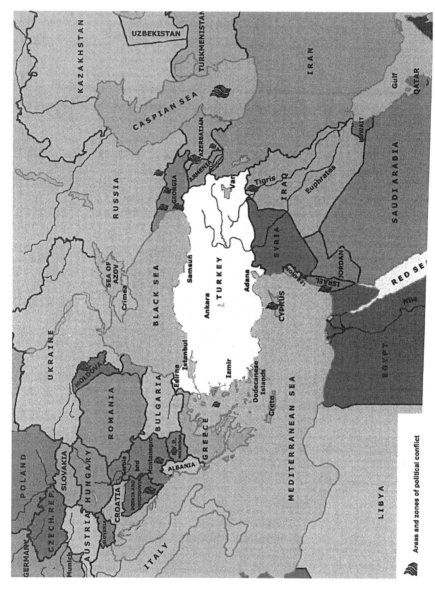

Map I.1 Turkey and Her Neighborhood

to Turkey as constituting the northern frontier of the Middle Eastern others refer to it as belonging to southeastern Europe, the Balkans, or the Black Sea region. Probably all of those designations are correct. In the meantime, all such depictions also emphasize the multifaceted regional and international relations Turkey plays in the Balkans, the Caucasus, and the Middle East.

The political geography of Turkey was determined by means of major international conflict, power struggle, and diplomacy of the nineteenth and early twentieth centuries. The Republic of Turkey was established on the ruins and legacy of the Ottoman Empire in the aftermath of World War I. Consequently, the political geography, culture and history of the Turkish Republic have been deeply influenced by the saga of the Ottoman Empire.

The French Revolution of 1789 opened the Pandora's box for all Empires of Europe, including the Ottoman Empire. The Ottoman Empire had emerged as a patrimonial kingdom at the end of the thirteenth century,[11] and eventually expanded to control vast swathes of land from parts of current day Hungary, Serbia, Moldova, and Romania in eastern Europe to Crimea and the northern shores of the Black Sea to the Caspian Sea and parts of current day western Iran to the Gulf and Yemen in the southern tip of the Arabian peninsula, except for the inner desert the current day Saudi Arabia, and all of the rest of the Arabian peninsula to Egypt, Libya, Tunisia, and Algeria, at the apex of its power in the middle of sixteenth century. Even before the French Revolution, the Ottomans had been suffering military defeat in the hands of their adversaries in Europe and Asia. Austria-Hungary, Russia, and Iran had stopped the advances of the Ottoman armies, and pushed them back in the seventeenth and early eighteenth centuries. The Russian policy of reaching "warn water ports" had led them battle the Ottoman forces for the control of the Black Sea and eventually the Balkans. However, the French Revolution provided the Austrians and Russians with a new opportunity to undermine the Ottoman Empire, nationalism.

The Austrians and Russians began to suppress nationalist movements over their territories, on the one hand, and vehemently support all forms of nationalist forces in the Ottoman lands to undermine its territorial integrity. The Greek orthodox communities of the Ottoman Empire were the first to establish a "nation-state" through a protracted struggle, which started in 1821, with the help of Russia, and came to an end in 1830, with full independence accorded to the budding state of Greece. In the same year, the Serbians were accorded autonomy, which eventually led to full independence of Serbia in the aftermath of Russo-Ottoman war of 1877–1878.[12] The other Orthodox communities, such as the Macedonians, Montenegrins, and Bulgarians developed their own national movements and struggled to establish their independent states in the nineteenth century. Wallachians and Moldavians joined the southern Slav Orthodox communities in establishing their own national movements at about the same time.

It was only a matter of time before the Albanian Muslims emulated their Christian neighbors. Furthermore, the Bosnian and Herzegovinian nationalisms joined in the fray in the nineteenth century. All of those communities, eventually, managed to secede from the Ottoman Empire and establish their independent nation-states. Some, such as the Bulgarians and Albanians had to wait until the twentieth century to develop legally independent and formally established nation-states. However, by the end of the Balkan Wars of 1912–1913 and the beginning of World War I, the Ottomans could only manage to hold on to a small piece of Thrace, on the southeastern tip of the Balkan Peninsula.

The process of establishment of the Balkan nation-states was a tormenting experience for all parties involved. The Ottomans lost territory. The Muslim communities of the Balkans, and the Turks in particular, lost their lives, livelihoods, homes, and other possessions. They were pushed out of the Balkans and most of them found their way to where their compatriots had been living in large numbers in Thrace and Anatolia. The expulsion from their homelands, and the sudden and unexpected loss of territory in the Balkans led to a great loss of morale among the Ottoman political elite and intellectuals. The impact of the Balkan tragedies on the psyche of the Turkish elites and nationalists continued well into the Republican era.

THE CHALLENGE OF TERRITORIAL INTEGRITY

The Ottomans were faced with two existential challenges in the nineteenth century. One was the revisionist foreign policies of its northern neighbors of Austria-Hungary and Russia, which constantly pushed toward the south into the Ottoman territories, and the other was the development of Balkan nationalisms. The Ottoman reactions to those two existential challenges may best be summarized as the erection of a modern army to halt the advances of Austrian and Russian armies, and devising new ideologies to rally the Ottoman population around the Imperial state.

The efforts at modernizing the army had started in the eighteenth century, yet they had also run aground when the traditional armed forces successfully risen up to defeat the new army, oust Sultan Selim III from the throne, and execute him. However, his nephew Mahmut II did not repeat his uncle's error, and first got rid of the traditional (*janissary*) forces in 1825, and then began to establish a modern army, with the help of the French army corps. However, even with the help of the French and eventually the German army corps the Ottoman army could not develop to an extent to cope with not only the major challenges of the Russian army, but much lesser challenges put forth by the Egyptian army. In 1838 the Egyptian army was able to destroy the Ottoman armed forces in the middle of Anatolia (*Kütahya*), and if it were not for the British intervention, the Ottoman dynasty would have come to an end there and then.

The Ottomans were not much more successful in dealing with the ideological and political challenge of Balkan nationalisms. Three major ideological developments, and some minor ones, occurred in the nineteenth century to forge unity in the Ottoman lands. One of them was Ottomanism (*Osmanlıcılık*). It was proposed as an "imperial identity" to supplant all national, ethnic, and religious identities of the Empire. However, it never attracted much appeal for the very term "Osmanlı" was closely connected with the palace and the power elite who were strategically situated around the Sultan and his palace. The subjects of the Sultan failed to define their identity through something they were so removed from and alien to. It did not gain any momentum from the beginning.

Second to develop was Islamism, which later on developed into a political movement of union of Islam (*ittihad-ı Islam*). Islam as a flag to rally around was most effectively hoisted under the reign of Abdulhamid II (1876–1909). Third to develop was Turkish nationalism (*Türkçülük*). It began as an ethnic or even racist nationalism, through the intellectual works of Ismail Gasprinsky, Akçuraoğlu Yusuf, Ziya Gökalp, and others in the nineteenth century, and grew into a major political movement in the aftermath of the Balkan Wars of 1912–1913.

Socialism, corporatism, and so on also developed as new ideological currents, which attracted very few supporters, when compared with either Islamism or Turkish nationalism. The latter two ideological currents played a critical role in the establishment of Republican Turkey and still continue to fuel the emotions and imaginations of the Turkish political elites and masses alike. Therefore, they warrant a much closer examination, and we examine their development and interaction in chapter 1 of this book.

The Ottomans were not able to ward off the nationalist challenges in the Balkans, and they were finally driven out of their Balkan possessions, except for the eastern Thrace, which is still a part of Turkish territory, by means of the Balkan Wars of 1912–1913. The victory of the Balkan armies, without the support of the Russian armed forces came as an unanticipated and totally unexpected blow to the Ottoman state and elites. The Ottoman armed forces were by far the superior of the Balkan armies, and they had been occupying strategically superior positions at the start of the Balkan Wars. However, their performance during the war was dismal, and they suffered another major defeat. Almost a century after the initiation of the modernization project of the armed forces, they still failed to perform well against far weaker forces at war. The psychological shock waves of the defeat traveled far and deep. The Republican elite felt it in their minds and souls for many years to come. The Balkan Wars are still being taught in the Defense Colleges of Turkey as a lesson in failure. In chapter 1 we also examine the Balkan Wars briefly.

World War I brought new destruction and misery to an already battered people and the dilapidated Ottoman state. It also paved the way to the collapse of the latter, though, ironically, only after its major adversaries experienced the same fate as the Ottomans. The end of the World War brought new political realities, which fuelled Turkish nationalism to an extent that no pundits had anticipated. The armistice Treaty of Mudros (1918) and the peace Treaty of *Sevrés* (1920) stipulated that Ottomans territory be divided up between the victorious powers of the World War.

Consequently, except for a small enclave in central Anatolia the Ottoman territory was occupied by the British mandate over Mesopotamia, which eventually became Iraq, Transjordan, and Palestine; and the French mandate over Syria and Lebanon. Eventually, the Armenian, French, Greek, and Italian troops began to occupy parts of Anatolia, in 1919. Such occupation began to incite resistance and initiate organization of forces of nationalism. A national movement of resistance was eventually established through the enterprising efforts of an Ottoman general, Mustafa Kemal Atatürk.

Kemal organized the nationalist resistance and the War of Liberation was fought against under his command with very powerful states and armies, with very little human, financial, and political resources at the disposal of the nationalist forces. Many pundits thought that the nationalists had no chance to succeed. Indeed, the Sultan and his government had joined ranks with those who thought that national resistance to such superior forces was no less than folly. Therefore, the Sultan's government seemed to cooperate with the terms of the armistice treaty of Mudros, and the peace Treaty of *Sevrés* and fought to put down the nationalist resistance as well. However, the Turkish nationalists won the War of Liberation (1919–1922), and negotiated a peace treaty (*Lausanne*) successfully. It was the Turkish nationalists who abolished the Sultanate in 1922, and the religious institution of Caliphate closely tied to it in 1924. In chapter 1, we examine the Ottoman collapse and the War of Liberation at length.

The Republican regime was established on October 29, 1923. A new political regime based upon the principle of national self-determination as crystallized in the national legislature (Turkish Grand National Assembly, TGNA), and a form of government that implied a form of Westminster model of parliamentarism operating through a unicameral legislature was incorporated in the first Constitution (1924) of the country. However, the Cultural Revolution initiated in 1924 with the ouster of the religious institutions, which had been used by the Sultan's men to undermine the nationalists during the War of Liberation, began to create new worries for the Republican government.

An ethno-religious uprising in the eastern provinces of Turkey precipitated the government to take extraordinary measures, and abolish all opposition to the Republican People's Party (CHP) government. A one party rule that would last for the next two decades or until the end of World War II started. This was a period of charismatic leadership of Mustafa Kemal Atatürk, single party rule though the unicameral TGNA, and Cultural Revolution. We examine in chapter 2 the developments of the interwar period, which coincided with single party rule and Cultural Revolution.

World War II brought about new challenges. Turkey encountered new demands for territorial acquisitions and troop deployments from the Soviet Union. In the meantime, the Turkish economy suffered from almost six years of war in which Turkey followed a neutralist policy successfully, yet lost its access to its regular foreign markets, and kept a large army under arms. Consequently, the welfare of the population suffered dearly during World War II. A burgeoning middle class had emerged throughout the War, which began to demand for the opening up of the single party regime to new political parties and movements. Turkey hence moved toward a multiparty democracy, as the country also vied for an alliance with the club of democracies led by the United States. Soon after, a democratic election brought about major changes in the country as the RPP was toppled and the Democrat Party (DP) came to power in 1950. In chapter 3, we analyze in greater depth the first attempt at instituting democracy in Turkey.

The change of the party in government brought about an unexpected change in the socioeconomic development of the country. The economic and social policies of the DP governments precipitated increasingly rapid social mobilization of the Turkish population, which resulted in rapid urbanization, industrialization, and rapid spread of means of telecommunication, especially since the 1980s. We examine the impact of rapid social mobilization on the Turkish society and polity in chapter 3. Since social mobilization has been an unfolding process its role in the Turkish society and polity are followed through in chapters 4 through 6 of this book.

The Turkish political system failed to cope with the challenges of democratization and rapid social mobilization. In 1960 the first attempt at instituting multiparty democracy came to an end by means of a military coup. The military junta co-opted the students of constitutional and public law to draw up a new constitution in 1960. In 1961 the country adopted a new constitution through a popular referendum, which turned out to be the most liberal constitution country has ever had. However, the liberal multiparty democracy of the 1960s came to a sudden halt with a new ultimatum of the military in 1971. However, that military interruption was brief and Turkey reverted back to multiparty democracy in 1973. Unfortunately, the Turkish democracy was not really out of the woods yet. The oil crisis brought about new economic challenges.

The Cyprus crisis of 1963–1974 and the Turkish intervention in the crisis as a guarantor of the status quo on the island of Cyprus in 1974, when failed to be managed by the Turkish governments created a relative isolation of Turkey from the international community, and a concomitant downturn of the economy under the influences of the oil and Cyprus crises. The political consequences of the economic downturn were dismal. The country veered toward a civil war like blood bath between the forces of the left and right. As the death toll increased and the political system gave all the signs of paralysis to act, the military stepped in for a third time on September 12, 1980. In chapters 4 and 5 we examine the unfolding of events in the 1960s through the 1980s.

The country veered away from democracy for the next three years, and gradually eased back into it in 1987. The 1980s was more or less a transition to democracy period for Turkey. In the 1990s the Cold War ended and Turkey found itself encountered with a new world order in which the old borders are increasingly questioned, the inviolability of the borders in Europe was no longer generally accepted. The international embargo on Iraq after the Gulf War of 1991, in which Turkey participated, led to a sudden downturn of the economy of the southeastern parts of Turkey, where large groups of Kurds reside.

In a matter of a year or two the effectiveness of the Partiye Karkeren Kürdistan (Workers' Party of Kurdistan) PKK and the local sympathy for it increased, and so did the death toll. Turkey began to drift further into the politics of the Middle East, vis-à-vis the influences of Iraqi, and Syrian Ba'athi regimes of the 1990s. The bloodbath precipitated by the terror campaigns of the PKK coincided with the genocidal treatment of the Muslim Bosniaks in the hands of the Serbs and Croats in Yugoslavia, which started to fall apart in the early 1990s, whose cultural ties with Turkey deeply influenced the Turkish Muslims whether Bosnian or not. Under the circumstances the citizens and the state in Turkey alike were pressured to redefine the core values of Turkish identity, while nationalism and Islam started to emerge as the main ideological currents in the Turkish political arena once more. They began to divide the Turkish society along cultural fault lines that have been crisscrossing the Ottoman and Turkish political landscapes for the last 300 years.

Turkey began to experience an increasing pressure to cope with a Marxist–Leninist, Kurdish peasant movement called the PKK, and other spillover effects of the Gulf War of 1990–1991. What had started as a small band of Maoist Kurds with hazy ideas on defying the Turkish state in the late 1970s grew into a major political movement and campaign of terror in the early 1990s. The Gulf War and the establishment of a safe haven for Kurds in the north of Iraq rendered a great opportunity for the PKK to set roots there and launch a campaign of terror against Turkey with the backing of the Syrian regime of Hafez Assad.

The PKK threat and the post–Cold War developments in the Middle East and the Balkans led to unanticipated developments. Social democracy lost its appeal in the eyes of the voters. The left-of-center parties began to lose ground in domestic politics in the 1990s. As class-based understanding of politics waned, cultural characteristics, such as ethnicity and religiosity emerged to dominate the Turkish political scene once more. The left-of-center parties began to shift gear to reemerge as the champions of secularism and Turkish nationalism. However, in the meantime, the networks of religious orders began to emerge to provide valuable services to masses of people who recently migrated to major cities of the country.

In the 1980s the military government of Turkey, which had championed secular values of the Turkish Republic and the messages of the founding father of the Turkish Republic, Mustafa Kemal Atatürk, had also used the services of the religious orders to forestall "the peril of communism." Consequently, the Sunni-Islamic religious orders had received a major support from the military establishment to establish their networks, school systems, and communities throughout the country. The right-of-center parties were the first to benefit from the increasing reach and effectiveness of religious orders at the polls. However, the right-of-center party governments failed to heal such economic woes of the country as sustained by "stable" high consumer price inflation and deal with emerging cases of political corruption. The religious (Sunni Muslim) rightwing parties emerged to challenge the corrupt political order and promote religious values to deal with several ills of the country.

The religious rightwing parties proposed to reinvent political integration of the country on the basis of Sunni Islam, a sect into which both the majorities of the Kurds and Turks in Turkey belong. They argued that secularism failed to provide for the sociopolitical solidarity of the Turkish population. Instead, their spokesmen proposed a multi-confessional legal system which people would be free to choose according to their sect and religion. That proposal was no more than the resurrection of the former "millet system" of the Ottoman Empire, which we examine in the following two chapters of this book. However, their emphasis on religious solidarity seemed to attract the majority of the Kurdish Sunnis. They seemed to be ready to integrate with the rest of the Turkish society on religious grounds; though they negated any nationalist integration formula, for they considered such a move to be inimical to the survival of their ethnic identity.

In 1991 religious right started to gain electoral grounds. However, in 1995 a major voter realignment occurred in Turkey, whereby the center of the left–right spectrum began to erode rapidly as large numbers of voters shifted their preferences to the right. Amazingly enough, in the 1999 elections, especially due to the immediate circumstances predating the elections, the left-of-center Democratic Left Party (DSP) was able to win a plurality of the vote, and the religious rightwing lost votes. However, they were quick to regain lost ground. A devastating earthquake in August and another in November 1999 shattered the confidence in Prime Minister Ecevit of DSP and his coalition government. The corruption claims directed at various members of his cabinet again printed an impression that left-of-center and right-of-center parties were too corrupt to rule the country. In 2001 a major financial crisis also bolstered the image of corruption and incompetence of the coalition government. The old guard of the religious rightwing was also perceived as being too insensitive to secular and non-Sunni voters to manage the affairs of the state in Turkey. It was at that juncture that the Constitutional Court banned the religious right wing Virtue party from politics.

The younger and upwardly mobile elite of the Virtue party split ranks under the circumstances and established a new political party called the Justice and Development Party (AKP) on August 14, 2001. They began to propagate a much more secular platform, with no ostentatious reference to Sunni Islam. They dropped their earlier negative attitude toward democracy. They called their new political stance as "democratic conservatism." It looks as if the voters considered them as a new right wing movement, one that could manage the affairs of the country and stabilize the economy, while refraining from undermining political stability. The economic mismanagement of Prime Minister Ecevit's coalition government brought about the final sway of votes away from those parties. The voter's state of mind and expectations favored a right wing party to win the votes that turned away from the previous parties in government. Hence, the AKP emerged as the winner of the majority of seats in the Grand National Assembly in the 2002 elections.

It is plausible to ponder whether the Turkish political drive toward a modern, secular nation-state with a democratic regime has come to an end, or not? Is Turkey now faced with the perils of being ruled by a religious government, which carries a hidden agenda to reimpose Şeriat (Sharia, Islamic law) upon Turkey? We examine the impact of the AKP in government on Turkish secularism, modernity, and democracy in chapter 6 and chapter 7.

In the meantime a heavy agenda awaits Turkey. The recent decision of the EU to start accession negotiations for Turkey failed to pave the way for a smooth transition of Turkey into that organization. The accession negotiations for full EU membership increased the relevance and importance of the EU in Turkish politics, and vice versa. European attitudes toward Turkey created a new soul search in the Turkish society over the core values of Turkish identity. Most Turks seemed to be willing to become full members of the EU, yet they had doubts about the sincerity and prejudices of the Europeans toward the Turks. Bitter memories of the nineteenth and early twentieth centuries, when the European powers tried to carve out the Ottoman Empire into many parts and subjugate the Turks to a colonial state of existence resurfaced. Many Europeans also demonstrated similar, serious doubts and concerns about Turkey's European vocation.

Turkey was in dire need of improved security and increasing support in combating terrorism that threatened Turkey, which seemed to emanate from Syria, Iraq, and radical, fundamentalist Islamic movements, such as al-Qaeda since the mid-1980s. Both the United States and Israel emerged as allies in dealing with the threat of the terror organizations of the Middle East. When European sympathies for the Kurdish nationalist PKK increased, it was the United States and Israeli support Turkey relied upon. As Turkey's relations with the EU became sour, particularly Israel emerged as an ally, providing Turkey with valuable information on terrorism and assist Turkey in modernizing its armaments. In the end, it was with the help of the U.S. forces in Kenya that Turkey was able to apprehend the leader of the PKK, Abdullah Öcalan in Nairobi in February 1999, which brought about the end of the PKK terror campaign soon after.

Turkey also relied upon the U.S. help in getting Azerbaijan and Georgia to agree on the construction of an oil pipeline from the Caspian Sea near Baku, Azerbaijan through Supsa, Georgia to Ceyhan, Turkey. Turkey also relies heavily on both Georgia and Azerbaijan for its eastern politics. Turkey has a very short border with Azerbaijan at Nakhcivan (see map I.1). Azeris also speak western Oguz Turkish, which is akin to Turkish spoken in Turkey. It is not only oil, but also blood that ties the two countries together. However, similar cultural affinities have also been strengthened between the Central Asian states of Turkmenistan, Kirgizstan, Uzbekstan, Kazakstan, on the one hand, and Turkey, on the other. Turkey shares similar ethnic stock, and cultural characteristics with those states.

The collapse of the Soviet Union provided Turkey with new economic and cultural opportunities to its East. Russia, which has traditionally viewed Transcaucasus and Central Asia as its backyard or soft belly has been anxious not to let its hegemony over those areas erode. Iran has also been traditionally interested with the developments of the same political geography. Therefore,

Turkey began to experience Russian and Iranian challenges to its encroachments to the Transcaucasus and Central Asia. Under the circumstances the United States seemed to be a plausible NATO ally for Turkey to check and balance the power of Russia and Iran.

Under the circumstances one inclines to assume that such security concerns and foreign policy options created close and smooth relations between Turkey and the United States since the 1990s. There are many complications in the U.S.–Turkish relations. In the Transcaucasus the closest ally of Russia is Armenia, which is posed with hostility toward Azerbaijan. Armenians and Azeris fought over a region of Azerbaijan called Nagorno-Karabagh, and the former has invaded and occupied not only Nagorno-Karabagh, but also about 20 percent of Azeri territory. Armenians have used the former Soviet forces and Russian military and other assistance to counter balance the influence of Turkey in the region. Armenia also forged strong relations with Iran. Turkey considers the current revisionist Armenian government a threat to peace and stability in the region. The United States, which hosts politically well-organized Armenian communities, has a different image of Armenia. In the U.S. eyes Armenia is a small country squeezed between major regional powers and often mistreated by them. The United States often pressures Turkey to act like a "big brother" in full confidence and show magnanimity toward Armenia, which Turkey rejects until and unless Armenia drops its revisionist foreign policy and accepts its internationally recognized borders with Azerbaijan and Turkey as legitimate.

The U.S. governments have also publicly tried to promote Turkish membership in the EU, which has often prompted a negative reaction from the EU. However, a closer union of Turkey with the EU further complicates the relations between Turkey and the United States. For example, Turkey although a close ally of the United States in the "war against terror" since September 11, 2001, wavered over sending troops into Iraq, and also dithered over the issue of providing passage rights to the U.S. troops through Turkey into northern Iraq in March 2003. Turkish government and masses alike calculated that their national interests precluded Turkey from becoming involved in the coalition of the willing to invade Iraq. Turkey seemed to be more interested in prolonging the economic embargo and diplomatic pressures on Iraq, rather than fight a war with its neighbor. Hence, Turkish position seemed to veer closer to that of the French–German entente against the United States in 2003.

Turkey had already been given December 2004 as the final date for the EU to decide on its readiness to start negotiations for accession to full membership in the EU. Turkish foreign policy stand vis-à-vis Iraq seemed to have contributed to convince the EU heads of state that Turkey is serious in becoming a democratic country with European credentials. Turkish government also took additional steps, such as agreeing to a settlement of the conflict brokered by the United Nations (UN) between the Greek and Turkish states and communities on the island of Cyprus. On the domestic front Turkey abolished the death penalty, and made major changes in its illiberal Constitution to promote individual, associational, and cultural rights and liberties. The goal of EU membership seemed to have been providing the necessary incentive for Turkey to adopt the European standards for democracy and rule of law, otherwise known as the Copenhagen Criteria.

Consequently, Turkey's relations with its neighbors and allies have become much more challenging and complicated. In chapter 6, we analyze the forces that have been at play in the current Turkish society and politics, before we draw up the main conclusions of this brief study of Turkish sociopolitical developments in chapter 7.

1

From Collapse to Liberation

The Slippery Slope to Ottoman Collapse

The end of the nineteenth century was replete with dramatic developments in the domestic political life of the Ottoman Empire. The modernizing reforms had run their course and culminated in the first constitution and the establishment of the first legislative institution, the Imperial Assembly (*Meclis*) of the Ottoman Empire by 1877. The term "Ottoman" in the text of the Constitution,[1] yet it failed to make any difference on how the "Ottoman subjects" perceived their identity. Ottoman "citizenship" never seemed to be sufficient in providing an idea around which the myriads of religious communities (*millets*), ethnic groups, tribes and clans united, nor were democratization on firm ground. The Ottoman bicameral *Meclis* met in 1877 with the election of deputies from all over the Empire from Arabia to Serbia. However, the eruption of the Russo-Turkish War of 1877–1878, and the Constitution's entrusting the Sultan Abdülhamit II with excessive powers, shortly after led to the suspension of the activities of the *Meclis*, when the deputies started to level criticisms of the Sultan's handling of the Russo-Turkish war, until 1908.[2]

The *Hamidian* period of de facto absolutism in a legal cloak started in 1877, and lasted for 31 years.[3] It was a period that undermined the legal and constitutional developments of the country, while continuing with its social and physical modernization. The Ottoman Empire veered toward a form of absolute monarchy, which was unacceptable to some of the political and intellectual elites of the land, who started an opposition movement against the Sultan. However, this stirring was confined to the elites and university students at best, and failed to ignite much mass involvement until the very culmination of the political movement in a military uprising in 1908.[4] Ironically, the backward looking political style of the *Hamidian* government consolidated its power and increased its effectiveness to deal with opposition, as the adoption and importing of all sorts of fruits of modern day technology from railroads to telegram enhanced control from the Center. Even education reform can be cited as an example to the continuing efforts at modernization of the *Hamidian* regime. Although most of those efforts were concentrated in the field of natural sciences, a new school of public administration, and a brand new Ottoman University were also established during Abdülhamit's reign.

However, two political measures, which had been widely wielded by the government at the time, remain as ominous legacies of the *Hamidian* regime in the Turkish political culture. They are political censorship (*sansür*) and informants spying on everyone, including their own family members, in return for material or political gain (*jurnalcilik*). Both of those practices have been abundantly used, especially in times of political crises in Turkey throughout the twentieth century.

An important characteristic of the *Hamidian* style of government was the erection of political committees serving as the place of political decision-making, insulated from the prying and vigilance of the public bureaucracy.[5] Abdülhamit II established a small circle of loyal officials around him in the Palace. The result, according to Berkes, is that "This became the weakest and most oppressive part of the system because of the absence of the means, the methods, and the personnel of a rational administration."[6] Although the practice was dropped after Abdülhamit II was ousted from the throne in 1909, we observe the same practice reemerging, as a new form of Hamidianism (neo-*Hamidianism*) as late as the 1980s and the 1990s in Turkish politics (see chapter 5 of this book).

A new emphasis on Islam emerged as the main tool of mass mobilization. Abdülhamit II would now be the "pious" Sultan and exalted Caliph. The new policy of "Islamization" was designed not only to enable the Sultan to attract the support of the conservative-minded masses, but as a foreign policy tool oriented to the double objectives of undermining the British *Raj* in India and the Russian hegemony in Central Asia.

Outside of the Ottoman Empire, the Russian and the British Empires had become the two rival powers ruling millions of Muslims in the latter half of the nineteenth century. The Russian Empire had extended its sovereignty over Central Asia, where large communities of Muslim Turks lived. The image of a pious Sultan and Caliph would be attractive to Central Asian peoples that have recently come under the Russian rule, and so would be the Indian, Egyptian, and other Muslim communities under the British rule. If Abdülhamit II could attract the support of such Muslim communities outside of the realm of the Ottoman Empire, he could wield a strong lever to counterbalance the interventions of Russia and Britain by inciting or igniting protests in Central Asia, India, Egypt and elsewhere when threatened by Russia and Britain. Hence, Islamism (*Islamcılık*) became official state policy under Abdülhamit II. "Abdül-Hamid, . . . founded a system closer to what the Islamist Young Ottomans conceived as *meşveret* (counseling), the essence of Islamic constitutionalism."[7] Islamism as state policy was also abandoned after Abdülhamit II was deposed. However, Islamism remained in the glossary of the political culture to be appealed to by various governments throughout the twentieth century, and even as late as the 1980s and the 1990s.

Consequently, a relatively modern form of despotism combined with technological modernization, political traditionalism, which heavily emphasized and reinforced Islamism emerged under the reign of Abdülhamit II.

However, in spite of all the censorship of the press (*sansür*), spying (*hafiyelik*), informing suspects (*jurnalcilik*), and suppression of political opponents, the opposition to the *Hamidian* regime eventually gathered steam. One main force behind the opposition consisted of the very students of the modernized colleges, such as the Royal Medical School, and the Military Cadets, who established their clandestine political organizations and joined the ranks of the opposition. Although political activism of the college students was not a new phenomenon in the Ottoman Empire, that practice was rejuvenated in the last decade of the nineteenth century, and continued to be a strong force in Turkish politics ever since.

The most important outcome of the political activism of college students was the Association of Union and Progress (*Ittihad ve Terakki Cemiyeti*, ITC). It did not take long for the *Hamidian* regime to deal with the students though. The ITC collapsed in the Ottoman lands within a year of its establishment. However, with internal fissure, strains, and domestic bickering the Paris branch thrived and ceaselessly tried to establish links with the intellectual elites in the Ottoman lands. The exile in Europe of the "Young Turks" had its unexpected consequences. The most important political outcome was the slow development of sense of "national" identity and nationalism of the Turkish students in exile.[8]

FROM THE "STUPID" TO THE "GRAND" TURK

In the eyes of the Turkish subjects of the Empire, the Ottoman Sultans were not only their temporal rulers, but also as Caliphs they were spiritual leaders of the Muslim *ümmet* (*umma*, community), to which they loyally belonged. Most Turks seemed to have believed that they shared the same ethnic origin with the Ottoman dynasty (which after so many years of multiethnic marriages of the Ottoman Sultans was no more than a myth). Moreover, most Turkish subjects of the Empire, and particularly the learned men among them failed to pay any attention to their ethnic origins until the late nineteenth century.[9] Until that time most references to Turks, even by those learned gentlemen of the Ottoman Empire from Turkish backgrounds were quite demeaning. The identity of a "Turk" was more to do with the nomadic Turks (who were and to a certain extent still are referred to as "Turkmen" in some parts of Turkey), rather than the gentile power elite of Istanbul, to a certain extent, had descended from the same ethnic stock.[10] It was the success of Turkish nationalism that dramatically transformed such a lowly image of the "Turk" in the Ottoman Empire to an ideal or even an idol of a "Grand Turk" in the eyes of the masses and the elites alike, in a matter of a decade's time.

Ethnic or other lineage group identification connoted tribalism, which Islam condemned as a major sin, for such affinities would drive a wedge among the Muslim *ümmet* and undermine the solidarity of the Muslims in the world.[11] Therefore, it is no surprise that the Ottoman state officially recognized one division in society, which was based on religious identity or community (*millet*). The subjects of the Ottoman Empire, irrespective of their ethnic background had been socialized into accepting such a perspective on society. There were four major millets in the Ottoman Empire, and they were the Armenians, Greeks, Jews, and Muslims.[12] In essence, the Ottoman *"millet* system" seemed to have enjoyed widespread legitimacy in the eyes of all communities under the Ottoman jurisdiction until the nineteenth century.[13]

Even when the nationalist movements began to sprout in the Balkans, it was no coincidence that they followed the old divisions of the *millet* system for a while. Churches played some role in mobilizing the national movements against the Ottoman Empire, a form of "religious nationalism" emerged in the Balkans, and spread to the rest of the Ottoman Empire. "This brand of nationalism, however, was generally intolerant of religious and ethnic diversity and focused most explicitly on territorial issues."[14] Consequently, peace became increasingly difficult to preserve between and within nation-states in the Balkans, and hence the term "Balkanization" was thus coined to refer to the development of many political systems, which are in constant political bickering and conflict with each other.

It was not difficult for the Christian and Slav, Greek, Albanian etc. communities of the Balkans to be mobilized against the "foreign yoke" of the "Muslim" and/or "Turkish" Ottoman Empire by their indigenous nationalist leaders. Although some Turks increasingly resented the "arbitrary style of rule" by their patrimonial Sultans throughout the nineteenth century, there is scant evidence at the time that they dreamt of getting rid of the Empire, of the Ottoman dynasty, or the Caliphate. They were more concerned with the viability of the Empire, which under the challenges of the modern armies of Russia, France, and Austria, was slowly crumbling, the Turks seemed to have sufficed by participating in reform movements. Reforms aimed at modernizing the military and the medieval officialdom of the ruling institution, introducing constitutional monarchy and limit the powers of the Sultan, and overhaul the legal and educational systems rapidly.[15]

At first, the Turkish members of the Ottoman government and central administration when confronted with the challenges of the international system, in the form of military defeat abroad, and of the nationalist uprisings mainly in the Balkans, rallied around the Sultan. In the aftermath of the French Revolution of 1789, when the existential concerns of the Ottomans became much more critical, the Turkish subjects labored to save the Ottoman state and their own homeland (*vatan*) from the encroachments of their foreign and domestic enemies. They seemed to have been loyal to Sultan Mahmut II, the most daring reformist Sultan of the Ottoman reign in the early nineteenth century. Most of those dramatic changes in the Ottoman political and administrative institutions and political culture were received well by the Turks. Even those Turkish intellectuals who were critical of the pace and scope of the reforms seemed not to suggest a Turkish "ethnic" nationalist program in the early nineteenth century. Their main qualms were with the "modernization as Westernization" content of the reforms. Some objected to those measures and policies of the state that veered away from the established traditions and practices of the Ottoman Empire. Their objections seemed to be less directed at the political reforms, but more directed at the sweeping legal and educational reforms of the 1840s and 1850s, which undermined the status of the religious establishment of the Empire.

When the modernizing *Tanzimat* reforms (1839–1877) as whole introduced the idea of limited government, adopted the principle of proportionality between crime and punishment, and most important of all, reformed the Ottoman "slave official system" and introduced the idea of rule in accordance with the law, the proportionality between crime and punishment, and equality before the law for all members of the *millets*, which meant that the arbitrary rule of the Sultans, and the practice of political executions of the officials would come to an end.[16] These were changes in the rules of the game of government and politics. They were carried out to render the Ottoman public administration modern and viable. However, other sweeping legal reforms followed soon after. The commercial and the criminal codes, and even the civil code, which has always been under the influence of religion, were all reformed, or in fact, imported from Italy, Belgium, France, and other European countries, with often minor adaptations.[17] The newly established educational institutions started to follow a curriculum that emphasized science and reduced religious education by the latter half of the nineteenth century.[18] Initially the Muslim subjects of the Empire stayed away from such schools. However, by the latter half of the nineteenth century increasingly larger number of Muslim and Turkish students started to be enrolled in the modern educational institutions. The modernized officialdom required potential candidates to master a solid background in science and foreign languages, preferably French. The new schools became conveyor belts to prestigious jobs in the government bureaucracy, and acquisition of power and wealth, which due to the primacy of politics always required some government job to marry those two values.[19] Hence, in the latter half of the nineteenth century anybody who would want his son to be somebody in the Ottoman Empire tried to enroll him in the new and modern educational institutions, such as the "*Sultani* Schools."

The overall impact of those reforms was to diminish the power, wealth, and prestige of the religious establishment, though its schools and other institutions were left untouched by the reforms. The Ottoman *millet* system had created a decentralized educational system. The Muslim subjects of the Sultan were freeborn individuals, and hence it was out of question for them to be recruited into the medieval system of "slave" officials that ran the Empire. The Sultan required undivided loyalty of his officials to serve their patrimonial master with devotion, fealty, and self-sacrifice. Hence, the Sultans needed slaves, over who they would have the prerogative of life and death.[20] The slave officials were recruited through a procedure of conversion (*devşirme*) from among the Christian communities, especially from those communities who became Christians after the revelation of the Holy Qur'an, such as the Serbians, Bulgarians, and Albanians in the Balkans.[21] Once converted into Islam at a very young age, the boys were trained in martial arts and sciences, mathematics, theology, religion, and so on and prepared for a career in the state service. Those who turned out to be bright advanced their education and often managed to serve in the higher echelons of the political establishment of the Empire. The brightest would eventually ascent all the way to the second most powerful political position to that of the Sultan in the "Ruling Institution" and become a Grand *Vizier* (Premier). However, even a *devşirme* Grand *Vizier* was no more than a slave of the Sultan, who could at any instant be politically executed.[22] The worldly possessions of the slave official would then be returned to the treasury of the state (palace), and thus, the family of the official would not be allowed to inherit the worldly possessions of the official in question.

Consequently, the main ladder of upward social mobility that was provided for the Muslim subjects of the Sultan was the religious institutions and the related legal profession (judiciary). They could and would join the *ulema* (clergy), and if bright and successful enough one could rise up to the position of a judge (*kadi*), higher court judge and cleric (*müftü*) or even become a *Şeyhulislam* (Grand *Mufti*) of the Ottoman Empire. Although the position of *Şeyhulislam* enjoyed prestige and clout within the religious institutions, yet compared to the Sultan, *Şeyhulislam* was not necessarily much stronger than the highest ranked slave official, the Grand *Vizier*. On occasions Sultans were able to dispose off the *Şeyhulislams*, with the same kind of arbitrary decisions, and had them executed.[23]

As the influence in the educational and judicial institutions of the Empire of religion diminished in the latter half of the nineteenth century many Turkish-Muslim subjects of the Sultan took part in the social and political protests believing that Islam and the traditional order closely intertwined with it were at risk. Modern laws and practices were introducing Western institutions and morals to an Islamic society and undermining its traditional core. Modern versus traditional, West versus Islam, progress versus going back to the golden ages of the Ottoman grandeur, and other variations of the same theme emerged to divide the Ottoman society into two major *kulturkampfs*.[24] Those who aspired to be modern and believed in an "Image of Good Society" built around science versus those who defended the idea of preserving the traditional social order, which inherently possessed an "Image of Good Society" built around religion as tradition gained stability and visibility. Interestingly enough, those on both sides of the divide were still motivated by the goal of rendering the Ottoman political system viable. Neither the modernists, nor the traditionalists seemed to vie for a nationalist solution. Their solutions were more along the lines of manufacturing an Ottoman identity or Ottomanism (*Osmanlıcılık*), or creating or reinforcing Islamic morals and society or Islamism (*Islamcılık*).[25] However, eventually a third way was invented to supplant both of the former two: Turkism (*Türkçülük*).[26]

THE RISE OF TURKISH NATIONALISM

The Turkish subjects of the Ottoman Empire had to cope with the rising tide of Balkan nationalisms. Turkish peasants and townsfolk living in the Balkans constituted a large minority in the Balkans. They were no less than 32 percent of all the population in the Balkans in 1820s, and their numbers swelled to 43 percent in the 1870s, and eventually to 47.5 percent of the Balkan populations in the 1890s.[27] They learnt about nationalism from their Greek and Slav Christian neighbors the hard way. Under the increasing influence of pan-Slav or indigenous religio-ethnic nationalisms the Christian populations of the Balkan lands started to show increasing signs of hostility, and intolerance toward their Turkish neighbors, and other minorities, such as the Jews. Consequently, when the Russian troops invaded the Balkans during the Russo-Ottoman War in 1877–1878, the Muslim population of the Balkans suffered dearly: "Approximately 250,000 to 300,000 Muslims, mostly ethnic Turks, were killed, and about 1.5 million were forced to take refuge in the Ottoman domains."[28]

The loss of the Balkan territories in the nineteenth and early twentieth centuries led to huge dislocations of population from the Balkans toward Istanbul and Anatolia. Many Muslim Turks were forcefully evicted from the newly established states or faced massacre. More than a million fled their homelands in the Balkans toward where Muslim Turks constituted the majority of the population, which happened to be in Thrace, Istanbul included, and Anatolia. The migrants now had a strong sense of identity being forced upon them by their Christian neighbors in their old homelands. They were new to Anatolia, and the only reason they were there was the rising tide of nationalisms in the Balkans. They were hated, threatened, massacred, and eventually forced out of their homes, only because they were "Muslim and/or Turks." The ardent Turkish nationalist intellectuals and leaders could not have dreamt of such an effective instruction of nationalist fervor and ideology in their wildest dreams.

Second, the Turkish officers and soldiers serving in the Ottoman army, who were assigned to various posts in the Balkans, experienced the rising tide of nationalism in their professional line of duty. They had been educated by French and German officers as cadets in the nineteenth century, became increasingly well versed in French and German, could follow the foreign press and literature, and hence inquire into the ideology of nationalism of the time.[29] There was only a small step between inquiring about "nation," "national identity," "and nationalism" in general terms, and inquiring into one's own national identity. Curiously enough, it was the secessionist movements and the "enemy" of the Ottomans, which seemed to have precipitated a deepening curiosity in nationalism in the minds of the Turkish intellectuals and officers in the Ottoman Empire.

If Balkan nationalisms were one source that triggered the curiosity of the Turkish subjects of the Empire in their ethnic origins and national identity, the increasing interactions of the Turkish subjects of the Empire with Europeans constituted another. In the second half of the nineteenth century young Turkish men were sent to Europe for college education. Others got embroiled in the fight against the reign of Abdülhamit II, whose regime veered away from constitutional monarchy and reverted back to the absolutism of an earlier era, and fled from the Ottoman territories to take refuge in Europe. Hence, the term "Young Turk" was eventually coined by the Europeans to refer to the increasing number of Ottoman students, activists, freedom fighters, and the like who took refuge in Europe, and conspired to oust the absolutist Sultan from his throne. The ethnic Turks among the "Young Turks" were eventually exposed to nationalist ideas and concepts in Europe. For example, "when a group of such students were asked what their nationality happened to be by a librarian most failed to suggest any answer other than 'Islam' or 'Muslim' to a question of their 'national identity.' They were quickly reminded that "Islam" was a religion, not nationality. Eventually they managed to discover that what the European librarian was inquiring into was their 'Turkishness.' "[30] Their curiosity was triggered through such instances and they started to inquire into, deliberate and debate about such concepts as nationality, nationalism, homeland, nation, and nation-state.

In the beginning they did not even have a word in Turkish, or the Ottoman court language *Osmanlı* (which was a hybrid "language" composed of Arabic, Farsi, and Turkish), that coincided with the concept of "nation." After much debate they decided to translate the concept of nation as "*millet*," which obviously had a strong religious connotation. It clearly demonstrated how strong the Ottoman "*millet* system" idea was in the latter half of the nineteenth century. Such a conceptualization also demonstrated how closely sociopolitical identity of the Ottoman Turks was related to their religious affiliations.

Ironically, another major source of inspiration that contributed to the development of Turkish nationalism was the works of the European orientalists.[31] The European increase in the scholarly efforts at unearthing the origins of the Asiatic peoples, their languages, and cultures had contributed to the awakening of Turkish nationalism.[32] European converts to Islam, such as Mustafa Celaleddin Paşa, a Polish national by birth, also labored to unearth the contribution of Turks to civilization.[33] It was another orientalist, *Arminius Vambery* who argued that Turks belonged to the same "Turanian" group as the Hungarians, Finns, Estonians, and other peoples.[34] Young Turks could read the works of other orientalists in their exile in Europe, which increased their curiosity and awareness of their ethnic or racial origins. "The scholarly works of orientalists acquainted Ottoman Turks with their language and ancient history, and with the contemporary Turkic-speaking peoples living outside the boundaries of the Empire in Central Asia, the Volga Region, the Caucasus and Iran."[35]

Coincidentally in the latter half of the nineteenth century another critical development increased the awareness and familiarity of the Ottoman Turks with their brethren living outside the Empire. It was the drive of the Russian armies into the Central Asian *Khanates* of *Khokand* and *Khiva* in *Turkistan*, which precipitated appeals for help in the name of Islamic solidarity, from those lands to the Ottoman capital by the 1860s and the 1870s.[36] Humble military missions, diplomatic envoys were sent to Central Asia in those years, which further increased the awareness of the plight of Muslim Turks elsewhere. "A further impetus, and possible most crucial one, to the growing Ottoman familiarity with Turks living outside the Empire, was the increasing flow of intellectuals and men of letters from Turkish provinces in Russia into the Ottoman Empire, especially toward the end of nineteenth century."[37] Hence, a new breed of nationalist intellectuals and leaders arrived from Russia about the same time as the masses of Turks were forced to flee the Balkans and settled in Istanbul, Thrace, and Anatolia. Ismail Gasprinski of Crimea was among the first group of early Turkish nationalists whose ideas of unity of Turks and modernization of Islam was widely read among the Turkish subjects of the Ottoman Sultan.[38] Others followed soon. Among them Gasprinski's nephew Yusuf Akçura, and Ağaoğlu Ahmet of *Nagorno-Karabag*, Azerbaijan made relatively big impact on the development of Turkish, or even pan-Turkish nationalism. In fact, the most important impact of the Turks outside of the Empire was the development of a new brand of Turkish nationalism, which was deeply inspired by pan-Slavism of Russia, and developed as a counter ideology to cope with the challenge of the former.[39]

Yusuf Akçura had an interesting life. His father who was a rich business-man in *Kazan* passed away when he was only two years old (1878). His mother could not manage their family business, and soon migrated to Istanbul in 1883. His childhood and adolescence passed in Istanbul, where he attended the military college, yet he was involved in the political campaign against the absolutist regime of Sultan Abdülhamit II. He was caught and expelled from the army, and was sent to exile in *Tripoli*, Libya. He fled to Paris soon, where he attended college and earned a degree in political science. He eventually found his way to Crimea, where he started to work as a teacher of history and geography. However, his contacts with the Young Turks continued all along. Furthermore, he provided one of the most rigor-ous arguments for Turkish nationalism in a treatise called "*Üç Tarz-ı Siyaset*" (Three Ways of Policy), which was originally published in a daily called *Turk* in Egypt.[40] He rose to further prominence in Turkey after Abdülhamit II was ousted from government, and when he participated in the War of Liberation (1919–1922) and served as a deputy of the Grand National Assembly before and after the establishment of the Republic in Turkey.[41]

Akçura's treatise focuses on the three ways of development suggested since the beginning of Westernization in the Ottoman Empire. He enu-merates them as follows. The first is to integrate many nations under the Ottoman sovereignty and create a single amalgam of "Ottoman nation" (*Ottomanism*). The second way is to unite all the Muslim of the world under the political administration of the Caliph (*Panislamism*). The third way is to establish a political union of a Turkish nation based on race (*Panturkism*).[42]

He argued at length that the first of those three ways had indeed been tried by the Ottoman governments of the nineteenth century and failed. He further argued that it was the failure of the policy of creating an Ottoman nation that led to the devising of the second policy of *Panislamism*.[43] He went on to argue that such a policy would mean no more than establishing a theocratic state based upon a blatant form of discrimination of non-Muslims and the absolute rule of a despotic ruler, which he and most of his Young Turk associates loathed.[44] Instead, inspired by German nationalism, he suggested a third and a novel idea of establishing a Turkish nation on the basis of race.[45]

Akçura suggested that the only beneficial road to take is to establish the unity of all Turks around the globe under a single political union. Although he considers Islam as a potential factor promoting unity of Turks, and he deemed Islam as a shared characteristic of all Turks, he identified race as the most important contemporary glue that enhanced the solidarity of a nation.[46] His main argument seems to be that religions had been becoming less communitarian and more individualistic belief systems in late nineteenth and early twentieth centuries, whereas racial characteristics emerged as the most effective characteristic of human societies that promote unity and solidarity.[47]

It did not take long for the Ottomans to develop their own brand of pan-Turkism. Ironically, it was an ethnic Kurd, Ziya Gökalp who emerged as the most important intellectual champion of pan-Turkism, whose calls for the establishment of a single Turkish Empire (*Turan*) across the Ottoman Empire and Central Asia, inspired large numbers of young Turks, politicians, including Mustafa Kemal Atatürk, the founding President of the Turkish Republic, social and political thinkers of the Ottoman Empire in the early years of the twentieth century.[48] Influenced and inspired by the patriotic writings of Namık Kemal (a nationalist poet and thinker of an earlier generation),[49] and by the sociological thinking and ideas of the French sociologist Emile Durkheim, Gökalp began to emerge as the ideologue of the Young Turks by 1912,[50] on the one hand, and the founder of the first Department of Sociology in the Ottoman lands at Istanbul University, on the other.[51] He had a colorful political career as well. He functioned as a member of the executive board of the main political organization and later party of the young Turks, the party of Union and Progress (ITF), and was behind many social and political reforms that ITF carried out between 1912 and 1918. In 1919, he was arrested by the British occupation forces as one of the main culprits of the Ottoman war atrocities and incarcerated in Malta. He was released from the British prison in Malta in 1921 for the British prosecutor assigned to the case could not find enough evidence to press charges against him and others who had been arrested with him.[52] He was elected as the deputy of the Grand National Assembly of the young Turkish Republic from *Diyarbakir* in 1923, and passed away in 1924, at the young age of 48.[53]

Gökalp was a prolific social thinker and nationalist intellectual. He published many books, novels, and poems. Gökalp's works reflected his reactions to and views about the turbulent and tragic developments of his lifetime, most specifically during the last three decades of the Ottoman system, and the Islamist, Ottomanist and the pan-Turkist (*Turanist*) ideas and ideologies of his time. His poetry reflected the influences of these currents of thoughts on his thinking, for his poems clearly demonstrated the impact of the Young Turk poet Namık Kemal's patriotism and utopian

Islamism, as well as Western humanist and Sufi thinking of his time.[54] After grappling with all those different strands of thinking, his intense patriotic upbringing and his experiences in *Selanik* (*Thessalonica*), with the non-Muslim Balkan nationalisms veered him toward Turkish nationalism and even pan-Turkism.

Gökalp argued that ". . . Nationalist movements in Turkey thus started first as movements of religious autonomy, and then as movements of political autonomy and independence . . . We know that Turkish nationalism started as a cultural movement. One of its early fathers was the founder of our oldest university, and the other that of our military schools."[55]

Gökalp believed that nationalism grew from a nebulous cultural movement into a mass political ideology and phenomenon in Turkey just as the germination of a seed would: "A people without a national character is comparable to the seed before it becomes a living organization . . . Nations, too, need to pass through the stages of germination and growth . . . When a nation experiences a great disaster or when it is confronted with a grave danger, individual personality disappears and becomes immersed in society . . . In time of a crisis a person does not worry about his own liberties, but thinks only of the survival of national independence. . . . Ideals are always created in such critical moments. They are born in hearts in communion—hearts unified by national disasters which created one single heart."[56] He often substantiated his arguments with the German situation in the Napoleonic wars, Japanese experiences of threat in the nineteenth century, Jews in Egypt before the arrival of Moses to save them etc. Indeed, it seemed as if the turbulent times of the 1910s and the 1920s were replete with such calamities for the Turkish people, who at a time of disaster were destined to unearth its own nationalism. He thus firmly believed that the time was ripe for the growth of Turkish nationalism into a full-fledged political ideology or even the "Ideal" of the state.

Gökalp labored to prove that Turkish nationalism would not undermine the interests of the Ottoman state ". . . Turkism is the real support of Islam and of the Ottoman state, and it is against cosmopolitanism."[57]

Gökalp went on to argue that ". . . as the newspaper helped the rise of the ideal of nationalism by expressing the social and local sentiments of the masses in a colorful way,"[58] books produce internationality, and modernity is brought about by technology. He further maintained that ". . . For us today modernization . . . means to make and use battleships, cars, and aeroplanes that the Europeans are making and using. However this does not mean being like them only in form and in living. When we see ourselves no longer in need of importing manufactured goods and buying knowledge from Europe, then we speak of being contemporary with it."[59]

Gökalp's formulations about nation, nationalism, culture and civilization have deeply influenced the establishment and development of the Turkish Republic. He argued that nationalism was a cultural creation. He especially labored to explain that culture and civilization shared a lot of common features. Both culture and civilization related to religious, moral, legal, economic, linguistic, and similar realms of social life. However, Gökalp built upon his original argument that culture is national and civilization is international. For him civilization was a consciously created artifact of the human reason, whereas ". . . The elements that constitute a culture, on the other hand, are not creations of conscious individual actions . . . so the elements of a culture rise and grow spontaneously."[60] He suggested the example of language. Individuals may propose new terms or even grammatical rules, yet they may or may not be accepted by the people. The changes in language occur spontaneously by themselves, while an individual member of the community pacifically watches on. Whereas civilization often hosts such invented terms, as individuals who make up specialized groups, such as scientists, artists, musicians, and the like often produce invented terminologies, which are used internationally. Consequently, Gökalp concluded that ". . . culture is composed mainly of emotional elements, while civilization is composed of ideas."[61] So, according to Gökalp, there is no anomaly in arguing that the Turkish nation simultaneously belongs to the *Ural-Altai* group of peoples, to the Islamic *ümmet*, and to Western civilization.[62]

In short, Turkish nationalism shares the same origin as the Balkan religio-ethnic nationalisms. Ethnic characteristic of Turkish nationalism, which even veered toward racism for a while, developed with the advent of secularism, on the one hand, and the atrocities that the Turkic peoples of Russia suffered in the hands of the Russian governments in the nineteenth and twentieth centuries, on the other. This new breed of ethnic-nationalists was able to gain respect and status in Istanbul's intellectual and political circles. Eventually, they were able to find large numbers of Turks ready to be fired up with their pan-Turkic ethnic nationalist ideas and ideologies. Hence, it was no coincidence that Turkish nationalism became a mass movement by 1912–1913. The Union and Progress party, which was the most effective political force of the country at the time, gradually adopted Turkish nationalism as its ideology. ITF came to power by means of a military coup d'état in 1912–1913 and stayed in power before and during World War I. The hardships of the World War, the humiliating defeat of the Ottoman army in the Middle East, and the War of Liberation further contributed to the transformation of Turkish nationalism and to the establishment of a Turkish nation-state, over the territories of Eastern Thrace and Anatolia.

Turkish nationalism developed from a religious nationalist model of Balkan origins, adopted a pan-nationalist dimension by the early twentieth century, while preserving Turkish-speaking Muslim subjects of the former Ottoman Empire as its core clientele. However, by the end of the War of Liberation it developed into a modernist, and secular movement in the Republican Turkey. How was such a transformation possible? Chapters 1 and 2 of this book examine the reincarnation of Turkish nationalism in the War of Liberation and the Republican Turkey.

UNION AND PROGRESS VERSUS POLITICAL ISLAM

The real danger from the ITC finally emerged for the *Hamidian* regime, when seven officers of the Third Army and three civilians established the

Ottoman Freedom Society (*Osmanlı Hürriyet Cemiyeti*, OHC) in *Selanik* (*Thessalonica*) in 1906.[63] Within a year many more officers and members of the Ottoman public administration joined its ranks. It was then that the Parisian Committee of Union and Progress and the OHC started to negotiate a merger, which happened soon, under the banner of *Ittihat ve Terakki Cemiyeti* (ITC) in 1907.[64] Only one year later, in July 10, 1908 the ITC publicly challenged the Sultan to reinstate the constitutional monarchy. When the general director of the *Rumeli* province,[65] Hüseyin Hilmi Paşa was ordered by the Palace to outlaw and destroy all clandestine organizations, his response was telling of the power, effectiveness, and prestige of the ITC. He responded that the ITC was not only well organized, but even the governors of the districts of the province under his command are its members, and he has no means to order them to surrender their membership![66]

The members of the organization varied in their motives and objectives.[67] If there was one ideal they all seemed to share it was the loosely and hazily defined concept of "liberty," which obviously had different connotations to different members of the organization. They all seemed to be inspired by the French Revolution, and influential members of the ITC who had spent a long time in France and elsewhere in Europe seemed to have picked up the positivist and Jacobin value orientations to politics.[68] The ITC started out with the intent of emancipating the Ottoman peoples from the despotic regime of Abdülhamit II, and usher in a period of constitutional regime endowed with "liberty, equality, fraternity and justice."[69] The Sultan Abdülhamit II caved in to their demands and reestablished the constitutional monarch on July 11, 1908.[70]

LIBERTY AND THE ISLAMIST UPRISING OF "MARCH THIRTY-FIRST"

The transition from the Abdülhamit's absolutist regime to constitutional monarchy and multiparty democracy was anything but smooth. The ITC did not oust the Sultan immediately after the reinstatement of the 1876 Constitution. A state of anarchy emerged by late 1908 and early 1909, and in less than a year the ITC government established limits on individual liberties, by imposing a new regulation which demanded that all congregations must seek the approval of the authorities 24 hours before they meet.[71] However, it was not enough to control the events to follow.

The soldiers of the First Army in Istanbul rose up against their officers, and others from the city joined them on the early morning hours of Tuesday March 31 (lunar calendar, April 10) 1909 in their zeal to establish "the rule of *Şeriat*" (Islamic law). In the liberal practices of early 1909 a voluntary association called the Society of Islamic Unity (IMC) was established. IMC had members among the ranks of the First Army of Istanbul, as well as the soldiers of army units, which had recently arrived from the Balkans.[72] There was some evidence that IMC had been involved in the uprising, and the son of Sultan Abdülhamit II was also a member of the IMC, which leaves little room for imagination as to where Abdülhamit stood on this matter.[73]

The officers of the rebel troops had earlier taken part in the revolution of July 10, 1908 and the reestablishment of constitutional monarchy. They became the target of hostilities of the soldiers and crowds who demanded the reinstitution of "*Şeriat.*" Soon after the uprising started the soldiers came under the rule of their petty officers. They eventually attacked the *Meclis* (the Imperial Assembly) and on their way those officers, who tried to order their troops back to their barracks, were murdered. In the *Meclis* they attacked the deputies and killed three of them. The rebels gradually turned to the ITC and attacked whoever resembled a member of that Young Turk organization in their eyes.[74]

The news of the uprising traveled fast. The Third Army in *Selanik* immediately sent troops, known as the *Hareket Ordusu* (Operation Army), to rid Istanbul of the rebels and the reign of terror in the name of "*Şeriat.*" They moved into the city on April 11 (lunar calendar) and fought with the rebels until April 14, 1909. The two weeks of reign of terror in the name of "*Şeriat*" came to an end, and so did the reign of Abdülhamit II, who was ousted from the throne by a unanimous decision of the *Meclis* and sent to exile in *Selanik*.

The events known as the "March thirty-first incident" (*Otuzbir Mart Vak'ası*) constituted another major milestone or marker that constructed the elite political culture of Turkey in the twentieth century. They constituted the first serious encounter and clash of the modernist and secularly oriented members of the political elite with the Islamists in the twentieth century. However, it would not be the last. The relations between the nationalist–modernist elites, on the one hand, and the tradition bound masses, on the other, throughout the Turkish War of Liberation and beyond further crystallized the destabilizing role that religion can play in mobilizing the masses to rise up against the establishment in the eyes of the state authorities in Turkey.

The Second Constitutional period of the Ottoman Empire was its last. It began in 1908 and with the defeat of the Ottoman armies in World War I it ended in 1918. The ITC was instrumental in the lifting of the suspension of the *Meclis* and the initiation of new elections in 1908. In 1909 the Constitution of 1876 was thoroughly amended, and a multiparty system was put in place. However, the pluralist democratic political life of the Empire survived until the 1912 elections or at most up to the 1913 military coup, which installed the Union and Progress Party (ITF) in government, as the one-party system started to take hold.

It was the load of international politics, and the decrepit economy, which failed to provide the government with the capability to meet the international challenges that seemed to have contributed lavishly to the collapse of the budding Ottoman democracy. Most of the Balkan territories had been lost to domestic nationalisms and foreign plots before World War I. In that process Ottomans wasted a lot of financial and human resources to hang on to the Balkan territories. The push of the Russian Empire to the south could only be averted at a very high human, financial, and territorial cost. For example, during the Russo-Ottoman war of 1877–1878 the island of Cyprus, a *bona fide*

Ottoman territory since AD 1571, was leased to the British Empire, "which was to occupy and administer the island in exchange for a promise to help Turkey to defend itself against the Russian expansion."[75] The lease was converted into a permanent occupation by the British, and at the outset of World War I, Britain annexed the island (1914). Cyprus legally became a British crown colony in 1925, and was granted independence by Britain in 1960.[76] Nevertheless, the Ottoman Empire still had sovereignty over Macedonia, Bulgaria, and Albania, as well as Tripolitania and Cyrenaica (currently parts of Libya) and most of the Arabian Peninsula at the beginning of the twentieth century. However, worse was to come in a very short while.

The last main Ottoman territory in North Africa (Tripolitania, Libya) came under the attack of the Italian armies, when Italy decided to join the "other Great Powers of Europe" in the "Scramble for Africa" in 1911.[77] The Ottomans had no means to defend Tripoli and its vicinity properly, where the Italians had landed troops. Only a small group of patriotic soldiers and among them the future founding father of the Turkish Republic, Mustafa Kemal (Atatürk) rushed to defend Tripoli and environs. With no professional troops at hand, they managed to get gather a ragtag army of local tribes and put up a stiff fight. However, they were in no position to defeat a contemporary army. Eventually, the Italians were able to beat the tribal troops and control the coastal zones of Libya. The Ottomans signed the treaty of *Ouchy*, not only ceding their rights over Tripolitania and *Cyrenaica*, to Italy, but also relegated the possession of the *Dodecanese* islands in the southern Aegean Sea, right of the southwestern coast of Anatolia, to the Italians on October 15, 1912.[78]

Just as the hostilities with Italy were dying down, the Balkan Wars erupted in 1912. The major issue that seemed to have finally broken the camel's back was the status of Macedonia, which was, legally speaking, under Ottoman jurisdiction, but was desired by all of its Balkan neighbors. The hostilities over Macedonia boiled over in 1912, when the four Balkan states finally agreed upon how to split Macedonia among themselves (or so they had assumed), and attacked the Ottomans.[79]

Presumably, the Ottoman armies had been completely renovated, and developed into a contemporary fighting force. It had almost been a century (86 years) since 1826, when Sultan Mahmut II managed to have the medieval Janissary troops destroyed, and initiated the most comprehensive military reorganization of the Ottoman armed forces. The Ottoman officer corps had been trained first by French and later by German officers in the meantime. However, the performance of the Ottoman armies in their defense of the Ottoman realm against the Egyptian army in 1838, and the Russian armies in the Crimean War of 1854–1856, and in the Russo-Ottoman War of 1877–1878 left much to be desired. The Ottoman army was not employed in any major war between 1878 and 1912, except for a victory against the Greek army in 1897.

It was widely believed that the Ottoman troops were no less trained, numerous, and equipped than the Balkan armies they fought in 1912.[80]

Furthermore, they were better located to defend their territory. However, the Ottoman army once more caved in under the attacks of the Balkan armies. In fact, the defeat was so comprehensive and quick that, it came as a major shock and even a quagmire for the Ottoman political and military establishment.[81] The human tragedy that followed was also heart breaking. Millions of Turks residing in the Balkans were forcibly evicted from their homes, once more. As millions rushed in sheer panic to Thrace, Istanbul, and Anatolia to avoid the wrath of Greek, Bulgarian, Serbian nationalists, many were massacred, raped, and even trampled over by the mass exodus.[82]

The living conditions they found themselves in, once they arrived in their new homeland were pretty dismal. The Ottoman Empire had been without sufficient economic resources for years. Indeed, the state finances were in shambles between 1847 and 1875, the year when finally, the Ottoman state defaulted its debts.[83] Eventually, a debt administration (*Düyunu umumiye*), which was run by the foreign lenders to the Ottoman Empire, was eventually established in 1882.[84] The Ottoman economy and even politics, to a great extent, came under the influence and directives of that debt administration, managed by French, British, German, and other European administrators appointed by the financial institutions of the lenders.[85] What little the Ottomans had as resources could not be stretched far enough to alleviate the sufferings of the Muslim-Turkish refugees of the Balkan Wars.

However, the previous images of the "Christian" Bulgarians, Greeks, Serbians, Montenegrins, on the one hand, and the "Muslim" Turks, on the other, were shattered for good at the end of the Balkan Wars. Indeed, Donald Quataert reports the interviews with two elderly Christian Bulgarians of the intercommunal relations between "Christians" and "Turks" in Bulgaria during early 1900s: "Turks and Bulgarians lived together and were good neighbors. On holidays they exchanged pleasantries. We sent the Turks *kozunak* and red eggs at Easter and they sent us *baklava* at *Bayram*."[86] The residential settlements seemed to have corroborated the same amicable relations between religious communities in the Empire in the Balkans and elsewhere. Quataert argues that, ". . . there was a high degree of residential mixing . . . Ottoman families chose their home sites, they used a host of criteria and simply not religion."[87] The Muslim Turks who were forced to vacate their homes in the Balkans and met with enormous hardships and mistreatment on the way to Thrace, Istanbul, and Anatolia, and some even continued to suffer during and after they settled at their new homes. They eventually turned their hatred to Christian communities residing at their new neighborhoods. In place of the older amicable intercommunal relations emerged hostile and intolerant Muslim attitudes toward the Christian communities of Thrace, Istanbul, and Anatolia, and vice versa.

In 1913 the victorious powers of the First Balkan War fell apart over the distribution of the spoils of war. The Second Balkan War erupted. It was the opportunity that some young officers in the Ottoman army were dreaming for.[88] It was the daring act of those officers, which resulted in regaining some small parcels of territory in and around the city of *Edirne* (*Adrianapolis*) on the river of Maritza back.[89] This daring attack led by a young officer by the name of Enver (who eventually became the son-in-law of the Sultan), made him an instant hero and contributed to his stellar rise to the Ottoman Cabinet soon after.[90] A military coup he participated in also seemed to have helped Enver Paşa to become an influential member (Minister of War), in the Ottoman Council of Ministers,[91] which declared war on the Entente Powers in World War I, which in turn, paved the way to the collapse of the Empire.

With all its tragedies and drama the Balkan Wars have been one of the most important events that shaped the thinking of the Turkish political elite and the masses alike, ever since. Some of the more perceptive officers who took part in the war arrived at the conclusion that the main reason why the Ottoman armies lost the war was not their lack of training, or lack of resources, logistics, and other capabilities. Their dramatic defeat was a direct result of the involvement of the officer corps in domestic politics.[92] It became clear after the war that the strategic planning and discipline was undermined by political corruption and incompetence, which was fueled by involvement of the officers in domestic and partisan politics.[93] The command and coherence of the army collapsed under the pressures of war, and the defeat followed immediately after. The moral of the story seemed to be a foreseeable disaster, which had been earlier outlined by none other than the founding father of the Turkish Republic to be, Mustafa Kemal (Atatürk) in 1909: When politics and military service mix, they produce a recipe for disaster![94] Mustafa Kemal (Atatürk) had been proposing to sack the soldiers involved in politics from the military profession since 1909, and he arrived at the conclusion that the Balkan Wars were just a living testimony of the disastrous outcome of politicization of the military.[95]

World War I that followed immediately after the Balkan Wars further solidified and deepened the animosities of the confessional and ethnic communities, which simply persisted during the Turkish War of Liberation and beyond. Muslims and Christians suffered reciprocal mistreatments, massacres, and deportations from 1912 to 1922. Population exchanges between Turkey and Greece continued until the 1930s, and deportations of "Muslims as Turks" from the Balkans occurred in the 1950s from Bulgaria and Yugoslavia to Turkey, from Bulgaria to Turkey in the 1980s. Ethnic cleansing in Bosnia-Herzegovina, Serbia and Macedonia led to further migration from those lands to Turkey in the 1990s.[96] The residence permits of Greek citizens residing in Turkey at the restart of the Cyprus conflict were cancelled in the 1960s, and thus 9,000 Orthodox Greeks left over in Turkey and mainly in Istanbul from the Ottoman Empire were deported in 1964. In a sense, Balkan nationalisms, of which Turkish nationalism is a sort, continued to threaten and undermine the relations among the Balkan nations, Turkey included, throughout the twentieth century.

When the Balkan Wars and tragedy were over and the ITF was faced with the daunting task of steering the decrepit Empire through the turbulence of the approaching World War. The ITF was the first example of a political party that championed liberty and ended up in establishing an illiberal regime of its own in Turkish politics. Others, such as the Democrat Party (DP) of the 1950s, were to trek down the same route in the rest of the twentieth century.

The debate over whether ITF could avoid taking the Ottoman Empire into World War I still simmers among the pundits of Ottoman history. The decision to grant refuge to the German cruisers *Breslau* and *Goeben*, and their eventual bombardment of the Russian Black Sea shore with their Ottoman flags hoisted indicated more of a choice than inevitability.[97] However, Russia was very eager to dispose off the Ottoman Empire, which it had considered as the "sick man of Europe" in a way it saw fit, and the Germans were also looking for an opportunity to get the Ottomans to enter the war as their ally.[98] Whatever the truth may be, the Ottomans found themselves in alliance with the Germans, Austrians, and Bulgarians, and began fighting against the Entente of the British, French, Russian, Italian, and Greek armies in Europe, the Middle East, and the Eastern parts of Anatolia.

THE WORLD WAR AND THE COLLAPSE

The Dardanelle is the strait that connects the Marmara Sea with the Aegean and eventually the Mediterranean Seas. If penetrated, Istanbul, the capital city of the Ottoman Empire could be invaded easily, and the Ottomans could be knocked out of the war in 1915. In fact, the dismal performance of the Ottoman armies in the Balkan Wars only three years previously indicated that they were no match for the British and the ANZAC (New Zealand and Australian) forces. However, the Ottoman armies, their German and Turkish commanders turned out to be much more determined and capable than the British government had anticipated. Indeed, the British were stopped at the entrance of the *Dardanelle*, at *Gallipoli*. The whole military campaign was such a disaster for Britain that one of the masterminds of the campaign, Sir Winston Churchill, almost had his political career ended there and then. However, in Eastern Anatolia and the Middle East the performance of the Ottoman armies and the Entente forces led to totally different outcomes.

Both of the military campaigns in the east and the Arabian Peninsula in the south turned out to be replete with tragic failures for the Ottoman armies. In both theaters of war the Ottoman forces were faced with far superior fighting forces. The Ottomans started to run out of resources and logistic support for their armies as the war continued. The non-Turkish and/or the non-Muslim communities hosted nationalists, who viewed the approaching armies of Russia and Britain as saviors, and cooperated with the enemies of the Ottomans. Hence, the Ottomans had to deal with what they considered to be seditious activities of local nationalisms and the onslaught of the Russian and British troops simultaneously. The Armenian nationalists in the east and the Arab nationalists in the south emerged as the most important domestic challenges during World War I.

The Russian army advanced rapidly in eastern Anatolia in 1914 and 1915, while the Armenian nationalists perceived the developments as their long awaited opportunity for struggle for independence.[99] As Bernard Lewis points out "In 1914 the Russians formed four large Armenian volunteer units, and three more in 1915. These . . . , included Ottoman Armenians, some of them deserters, some of them well-known public figures. . . . Armenian guerilla bands were active in various parts of the country and, in several places, Armenian populations rose in armed rebellion, notably in the eastern Anatolian city of Van and the *Cilician* town of *Zeytun*."[100]

Pressured by the British in the west and the south, and the Russians in the east, the Ottoman government decided to use an old and thoroughly tested, and institutionalized method of "deportation and resettlement" to deal with what it perceived as a communal (*millet*) insurgency. The Armenian communities in the east[101] were subject to forced migration (*tehcir*) to *Zor* in Syria, still a part of the Ottoman territory in 1915.[102] One student of Ottoman history unearths that ". . . Order after order speaks of the need to guard the deportees and their property and assure their safety. Those deported often walked, since there were few trains in these areas. As they walked, they suffered and some died of malnutrition or an accompanying disease while others were killed in the hands of bandits who preyed on the weak. But, the solicitous state documents not withstanding, Ottoman officers, soldiers, and civilian officials—the very persons who had the sworn responsibility to defend and protect the lives of all Ottoman subjects regardless of religion or ethnicity—murdered vast numbers of Armenian civilians, men, women, and children alike."[103] Another prominent student of Ottoman history, Bernard Lewis gives a slightly different account of what transpired: "In an embattled empire desperately short of manpower, neither soldiers nor gendarmes were available, and the task of escorting the deportees was entrusted to hastily recruited local posses. . . . Many succumbed to hunger, disease and exposure; great numbers were brutally murdered, either by local tribesmen and villagers, through the negligence or with the complicity of their unpaid, unfed, and undisciplined escorts, or by the escorts themselves."[104]

Indeed, a total of about 600,000 Armenians perished from the population records during period that spans across World War I and the War of Liberation, which constituted about 40 percent of the Armenian population of the area.[105] Zürcher argues that the figure may be as high as 800,000[106] and Lewis talks about hundreds of thousands and perhaps over a million who perished during deportation,[107] though the latter two cited no demographic study to back up their claims. Zürcher also clearly argues that there is no evidence that there was any systematic annihilation of the entire Armenian population as state policy by the Ottoman authorities.[108] Lewis[109] and Quataert[110] seem to concur. Nevertheless, some among the *Ittihat ve Terakki Fırkası* Special Organization (*Teşkilat-ı Mahsusa*), which seemed to have functioned as a "state within the state" during the one-party rule of that party after 1913, might have organized the mass killings of the Armenian civilians in various locations in eastern Anatolia.[111] However, as Zürcher, who believes in the complicity of the Special Organization[112] and others[113] indicate that no records of the ITC party archives or of the Special Organization exist on the matter, and no authority, including the British

Forces that occupied the Ottoman capital were able to unearth any evidence of a state conspiracy to annihilate the Armenian population of the Ottoman Empire.[114]

It is also a matter of fact that, in the same period, about 1,000,000 Muslims also disappeared from the population rosters of the Ottoman Empire in the same eastern provinces.[115] The Muslim losses amounted up to 60 percent of the Muslim populations in some of the same eastern provinces where *Dashnaks* (Armenian nationalists)[116] were active between 1912 and 1922.

The tragic events of World War I were another staging of the same nationalist scenario that had been successfully executed in the Balkans until only a decade or so ago. However, this time the potential mentor of the Armenians, the Russians could not survive long enough to "liberate" them, as they had done so earlier for the Moldavians, Romanians, Bulgarians, and others in the Balkans. The Russian armies collapsed under the load of the World War. The dire economic conditions of Russia precipitated the simmering discontent into a social revolution in the middle of the war, and by 1917 Russia quit fighting the Ottoman armies. The Russian forces vacated the whole of eastern Anatolia and the Caucasus before the end of the war. Hence, from 1917 to 1922, when the Red Army fully reclaimed the southern Caucasus and the Turkish–Soviet border was legally redrawn, the area turned into a battleground of tribal and primordial wars, where savagery reigned. Many more Armenians and Muslims died in reciprocal massacres. However, in the meantime the Armenian nationalists, mainly the *Dashnaks* lost the war they fought with the Ottoman state and the Muslim *millet* of the Ottoman Empire in eastern Anatolia. Innocent bystanders, Armenians and Muslims alike, suffered dearly in that process.

The Arab nationalists also had a more powerful mentor to count on, the British Empire. The British had done their homework well before the war. The famous saga of Lawrence of Arabia is just one piece of evidence of how well the British intelligence had worked through the area. The British approached Sharīf Husayn of *Hijāz*, who had been known for his zeal to establish the ruling dynasty of Arabia. The letters of Mac Mahon, the British governor of Egypt to Sharīf Husayn promised him just that in 1915–1916.[117] It did not take long for Husayn and his sons to join ranks with the British forces and fight against the Ottomans. However, it is wrong to assume that all of the Arabs were ready to end the Ottoman "yoke." Although there were many nationalists in Syria, Lebanon, *Hijāz* and elsewhere, many more seemed to be happy with their lifestyle, the state of affairs, and they seemed to have stuck with the Ottomans until the very end of the war.

The Ottoman authorities perceived the attacks of the Arab nationalists, and the tribes that joined them as an overall revolt of fellow Muslims acting in full complicity with their enemy in war, and dealt with them as harshly as they could. The Arabs still resent the heavy-handed rule of Cemal Paşa, who was the general commander of the Ottoman armies of Middle East in the war. He did have many Arab intellectuals arrested, tried for treason and executed for their complicity in the Arab revolt. The Arab intellectuals and elites eventually concluded that the Ottomans had increasingly come under the influence of Turkish nationalism. They more and more perceived the Ottoman authorities as a "Turkish elite" imposing a foreign rule on the Arabs. Those Turks who participated in the military campaigns of the Arabian Peninsula also developed an impression that the Arabs betrayed the Ottoman Sultan and their Caliph, and stabbed them in the back. When the war ended, the Turkish majority to the north and Arabs to the south had been left with not much motivation to live under a single political authority.

The overall impact of the atrocities committed in the east and the south against the Muslims and Turks culminated in a state of mind deeply influenced by fear, which occasionally reaches levels of paranoia, of a loosely defined threat of "division" or secession from the union of some ethnic or religious community in modern day Turkey.

THE TURKISH WAR OF LIBERATION

In the middle of World War I, the Foreign Ministers of France and Britain had drawn up a plan to redesign the Middle East and Anatolia to their interests and aspirations after the war. This plan is referred to as the Sykes–Picot Agreement of 1916, after Mr. Sykes of Britain and Monsieur Picot of France. When the British emerged as the victorious side in the Middle East at the end of 1918, the Allies had the opportunity to implement the Sykes–Picot Agreement, which eventually culminated in the design of the Treaty of *Sèvres* (1920) (see map 1.1).

However, the redrawing of borders had started even before the *Sèvres* Treaty, and almost immediately after the signing of the *Mudros* Armistice Treaty with the Ottoman Empire (October 30, 1918). The French had invaded Syria, Lebanon and parts of what is now southeastern Turkey. The British had established their rule over Iraq, Transjordan, and Palestine, and occupied Istanbul by March 1919.

Various negotiations and deliberations continued from the signing of the *Mudros* Armistice to the drawing up of the Treaty of *Sèvres*, which reinforced the picture that had been drawn up in the Sykes–Picot agreement and the *Mudros* armistice. The Arab provinces were finally severed from the Empire.[118] The Thracian and Anatolian territories of the Ottoman Empire were divided up between Greek, French, Armenian, and British occupation zones (see map 1.1). The straits of Bosporus and Dardanelle, and Istanbul, the capital of the Ottoman Empire were placed under the control of the Entente forces led by the British. The style with which the Treaty of *Sèvres* was designed may best be defined as vindictive.[119]

It was the last step, which the Ottoman government took by signing and ratifying the Treaty of *Sèvres* that completely dashed all hopes of establishing a united resistance to the occupation in the eyes of the Turkish nationalists. Two events flared up nationalist zeal to resist the occupation forces in Anatolia and eastern Thrace. One was the landing of the Greek troops at İzmir on May 15, 1919, and their mistreatment of the population in and

36

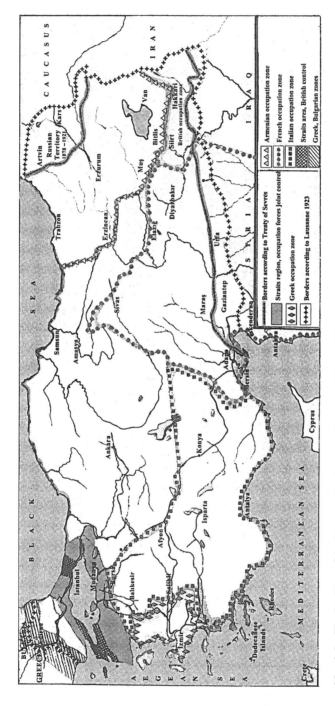

Map 1.1 The Partition of the Ottoman Empire According to the Treaty of *Sevrès*

Source: Maarif Vekaleti, 1931: 152–153.

around *İzmir*.[120] The second consisted of the atrocious acts against the Muslim men and women committed by the Armenian nationalists in various garbs, from those of the official Armenian army in the eastern Anatolia to those of the French army in the south and southwest of Anatolia.[121] The Turkish nationalists showed signs of organizing local and regional organizations to resist the occupation forces (*Müdafa-i Hukuk ve Reddi İhak Cemiyetleri*) as early as May and summer of 1919.

The signing of the Treaty of *Sèvres* in August 1920 led to the severance of relations between Istanbul (Ottoman) and nationalist resistance in Ankara. Now, the nationalists could explain their position with greater clarity, and ask the support and participation of the demoralized and downtrodden masses in their efforts to revoke the Treaty of *Sèvres*. The Treaty of *Sèvres* was identified with unfair punishment, immoral treatment, humiliation, and defeat in the eyes of the Turkish nationalists. Resisting, repealing, and preventing the conditions of the Treaty of *Sèvres* became a major objective of governments and all nationalist political forces in Turkey ever since. From 1920 onward Turks developed a deep suspicion of the true motives of the major powers of the world. Sometimes loosely referred to as the "*Sèvres* syndrome," has become an integral part of the Turkish culture and the political psyche ever since August 10, 1920.

When, as some believe, "the first bullet" was fired, by a journalist, Hasan Tahsin at the Greek troops landing at the *Izmir* harbor, his daring act seemed to have fired up the pent up nationalist fervor among the young Turkish nationalists.[122] In fact, even before Hasan Tahsin fired shots at the arriving Greek troops, small groups of nationalist activists gathered in organizing clandestine organizations to resist occupation in the Aegean and Thracian regions of Turkey.[123] The Hasan Tahsin incident and other similar events provided the nationalists with the opportunity to mobilize others and enlarge their ranks. However, the leader of the nationalist resistance emerged only after Mustafa Kemal Paşa (Atatürk) was sent to the Black Sea port of *Samsun* as a military inspector, on the order of the Sultan on May 16, 1919 from Istanbul. It was Mustafa Kemal who managed to unite the local and regional movements of nationalist resistance into a single national movement (*kuvva-i milliye*) between May 1919 and April 1920.

Mustafa Kemal found himself in conflict with the Palace soon after he started to organize nationalist conferences and congresses in *Erzurum* (July 23, 1919) and *Sivas* (September 4, 1919), on the way to organizing a liberation movement. After he fell apart with the Palace and the government in Istanbul, he took the opportunity to set up a nationalist government in Ankara. The *Meclis* (Ottoman Imperial Assembly) in Istanbul had new elections in 1919. Mustafa Kemal and nationalists were able to mobilize enough support for their movement by then to have the majority of the deputies of the new and the last Ottoman *Meclis* to be elected from among their ranks. It was that Ottoman *Meclis*, which adopted the National Pact (*Misak-ı Milli*), which served as the basis for organizing the nationalist struggle for liberation. It was the "National Pact" which defined the borders of the national homeland of Turks and asserted the right to self-determination of Turks in their homeland. Espousing the principles of the U.S. President Wilson the nationalists called for the right to resist occupation and establish a nation-state on the national homeland of Turks.[124]

However, the declaration of the Nationalist Pact was more than the British could tolerate. They attacked and captured as many of the deputies of the *Meclis* as they could, though some were able to flee Istanbul and join the nationalists in Anatolia. The British incarcerated the deputies of the *Meclis* they arrested in Malta.[125] This British move enabled Mustafa Kemal and the nationalist elite to organize a new *Meclis* in Ankara. The Grand National Assembly (BMM) convened on April 23, 1920. Hence, thanks to the British, the small town of Ankara in the middle of Anatolia, which had been the organizational headquarters of the nationalist movement, now became the seat of the nationalist government, which functioned as an alternative government to the Ottoman government in Istanbul, and hence it is often referred to as the "Ankara government," until the declaration of the Republic in 1923.

At the time the Sultan and his "Istanbul Government" accepted the conditions of the Treaty of *Sévres*, the nationalists had established their legislature with the claim of representing the "will of the nation," and a government consisting of the Grand National Assembly (BMM), which functioned in unison as the legislature, executive and judiciary, simultaneously. Mustafa Kemal also set out to establish a national army under the command of the BMM. It took much longer for the various guerilla forces fighting in different parts of the country to be united under the umbrella of a single command of the national army. Some guerilla groups resisted the idea and they had to be eliminated by force.[126] A disciplined, trained and veteran army was eventually established by 1922. In the meantime fighting had been continuing, at least, on four different fronts between 1920 and 1922.

One of those fronts was established in the east, where what was left over from the Ottoman army, under the command of General Kazım Karabekir engaged the Armenian armed forces. The *Mudros* armistice treaty stipulated the disbanding and demobilization of the Ottoman armed forces, and control of all lines of communication and transportation, including the straits by the Entente forces.[127] General Karabekir had not heeded the terms of the *Mudros* Armistice Treaty and continued to keep his forces under his command in battle ready conditions. They soon found themselves at war with the armies of Armenian state, which started to invade eastern Anatolia. The Treaty of *Sévres* foresaw the allocation of large swaths of eastern Anatolia to Armenia. However, the Armenian armies lost the war and eventually the Ankara and the Armenian governments negotiated and signed a peace treaty (Treaty of *Alexandropol/Gümrü/Gymry*), in early December 1920.[128] It was ratified by the "Ankara government," but could not be ratified by Armenia, for the latter was reoccupied by the Red Army in the beginning of 1921. The Soviets eventually accepted the terms of the Treaty of *Alexandropol (Gümrü)*, and the border between Turkey and Armenia was legally recognized as part of the Turkish–Soviet border until 1945. However, the early settlement of the eastern question relieved Karabekir's troops from active duty, and enabled them to be deployed in the west against a much more severe threat posed by the Greek invasion forces.[129]

The second front emerged in the south, where local guerilla resistance engaged the French forces in the provinces of *Antep*, *Maraş*, *Urfa*, and to west, in the region of *Cilicia*. It did not take long for the Armenians serving in the French army to start to settle their old accounts with the Muslim populations. Muslims began to resist the French rule, which tolerated the Armenian attacks on Turkish civilians in 1919 and 1920. The French had made a big miscalculation, for every Armenian attack further drew Muslims to the ranks of the Turkish nationalist resistance. Finally, in 1921, the French offered the Ankara government a new border, which was eventually accepted by the latter. The Treaty of Ankara (1921) reestablished the border between Syria and Turkey, and the French pulled out of *Antep*, *Maraş*, *Urfa*, and most of *Cilicia*. Hence, the Treaty of Ankara documented that the French recognized the terms of the Turkish National Pact, and broke ranks with the Entente and the British. However, Turkey continued to demand a plebiscite in the district (*sancak*) of *Alexandretta* (*Hatay*) to determine the legal status of that autonomous region of the French Mandate of Syria until 1936. The French agreed to a plebiscite, which was held in 1938, and the results indicated a slight majority of Turkish representation in the parliament of *Hatay*, which then convened and voted to join Turkey.[130] Hence, the *sancak* of *Alexandretta*, which had been an autonomous part of the French Mandate of Syria until 1939, legally became the *Hatay* province of Turkey in that year.[131]

The third front was established in the west, where guerilla forces, and eventually the regular, nationalist army of the Ankara government fought the Greek forces. The Greek forces were well equipped, trained, and seemed highly motivated with the idea of reestablishing their ancient Empire under a new guise. Indeed, they put up a stiff fight. They seemed to have the upper hand until 1922. However, the more they pushed into Anatolia, the more the Turkish forces hit and retreated. Soon they were too far away from the Mediterranean and the Aegean coasts for their logistic support to be sustained without trouble. After fighting nonstop for about three weeks, day and night during the Battle of *Sakarya* (August 23–September 13, 1921), the Greek army seemed not to have won a victory instead they seemed to have run out of food, ammunition, morale, and capability to pursue the Turkish nationalist army.[132] The Greeks had to pull back to the west of the river, and defend their western Anatolian possessions. They were considered to be in an impeccable defensive position. However, the attack of the Turkish army on August 26, 1922 proved that assumption wrong. The Greek forces had to pull out of Anatolia in a hurry or surrender. They departed from Smyrna (*Izmir*) on September 9, and *Bursa* on September 13, 1922. A new Armistice Treaty was signed in the small coastal town of *Mudanya* (a town near Bursa on the *Marmara* Sea coast), was signed between the British and the Ankara government soon after (October 11, 1922), which ended the military campaigns of the War of Liberation. In the meantime, the Turkish nationalist forces had landed on the European side of the city of Istanbul on October 6, 1922.

The Sultanate was abolished by means of a simple resolution of the Grand National Assembly on November 1, 1922. The Sultan and his family were exiled. A new Caliph, Abdülmecit Efendi was selected on November 18, 1922. The Caliphate lasted for another two years, until 1924, and it was also abolished by the young Republican regime, which in turn, was established on October 29, 1923. The fate of the Sultan and Caliph had a lot to do with the fourth front of the War of Liberation. This front was established all over Anatolia. Indeed, it was more or less an internecine struggle or civil war. What were at stake were the souls and minds of the people of Anatolia. The battles were not only fought by guns and bullets, but also by religious decrees (*fetvas*). On 19 occasions massive uprisings took place against the authority of the government of Ankara.[133] In all of those cases, those who participated in the uprisings alluded to the superior authority of the Sultan and the Caliph. Most accused the nationalist as "heretics, bandits, and pagans," who perpetrated a grave sin by disobeying the authority of the "*amir-ul muminin*" (the leader of the Muslims), who was none other than the Sultan and Caliph in Istanbul.[134] The nationalists had to respond to this grave challenge by the help of the Muslim clergy (*ulema*), whose credentials and opinions they needed to prove that they were indeed involved in a pious activity, whereby the Caliph and Sultan was under the control of the British in Istanbul. Hence, the attitude of the Islamists and the nationalists completely diverged to create an internecine conflict over the status of the Treaty of *Sévres*.

In the eyes of the Sultan the conditions of the Treaty of *Sévres*, which left the capital city of the Empire under the British occupation and his government subservient to the British, and large swaths of Anatolia to Armenian, Greek, French, Italian, and other occupation forces was no different than the previous treaties and defeats of the Empire. The Islamists (*Islamcılar*) adopted the same position as the Sultan and Caliph in Istanbul toward the Treaty of *Sévres*, while Ankara government and their allies considered it an affront to the Turkish nation.

Islam was again employed as a powerful tool by the Ottoman government in *Istanbul*, with the full blessing of the British occupation forces to challenge the nationalist war efforts.[135] They tried to suppress the nationalist forces, and the nationalists had to fight back with the same means to eliminate that grave danger. However, it was the second time in a decade that Islamists had turned out to be a grave hazard for the modernist elites since the "March thirty-first incident." The Islamist challenge to the nationalist elites and army in the War of Liberation further reinforced the image of the Islamists in the eyes of the nationalists, as the lackeys of the foreign forces, always ready to be mobilized to undermine the national interests of Turkey. Islamism was thus identified with restiveness, rebelliousness, and popular uprising against the nationalist policies and programs, independence, and eventually the Republic in Turkey. Once the Islamist challenge was defeated in the War of Liberation, the nationalists dealt with them in the same way they dealt with all others, who they had considered to be involved in treason.

The nationalist elites also had to deal with another domestic challenge, and that was much more of a competition, than a mere confrontation. The leaders of the ITC had also fled after World War I. Among them, Enver had ended up in Russia. As a Turkish ethnic nationalist he seemed to have taken the idea of establishing a state of and for the Turks in Turkistan, more or less along the lines the original brand of nationalists had argued for the Turkish homeland of "*Turan.*" Enver seemed to continue with his project of salvaging the lands of Central Asia, Azerbaijan, and the rest of Transcaucasus, and Anatolia to merge them under the flag of *Turan*! He seemed to make various gestures to cajole the nationalists fighting the War of Liberation to his idea. Mustafa Kemal Atatürk had always considered him as a rival and dangerous man to deal with. He and his close circle were tremendously alarmed of Enver's activities, and seriously resisted his encroachments and attempts to return to Anatolia. Eventually, Mustafa Kemal was successful from fending Enver off from his nationalist movement and Anatolian territory. Enver nevertheless went on with his idea and tried to "emancipate" Central Asia from Russian dominance, and was killed near Dushanbe (currently in Tajikistan), in June 1922 by the Red Army.[136]

THE TREATY OF *LAUSANNE*

If there are any catchwords in the lexicon of Turkish political culture that identify where one stands on nationalism, they are the "*Sévres*" and the "*Lausanne.*" What "*Sévres*" stands for should be pretty obvious in light of the preceding examination of the conditions of the War of Liberation. The Treaty of *Lausanne* is the crystallization of what the resistance to occupation managed to win. After the signing of the armistice Treaty of *Mudanya* (1922), the Ankara government tried very hard not to lose what they had gained at the battleground against enormous odds, during the peace negotiations at *Lausanne.*

The nationalists had no one to turn to for advice in the negotiations, and no example to follow in *Lausanne.* The Ottoman diplomats had long forgotten what it was like to drive a hard bargain with Britain, France, and other major powers of the time. The only other new state of the time was the Soviet Union. Although Turkish nationalists had signed a treaty of friendship, and nonaggression, with the Soviets in 1921, the long history of enmity between Russia and the Ottomans led them to be cautious toward the Soviet Union. Hence, the peace negotiations took almost a year to complete and they were terminated once during that year. Eventually, the Turkish delegation came to terms with the victorious powers of World War I, and the Treaty of *Lausanne* was signed on July 24, 1923.

The signing of the Treaty of *Lausanne* resulted in the realization of one of the major objectives of the nationalists, namely, repealing the terms of the Treaty of *Sévres.* Second, the Treaty of *Lausanne* accepted the right of the Turks to self-determination and their sovereign rights over their homeland. However, the definition of the national homeland, which the National Pact (*Misak-ı Milli*) of 1919 had adopted, did not fully coincide with the terms of the Treaty of *Lausanne* on the territory of the new Turkish state. For example, the province of *Mosul*, which is populated by Kurds and Turkmen, and now is in northern Iraq, was designated on demographic, cultural, and historical grounds as part and parcel of the Turkish national homeland in 1919. However, the British had invaded city of *Mosul* (November 15, 1918), and swiftly moved their troops to further north of the city, in violation of the Treaty of *Mudros*.[137] The negotiations in *Lausanne* failed to clarify the status of *Mosul*. Second, the status of the autonomous *sancak* of Alexandretta between the French mandate authority in Syria and the Ankara government was also far from being successfully resolved in *Lausanne*. Some of the Aegean islands, which had been declared as part of the national homeland by the National Pact, were also left outside of its realm. Consequently, the Treaty of *Lausanne* did not fully coincide with the demands of the National Pact of 1919. However, there was sufficient coincidence for the nationalists to be realistic about the situation, and accept to refer the case of *Mosul* to the League of Nations, although Turkey was not yet a member of that organization at the time. The Ankara government also accepted the autonomy of the *sancak* of *Alexandretta*, which was assigned to the French mandate authority in Syria, for the time being. The newly established Turkish Republic saw little benefit in prolonging conflict with the British and French mandate administrations to their south, and swiftly moved to settle the territorial disputes.

The *Mosul* issue was resolved in favor of the British mandate in Iraq by the League of Nations, after three years of inquiry, negotiations, and some tension by 1926. An ethno-religious uprising in eastern Anatolia delivered the message to the Turkish nationalists that if they pursued a policy of non-agreement over the drawing of the border with Iraq, the British will continue to destabilize Turkey.[138] The Turkish Republican government had other domestic and international woes, such as the belligerence of the Italian dictator Mussolini, who had started to make imperialist demands in a speech he delivered in Tripoli (Libya) in 1926, to deal with.[139] Agreeing to the proposals of the League of Nations over the issue of *Mosul* would have introduced some stability in Turkish–British relations, and it indeed did so.[140]

The borders of Republican Turkey, now fully extended legitimacy and legality through the Treaty of *Lausanne*, made her neighbors to most of the major powers of the time. Turkey had the Soviet Union as her northern and eastern neighbor, and Iran as her southeastern neighbor. The southern borders made Turkey a neighbor of Britain and France, and of Italy ruled by Mussolini in the southwest (for Italy was in possession of the *Dodecanese* islands). In the west, Turkey shared a long border over land and sea with Greece and Bulgaria. Turkey also shared the Black Sea with Bulgaria, Romania, and the Soviet Union in the north. Consequently, it became imperative that Turkey followed a very cautious foreign policy that would minimize friction with the major powers of the interwar era.

In the meantime, Turkish nationalism went through a metamorphosis and rescinded all claims beyond those that failed to coincide with the National

Pact and the Treaty of *Lausanne*, such as that of the establishment of a Grand Turkistan (*Turan*). Fully distancing itself from any form of pan-nationalism, and mainly focusing upon protecting what it could salvage from the encroachments of the major powers of the time provided an opportunity to develop a civic form of nationalism in Turkey. Consequently, protecting the national homeland, improving the welfare of the population residing in Anatolia and western Thrace, and the rights enshrined by the Treaty of *Lausanne* gained penultimate importance. Ethnic nationalist character of Turkish nationalism eroded rapidly to make room for a civic content to develop immediately after the Republic was established. The next chapter of this book concentrates on the establishment of the historical and cultural baggage that the Republic inherited from its Ottoman past, and the nature of the Republican political regime, Anatolian society, and the Turkish economy in the first years of the Republic.

2

FOUNDING THE REPUBLIC AND THE CULTURAL REVOLUTION (1923–1946)

The Republic of Turkey (*Türkiye Cumhuriyeti*) was established on October 29, 1923. The Treaty of *Lausanne* (signed on July 24, 1923), designated the new government in *Ankara* as the legal and legitimate heir of the Ottoman Empire, for the latter had been abolished in 1922 and thus was not a party to the Treaty.[1] The new Turkish government would rather sever its ties with the decrepit and by then abolished Empire. Indeed, most enterprises and policies designed by the Turkish government after 1923 were to serve that purpose.

Atatürk played a major role in calculating, timing, and devising the daring steps of a modernizing and secularizing cultural revolution, which lay the foundations of the Republican political system.[2] The relative dearth of well-trained and skilled personnel at the disposal of the Turkish state, who could have assisted the President and his close company in the early days of the Republic constituted a serious problem.[3] The Balkan Wars, World War I, and the War of Liberation resulted in ". . . both mortality and physical destruction, the events that overtook Anatolia between 1912 and 1922 were among the most disastrous . . . In Anatolia, out of a prewar population of 17.5 million, nearly 3 million Muslims, nearly 600,000 Armenians, and slightly more than 300,000 Greeks were lost . . ."[4] Not only manual labor pool was devastated but also the pool of skilled labor, and most specifically the few college educated members of the former Ottoman society perished in the wars, most of who served as reserve officers (third lieutenants), who led the troops to battle, and often died at the very first instance of battle. Some of the Republican leaders were graduates of the Ottoman military academies, and few had any depth of knowledge about secularism, republicanism, nationalism, science, and so on. Relative to his associates, colleagues, and advisers, Mustafa Kemal Atatürk seemed to be unique. Mango stated his characteristics the best: "Atatürk was a competent commander, a shrewd politician, a statesman of supreme realism."[5]

ATATÜRK AT THE HELM OF GOVERNMENT

Atatürk seemed to analyze the political context within which he operated. From the perspective of a staff officer he possessed the ability of logical inference, which enabled him to take the radical and sometimes even daring, and usually unanticipated decisions. He was also quick to adapt to the changing times. He was no philosopher. He seemed to have followed, intensely thought about the developments, and deliberated suggestions, proposals, propositions and policy suggestions made by the others. He came to believe by 1918 that the Ottoman system was a liability, rather than an asset, which would best be discarded with, as quickly, clearly, and effectively as possible.[6] Once he had arrived at a conclusion, he seemed to have never looked back. Those who failed to see through his spectacles were cast aside, even if they had been in his close circle earlier on. His classmates from the Defense Academy, his colleagues in many of the wars he took part in either drifted away or dithered and were cast off by Atatürk and his closest military and political aide İsmet İnönü, as Atatürk prodded on with the cultural revolution of the 1920s and the 1930s.[7] The few who stood by him until his death functioned more in the capacity of his subordinates than his coequals.[8]

Atatürk's political style of rule incorporated a mixture of personalism and commitment to institutionalization of modern representational structures.[9] He was also keen at creating political structures, such as a national legislature (the Turkish Grand National Assembly, TGNA), where all political legitimacy legally, and theoretically rested, a political party (Republican People's Party, CHP) as a popular mobilizing agent, and an army that effectively and loyally serves the National Assembly. However, Atatürk's charisma, especially when he served as the President of the Republic, was larger than life, and this had curbed the free play and corresponding development of those political structures. He was able to wield enough influence over the political groups, structures or institutions, through the support of the CHP deputies in the TGNA, so that his personal style of rule made its imprint on the developments of the formative years of the Republican era.

There is some debate whether Atatürk was a dictator of the 1920s and the 1930s, or a democrat in disguise whose efforts at the establishment of democracy dismally failed due to the cultural and political constraints of the interwar era. As a charismatic leader Atatürk was definitely more dedicated to modernization than to liberal democracy. However, there is no evidence that he was emulating Lenin, Stalin, Mussolini, or Hitler of his time. He seemed to have reasoned that unless a modern, secular, and national culture is solidly established, a modern political system, potentially hosting some form of democracy,[10] could not have any chance of survival. Hence, he opted for one-party rule, with a party mostly composed of many junior members attracted to his charisma,[11] and a cultural revolution that would establish a modern nation-state in Anatolia and eastern Thrace. His efforts were also focused on the establishment of a strong centralized public bureaucracy that would penetrate the periphery, and with the help of the Republican People's Party, shape it after the image of "Good Society" he had envisioned for the young Turkish nation-state.[12] The attempt to institute democracy was carried out by his Prime Minister and later President (1938–1950) İsmet İnönü, almost immediately after World War II.

In short, the priority of the new leadership, spearheaded by Atatürk himself and the republican political elite was to consolidate power at home and put their hard won territory on track for a socioeconomic and cultural transformation that would deliver the fruits of Enlightenment in a few decades. Hence, they preferred to bury the hatchet and trek a peaceful foreign policy vis-à-vis the neighbors of Turkey. The domestic political and socioeconomic conditions required immediate attention, while the nation-state trekked a careful, legalistic and peaceful foreign policy, which Mustafa Kemal Atatürk eventually formulated as "Peace at Home, Peace Abroad" (*Yurtta Sulh, Cihanda Sulh*). Such a status quo orientation in Turkish foreign policy made an indelible mark that even when Turkey decided to take part in the UN forces in the Korean War (1950), and was forced to take action in Cyprus (1963–1974), Iraq (1990, 2003), Balkans (1992–1996), and elsewhere, the consternation of the public and elites alike have created a major factor for the Turkish governments to cope with.

CONSOLIDATING POWER AT HOME

Soon after the ratification of the Treaty of *Lausanne*, the Republican leadership started to deliberate the normalization of the political system of the new nation-state. The Republic had inherited a war-ravaged territory with scant human resources, and devastated economic infrastructure due to the Balkan Wars, World War I, and the War of Liberation. However, the most severe challenge for the young Republic emerged from the ranks of the ethnic and religious communities and movements in the country that were still attracted to the appeal of the Ottoman religious establishment. It did not take long before they started to challenge the territorial integrity and political authority of the Republican state. The Turkish political elite confronted the challenge of ethnic separatists, mainly the Kurds, and religious revivalists, mainly the Sunni religious orders, which often colluded to strive to reestablish the Ottoman system under some new guise.

In the background stood the looming problem of the status of the Caliphate and the separation of the realm of religion (caliphacy) from the realm of politics (government in Ankara). Secularism was not a new issue, and indeed it had been a burning political matter for a long time. About a century ago, the *Tanzimat* Reforms (1839–1876) had elevated the issue of secularism to a new level.[13] Indeed one of the main influences of the *Tanzimat* Reforms was to diminish the control of the legal institutions and procedures by the Ottoman religious establishment.[14] Similarly, the educational institutions had also been removed from the monopoly of the religious establishment, which had not taken this affront lightly. It had tried to regain lost power, prestige, and wealth at many instances.

However, religion still continued to function as a major political force in the Ottoman society. In the War of Liberation, the Sultan and the Ottoman government in Istanbul had tried to use the spiritual vehemence of the institution to organize uprisings to stifle Turkish nationalist forces. Although the forces of national resistance were able to crush such ominous influences of the Ottoman government, such dire doings seemed to have managed to undermine the remaining credibility of the caliphacy in the eyes of the nationalist elites, while failing to curb their zeal and success at resisting foreign occupation.

The Caliphate started to show signs of providing the monarchists, who were motivated with the objective of reviving the Ottoman Empire, with a legitimate cover to operate against the republican regime.[15] It did not take long for the republican government to react to the moderate demands of the caliph to extend the privileges of the caliphate. Mustafa Kemal's response to the appeal of the last caliph Abdülmecit Efendi clearly demonstrated how the republican leadership perceived the situation: "We cannot expose the Turkish Republic to any sort of danger to its independence by its [Caliphate's] continued existence. The position of the caliphate in the end has for us no more importance than a historic memory."[16] On March 3, 1924 the TGNA abolished the Caliphate, and transformed the Ministry of Religious Affairs into a department of the state and entrusted the religious endowments (*evkaf*) under the jurisdiction of another department of the state. The caliph and his family were also sent to exile. The last main institutional vestige of the Ottoman Empire, the institution of Caliphate, which had already been relegated to a position of relative irrelevance in the Muslim world,[17] was thus eliminated from the realm of the young Turkish Republic.

THE REVIVALIST CHALLENGE AND THE REPUBLICAN REACTION

The more pious among the Sunni Muslims of Anatolia did not take the decision to abolish the Caliphate lightly. There was increasing criticism of Mustafa Kemal Atatürk and the Republican regime among those affiliated with the religious establishment of the *ancién regime* of the Ottoman Empire. The most important and even critical development, which directly challenged the legitimacy of the Republican regime, occurred soon after the Caliphate was abolished, in eastern Anatolia. Şeyh Sait, was a revered leader (*şeyh*, sheik) of the *Nakşibendi* religious order (*tarikat*) rose up against the Turkish government. The gist of his political claim was that the Republican government had abolished the Caliphate and was on its way to undermine religion (Islam) completely.[18] He was suggesting that the Republican government was in the hands of infidels (*kâfir*), thus it is imperative upon all Muslims to rise up against it and replace it with the "rule of *Şeriat* (*Sharia*)."[19]

McDowall is of the opinion that the acts of Şeyh Sait indicated that, "he acted less on 'Kurdish' ethnicity per se than on Kurdish religious particularism . . . this was expressed in Kurdish devotion to the Shafi law school, which unlike the Hanefi school, made a distinction between devotion to the person of the caliph and acknowledgement of the preeminence of the state."[20] The uprising found sympathizers and participants from among the Kurdish tribes in southeastern Anatolia. The demands of the Şeyh Sait uprising were the reestablishment of the Caliphate and of the "rule of *Şeriat*."[21] In practice, Sait himself seemed to be asking for the reinstitution of the privileges of the religious establishment of the Ottoman system. He argued that, "the *Medreses* (Higher Educational Institutions of Islamic Theology) were closed up. The Ministry of Religious Affairs and Charitable Endowments (*Evkaf ve Şeriye Vekaleti*) was abolished. Religious schools were put under the authority of the Ministry of National Education." He further argued that some journalists had started to insult Islam and criticized Prophet Muhammed.[22]

There had been some form of activism among the Kurds in the final years of the Ottoman Empire and during the War of Liberation. A relatively small but well-educated elite established Kurdish associations in Istanbul, various provinces in Anatolia, Europe, and elsewhere.[23] Some of those associations had a declared aim of establishing an independent nation-state of Kurds, over the Ottoman territories of eastern Anatolia and *Mosul*,[24] and they seemed to have received encouragement and support from the British authorities during the War of Liberation.[25] It is also untenable to argue that Şeyh Sait and others who rebelled in the east of Turkey as early as 1924 and as late as 1937 were all champions of Kurdish ethnic nationalism. What has so far been documented about the Şeyh Sait's "*Nakşibendi—*Kurdish Uprising" seemed to indicate that he and his followers were more concerned with the defense of a lifestyle, society, and culture deeply influenced by their Sunni (*Shafi*) Muslim values.

The French missions in Syria and Lebanon had also been monitoring the developments in northern Iraq and southeastern Turkey with utmost rigor. Their reports to Paris seemed to indicate that the British probably did not encourage the Kurdish nationalists to take action against the young Republican regime in Turkey, but tolerated or even benefited from the internecine conflict between the Kurds and the Turkish government. The French were of the opinion that the British could exploit the Kurdish–Islamic restiveness of the area to prove that the Turkish government was even unable to establish law and order among its own Kurds.[26] The French further seemed to believe that the timing of the uprising was immaculate for the British to demonstrate to the League of Nations that the Turkish government would be incapable of ruling *Mosul*.[27]

The Turkish authorities further assumed that they were not only challenged by the usual religious suspects, but also by some Kurdish nationalists.[28] They tended to assume that the Islamic propaganda leveled against them was a smokescreen to hide the true feelings of the Kurdish leaders, who would establish a Kurdish state, under the guise of a "*Şeriat* state" for the Kurds. Kurds had been a tribal people, whose identity was deeply influenced by Islam. The Kurdish intellectual nationalists assumed that the only way to mobilize the tribes was to rally them under the flag of Islam, for their ethnic identity did not seem to transcend beyond their tribal allegiances. In this context, such religious figures as Şeyh Sait, who was the leading Islamic scholar of the *Nakşibendi* sufi order (*post-nişin*) of his time, seemed to have come in handy for the Kurdish nationalists to exploit. Sait could fire up the people, mobilize various Kurdish tribes and orient them to cross-tribal, yet religious goals. Once successful, some nationalists assumed that they then could conspire to dislodge and replace the religious leaders of the uprising.

Therefore, it was not at all surprising to observe many and disparate forces at work rallying around Şeyh Sait. There were some motivated with the idea of salvaging Islam from the rule of the "infidels in Ankara," others who were after establishing an independent Kurdish state, yet others who would seek material benefits and take their share of the plunders in the name of "jihad," and so on. Was it religion, ethnic nationalism, destitution, or some sort of foreign espionage that functioned as the "genuine" cause of those uprisings? There still is no clear-cut answer to such a question. Each and every one of those factors might have contributed to one or two or all of those more than 35 uprisings that took place in the east of Turkey. They played a major role in determining the nature of political regimes, institutions and policies in the Republic ever since. The Republican elite perceived of a major or even existential religious, and a similar Kurdish nationalist challenge from the very beginning of the establishment of the Republican regime. The reaction of the Prime Minister İnönü, the CHP elite, and the TGNA was to send major army corps and employ the air force to deal with the rebel army of Şeyh Sait, on the one hand, and adopt new legislation, the Law on the Maintenance of Order (*Takrir-i Sukün Kanunu*) to outlaw almost all forms of opposition to the Republican government, on the other.[29] Consequently, once the Sait uprising was suppressed expeditiously, the road was cleared for Atatürk and his loyal CHP government to launch its project to "create the Republican man" from 1925 onward.

AN OTTOMAN LEGACY: CLASH
OF THE *KULTURKAMPFS*

It goes without saying that the Turkish Republic inherited the sociopolitical characteristics of the Ottoman Empire. The new politics of the Republic was established on the former cultural divide of the Ottoman system, which consisted of two irreconcilable *kulturkampfs*.[30] The seat of the Ottoman Empire (*Dersaadet*) had created its own culture, complete with its own court language, *Osmanlı* (which was only intelligible to the learned members of the power elite), its own tastes for music, arts, literature, food, and so on; thus a whole style of living evolved, which was far removed from the pristine *Oguz* (Turkish), and the nomadic warrior (*Gazi*) culture of the former kingdom. The Periphery (*taşra*) remained aloof from the culture of the Center, and evolved spontaneously through its own domestic and even local dynamics. However, the land tenure system, the tax-base it provided, and the needs of the army kept the center and the Periphery in systematic contact. Religion also seemed to function, nominally even if not substantially, as the main hinge that connected the political center of the Empire to the rest of its society (*taşra*). The Sultan as the Muslim ruler of the Empire, who was also the Caliph after the sixteenth century, occupied the strategic seat of power at the very hub of the Center. The main churches of the Orthodox (Greek) and Gregorian (Armenian) communities were also part of the religious establishment of the same Center. The Ottoman *millet* system provided identity and status to all the subjects of the Empire. Even the practice of religion (high culture) at the center, and the periphery (low culture) differed in substantial ways.[31]

The outcome of the nineteenth-century reform movements had been the further complication of the cultural divide of the Center and the Periphery of the Ottoman society and polity. Eventually, two completely different and even irreconcilable images of "good society" began to take root during the nineteenth century. One of those images was built around the nineteenth-century conception of "science and progress" as the core value that defines the substance of human existence, nature, society, and politics.[32] The proponents of the "science" camp tried to use social science and reason to diagnose and treat the ailments of the Ottoman system.[33] Most were motivated with the idea of saving the "Ottoman system" from its decrepit state of existence, and render it viable.

In opposition to that camp emerged the rival *kulturkampf* of those who were attracted to the image of good society constructed around the preservation of the traditional lifestyle, its corresponding values and understandings of morality, work, family, and other aspects of life. Such an image of good society had been deeply influenced by the tradition-mindedness of the Ottoman masses and the Ottoman religious establishments. Such an image was somewhat Platonic, for it assumed that a perfect state and corresponding lifestyle were preserved in the traditions of the community and the state, of which the individual is a subject.[34] Another version of this idea has been that the "Perfect State" and society had existed in the Ottoman Empire at some point of time, in the past. Hence, if the contemporary Ottoman/Turkish society and its culture could be re-created with that "medieval image of good society" in mind, a just political and socioeconomic order could be reerected. This seems to be a call for "Back to the Future of the Golden Past." Religious education and thinking, preserving and protecting the moral standards from the corrosive impact of the "decadent West" have been at the core of such a cultural image. It also hosts values, which emphasize conservation of the folklore and traditions, and promotes simplicity of lifestyle, which often goes with an attitude of doggish loyalty to the routine.[35] An unconditional devotion to tradition and a corresponding attitude of thankfulness (*şükretmek*) to one's place in society seemed to be the most critical mental qualities of such a traditional understanding.[36] The goal then becomes to turn to agricultural production and society, small manufacturers and their guilds, or going back to the medieval virtues of the Ottoman past.[37]

I will call the former camp as the "secular," and the latter as the "revivalist" *kulturkampfs*, a la Andrew Davison[38] in the rest of this book. Although the cultural cleavage deepened and even widened over time, it also showed remarkable twists and bends. The pristine nature of the *kulturkampfs* has been lost over time, while they borrowed ideas and behavior from each other.

Currently, "the revivalists" have been most eager to use modern technology, such as computers, VCRs, DVDs, and the like, while the secularists seem to pay some more attention to religious values. Various political movements emerged from among the ranks of the two *kulturkampfs*, which seemed to promote values and ideas that were less than a simple extension of their core values, but a mix of both.

Nevertheless, the two *kulturkampfs* clash almost incessantly, yet their struggles tend to have ebbs and flows. Occasionally, their conflict reaches a crescendo, or a milestone, and then settles into their usual, more moderate pattern. The War of Liberation, the May 14, 1950 national elections, the 1960 and 1980 military coups, and the December 24, 1995 elections were such milestones.

There have been three driving forces which seemed to have determined the pace and nature of the conflict of the *kulturkampfs*. One such force consisted of the deep running socioeconomic transformation for the last 80 years. The Turkish society has been evolving from an agricultural to an industrial one. The painstaking jettisoning of the traditions, institutions, and folklore of an agricultural society, which is supplanted by an industrial one, has caused rapid social mobilization of the population of the country. New and rising expectations, and their lack of satisfaction, which led to deepening social frustration of the masses opened up new opportunities to draw up new agendas, and recipes for miracles by the new political parties and movements. Second, disasters either caused by international political affairs, such as war, civil war, or natural disasters, such as earthquakes, flooding, forest fires, and the like have constituted a major determinant of the severity of conflict between the *kulturkampfs*. The people's perception and expectations of the government's performance under the duress of the time have often determined whether there would be new battles fought between the *kulturkampfs*. Third, Turkey moved from a single party system of "CHP dominated State" to multiparty democracy in 1946. Democratization has been a long and arduous process for the Turkish political system to trek. However, in a very short period of about a year (1945–1946) the *kulturkampfs* discovered themselves in the midst of a new game, with a new playground, new players, and with new rules. Their adaptation to the game of democracy was difficult, and painstaking, thus they suffered through two and a half military coups, or democratic breakdowns between 1946 and 1980.

The War of Liberation provided the first context in which, the great legacy of the clash of the *kulturkampfs* was carried over from the Ottoman to the Turkish Republican culture. At the end of the War of Liberation the Republican elite had developed an image of the revivalist camp and all their sympathizers as the "traitors and spies of the occupying forces." The uprisings in the eastern parts of the country further reinforced the image that the revivalists would continue with their restiveness. Their rebelliousness not only created grave dangers at home, but they also provided excellent opportunity for the neighboring powers of Britain, France, and Italy to exploit the restiveness of the revivalists and continuously pressure the Republic to extract new concessions in the conflicts that simmer between them and Turkey. For example, the Treaty of *Lausanne* had left the status of the *Mosul* province of the former Ottoman Empire in the limbo. The Şeyh Sait rebellion coincided with the activities of the League of Nations Commission, which had been assigned the task of devising the conditions for a peaceful settlement of the *Mosul* issue. The Turkish political elite suspected that the Sait incident was related to the issue of *Mosul* and pointed to a conspiracy of the British Empire. Hence, they perceived the revivalists as a liability for the Republican regime and its declared goals. One obvious conclusion was to delegitimize and liquidate the forces of "traitors, and spies" (the revivalists), who were operating under the veil of religiosity. The tool to be used for such an operation would be the establishment of a secular order.

THE GENESIS OF SECULARISM IN TURKISH SOCIETY AND POLITICS

The Ottoman modernization, which had started with the reform or reorganization of the military and other institutions of the state, had left the religious institution of the state mostly unscathed. This resulted in dualism of state structures in which secular institutions existed side by side with the traditional religious ones throughout the nineteenth century. Not only their conflicting images of "Good Society," but also their interests had started to diverge and clash as the resources of the Ottoman state had been hard hit with devastating wars, loss of territory, and agricultural revenue.[39] State officials, hard pressed with demands to raise increasing amount of revenues from a dwindling agricultural economy, began to apply excessive pressure to extract more resources from a shrinking economy. The arbitrary nature of the patrimonial style of rule of the Ottoman state made matters even worse.[40] Corrupt and callous state officials turned into plunderers of their own society by the nineteenth century.

The religious officials of the Ottoman Religious Institutions played a dual role. The Muslim clergy (ulema) served both as the *kadı* (judge) and *imam* (prayer leader) in the Ottoman system. As the *imam* of a locality they functioned as the learned men of Islam, helped the locals to practice religion, gave them moral advice on matters of life and death, educated the young, provided them with social leadership, and carried out various social and legal services. In the capacity of a *kadı* they adjudicated the religious law (*şeriat*),[41] helped to resolve conflicts and functioned as the facilitator of communication between the people and the Sultan and his palace. In that latter capacity *kadı* was probably the only man who was proficient in *Osmanlı*, in the locality he served. Hence, he wrote the petitions of the peasants (*reaya*) and communicated them directly to the Sultan or the Grand *Vizier* (premier). Traditionally, the *ulema* provided a valuable link, hinging the Center with its Periphery. However, when the Center began to pressure the Periphery to extract more resources some of the *kadı* joined the plunder of the Periphery to collect their share of the bounty.[42] It is small wonder that there were widespread desertions of the villages and various peasant uprisings between the sixteenth and the nineteenth centuries in the Ottoman Empire.

Intriguingly enough, some Muslim clergy sided with the peasants and the other downtrodden subjects of the Ottoman Empire, and tried to protect them from the excesses of the state officials. Incidentally, they were already sharing the same lifestyle and socioeconomic conditions with the locals. They experienced the good and the bad times simultaneously with the peasantry. They were there to chant the life of Prophet Mohammed (*Mevlut*) at such festive occasions as a wedding ceremony, birth of a child, or such sorrowful times as one week after the death of a person. It is wrong to assume that all *imams* gained the respect and confidence of the local communities they served. However, where they excelled with their theological knowledge, integrity, decency, humaneness, and other qualities, they became local leaders. When the modernization project began in the end of the eighteenth century and followed through the nineteenth, the role of the clergy, including the Muslim *ulema* took a new twist.

Laicism: A Remedy for Islamic Revivalism?

Once the Ottoman Empire and the Caliphate were abolished, it was only a small logical step to eradicate all of the remaining institutional agents and vestiges related to them. What seemed to have prompted Mustafa Kemal Atatürk was a belief that preserving the Caliphate would expose Turkish politics to various influences and interventions of the Muslim communities and states all over the world.[43] Soon after the *medreses*, and such organizations of the religious orders as *tekke* and *zaviye*, which had belonged to the *Sufi* orders (*tarikat*) were closed down. When the Şeyh Sait uprising occurred, it further strengthened the resolve of the secular camp that more radical steps would be needed to undermine the power of the clergy over the Muslim communities in Turkey. This was done by removing the last realm under the control of the religious clergy, their legal authority in the realm of family law and the civil code (*mecelle*) of the country. The Swiss civil code was translated with minor modifications and adopted as the civil code of the Turkish Republic as of February 17, 1926.[44] The legal system of the Turkish Republic was thus based on completely secular principles. All linkages between religion and law were severed. The clergy was left devoid of any legal authority to exercise over any realm of life. The legal and religious authority of the religious institutions of the *ancién regime* was thus completely eradicated. Hence, the adoption of the Swiss civil code as the civil code of the country completed the first radical step in erecting a secular political and legal regime in Republican Turkey. From then on, all other steps taken by the government and the TGNA were the adaptation of the rest of the system to the core necessities of the new secular order.

The revolutionary steps in establishing a lay political order ushered in a new definition of political legitimacy solely based on the will of the nation, unchecked by any traditional force or religion. Having removed all of the educational and legal authority vested in the religious clergy, the Republic relegated the revivalist *Kulturkampf* to a point of political irrelevance. Hence, the article of the 1924 Constitution, which had referred to Islam as the religion of the state, was eliminated with the 1928 amendment, with no popular resistance. Furthermore, the state changed its legal character to a lay state, theoretically equidistant to all people of different beliefs and conscience, all religions, and sects of Islam, and thus bearing no special ties with any religion.

The institution of the *kadı* was also eliminated in the same revolutionary process. All of the Islamic characteristics of the legal system were removed, as all realms of the law came under the jurisdiction of the secular judges serving in the judiciary of a unitary state. The role of the *imam* survived the revolution. Nevertheless, *imams* were no longer entrusted with the formal role of educating the young or carrying through marriage ceremonies, for the religious weddings were outlawed as of 1926. Yet, they are still entrusted with the role of leading communal prayers in the mosques, and in delivering their Friday prayer sermons, and so on. However, they are strictly monitored by the Directorate of Religious Affairs (*Diyanet İşleri Başkanlığı*, DIB), which even provides the Muslim clergy with the text of their Friday sermons. The Christian and Jewish clergy have kept their autonomous status, and their congregations are legally considered as "the minorities" of Turkey, due to the stipulations of the Treaty of *Lausanne*. The funeral ceremonies were among the few acts the role of *imam* preserved as part of its prerogative. The informal role of *imam* as the leader of the local communities they served also persisted with some variation.

The Republican Directorate of Religious Affairs is a regulatory mechanism, which is instituted to check and control the Sunni clergy and the Sunni communities, on the one hand, and through sermons of the *imams* and the publications of the DIB provide theological and moral guidance to the Sunni masses in secularism and Islam, and ensure that the secular principles of the Republican state are not breached in any way, on the other. There has not been any systematic effort to regulate the activities of the *Alevi* communities by the Republic, which constitute the non-Sunni Muslim sect of Islam in Turkey. The *Alevis* had suffered dearly in the hands of the Sunni establishment and the masses of the Ottoman Empire, which perceived them as an extension of Shi'ite Iran into the Anatolia and even heretics; and treated them as more or less a fifth column of Iran, and banned and repressed the *Alevi* communities, and even occasionally massacred them. The *Alevis* welcomed the secularism of the Republic. For the first time in the last few centuries the *Alevis* were able to gain recognition and autonomy from state intervention, and could practice their religion free of political harassment. However, social segregation, tension and lack of tolerance of the Sunnis and *Alevis* respectively persisted in the Republican era as well. Those tensions were eventually exploited by rival political leaders and parties, which led to occasional sectarian violence in the country in the 1970s and the early 1990s.[45] The Treaty of *Lausanne* defined the status of the Christians and the

Jews; and they have not been regulated by the DIB. They kept their old churches and synagogues. However, according to the system envisaged by the Treaty of *Lausanne*, the ties of the former Christian and Jewish *millets* to the new Republican Center were fully severed. Most former ecumenical authorities of the minorities were even placed under the authority of the governors (*kaymakam*) of the subprovincial districts (*ilçe*), where their churches are located.

The objective of the Republican regime, which by now became fully controlled by the secularist camp, was to roll back the realm of religion into the private lives of individual citizens, as much as possible. The expectation was to impede religious interests, particularly the mass mobilization capability of the *Sufi* orders (*tarikats*), from being influential in the realm of politics. A series of new steps were taken to eradicate the religious symbols and related revivalist markers from the realm of public life. One such symbol was directly related to the attire of the people. The Ottoman society had different dress codes for different professions and members of different *millets*, which helped to identify the social identity of a person in public space. From 1925 till 1935 various laws were promulgated, which outlawed the clergy from donning religious attire outside of such buildings and facilities where religious ceremonies were carried out as temples, funeral homes, and graveyards.[46] The *fez*, which had earlier been introduced, as a modern headwear had become a symbol of revivalism by the 1920s, was also outlawed for men. Instead, hat and cap were introduced as new and legal headwear for men. The veil was also outlawed for women.[47] The clergy were also banned from using their various titles, and all other Ottoman titles such as *efendi*, *bey*, and *paşa* were also outlawed.[48]

If eradicating religious symbols from public life was one motivation for the republican regime to outlaw them, another motive seemed to be the elimination of all cultural marks that accorded some form of distinction and identity to some vocations. The nationalist creed of the secularists was also at work here. They were creating a national society of equal citizens. Hence, no vocation could brandish itself as a distinct group requesting deference, privilege, and authority, or some form of favor from the rest. The clergy constituted such a class of people, who would have themselves distinguished from the rest of the public by their looks. Veil also signified that women should be segregated from the rest of the society, and be relegated to a status of secondary importance in society. Veil and covering themselves up in a dark colored (usually black), textile (*çarşaf*) signified that they are not to be taking part in every realm of life. Such a style of dress indicated that women were to be protected and hidden (*kaç-göç*) from the male members of the society, and thus kept at home. The secularists perceived such a style of dress as cultural impediments to equality of citizens, social participation, and integration of half of the population to the national economy and polity. Hence, in 1930 women were extended the right to participate in the local elections and in 1934 to participate in the national elections as candidates and voters.[49] Furthermore, the overall goal of the secularists in power was to integrate into

Europe or the "West." Hence, they assumed that the outlook of the people would constitute a psychological impediment to such a goal, if they continued to don their traditional dresses.[50] However, such a transformation would require more than just the alteration of the dress codes. People should not only look like Europeans, but also think like Europeans. The obvious step to take was to institute new schools and curriculum, which would instill nationalism, secularism, and science in the minds of the students.

The Republican government took another radical decision and put all schools under the jurisdiction of the Ministry of National Education in 1924. However, eventually the practice of providing some students religious education, while educating the rest in secular, science education, and instilling a nationalist creed in the minds and hearts of both groups of students seemed not to be feasible. Hence, the government adopted a policy of mainly educating the students in science, arts and humanities compatible with the nationalist creed of the regime, and permit religious instruction as much as feasible under the circumstances.[51] Religious institution diminished in numbers and the size of the student body instructed in religion also diminished sharply in the 1920s and the 1930s.

In the meantime, new institutions of secondary education, such as the Teacher's Academies and Village Institutes (*Köy Enstitüleri*) were established to provide new opportunities of education to students from the lower classes and peasant backgrounds. The main rationale behind that decision was to provide national education to the new generation of teachers, who would socialize a new generation of students with nationalist, and secular ideas of the regime. They would also provide upward social mobility for the have-nots in the Turkish society, whose only venue of upward mobility had been religious education and theology in the previous Ottoman system.[52] The Village Institutes were also designed to educate teachers who would educate the peasants in modern agricultural technology, citizenship, nationalism, and secularism. The Republican elites under Atatürk's leadership had assumed that such an endeavor would provide for much needed increase in agricultural production and rural development, while inculcating a strong sense of nationalist ideology among the peasants, who constituted the vast majority of the citizens of the young nation-state.[53] In a sense, the Village Institutes project was a crucial means of implementing the policy of populism, secularism, and nationalism at the grassroots. However, the Village Institute project failed to survive much beyond the lifetime of Atatürk.

Finally, Atatürk and followers took another radical step to undermine all chances of resuscitation of the authority of the revivalist camp, and facilitate literacy through adoption of the Latin alphabet instead of the Arabic letters that had been in use by the Ottomans in the past. The transition turned out to be easier than expected for two main reasons. The 1927 Census registered the literacy rate at a dismal 11 percent. Hence, nine out of ten people were in no position to object to the change on the grounds that they needed to invest time and energy to relearn the alphabet. Second, most intellectuals who knew *Osmanlı* were also fluent in French, for French was the language of science in the Ottoman Empire, and thus they were familiar with the Latin alphabet as well.[54]

The alphabet reform seemed to have served the intended policy goal of the government at that time. The ties with the immediate past were severed. Religious and other non-secular and nonnationalist texts of the past became increasingly harder to influence the new generation of the Turkish Republic. However, although the literacy rate increased from 29.4 percent of the males and 9.8 percent of the female population of the country in 1935 to 93.9 percent of the male and 80.6 percent of the female population in 2000, the literacy rate did not increase monotonically throughout those years.[55] The lingering problems of education indicate that the literacy rate of the country has been sensitive to nontechnical, and more socioeconomic and cultural factors.

Education reforms encompassed a wider range of cultural issues, such as history and language. Purification of the "Turkish language" by means of eradication of Arabic and Farsi words from *Osmanlı* and replacing them with the words and concepts of the Turkish peasants and nomads, on the one hand, and making up new words, on the other, constituted the core activities of the language reform of the 1930s.[56] Eventually, a transliteration of the Holy Qur'an in Turkish was produced in 1928, and by 1932 the Holy Qur'an was cited in Turkish in the mosques of Istanbul.[57]

Simultaneously, a reconsideration and even reinvention of the "origins of the nation" constituted the essence of a reformed understanding and instruction of "Turkish History" at schools.[58] The pre-Ottoman and pre-Islamic origins of Turks were emphasized to further break the cultural ties with the immediate Ottoman past. A glorious past extending all the way to Central Asia, which was not only connected with the establishment of the Seljuki Empires of southwestern Asia, but also with many tribes that founded various European kingdoms were "re-discovered."[59] Studies that established linkages between contemporary European peoples and the Turks, such as the Bulgarians, Hungarians, and the Finns were funded and encouraged. Most emphasis was put on the role that the Turkish tribes played in the advent of civilization, for example, there followed the discovery of a Turkish alphabet, various relics of ancient Turkish or Turkic civilizations. In the meantime, the Hittite, Sumerian, Phrygian, and Lydian civilizations were also grafted onto the cultural heritage of the Turkish nation.[60] Such efforts were meant to prove to the citizens of the Turkish nation-state that they are the current ethnic stock of a civilized people, with which they should take particular pride. They were also led to believe that there was not that much of a difference between their national culture and the cultures of Europe. Hence, Ottoman past was to be jettisoned in favor of a future integration with the "Western" and the "only" contemporary civilization of the time.

SINGLE PARTY AT WORK

The steps taken to oust and eventually root out the vestiges of the Ottoman culture, and most specifically those of the rival camp of revivalists eventually culminated in nothing less than a cultural revolution. There is little evidence that all of the steps taken in the 1920s and the 1930s had been carefully designed as a philosophical system in the turbulent years of the War of Liberation. Most measures were identified as the remedy to maladies of the times or of the remaining legacy of a corrupt, and debilitating past. The overall objective of modernity was eventually brought out into the limelight of politics as a guiding principle. There was a sense of pragmatism and ad hoc problem-solving in the initial phases of the reforms. Hence, the record of the 1920s and the 1930s was substantially determined, not so much by a philosophy and social analysis and the concomitant ideological principles deeply embedded in such roots (e.g., the way in which the Stalin was executing another revolution in the Soviet Union), but by reacting to the international and domestic developments, and by way of trial and error. Probably the most significant outcome of this approach was the single party system and the party state of the 1920s and the 1930s.

It looked as if the Republican regime would be another version of the Westminster model of democracy in 1924.[61] The Constitution adopted by the TGNA was drawn up to host a unicameral two-party system, independent judiciary, and fusion of executive and legislative power. An opposition party of the disgruntled participants of the War of Liberation was established, Progressive Republican Party (TCF) in 1924. One of the parliamentary initiatives of TCF, which was eventually adopted by the TGNA, was to depoliticize the military by forcing the commanders of troops to resign their military posts in order to serve in the TGNA.[62] Indeed, leaders of the TCF had adopted the policy of separation of military and political careers, and had retired from the armed forces and became deputies of the TGNA. They had considered themselves as comrades at arms of Marshall Mustafa Kemal and while Atatürk had been accorded with highest honor, prestige and power of the land, they were relegated merely to a relatively humble position of being opposition deputies of the TGNA. Their opposition to the policies of the CHP government became acerbic and vocal over time, and vice versa.

The TCF elite seemed to be considerably conservative, and some were even devoutly pious Sunni Muslims. It seemed as if they were of the opinion that they had participated in the War of Liberation just to save Islam from the occupation of the infidels. They seemed to be more ready and willing to seek compromise with the Caliph in the aftermath of the War of Liberation. Their opposition seemed to propagate revivalist values at about the same time as the revivalist Şeyh Sait rebellion in the East. Though they had supported the declaration of the martial law and other military measures taken by CHP government, they were deeply suspicious of what they perceived to be the hawkish attitude of that government.[63] As if that was not enough, the TCF seemed to open up its ranks to the former Union and Progress Party (ITF) personalities, who had a long history of rivalry and hostility to Mustafa Kemal Atatürk personally.

The attempted assassination of the President and the founding father of the Republic Mustafa Kemal Atatürk at *Izmir* (Smyrna) in 1925 seemed to implicate some high-ranking members of the TCF, including those with impeccable credentials as General Kazım Karabekir, and General Ali Fuat Cebesoy.[64] Although they were exonerated from any wrong doing eventually, some members of the TCF, who had been active as the hired guns of the former Union and Progress Party (ITF) of the Ottoman Empire, were implicated with the conspiracy. The TCF seemed to harbor shady characters that were ready to use any method to oust their rivals as they had done so in the past. Hence, President Atatürk, PM Ismet Inönü, and the CHP elite perceived an existential threat emanating from the ITF and its former hit men, and took all the necessary measures to exact severe punishments for them. Not only were the remnants of the ITF eliminated, but the TCF was also forced to close down its operations as of 1925. Hence, Turkey adopted a single party system in 1925, which was to last for the next two decades.

Curiously enough, another experiment with a two-party system was carried out when the *Free Party* (Serbest Fırka, SF) was established in 1930.[65] Almost instantaneously an upsurge of criticism for the CHP rule and support for the SF occurred especially in the western provinces of the country. However, SF also proved to be much more influential in opposing the regime than the CHP state could tolerate.[66] Hence, the SF having performed quite well in the local elections stopped short of challenging the CHP at the national elections and decided to close itself down, barely three months after its establishment.[67]

Although there was no evidence that would implicate the SF in any way, on December 23, 1930 another morbid development occurred in a small western town of Turkey. In the small town of *Menemen* a group of Sunni Muslims, led by a cleric precipitated a protest rally, which demanded the reinstitution of the "*Şeriat* state." The ten men military team led by a college graduate reservist officer (third or reserve Lieutenant Mustafa Fehmi Kubilay), intervened to calm the protestors. However, they were not only unable to control the rally from developing into a lynch mob, but the reservist officer Kubilay was murdered; his head was sawed off, placed on top of spears and brandished in the streets by the protestors. The uprising was eventually suppressed. Some of the culprits were killed in the fighting and others were arrested, tried, sentenced to death, and executed soon after.[68] Kubilay was declared as a "Martyr of the Revolution" (*Devrim Şehidi*), and the incident has been commemorated every year as a reminder of the threats that the revivalist camp can muster against the Cultural Revolution ever since. In essence, that incident was more of the same sort of anti-secular anomic protest, which could be unleashed against the secularist camp, quite like the "March 31st, 1909" incident of the earlier times. When viewed from the perspective of the Republican establishment of 1930, the developments of that year hardened their resolve that cultural revolutions were not yet complete and more needed to be carried away to consolidate them. Indeed, the rule of the CHP government became less tolerant of criticism, more authoritarian, and the party itself got more intertwined with the state during the rest of the 1930s and the 1940s,[69] on the one hand, and the divide between the two *kulturkampfs* kept its relevance, as the "revivalists" further sank into the underground, on the other.

MANAGING THE ECONOMY

If establishing the territorial integrity and national integration of the young Turkish nation-state was one major concern of the CHP governments in the 1920s, to establish a viable economy and produce sustained and rapid economic growth was another. Indeed, both objectives were interlocked and existential concerns for the young Republic. The role that the economy played in the eyes of the nationalist political elite can be best symbolized in the convention of a major "Congress of Economy in Izmir" during February 1923, almost six months before the Treaty of *Lausanne*, and more than six months before the promulgation of the Republic.

The İzmir Congress was not only high on symbolism, but also produced an arena where representatives of the main sectors of the Ottoman economy were invited to air their views and discuss the economic issues and woes of the day.[70] The participants were hand picked by the nationalist government, and it seemed to have produced the opportunity for the Turkish-Muslim members of the Ottoman economic elite to establish links with the Ankara government for the first time.[71] The overall emphasis was on taking measures to establish a national economy, create a Muslim-Turkish middle class, protect the budding industry against foreign competition (which could not be implemented until 1929 due to the stipulations of the Treaty of *Lausanne*), provide assistance to farmers, and create an economic environment that would attract foreign capital investments.

The Treaty of *Lausanne* also influenced the performance of the Turkish economy in the 1920s, for it imposed free trade practices on foreign economic relations of Turkey until 1929, and Turkey was also held responsible for the servicing of the Ottoman debt. The first installment of the payment of the Ottoman debt had also been marked for the year 1929. It was such a dire coincidence that the Great Depression coincided with the first installment of the payment of the Ottoman debt. The overall economic context of the 1920s was also terribly grim.

At the end of the War of Liberation Anatolia was depleted of its human and some natural resources. After their sudden defeat at the end of August 1922 the Greek army tried to make sure that the most fertile lands of the western Anatolia, where relatively modern farming had started before World War I, would be turned over to the Turks as a wasteland. "British and American observers reported that Greek soldiers with dynamite destroyed the buildings and whole towns. Special kerosene pumps were used to spread fire among wooden houses. . . . Livestock could seldom be taken away quickly, it was slaughtered in the fields. Trees were chopped down or sprayed with kerosene and burned. . . . the American consul at İzmir, Park, a man who disliked Turks and had completely supported the Greek cause, reported that Greeks had destroyed everything they could as they retreated. He stated that he had observed the results in four cities, the Greeks had destroyed 90 percent of the cities of *Manisa* and *Kasaba*, 70 percent of the city of *Alaşehir*, and 65 percent of the city of *Salihli*."[72] The eastern provinces of Turkey were hardly in any better shape after many years of fighting between the Russian and Ottoman armies, the Armenian army and the Turkish resistance forces. The survey of the American government of the area soon after World War I reported widespread famine and starvation among the inhabitants of *Erzurum* and vicinity, and sheer devastation.[73] The figures reported by Emory Niles and Arthur Sunderland of the U.S. government helped to draw up an appalling picture.[74] For example, of the 6,500 Muslim houses in Bitlis that had existed before 1914 none was standing in 1919, and of the 1,500 Armenian houses 1,000 were still standing, yet of the 30,000 Muslims who lived in that Province before World War I only 4,000 remained alive in 1919, and of the 10,000 Armenians none was alive in 1919.[75]

Consequently, the economic structure inherited by the Republic from its Ottoman predecessor was in complete shatters. Almost all livelihood of the population of Anatolia was devastated by the wars that ravaged through the land in the 1910s and the 1920s. Grain seed, olive trees, arable land, agricultural infrastructure, and the population to till the land were heavily battered, and thus Anatolia had been depleted of valuable human, natural, and financial resources between 1914 and 1922.

A large-scale population exchange was carried out between Turkey and Greece, as foreseen by the Treaty of *Lausanne*. The objective of the parties to that Treaty was to disengage the Muslim and Greek Orthodox *millets*, and avert new potential for ethnic strife and political conflict to unfold in the years to follow. The political elites of both countries had arrived at the opinion that too much ill will was spilled out between those *millets* for them to coexist in a state of peace and tranquility in their old neighborhoods. Once more, the Muslim population of Greece and Greek Orthodox population of Turkey had to emigrate and resettle in foreign and even hostile lands in 1923.[76]

The economy grew by an average of 8.6 percent, while agriculture grew 8.9 percent, and industry grew by a staggering 10.2 percent per annum between 1924 and 1929.[77] However, it ran into serious difficulty by the late 1920s and the early 1930s because of the dire influences of the unanticipated Great Depression.[78] The economy slowed down by half the pace of the 1920s. The liberal foreign economic regime of the 1920s was dismantled and private initiative, although not discouraged was no longer treated as the engine of change in the years that followed. Instead, a major step toward "state led economic development" was taken. The major economic legacy of the 1930s was the establishment of large-scale state enterprises in all of the critical sectors of the economy from mining and steel production to banking and air, rail and marine transport industries. They helped Turkey to rekindle rapid industrialization and economic growth in the 1930s.[79] However, the State Economic Enterprises (KIT), and the overwhelming weight of the state and state regulation in the economy failed to protect Turkey from the dire influences of World War II.[80] However, the state economic enterprises, and state-owned banks established in the 1930 and the 1940s have dominated the Turkish economy ever since. Though Turkey has been trying to privatize them since the early 1980s, the outcomes of those efforts have been erratic and humble.

THE END OF THE FORMATIVE YEARS

Mustafa Kemal Atatürk, the charismatic leader and the founding father of the Republic passed away at a relatively early age of 57 on November 10, 1938. In his lifetime the political consolidation of the republican regime and the national integration of new state had robustly progressed. However, it would be far fetched to argue that the Turkish nation-state had been out of all trouble by the late 1930s. In fact, within a few months' time of Atatürk's death Turkey encountered another major challenge. World War II erupted in September 1939 and within a year both Bulgaria and Greece came under the invasion of the armies of the Third Reich, while the Red Army moved south to control the northern half of Iran, as well. Turkey found itself encircled in the middle of a huge pincer, between the German armies to the west and the Red army to the east. Twenty-six years ago in 1914 a similar context had led to a huge devastation when the Union and Progress party government of the Ottomans had declared war on Russia. Was the history going to repeat itself? Did Turkey have any choice?

Indeed, Turkey had signed and ratified a friendship treaty, popularly known as the Treaty of Moscow, with the Soviet Union on March 16, 1921, which was still valid in 1940.[81] Soviet Union under Lenin and later Stalin had supported republican Turkey, as an anti-imperialist, developing country, resisting western hegemony. Turkey had also signed a similar treaty with France and Britain in 1939, and France had accepted to hold a plebiscite in the autonomous region of Alexandretta (later the province of *Hatay* of Turkey). The status of Alexandretta (*Hatay*), just like that of *Mosul*, had not been solved in the Treaty of *Lausanne* either. The French had controlled Alexandretta as an autonomous entity, independent of both Syria and Turkey until 1939. Both Turkey and Syria considered Alexandretta/*Hatay* as part of their national homelands. In 1938, before Atatürk's death, the French agreed to hold a plebiscite in that autonomous province to determine the legal status of that territory. The plebiscite indicated that the people of Alexandretta/*Hatay* voted in favor of joining Turkey and by 1939 *Hatay* became a province of Turkey. Turkey's relations with the Third Reich were also devoid of hostility. However, Turkish–Italian relations were full of stresses and strains throughout the late 1920s and the 1930s.[82] Thus, the current borders of Turkey were determined (see map 2.1).

Turkey followed its carefully designed status quoist foreign policy throughout World War II. The greatest motive was to spare Turkey from the sorrows and devastation of another war. It is not so difficult to appreciate the way the new President of the country, İsmet İnönü (1938–1950), who also functioned as the new leader of the CHP and assumed the title of "national

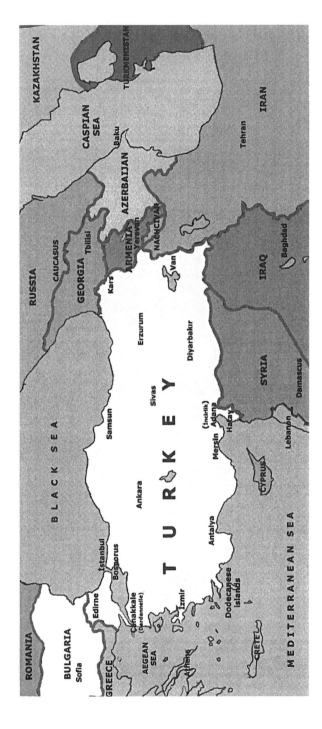

Map 2.1   Post–Cold War Turkey

leader" (*Milli Şef*), perceived the risks of running the foreign policy of the country in 1939–1940. Turkey performed a tight rope act not to test the power of either alliance, whose armies were deployed right next door. İnönü and the government resisted pressures of the British PM Churchill and Hitler to join the World War. When approached twice by Churchill to enter the war on the side of the Allies, the Turkish government requested from Churchill major equipment and air cover to attack the armies of the Third Reich, for the Turkish army was not a modern force that could cope with the challenge of the German army. The Allies lacked the resources to supply Turkey with such help. Hence, the Turkish army stayed put, and out of the conflict throughout World War II.[83]

However, the Turkish armed forces were fully mobilized and put under a state of alert during World War II, and all of the normal trade practices in the international and domestic markets were disrupted. Indeed, the Turkish economy suddenly began to experience what may best be termed a "war economy" with all of its dire consequences.[84] If the level of industrial revenue is to be assumed as 100 in 1938–1939, it fell down to 77 by 1944–1945, while the price index of industrial goods increased from 100 to 357 in the same period.[85] The major staple food production similarly suffered. In the same years wheat production index fell from 100 to 63, while wheat price index skyrocketed from 100 to 568.[86] Concomitantly, the overall agricultural revenue index took a similar dip as it fell from 100 in 1938–1939 to 69 in 1944–1945, while real national income dropped from 100 to 75 in the same period.[87] The newly established state enterprises started to suffer from lack of demand and labor input, as all channels of import were severely curtailed under the spread of hostilities all around Turkey in the Balkans, Middle East, and the Caucasus.[88] Six years of war from 1939 to 1945 delivered, probably not as harsh as the former world war, but yet another major blow to the infant industries and the fledgling economy of the country.[89]

Eventually the TGNA decided to declare war on the Third Reich in February 1945. The World War was practically over by then and no major casualties or collateral damage occurred in Turkey. However, when Turkey participated in the San Francisco Conference and the establishment of the United Nations in 1945, it was in a state of political isolation with a decrepit economy. Turkey failed to possess resources and capabilities to fend off all the pressures and challenges directed at her, on the one hand, but owned and controlled valuable strategic assets, on the other. The most critical and important geographical and strategic asset of the country has been the Turkish Straits, which consist of the *Bosporus*, the Sea of *Marmara*, and the *Dardanelle*, that connect the Black Sea with the Aegean and eventually the Mediterranean Seas. There had been a lengthy period of international pressure to limit and eventually avoid all forms of Turkish sovereignty over the Turkish straits since the eighteenth century,[90] which culminated in the establishment of an international regime over the Turkish straits in the Treaty of *Sévres*.[91] The Turkish government had negotiated an international treaty in *Montreux* in 1936, which provided for a maritime regime that had been agreed upon by all of the littoral states of the Black Sea.[92] However, the Turkish straits also constituted a major international route for a huge chunk of the international trade of the Soviet Union, and even currently that of Russia. Hence, the Turkish straits emerged as a strategic asset for Stalin's Soviet Union to venture for their control in the immediate aftermath of World War II. The Friendship and Non-Aggression Treaty negotiations came as a blow for the Turkish diplomats and government, who realized that the Soviets were considering to offer to place Red Army troops on both sides of the straits to "protect Turkey" as part of the renewed form of the treaty.[93] A new and a bold step needed to be taken by the government, which would end Turkish neutrality and place Turkey in a whole new web of relations, which still deeply influence the socioeconomic and political development of the country. We turn to those developments and analyze them in the next chapter.

3

DEMOCRACY AT WORK AND
AT RISK (1946–1960)

At the end of World War II Turkey found itself embedded in a context of uncertainty. It became clear that the British and the French mandates to Turkey's immediate south were crumbling, and so it was only a matter of time for the British and French to vacate the Middle East. Turkey was now faced with the prospects of being neighbors with the fully independent Arab nation-states of Iraq and Syria. Further south, in Palestine, the Arabs and the Jews were becoming increasingly poised to fight out their differences. The Soviet Army had occupied the north of Iran (Iranian Azerbaijan) in 1942, and encouraged the development of Kurdish autonomy, which eventually culminated in the establishment Republic of *Mahabad* further south in 1946.[1] At the end of the war the Soviet Army was dragging its feet in vacating Iran, which did not seem to be too different from the Soviet moves in Central and Eastern Europe, which in turn, could then be interpreted as Soviet encroachments into the Middle East. In the west of Turkey, Bulgaria had come under the rule of the Soviet forces, which had come to liberate it for a second time in less than 70 years (in the 1870s from the Ottomans and in the 1940s from the Germans). It seemed as if that the Bulgarian Communist party was in government for the long haul. In the meantime, Greece was slipping into a civil war. The two main parties of the conflict were the communists and the nationalists, and the Bulgarian communists seemed to be supporting the former. The Soviet Red Army even started to increase its deployment in Bulgaria in late 1945,[2] which also raised the prospects of further incursion of the Red Army into Greece, in one form or the other, and even an assault into Turkey.[3]

It was in that highly volatile and hazardous context that the Turkish diplomats started to test the waters in Moscow for the renewal or extension of the Treaty of Moscow of 1921. The initial signals indicated that there would be problems. Stalin and his advisers had calculated that Turkey was in a relatively isolated position. The circumstances looked ripe enough for new initiatives to be taken by the Soviets, including demands on control of the Turkish straits. These included the right of free passage for the Soviet navy and merchant vessels through the Turkish straits, as well as the establishment of Soviet bases on the straits (allegedly to protect Turkey from foreign threat), and handing the northeastern provinces of Turkey, *Kars* and *Ardahan* back to Russia, which had been returned to Turkey by Russia in 1921.[4] Hence, the Turkish government and President İnönü seemed to arrive at the conclusion that the Soviets were now suggesting to convert Turkey into either some kind of a satellite state. The negotiations in Moscow stalled as the Turkish government started to consider an appropriate response to Stalin. Eventually, the answer of the Turkish government was negative on all Soviet demands. The negotiations broke off soon after.[5]

It was crystal clear that Turkish–Soviet relations would never be what they had used to be in the interwar period. The Soviet Union was no longer the weak and timid state of the 1920s, in the grip of internecine conflict and under the threat of foreign invasion, when cooperation between Russia and Turkey, under the leadership of Lenin and Mustafa Kemal, had been established. The Soviet Union was now on the way to becoming a Super Power of a bipolar world. The Soviets were in the process of establishing a buffer zone in Central and eastern Europe between them and their Western adversaries to be. Good relations with Turkey lost the value the Soviets had attached to them in the 1920s and the 1930s. Turkey was no longer in a position to cope with the challenge of such a neighbor alone. Under the circumstances, it looked as if "Turkey's territorial integrity and its future as an independent state was gravely threatened by a resurgent Russia, and Turkey urgently needed to find allies to fend it off."[6] Hence, the Turkish government started to seek an alliance that would deter the burgeoning Soviet threat.

It did not take long for the British government[7] and eventually the United States to grasp the critical situation that Turkey was in.[8] If both Turkey and Greece were to join the newly emerging Soviet pact in the Eastern Mediterranean, it was a matter of time for the Middle East to come under immense Soviet pressure. In 1946, the battleship USS Missouri visited the Istanbul harbor, bringing the body of the former Turkish Ambassador to Washington, Mr. Münir Ertegün, who had passed away two years earlier in the D.C. but could not be sent back to Turkey due to the World War. This signaled not only rapprochement between Turkey and the United States but also of the U.S. support for Turkey and Greece.[9] In 1947, the U. S. President Harry Truman requested $400 million assistance be given to Greece and Turkey from the U.S. Congress until 1948, in the midst of a budget crunch, and declared the readiness of the United States to help "free countries" under threat, meaning Greece and Turkey.[10] Hence, what has been known as the "Truman Doctrine" since was thus formulated, and so began the Turkish and Greek journey to join the club of Western democracies.

TRANSITION TO DEMOCRACY

In the meantime, the political regime of Turkey started to veer toward multiparty democracy for the third and the last time. There had been a major cleavage developing among the ranks of the CHP (Cumhuriyet Halk Partisi, Republican People's Party) elite. The party group in the Turkish Grand

National Assembly (TGNA) was stirred with the proposals of four members of its prominent members, known as *Dörtlü Takrir* (Proposal of the Four) on June 7, 1945. The famous four consisted of the personalities of Mr. Celal Bayar (who had served as the Prime Minister under Atatürk during 1937 and 1938), Mr. Adnan Menderes (a young lawyer and landlord of a large farm in western Anatolia, who was destined to serve as the Prime Minister throughout the 1950s), Professor Fuad Köprülü (a history professor from a patrician Ottoman family whose line had a number of famous and influential Grand Viziers and himself a disciple of sociologist Ziya Gökalp), and Mr. Refik Koraltan (a veteran of the GNA of the War of Liberation).[11] If one reads the proposal of the four it sounds as if what they requested from the government was to end the extraordinary measures taken during the war, bring martial law to an end, especially in Istanbul, which had been suffocating the major powerhouses of the press located in that city, and provide more political and economic liberty.[12] The CHP government had been making several suggestions to liberalize the political system; faced with a proposal the government and the majority of the TGNA acted against it. The signatories were asked to explain their acts, or be disciplined by the party. Their defense and explanations were found unsatisfactory by the CHP establishment, and *Menderes, Köprülü* and *Koraltan* were expelled from the party in 1945. Bayar eventually resigned in the same year.[13] Within a month Turkey witnessed the birth of a new political party of the enterprising businessman Nuri Demirağ's the National Resurgence Party (*Milli Kalkınma Partisi*).[14]

It would be quite wrong to argue that the opposition within the ranks of the CHP emerged to defend political and socioeconomic liberties and human rights. Another row had also been developing within the ranks of the single party regime in the TGNA over government attempts at introducing a comprehensive "land reform project," which created grave concerns among the local notables with large landholdings, who served as prominent deputies of the CHP in the TGNA.[15] It was quite an irony that the bifurcated role of the local notables, which had existed in the Ottoman era, emerged once again in the Republican context. The local notables who had served to promote the policies of the CHP for two decades started to develop a stiff resistance to the ambitious plans of the CHP government to render the land tenure system more equitable in Turkey. The loyal local agents of the party state started to go through a change of heart and join the ranks of its main opponents in local and eventually in national politics.

The debilitating influences of the World War on the economy had also created another severe problem. The double hazards of high level of annual inflation of the general level of prices, and a concomitant scarcity of commodities had emerged to ravage the country. People experienced a severe shortage of purchasing power to afford such staple foods as sugar, shortening, bread, and the like, as the prices of such commodities took off during the early 1940s. They also became increasingly scarce, as an elaborate black market developed during the same period. The national income of Turkey fell considerably from 117.4 Turkish Lira (TL) per capita GNP in 1939 to 73.2

T.L GNP per capita in 1945.[16] Those few who could afford to purchase their needs from the black market continued to lead their prewar lifestyles and even prosper, while a huge majority of the population slid into a state of bare survival and destitution. The CHP government moved to alleviate the public discontent in the middle of the World War. TGNA legislated a "wealth tax" (*Varlık Vergisi*) in 1942 and an agricultural produce bill was tabled soon after in 1943 (*Toprak Mahsülleri Kanunu*), which was followed by a land reform bill (*Toprak Kanunu*).[17]

The objective was to break the backbone of the black market and punitively tax those who had accumulated wealth through black market activities,[18] on the one hand, and also collect new revenues for the spiraling military expenditures, on the other.[19] The legislative bill was designed to punish the "war rich" and redistribute income or the hardships of the war more evenly. However, a vast majority of the businessmen, both wholesalers and retailers alike were the members of the former Christian and Jewish *millets*, who have since been designated as the "minorities" of the country by the Treaty of Lausanne. They had continued to practice their traditional vocations after 1923. In spite of the fact that there had been a policy of "nationalization of economic enterprises" of the Turkish governments since the establishment of the Republic,[20] few Muslims, who in overwhelming numbers had functioned as bureaucrats, clergy, judges, soldiers, and so on in the Ottoman times, but hardly as merchants, businessmen, industrialists, and so on, had moved into trading and manufacturing since the 1920s. The "wealth tax" almost exclusively hit the Greek, Armenian, and the Jewish minority businessmen and their families in Turkey.[21] In practice, the tax levied was excessive and often much beyond the means of the taxpayers to pay. Those who could not pay the tax were tried in court, and if found guilty, were sent to hard labor, while their wealth was confiscated by the government. The *Varlık Vergisi* "disaster"[22] did not last long (1942–1943), yet the damage was done. Many minority families lost their lifelong earnings and wealth, and emigrated from Turkey, most specifically from Istanbul.[23]

However, the black market could not be destroyed. In the meantime, some Muslim entrepreneurs emerged to replace the dislocated minority business community. The land title registrations indicate that Muslim businessmen purchased two out of three pieces of real estate sold by the non-Muslim businessmen to pay the wealth tax.[24] The outcome was further Turkification of the business community of Turkey.

The interventions of the CHP government in the economy gave a clear signal to all members of the business community. Those who had accumulated wealth between 1939 and 1945 could no longer rely upon the good will of the CHP government or its leader and the President of the country, İsmet İnönü. The establishment of a legal opposition party that would effectively control the excesses of the CHP majority in the TGNA began to be felt by the business community of Turkey, and in Istanbul in particular. The domestic push for multiparty democracy coincided with the foreign policy objective of joining the club of democracies to cope with the challenge of the Soviet Super Power in 1945.

Soon after the purge of those who moved the "Proposal of the Four" in the TGNA from the ranks of the CHP, the Democrat Party was established under the leadership of Celal Bayar and his three associates on January 7, 1946.[25] The DP was another split from the ranks of the CHP. Soon after the establishment of the DP, Turkey experienced its first multiparty elections in 1946.

Unfortunately, the Turkish transition to democracy was not a well-orchestrated process. The President of the country, İsmet İnönü had a major role to play also in the capacity of the leader of the CHP, and so did the CHP elite.[26] It was İnönü's stamina, persistence, and adamant drive toward multiparty democracy that made the transition possible at the time.[27] The interwar period had witnessed an eclipse of the idea and performance of democracy. Indeed, totalitarian and authoritarian regimes flourished all over Europe, Latin America, and Asia in the 1930s. When the totalitarian forces, except for the Soviet Union lost World War II, the new regimes of Italy and Germany in Europe, and Japan in Asia faced the challenge of establishing democracy in cultures, which were, at best, not deemed fit for democracy at the time. Simultaneously, Turkey also encountered the very same challenge. The President of the country and the leader of the CHP, İsmet İnönü had witnessed the previous Turkish experiments with democracy as an officer of the Ottoman army, member of the TGNA and the Prime Minister of the CHP government.[28]

A Search for a Compromise on the Fundamentals

President İnönü seemed to have moved with the hindsight of the previous experiments with the TCF (The Progressive Republic Party) 1924 and SF (The Liberal Party) 1930, and tried not to repeat the same mistakes. Unfortunately that method had not spared him and his associates from making new critical errors.[29] When Bayar visited İnönü on the occasion of the establishment of the DP, İnönü seemed to be curious about two subjects; whether the new party, the DP was preparing to encourage religious revivalism, and whether the DP would be willing to support the foreign policy that the CHP had been following (1997: 145).[30] First and foremost, İnönü seemed to have been most concerned about exploitation of the religious feelings of the masses and the protection of the principle of secularism (*laiklik*).[31] One other topic, which seemed to have emerged during those interactions, seemed to be related with ethnic politics. İnönü seemed to have probed Bayar about refraining from organizing and mobilizing masses in the eastern provinces of Turkey, and especially in the areas close to the borders of the country.[32]

It seemed as if İnönü and Bayar were trying to establish the basis of a pact concerning sensitive cultural and foreign policy issues, which would be spared from exploitation by the politicians of the two parties in the election campaigns to come. The CHP started to vie for votes and began to exploit religious symbols for political purposes between 1947 and 1950, which was not only self-defeating, but boosted the morale and motivation of forces of political Islam and the sufi orders (*tarikat*), which had gone underground since the early 1930s.[33] ". . . In 1948, religious instruction was introduced for certain grades in elementary school, a Faculty of Divinity was opened a year later, a number of schools that provided religious training were allowed to conduct their activities freely."[34] In the beginning of 1949 the CHP government permitted the establishment of İmam Hatip courses (to educate prayer leaders and Quranic scholars), to function in eight provinces of Turkey.[35] In 1949, the PM Günaltay of the CHP government promised the institution of Faculties of Islamic Theology, one of which was immediately established at the University of Ankara the same year.[36] The struggle of CHP with folkloric religion as a fount of revivalism came to an abrupt and unanticipated end about the same time. The CHP government and majority in the TGNA amended the revolutionary act that closed down tombs (*türbe*), dervish lodges (*tekke*) and cells (*zaviye*) of the *Sufi* orders (*tarikat*) in 1924 and 1925, and permitted the tombs to be opened to public visits.[37]

Once the CHP began to exploit religion, the DP was morally and legitimately relieved from all restraints to exploit the religious symbolism of the majority of Sunni Muslims to its advantage thanks to the performance of the CHP governments of the late 1940s. It was a small step for the DP to reintroduce the call to prayer (*ezan*) to be chanted in Arabic, which had earlier been converted to Turkish, and start up new institutions of religious education.[38] Indeed, the DP had been occupying an anti-CHP stance on all issues, including secularism. The Democrats had cultivated special relations with many illegal *Sufi* orders, such as the *Ticanis*, who had been tried and imprisoned under the CHP rule.[39] The *Sufi* orders seemed to have received special and prestigious treatment by the DP establishment, although the DP could not go so far enough to annul the laws that abolished the religious orders as legal entities. It had become easier for the Sunni *Sufi* orders, though illegal, to become more active under the highly tolerant rule of the DP governments. The strict adherence of the CHP still under İnönü's leadership to secularist policies of the earlier era had been another cultural factor deepening the rift between the DP and CHP. When the economy went into a deep recession in 1954, and again plummeted into recession from 1958 to 1960, such cultural symbolism gained further recognition and began to poison the relations between the government and opposition.

Although, the CHP elite, and particularly İnönü vehemently criticized the DP government over their policies concerning secularism, they never could legitimately argue that the DP breached the İnönü–Bayar pact, before CHP did from 1947 through 1950. Such inconsistency and confusion over many issue and policy areas have been recurring characteristics of the CHP throughout the multiparty era. However, İnönü continued to argue systematically that "secularism was distancing of religion from state and politics"[40] to the point of being accused of being irreligious. Nevertheless, İnönü personally adhered to his understanding of secularism and resisted all attempts at employing religion as part of the CHP campaign in the multiparty elections until the end of his political career as the leader of the CHP in 1972.

The authoritarian nature of the CHP, which had existed for more than two decades as "the single party" functioning as the mobilizing agent of the Republican state until 1945, seemed to have contributed to the occurrence of various detours on the way to democracy.[41] The CHP elite had so much emphasized the unitary characteristic of the state and the "indivisibility of the nation" that, they failed to take the deep running sociocultural cleavages in the country into consideration in designing the political institutions of the multiparty era. Even if they were cognizant of the *kulturkampfs* (as they also belonged to one such camp), they seemed to have miscalculated the penetration and mobilization capacity of the opposing *kulturkampf* of the periphery. They had assumed that the periphery would not be veering away from them after more than two decades of efforts at penetrating and reshaping the periphery after their own image of good society. Some prominent CHP members even assumed all along that they could halt the transition to democracy and go back to some form of authoritarian CHP rule.[42] Hence, they opted for the Westminster model of democracy with a unicameral legislature.

Westminster model of democracy stressed rule by powerful majorities of the legislature. In Britain, where that model had originated, political culture and traditions have spontaneously erected checks and balances in the system, through trial and error,[43] and a host of values by the help of which various structures, such as the free press and the media, interest groups, independent judiciary, and a cantankerous electorate, act to monitor the government and the parliament actively and sanction it effectively.[44] However, Turkey lacked all such institutions and worse. Turkey had a long history of what Frey called an "in-group versus outgroup orientation," which had been inimical to any kind of open political competition, and undermined all semblances of legitimacy of the opposition (outgroup, enemy) in the eyes of the in-group (friends),[45] on the one hand, and had never practiced free press, freedom of association, freedom of speech, and so on until 1946, on the other. Therefore, there were no cultural, political, legal infrastructure, value system, and tradition of hosting structures or institutions that could check and balance the excesses of the majority of the TGNA. It was no surprise that the Turkish version of Westminster style of democracy quickly evolved into the tyranny of the legislative majority in Turkey. The unbridled one-party rule of the CHP was what the CHP elite had been yearning for under the guise of democracy in 1945. They got it for a four-year period after the 1946 elections, if not by popular vote, by Byzantine design and rigging the elections, which constituted another major flaw of the democratic transition process in the 1940s. The 1946 elections poisoned the relationships between the CHP and the DP for many years to come.

The other serious defect that the CHP elite had installed in 1945–1946 was the adoption of a majoritarian electoral formula they had devised for their model of democracy in Turkey. The original British majoritarian electoral formula is highly unjust, for it wastes a lot of votes (choices) of the people, in favor of rendering the election results clear, so that a winner (party government) emerges after the elections beyond the shadow of any doubt.

However, it seriously hampers different voices and opinions to be elected on their own platforms to the British Parliament, yet it produces clear winners and no problems over governability. The electoral formula adopted by the CHP elite in Turkey of 1946 was even more grossly unjust. First of all, the British first-past-the-post electoral system is carried out in single seat constituencies, whereas the Turkish majoritarian formula was implemented in multimember electoral districts. The voters were presented with names of candidates on party lists and the winning party list took a huge majority of the seats and often all of the available seats per multimember district.[46] Hence, even though the two political parties had not much difference in the total numbers of votes they obtained at the polls, the distribution of the seats were immensely skewed in favor of the front runner, which was CHP in 1946, or so it was officially announced. The official results indicated that CHP obtained 397, DP 61, and Independents 7 seats out of 465 seats of the TGNA in 1946.[47]

Unfortunately, the CHP government had contributed to another flaw in the electoral system by devising a system of "open ballots and secret vote count."[48] Hence, there was no secrecy at the polling booths or stations, for everyone could see who voted for which party list, yet the vote count was made by the state officials, formally under the supervision and oversight of the CHP elite, in secret. Many irregularities flourished in the 1946 elections, such as the disappearances of the ballot boxes, ballot boxes stuffed with the CHP ballots appearing a few days after the vote, and so on.[49] The DP vehemently protested the election results and condemned the CHP for rigging the elections. Hence, the first multiparty elections in Turkey were rendered neither free, nor fair. It was hardly an encouraging way to make a fresh start at democracy. Consequently, it is small wonder that Turkey paid a stiff price for the mistakes, flaws, and defects introduced or specifically designed with faulty assumptions of the CHP elite while the first timid steps were taken toward democracy.

An acerbic, abrasive, and belligerent DP opposition emerged in and out of the TGNA in the 1940s. The DP was critical of the style of rule of the CHP government, the election rules, the one-party legacy of the CHP, and most of all, economic policies of the CHP governments during the world war and beyond. "In a nutshell, the Democrats rejected the essential *dirigiste* approach of their predecessors, believing in incentives rather than directives as the driving force of national progress. They were determined to devote more attention to the problems of the neglected but electorally important agricultural sector and to encourage private industry at the expense, if necessary of state enterprises. To the conservative sections of the electorate they held out some, if vague, hopes of a limited relaxation of secularism . . ."[50] They had also promised liberty and democracy for all in Turkey. Indeed, the DP emerged as the party of the peasants, the neglected, and the downtrodden, businessmen, merchants, or in a nutshell, of the Periphery, challenging the arbitrary, callous, self-centered style of the party of the Center, the CHP, the public bureaucracy, which the DP was bent upon dislodging the latter from the centers of political power in Turkey.[51]

THE "WHITE" REVOLUTION: MAY 14, 1950

The elections of May 14, 1950 have been referred to as the "White Revolution" in Turkish politics, for they ended an era and ousted the most vehement political force in Turkey until that time, the CHP from power without any violence.[52] The CHP governments of the late 1940s had to function under severe and systematic criticisms of the DP opposition in the TGNA. One of the fruits of such an opposition was the partial amendment of the electoral rules. The 1950 elections had the same unfortunate majoritarian electoral formula, yet they incorporated secret ballots and public vote count.[53] The elections improved in being more fair and free. A huge vote swing seemed to have occurred as the DP scored a staggering landslide victory by obtaining approximately 53 percent of the valid vote (see table 3.1). The CHP was relegated to the ranks of the opposition in the TGNA, with about 39 percent of the valid vote, where they had to stay until 1961.

1950–1954 turned out to be a huge success for the DP government and leadership. The DP government decided to participate in the military campaign of the United Nations in the Korean peninsula, and sent troops to Korea, almost as soon as it ascended to power. The new Prime Minister of the DP, Adnan Menderes defended their policy as indicative of Turkey's resolve to be a part of the Western alliance, and North Atlantic Treaty Organization (NATO).[54] Turkey had applied for NATO membership earlier during May 1950 and

Table 3.1   National Election Results (1946–1957)

Election Year	Vote and Seat Shares (%)	Political Parties*					
		CHP	CMP	DP	HP	MP	Independent
1946	Votes	?	–	?	–	–	?
	Seats	85.4	–	12.7	–	–	1.2
1950	Votes	39.4	–	52.7	–	3.1	4.8
	Seats	14.2	–	85.2	–	0.2	0.4
1954	Votes	35.4	4.9	57.6	–	–	1.5
	Seats	5.7	0.9	92.8	–	–	0.6
1957	Votes	41.1	7.1	47.9	3.8	–	0.1
	Seats	29.2	0.6	69.6	0.6	–	0.1

Notes: In the table "Votes" refer to the percentage of the national vote the corresponding party obtained in the elections. "Seats" refer to the percentage of the National Assembly seats the corresponding party received in the national elections.

"?" indicates missing values. There are no records of how many votes or what percentage of the national vote any of the political parties that participated in the race obtained in the 1946 national elections.

"–" refers to nonexistence of the corresponding party at the time of the elections. For example MP and TKP (Turkish Peasant Party, *Türkiye Köylü Partisi*) merged in the early 1950s and formed the CMP.

* Political party names in the table are as follows: CHP (Republican People's Party, *Cumhuriyet Halk Partisi*), CMP (Republicanist Nation Party, *Cumhuriyetçi Millet Partisi*), DP (Democrat Party, *Demokrat Parti*), HP (Freedom Party, *Hürriyet Partisi*), MP (Nation Party, *Millet Partisi*). Only those political parties, which were able to win representation in the National Assembly, have been included in the table.

Source: Erol Tuncer, *Osmanlı'dan Günümüze Seçimler: 1877–1999* (Ankara: Toplumsal Ekonomik Siyasal Araştırmalar Vakfı (Tesav) Yayınları, 2002): 412–414.

repeated it in August 1950.[55] The Turkish troops, after suffering some difficulty in adapting to the long sea voyage to Pusan, Korea and to their new environment, performed extremely well in the Korean War.[56] On several occasions they managed to help the UN Forces stop the advances of the Chinese army, and gained the respect of the United States and other forces and commanders of NATO member countries. Turkish strategic location as an outpost very close to the Caucasus, which provided the opportunity of the use of airpower to undermine a westward attack by the Soviets, if the Turkish airfields could be used by NATO seemed to provide the final justification for the Turkish membership in NATO.[57] After trying so hard, Turkey managed to become a NATO member, simultaneously with Greece, on February 18, 1952, three years after the foundation of the NATO.[58]

The DP not only boasted about its bid to carry Turkey into full membership of the NATO alliance and alleviate the fears of communist takeover, but also of having designed and executed a foreign policy of being close and reliable ally of the United States and NATO. Consequently, Turkey neither showed much interest in the anticolonial struggles of the Third World countries, nor in the international organization of the Non-Aligned nations. Turkey as a NATO member country failed to cultivate any close ties with the emerging Third World states of Asia and Africa, with some which she had shared a long historical relationship under the Ottoman rule. Reciprocally, Turkey was perceived as a former imperial power and a contemporary friend of the "imperialist West" by the new states of Asia and Africa.[59]

THE ECONOMY TAKES OFF

The Turkish economy grew with leaps and bounds in the early 1950s (see table 3.2). A liberal economic regime, influx of foreign investment and loans, (including the Marshall Plan for European reconstruction), and free trade seemed to be delivering a steady growth, on the one hand, and the birth of a consumer society, on the other. The Periphery seemed to enjoy the fruits of development as well. The DP government seemed to be sensitive to the demands of the agricultural interests. The landlords with large farms benefited from the DP policies the most. Modern farming equipment, fertilizers, herbicides, and insecticides were imported in relatively larger numbers, and were made available to larger farmer communities, which could afford them. In the meantime both agriculture and industry seemed to gain from the policies of the DP governments (see table 3.3).

The DP government quickly realized that the U.S. government, through the famous Marshall Plan, other means, and facilities was eager to provide funds to boost agricultural production, trading, and the necessary infrastructural investments to boost trade in Turkey. The DP governments calculated that they could obtain funds from the United States to upgrade and extend the road system of Turkey, which would provide ease of transportation for the agricultural produce, on the one hand, and for the governmental services to reach the remotest hamlets of the country, on the other (table 3.4).

Table 3.2 Economic Growth Rates and Gross National Product (GNP) Deflator (1924–1960)

		GNP DEFLATOR	
	GNP	% CHANGE (Growth)	1987 = 100
1924	14.9	10.0	0.04
1925	12.8	12.4	0.05
1926	18.2	−8.5	0.04
1927	−12.8	2.2	0.04
1928	11.0	−0.1	0.04
1929	21.6	4.4	0.05
1930	2.2	−25.4	0.03
1931	8.7	−19.0	0.03
1932	−10.7	−5.7	0.03
1933	15.8	−15.9	0.02
1934	6.0	0.5	0.02
1935	−3.0	11.1	0.03
1936	23.2	5.0	0.03
1937	1.5	5.0	0.03
1938	9.5	−4.1	0.03
1939	6.9	1.8	0.03
1940	−4.9	22.5	0.03
1941	−10.3	38.9	0.05
1942	5.6	96.0	0.09
1943	−9.8	65.2	0.15
1944	−5.1	−23.7	0.11
1945	−15.3	−3.4	0.11
1946	31.9	−5.0	0.10
1947	4.2	5.6	0.11
1948	4.2	20.8	0.13
1949	−5.0	0.4	0.13
1950	9.4	−2.1	0.13
1951	12.8	6.5	0.14
1952	11.9	2.7	0.14
1953	11.2	4.8	0.15
1954	−3.0	5.1	0.16
1955	7.9	11.3	0.17
1956	3.2	11.8	0.20
1957	7.8	23.3	0.24
1958	4.5	14.2	0.28
1959	4.1	19.9	0.33
1960	3.4	3.3	0.34

Source: State Institute of Statistics and State Planning Organization (of the Turkish Republic) <http://ekutup.dpt.gov.tr/ekonomi/gosterge/tr/1950-01/>

The Turkish road system got its first push in the 1950s and increased in size dramatically to the detriment of the railroads ever since (see table 3.4).

Finally, the agricultural policy of the DP governments were based on two principles: "first, an increase in the supply of credit and the maintenance of high minimum prices by state purchasing agencies, so as to boost the resources available to the farmer, and secondly, a massive increase in the import

Table 3.3 Economic Growth in Turkey by Sectors (1923–1999)

Years	(1968 Prices, Million Turkish Lira)			
	Agriculture	Industry	Others	Gross National Product (GNP)
1923	4,900	1,100	5,400	11,400
1930	10,000	2,000	9,300	21,300
1940	15,000	4,600	14,100	33,700
1950	15,900	5,100	17,500	38,500
1960	26,800	11,400	33,000	70,000
1970	32,900	28,000	64,500	125,400
1980	42,100	42,400	102,900	187,400
1990	47,600	85,700	179,500	312,800
1999	57,796	118,894	236,138	412,828

Source: Oktay Yenal, *Cumhuriyet'in İktisat Tarihi* (Istanbul: Türkiye Sınai Kalkınma Bankası, 2001): 61.

Table 3.4 Transport Infrastructure in Turkey

AIR TRANSPORTATION (1)

Years	Number of Air Planes	Index	Number of Flights	Index	Number of Passengers	Index
1940	8	24	–	–	739	1
1950	33	100	10.242	100	86.331	100
1960	31	94	22.658	221	305.963	354
1970	17	52	29.458	288	1.095.191	1.269
1980	21	64	21.458	210	1.590.416	1.842
1990	35	106	44.496	434	4.574.497	5.299
2000	73	221	117.916	1.151	12.030.747	13.936
2001	69	209	108.918	1.063	10.277.423	11.905

DEVELOPMENTS OF RAILWAYS IN TURKEY (1923–2001)

Years	Length of Main Lines Passenger Transportation				Freight Transportation	
	(Km)	Index	(Thou. Person)	Index	(Thou. Tons)*	Index
1923	3.756	100	–	–	–	–
1930	5.632	150	–	–	–	–
1940	7.381	197	–	–	–	–
1950	7.671	204	53.130	100	8.681	100
1960	7.895	210	96.798	182	14.268	164
1970	7.895	210	104.041	196	14.898	172
1980	8.397	224	113.937	214	11.446	132
1990	8.429	224	139.089	262	13.464	155
2000	8.671	231	85.343	161	18.533	213
2001	8.671	231	76.400	144	14.800	170

Notes: * Excluding departmental trains of state railways.
(1) Data reflects THY figures including the planes rented.

Source: The Turkish Airlines, and <www.dpt.gov.tr/dptweb/esg/esgx.html>

Table 3.4 Transport Infrastructure in Turkey (cont.)

DEVELOPMENT OF MOTORWAYS IN TURKEY (1950–2000)

Years (1)	State Highways and Provincial Roads				Village Roads			Total	
	Highways	Asphalt	Total	Asphalt %	Asphalt	Total	Asphalt %	Km	Index
1950	–	1.624	47.080	3	–	41.735	–	88.815	100
1960	–	7.049	61.542	11	–	47.500	–	109.042	123
1970	–	19.226	59.453	32	–	162.055	–	221.508	249
1980	24	35.810	60.761	59	–	172.103	–	232.888	262
1990	286	47.597	59.128	80	21.374	308.597	7	368.011	414
2000	1.774	55.900	61.090	92	79.335	293.855	27	356.719	402
2001	1.845	56.619	61.305	92	85.563	291.217	29	354.367	399

Source: İlhan Tekeli and Selim Ilkin, "Türkiye'de Ulaştırmanın Gelişimi" in (no editor), *Cumhuriyet Dönemi Türkiye Ansiklopedisi* (Istanbul: Iletişim Yayınları, 1983): 2758–2768, and <www.dpt.gov.tr/dptweb/esg/esgx.html>

of tractors so as to extend the cultivated area, and thus raise production."[60] The number of tractors in Turkey jumped from 14,000 in 1950 to 44,000 by 1956; and the area cultivated by tractors rose from 8.6 percent of the arable land to 14 percent of it by the latter 1950s.[61] The living standards of the peasants and farmers improved throughout the early 1950s and stagnated beyond 1956.

The landless peasants, whose numbers increased with the rapid mechanization of the Turkish agriculture in the 1950s, constituted the main economic sector and social category who failed to benefit from the policies of the DP governments. Under the circumstances, an unanticipated development began to occur in the country. The DP government seemed to have assumed that the new road system would efficiently provide the much-needed public services to the rural areas. However, the rural population seemed to perceive the matters from a completely different angle. They seemed to have considered the new transport facilities as excellent opportunity to flee from their poor settlements for a larger share of the pie in the cities. Before the services and goods could appear in the remotest hamlets of Turkey, the inhabitants of those areas began to pack up and leave for such cities as Istanbul, Ankara, Izmir, and Adana, where those goods and services, and industrial job opportunities were already available. However, the DP governments had no plans or policies to cope with the increasing emigration of the rural migrants to the cities of the country. The social welfare system that the CHP governments had earlier erected was abandoned in the 1950s. Instead, family networks provided the only reliable system of social welfare in the country during the 1950s.[62] Nevertheless, the phenomenon of social mobilization began to deeply influence Turkish society, economy, and politics by the late 1950s.

SOCIAL MOBILIZATION AND THE ECONOMIC DOWNTURN

Increasing social mobility not only made the urban centers grow rapidly but also provided the large labor pool and cheap labor for industrialization.

Once social mobilization gained speed it became virtually impossible to stop it. The psychological factors, and specifically the rising tide of expectations and a concomitant rise of feeling of empathy motivated millions to consider living in the urban centers of the country.[63]

The attractiveness of the city life, with its relatively more accessible welfare facilities, such as relative ease of enrolling in a school and completing an educational program, obtaining healthcare, finding jobs in the developing construction sector, and so on, also seemed to have pulled the landless peasants to the big cities in droves. Kemal Karpat in a study he conducted in the 1960s calculated that about one out of eight Turks had migrated at least once by 1965.[64] From about three millions in 1950 to about six millions in 1960, the number of people living in the urban areas doubled (table 3.5). Hence, both the push of the rural areas and the attraction or pull of the big city centers seemed to have precipitated the start of massive migration out of the Anatolian countryside.[65] Similarly, industrialization also started to gain pace with urbanization (see tables 3.3 and 3. 5).

The U.S. Marshall Plan had rekindled the German economy, and the reconstruction of Germany necessitated an expanding labor force, beyond what German labor market could supply at home. Turkey provided a bountiful pool of unskilled and semiskilled labor. Hence, with the increasing demand and "pull" of the German market, the long odyssey of the "Turkish guest workers" started by the late 1950s. In 1961 the total number of Turks in Federal Republic of Germany was no more than 6,700, mostly skilled workers.[66] However, soon enough anyone who could pass the German health test could find his or her way to the payroll of a German company, and the number of Turks living in Federal Germany rose to 1,530,700 by 1987.[67]

From the fertile countryside of Anatolia, which produced a population boom of about 2.7 percent annual growth rate by the 1950s, emerged waves of emigration, which overwhelmed the Turkish and the German cities alike. Most peasants seemed to have moved away from their villages and small towns in search of jobs.[68] They seemed not to have intended to stay away from

Table 3.5 The Rising Urban Population (1950–2001)

	1950	1960	1970	1980	1985	1990	1997	2001 (3)
Total Population (1)	20,947,188	27,754,820	35,605,156	44,736,957	50,664,035	56,473,035	63,809,000	69,180,000
Urban Population (2)	3,035,961	6,053,448	10,221,530	16,064,681	23,238,030	28,958,300	37,023,189	45,430,954
Percent Urban	14.5%	21.8%	28.7%	35.9%	45.8%	51.3%	58.0%	65.7%
Rural Population	17,911,227	21,701,372	25,383,626	28,672,276	27,426,428	27,514,735	26,785,811	23,749,046
Percent Rural	85.5%	78.2%	71.3%	64.1%	54.2%	49.7%	42.0%	34.3%

Notes
(1) Estimate for year-end population from 1997 onward.
(2) Urban refers to areas with population of 20,000 or more.
(3) Estimate.

Source: State Institute of Statistics and State Planning Organization (of the Turkish Republic).

their land for long. They had hoped to earn much more than they ever could back at home, save most of their earnings, and then go back to their villages to buy some land, marry and settle. However, as time passed they became acculturated to their new jobs, environments, and lifestyles. Some went back home, but could not tolerate the small town or village life any longer, and moved back to the cities. Some never went back, but married and settled in the urban centers, or even in Germany and other countries of Europe, Asia, America, and even Oceania. The overall outcome was a grand transformation of the Anatolian landscape and demography once more.

Turkey began to possess metropolitan cities, such as Istanbul, Ankara, and İzmir, which grew in size rapidly. Lerner and others predicted that,[69] just like in Europe a century earlier, Turkey would also go through a similar process of modernization, industrialization, urbanization, and democratization.[70] Consequently, those who migrated to urban centers would have a chance to become literate, and under the influence of education, they would be seeking information, and thus follow the news and the media regularly.[71] Such educated and informed masses would be most inclined to develop a distinct sense of civic duty, which in turn would propel them to be involved in politics, participate in elections, run for public office, and so on.[72] Urbanization and industrialization would be expected to serve as the engine of modern political life, participation, and democracy. For a time in the early 1950s there were all the good signs of such a benign outcome of rapid social mobilization in Turkey. However, what the early researchers on modernization had not envisaged, or underestimated was the vicissitudes of the international economy.

Left alone and with some luck, such as good climatic and weather conditions, and large enough foreign currency reserves spent on tractors, the Turkish economy perhaps could have grown steadily enough in line with the expanding demands and increasing expectations of the population. However, the good weather conditions of the early 1950s and the foreign currency and gold reserves, which the previous CHP governments had accumulated through stringent spending, only lasted until the mid-1950s. Coincidentally, the world economic recession of the mid-1950s began to create dire economic challenges for the DP government. Under the circumstances, the free trade practices could no longer be sustained for much longer. The consumers began to discover that a variety of goods, most of which imported, could no longer be available or affordable. However, the DP was led to believe and expect that the economic policies of free trade, private initiative and capitalism, as the driving forces in a mixed economy, with a huge and still mismanaged public sector would deliver a consumer society and affluence. The Prime Minister of the DP governments in the 1950s, Adnan Menderes often boasted that there would be a millionaire per city district (*mahalle*), and that Turkey was on the road to becoming a "small America."

However, in 1956 even staple foods began to disappear from the market. Turkey needed American support to import staple foods from the United States and elsewhere.[73] Shortening, butter, cheese, and although not so much of a staple food, but definitely a cultural symbol, the famous "Turkish coffee" became almost impossible to find in 1958. Ironically, Turkey ran into difficulty to pay Brazil, from where the coffee beans for "Turkish coffee" were and still are imported. Concomitantly, Turkey started to experience price hikes for almost all commodities. Under the circumstances, the DP government had to call for early elections in 1957. They seemed to have calculated that, if they waited for the end of the legislative tenure of the TGNA until 1958, the economic situation would be far worse, and they could even lose the general elections, which for "the party of the people" would be both unthinkable and intolerable.

However, the "damage control" elections of 1957 did not help the DP much. There were fairly flagrant rigging at the polls,[74] which the CHP pointed to and condemned the DP with foul play. The DP was ready to lose a few votes here and there. However, it seemed as if they had lost far more votes than they had ever anticipated.[75] The opposition to the Democrat majority became much more effective or stiff, and the DP decided to reciprocate by curbing the press and muffling the opposition. The relationships between the government and the opposition parties of the country ebbed, while political tension between them grew with leaps and bounds. In the meantime, the economy failed to recuperate fast enough. The DP government had to devalue the domestic currency, the Turkish Lira, by 330 percent overnight, while the black market rate of the Turkish Lira spiraled to about five times of its official value by 1958.[76]

All those with fixed incomes lost a good chunk of their purchasing power overnight. The state employees and workers were the first and foremost among those who were hit the hardest. Among the state employees the military personnel were probably among the hardest hit. Some ominous signs of the dire economic conditions of the armed forces became visible for those who were eager to observe. The society columns of the Turkish dailies of the time indicated that the young officers were having a hard time to find suitable ladies to wed! Their social prestige seemed to be sliding down rapidly. The DP government did not seem to mind, and peculiarly enough, neither did the top brass of the military. They were to pay for their negligence dearly in a few years' time.

The DP had been taking harsh measures against its main opposition the CHP since 1953.[77] In 1955 the status of the island of Cyprus started to emerge as a major foreign relations burden for the DP government. On September 6 and 7 of that year the DP government instigated anti-Greek demonstrations in the city of Istanbul, which went out of control, and the houses and shops of all minorities and even some Muslims were seriously damaged.[78] The "incidents of September 6 and 7" further led to the increased intensity of the repressive measures applied by the government against the opposition. Another wave of emigration of the minorities from Istanbul took place in the immediate aftermath of that incident as well. However, tensions mounted to new heights between the DP government and the main opposition party, the CHP in the aftermath of the 1957 elections. The CHP started to question the dire economic conditions of the country's corruption, partisanship, and foreign policy performance of the DP government, as well as the irregularities in the general elections of 1957.

MAJORITARIAN DEMOCRACY BREAKS DOWN

The failing economic conditions increased the pressure on the DP government. The DP government was also led by a group of politicians who had been socialized into their political roles during the War of Liberation, the former CHP one-party rule, and they were not going to yield any ground to their archrival. The DP decided to fight the CHP opposition back, with the kind of tactics and measures they had learned to wield in the past, while serving among ranks of the CHP. The press was muffled through strict censorship. The university professors who dared to lecture about such "sensitive topics" as price inflation to their undergraduate students were fired. The measures became more oppressive and strict in 1958. It almost seemed as if the two political parties were involved in a no-holds-barred war against each other.[79]

In 1959 something quite like a miracle occurred. The Turkish Airlines plane carrying the PM Menderes, who was on his way to sign the London Accord with Greece, and Britain on the status of the Island of Cyprus, had a tragic accident at the Gatwick Airport near London, Britain.[80] Many members of the PM's entourage passed away, while he and some of the passengers emerged from the rubble of the plane unscathed. He signed the Accord in a hospital bed in London.[81] He was almost declared a saint by his followers, and his popularity increased with leaps and bounds for the last time. The opposition seemed to be inclined to show leniency toward the PM due to the shock he had experienced. İnönü greeted him upon his return to Turkey, and shook hands for the last time on February 28, 1959.[82] The relations between the DP and CHP seemed to have precipitated a final rapprochement and fraternity in early 1959. However, the thawing of the relations between the government and the opposition failed to last long.

In the spring of 1960 the parliamentary government started to show signs of breaking down[83] as college students demanding university autonomy, freedom of speech, freedom of the press, and the like began to hold protest rallies, demonstrations, and walkouts. Both of the major university campuses of the country, in the capital city of Ankara, and Istanbul were soon engulfed in the aura of student revolts. The DP initially tried to engage the students and placate them. However, it did not take long for the DP to change course and use force to suppress the student protests. The DP elite began to perceive the college students as part of a CHP conspiracy as well. Two students died in the clashes with the police and a few suffered spine injuries and others were severely harmed, and many more were injured. The newspapers were published with the photograph of the Rector of the Istanbul University being dragged on the ground near the university campus by the police seated in a jeep. The cities of Ankara and Istanbul were overwhelmed by rumors that the students were tortured, executed and their bodies were destroyed, as martial law was established in those cities. Coincidentally, a similar student uprising that had been taking place in South Korea about the same time led to a military coup in that country, and established Syngman Rhee to the helm of government in South Korea. That event was used as a reference by İnönü, when he argued that if and when the conditions for a military coup emerge, even he could not save the DP government.[84]

In the meantime, the relations between the DP and the CHP further deteriorated. The leader of the CHP, the former PM and President of the country İnönü was barred from the TGNA by the vote of the DP deputies, who constituted the majority. İnönü and the rest of the CHP leadership, almost all of them now barred from attending the National Assembly, took to the streets and started to organize public rallies to protest the DP government. However, they ran into strong government action against them. İnönü was prevented from entering the middle Anatolian city of Kayseri by the orders of the governor of that province, who could not but act with the orders of the government, for hours.[85] When İnönü continued his way by car, his way into Kayseri was cut off by military troops. İnönü walked out of his car and confronted the army major in charge of the troops and asked whether he will order his troops to fire on him, one of the foremost heroes of the War of Liberation and the man who signed the Treaty of Lausanne. The major responded that instead of firing at him, he would commit suicide; and thus İnönü's entourage went into the city of Kayseri.[86]

In another city in western Anatolia, mobs attacked and peppered İnönü and his entourage with stones, one of which landed on his head. The CHP vehemently argued that such activities were the work of the Democrats, who organized the mob to suppress the opposition.[87] The state radio kept the news of the opposition to a minimum or never reported their activities, while it announced huge lists of people joining the ranks of a Patriotic Front (*Vatan Cephesi*), which was established by the PM Menderes to cause a fusion (*tevhid*) of the forces of the triple formula of Ziya Gökalp, Turkism (*Türkçülük*), Islamism (*İslamcılık*) and Westernism (*Garpçılık*) in the person of the PM, Menderes.[88] Parliamentary democracy seemed to give every impression of a transformation back to single party government, with DP at the helm.

Under pressure PM Menderes offered his resignation to the President of the country, also the leader of the DP. President Bayar, who had served as a revolutionary within ranks of the Union and Progress Party of the Ottoman Empire, and as a guerrilla leader in the War of Liberation, and as minister and PM during Atatürk's reign, considered such a move as sign of weakness, and refused. The DP deliberated calling for early elections, just like they had done three years ago. The elections were scheduled to take place in 1961 by law. They could easily be moved to an earlier date in 1960. However, that move was also considered as a sign of caving to the pressures of the opposition. Furthermore, the DP considered that the mayhem of the spring 1960 was not a good time to call for early elections. The Democrats seemed to have considered the developments as a temporary outburst or just a fluke. The DP elite considered that their party was the party of the "people." What, they seemed to have thought, could a few student protests in the big cities and the desperate acts of İnönü and company do to hurt them? They seemed to have been in regular contact with the top brass of the military. The Chief of General Staff, General Rüştü Erdelhun pledged the allegiance of the "military" to the government, and acted in accordance with professional ethics and refused to be involved in politics in any way.[89] In true spirit of Mustafa Kemal's teachings, he and great majority of the top level commanders of the military seemed to have believed that the military should stay clear out of partisan bickering.[90] They could not be more wrong about the intentions of the middle ranked, younger officers.

A group of officers motivated more by ethnic Turkish nationalist feelings, some even on the verge of racism, and others anxious about salvaging the Cultural Revolution of the 1920s and the 1930s from the encroachment of the Periphery, had started to organize a secret society, or a military junta, as early as 1954.[91] The severe economic recession of 1955–1957 had increased the resolve of the junta and enlarged its ranks.[92] The military intelligence seemed to have infiltrated their ranks and passed on the information to the top brass of the military, and informed them of the conspiracy.[93] Amazingly, no one seemed to show any sign of concern.[94] Finally, there was only one Major General, Cemal Madanoğlu, among their ranks when they moved in May 1960 to oust the DP government. However, in the meantime a very popular soldier, the commander of the Third Army, General Cemal Gürsel (popularly known as Cemal Aga), had for his own reasons fallen apart with the other commanders and asked for early retirement. The junta was able to cajole and co-opt him to be their titular leader.[95] When the junta of young officers struck on May 27, 1960, they had few members of the army top brass, General Cemal Gürsel as the titular head, a Major-General Cemal Madanoğlu acting as the leader of the junta, a Brigadier-General Sıtkı Ulay, and the rest consisting mainly of lieutenants, captains, majors, some lieutenant colonels and colonels.[96] The May 27, 1960 "young officers' coup" became successful, and the DP government was not only ousted, but also the entire cabinet and the DP deputies of the TGNA, and the commanders of the armed forces, including the Chief of General Staff, General Erdelhun were arrested and tried.

It was obvious that the professional and institutional norms of the Turkish army collapsed as of May 27, 1960. A period of chaos reigned among the ranks of the armed forces of Turkey between May 27, 1960, through the uprising of February 22, 1962 and of May 20–21, 1963, when finally that last coup attempt led by an ethnic nationalist colonel Talat Aydemir was suppressed and the main culprits arrested, tried, and "seven of them were sentenced to death, twenty-nine to life imprisonment and seventy to various gaol terms."[97] A large purge from the armed forces and the cadets was carried out, which seemed to have ended the young officers' coup and movement once and for all only in mid-1963. The message became very clear by then. If the colonels were prepared to rise up against their superiors they would be facing death sentences.[98] Indeed, the coup attempt of May 20–21, 1963 was the end of the period of "young officers' coups" in Turkey.

However, the damage was done. The golden rule of the Republic, which stipulated that, those soldiers who intended to take part in politics must be ready to resign from the armed forces, was destroyed by the same soldiers who purported to have acted in the name of Atatürk's principles and revolution. They reasoned that the "National Unity Committee" of May 1960 acted to stop the bloodshed caused by the DP government of 1960, which had started to act as a party of a one-party regime and thus terminated the parliamentary democratic regime of the country and undermined its claim to political legitimacy. There is little doubt that Turkey was experiencing severe violations of such liberties as the freedom of expression, freedom of association, and freedom of the press by 1959.

THE MILITARY JUNTA AT THE HELM

On May 27, 1960 the military junta of the Committee of National Unity (MBK) acted efficiently and met with almost no resistance. The President of the Republic, the leader of the DP Celal Bayar was among the few who considered resisting arrest, though he was also detained without much difficulty. All of the deputies of the DP in the TGNA, all members of the Menderes Cabinet, and many members of the DP throughout the country were arrested. Personal friction and hostilities seemed to have played some role in the arrests of the rank and file members of the party. The DP was obliged to hold a convention every year by law. However, it had failed to do so. Soon after the coup a lawyer brought this matter up to the attention of the court, and the DP was closed down by a regular, civilian court decision for violating the Act of Associations. However, the founders and the most prominent members of the DP, such as the former President, Prime Minister, Ministers and Deputies of the TGNA were tried at a special court established at the island of *Yassıada*, close to the city of Istanbul in the Sea of *Marmara*, by the MBK during 1960–1961. The special tribunal after a trial period of 11 months, which was extensively covered by the press and the radio at the time, sentenced 14 members of the former DP, and the former Chief of General Staff, General Rüştü Erdelhun to death.[99] Three of the death sentences were commuted. The former Prime Minister Menderes, former Minister of Foreign Affairs Fatin Rüştü Zorlu, and Minister of Finance Hasan Polatkan were executed by hanging. They may be considered as the last example or legacy of an old Ottoman–Turkish tradition of "political executions" (*siyaseten katl*) in the Republican political culture. The overall impact of the executions on Turkish politics was the deepening of the cleavage between the *kulturkampfs*, which further poisoned the relations between the CHP and its opponents.

The legitimacy of the special "Yassıada Tribunal" has been questioned by the champions of the Periphery and right of center political parties in Turkey ever since the early 1960s. The Tribunal was considered as a "kangaroo court" by the DP sympathizers. They failed to live up to the expectations of the

CHP sympathizers as well. İnönü personally asked for clemency, yet failed to convince the MBK.[100] The saintly PM who survived the plane crash was turned into a timid figure in the trial, not because of the nature of the crimes he was charged with, but because of his frail posture. The former President Bayar showed enormous resilience and demonstrated courage during his performance at the Tribunal.[101] The complicity of the government in many of the cases involving "September 6 and 7," Kayseri, and similar incidents were proven to be correct.[102] Furthermore, instances of mismanagement and intolerance toward the political opposition within and outside the TGNA were also unearthed in the trials. The deaths and injuries suffered in the hands of the martial law administration of April–May 1960 obviously implicated the government. However, the horrible rumors of abduction and execution of the college students en masse through the employment of such horrific methods as eradicating evidence by the use of acid baths, meat grinders, and so on turned out to be totally devoid of truth.

In the end, the death sentences of the former political elite of Turkey have been considered by the people as too harsh a punitive measure to take. The tragic scenes of the hanged trio, which were published in the first pages of the Turkish dailies, also seemed to have increased a sense of pity, rather than propriety. There has not been any evidence that such harsh measures have provided a learning experience for the Turkish political elite. It is no secret that the variety and scale of corrupt practices perpetrated by the Turkish political elites increased rather than decreased since the 1950s. Relations between the governments and opposition parties and forces failed to improve much in the 1960s. In about ten years later another military coup (March 12, 1971) could not be avoided. Another and much more powerful military takeover of the government occurred in less than ten years following that (September 12, 1980). One cannot but conclude that the exemplary role of the harsh sentencing at the "Yassıada Trials" was at best negligible.

However, the military coup of 1960 brought the political careers of many DP elite to an abrupt end. A new power struggle erupted between the political forces purporting to represent the interests of the Periphery. Indeed, a younger generation of politicians began to fill the vacuum by mid-1960s, who dominated the Turkish political scene for many years to come. The military government of 1960–1961 did cause a partial purge of the Turkish political elite.

The military became a more visible and effective political force in Turkish politics after the coup of May 27, 1960. The military junta (MBK) was instrumental in setting up a pattern for future formulation or redrawing of constitutions. Their coup could not be legitimated under the 1924 Constitution of Turkey, and they had come to believe that it constituted a major source of the breakdown of democracy in Turkey. Hence, they concluded that Turkey needed a new constitution. They summoned a committee of academics, who set up a workshop in Istanbul, which produced a new draft constitution. Soon after, a "Constituent Assembly" (*Kurucu Meclis*) was established with the participation of CHP with 222 members, with 25 members from another opposition party of the 1950s, and 25 independents.[103] They were not elected though popular vote, but by a corporatist electoral process, in which bar associations, universities, press, veterans associations, and other non-governmental organizations took part in fielding and electing candidates, and acted as a lower chamber of the MBK.[104] The constituent assembly worked efficiently and produced the most liberal democratic constitution of Turkey in 1961. Turkey also had its first constitutional referendum on July 9, 1961, which resulted in the adoption of the new constitution with the approval of 62 percent of the voters.[105] The Constitution of Turkey that had been designed and implemented by Atatürk and other founding fathers of the Republic since 1924 was completely jettisoned and replaced by a new written Constitution designed by the Constituent Assembly on May 27, 1961. Ironically, the MBK and their hand picked academic consultants who were motivated by the ideas and ideals of Mustafa Kemal Atatürk dislodged the 1924 Constitution of the country. However, they made sure that all of the fundamental aspects of the Cultural Revolution were incorporated in the new text.

The military also became more eager and ready to fill in the political vacuum created by the inexperienced politicians, who managed to occupy public offices through elections and successful coalition bargaining, after the coup of 1960. The dismal performance of the Turkish governments in coping with the socioeconomic processes they helped to unleash through rapid social mobilization and further lack of capability in managing political instability produced a dysfunctional tendency among the political elite in Turkey. Governments of all political colors tended to invite the military to cope with political instability through declaration of martial law, which often constituted the first step toward a military coup. Declaration of martial law is a clear sign and indication of the incapability of the civilian politicians to manage the political affairs of the country through peaceful means. Such a dramatic measure not only places the military in an awkward position, that they are the authority of last resort before a state of chaos imposes itself upon the country, but also that the country needs to be saved from the perils of some looming danger, which the civilian government cannot cope with. Hence, the armed forces perceive of their newly acquired political role as not only legal but legitimate. They then set on the road of planning and running the political system to cope with the "peril" at hand. They demand many drastic and at times even draconian measures to be taken by the TGNA. When and if resisted by the TGNA and the ruling party or coalition of parties, they often tend to evaluate trepidation of the civilian politicians as further evidence of their negligence, lack of awareness, and ineptness, which required more pressure. If the frustration of the military runs deeper, they tend to go even further, topple the civilian government and take the necessary measures all by themselves. The eagerness of democratically elected governments to declare martial law to cope with political instability seemed to have precipitated the military to plan ahead to establish procedures, regulations, norms, and even institutions to manage the martial law administrations.

It should not be forgotten that the professional ethic and the hierarchical structure of the armed forces had been destroyed in the 1960 coup.

The generals, lieutenant generals, and other commanders of the armed forces were arrested, ordered around by their subordinates, tried with the DP elite, and the Chief of General Staff was sentenced to death! Professionalism, and institutional norms of the armed forces had to be resurrected, reestablished, and institutionalized only after 1963. From then on Turkey experienced two more military coups, but the top brass managed to avoid another "young officers' coup" from taking place. No Chief of General Staff dared to forget what happened to General Rüştü Erdelhun, and all tried to avoid such a calamity to take place as best as they can. The lesson to be learned was that the top brass of the military could no longer afford to stay out of politics completely, as Rüştü Erdelhun had done in the 1950s, nor could they let the professional norms be relaxed so that the middle ranked young officers attempt to make a coup again. Hence, they made sure to adopt norms that would ensure that the military establishment moved to oust civilian governments with full hierarchical and institutional command structure intact, in the aftermath of 1963.

The 1960 coup was also the first example of a NATO army acting in complete lack of discipline, which had never taken place in Turkey or any other NATO ally before. The 1960 military coup eventually got the seal of approval from NATO, and set up an example to be followed by other NATO armies. The Greek army was to follow suit soon in 1967, and so did the Portuguese army a decade later.

CONCLUSION

The initial attempt at transforming the political regime of Turkey from a one-party system to multiparty democracy broke down under the political strains and stresses produced in part by the economic recession and rapid social mobilization, and in part by the political culture of the elite in 1960. It was proven once again that old habits died hard. The DP was a new party with a relatively old program, established by politicians, who had spent a lifetime in the ranks of the Union and Progress (ITF) and the Republican People's parties (CHP). The leader of the DP, Celal Bayar was an archrival of the leader of CHP, İsmet İnönü almost throughout his political career. The chemistry between the two never contributed to their relations. Consequently, the DP was made out of the same cultural and political material as the CHP. Unfortunately, that failed to make DP act as any political party in a democracy, and neither could the CHP. The party elite of the DP had the instincts of political leaders leading a single party of a one-party regime, which considered any opposition to them as intolerable, reprehensible, and illegitimate.[106] There is scant evidence, if any, that CHP had any different composure in the 1950s.

The DP had emerged as the champion of "the people" (Periphery). Its program and election campaigns promised freedom from the stiff and rule-bound bureaucratic rule of the CHP, which had applied to the huge majority of the country, though a "happy minority" among the ranks of the CHP seemed to have lived "unimpressed" by those rules and laws. The DP promised that they would empower the people, if they come to win the elections. They won the elections in the 1950s. Consequently, the DP established an efficient popular patronage mechanism through its party organization, which delivered to the peasant majority what they had desired: freedom from regulations. The bureaucrats learned to obey their new political masters, and those who could not do so were sacked and replaced by others.

The DP also increased the role of free enterprise in the economy, and religious orders, especially the *Ticanis* and *Nurcus*, and anticommunist pressure groups in society and politics. The number of secondary schools providing religious education increased in number and geographical magnitude. In the 1951–1952 academic year there were only seven middle schools providing religious education to prospective "imams" (prayer leaders/clerics) with a total of 876 enrolled students in all of them.[107] Whereas in 1959–1960 academic year 19 middle schools and 16 high schools (*lycée*) with a total of 4,066 students and a total of 336 graduates of the "Imam-Hatip Schools" in the country.[108] Religious instruction and prayer instructions were both reverted back to Arabic.[109] Indeed, a report written by a former expert of the Ministry of National Education and published by a leading Association of Businessmen/women and Industrialists (TÜSİAD) concluded that the Imam-Hatip Schools eventually increased their capacity with leaps and bounds, enrolled and graduated far more prospective *imams* than can Turkey ever employ.[110] The report went on to argue that Imam-Hatip education had become another, alternative channel of education to the national and secular education provided to the students in Turkey.[111] Clerical versus anticlerical sentiments started to regain importance as a sensitive political issue of secularism in Turkey by the late 1950s.

A new constellation of political forces emerged in Turkey after the coup that ended the democratic regime of the 1950s on May 27, 1960. The armed forces began to play a more visible role in the politics of the country ever since. The relationship between the Center, Periphery and the armed forces needed to be reestablished or even reinvented in Turkey after the transition back to democracy started in 1961. The champions of the Periphery could no longer trust the military neither could the military be at ease with the agents of Periphery at the helm of government. A paradox started to take hold in Turkey ever since: The military trusted the CHP, the party of the Center, which the people have not usually been inclined to trust or support at the polls; while the people tended to trust the parties of the Periphery, such as the DP, and support them at the polls, which in turn have been viewed with great suspicion by the Center, the CHP, other agents, and parties of the Center, and the military. However, in the meantime, the Periphery continued to show remarkable confidence in the military,[112] yet continued to distrust the political parties and forces that rubbed shoulders with the military. How, then, could Turkey experience democratic government? In the next chapter of this book we examine the complications developing around the relationships between Center and Periphery in Turkish politics in the aftermath of the coup d'état of May 27, 1960.

4

THE SECOND REPUBLIC (1961–1980)

NEW DEMOCRACY AND THE OLD MALAISE

The Military Committee of National Unity (MBK) now confronted the question of how to construct a democratic regime that would not slide into the tyranny of parliamentary majority,[1] and endanger freedoms and human rights. Second, they addressed the question of establishing a democratic regime, which would guarantee that economic policies of the country would be rationally designed and professionally executed, without partisan meddling, to deliver sustained economic growth.

The breakdown of democracy in 1960 was the outcome of several factors. First, and probably the foremost political problem of the 1950s was the "unchecked and unbalanced" unicameral legislature, which had been notorious with its intolerance toward political opposition[2]. The majoritarian electoral system used in the 1950s disproportionately exaggerated the percentage of the parliamentary seats obtained by the party in government (DP) (see table 4.1). Similarly, the opposition party received disproportionately far less of the percentage of the parliamentary seats than the percentage of the national votes they got in the elections. Such an imbalance, which was not ameliorated by any institutional, cultural, and traditional norms and structures, was inimical to opposition, freedoms, and human rights.

Unchecked by a nonpartisan president, or any institution, structure, or political force other than the often despised and scorned opposition party in the National Assembly, the fusion of power between the legislative majority, the PM's office and the cabinet and of the office of the presidency led to the implementation of Lord Acton's law in Turkey in the 1950s: The absolute power of the parliamentary majority led to abuse of power. In the words of a famous student of Turkish politics, ". . . The government claimed obstruction while the opposition charged oppression."[3]

The problems of the 1950s could not be reduced to legislative politics. There were severe problems with the performance of the economy. With the implementation of the Truman Doctrine from 1947 onward, Turkey also gained from the Marshall Plan in Europe.[4] The American aid came with few strings attached. The American experts who had surveyed the Turkish economy prior to the implementation of the Marshall Plan stressed the need to reduce

Table 4.1 Turkish National Elections and Disproportionality of Representation

Elections	D^1	I^2	LSq^3	LD^4	R^5
1950	31,05	20,70	29,85	32,9	1,51
1954	35,05	17,53	33,13	36,60	1,46
1957	21,54	10,77	18,34	22,20	1,30
1961	2,55	1,28	2,32	2,40	0,36
1965	1,45	0,48	0,94	1,00	0,12
1969	13,45	3,36	8,79	10,30	1,14
1973	10,50	2,63	6,78	7,80	0,93
1977	10,20	2,55	6,41	5,70	1,03
1983	7,30	4,87	6,79	7,70	0,41
1987	18,90	12,60	20,86	28,60	1,13
					(1,79)*
1991	9,40	4,68	9,30	12,50	0,50
1995	16,10	6,44	9,78	7,30	0,51
					(1,34)*
1999	15,90	6,36	9,28	8,7	0,20
					(1,31)*
2002	22,35	22,35	24,22	31,7	0,25
					(1,92)*

Notes: Only those political parties that have obtained seats in the TGNA are included in the above-presented disproportionality calculations.
1. Loosemore-Hanby index (Lijphart, 1994: 58)
2. Douglas W, Rae index (Lijphart, 1994: 60)
3. Least Squares index (Lijphart, 1994: 60–61)
4. Largest deviation index (Lijphart, 1994: 62)
5. Range index = maximum S/V—minimum S/V (suggested by the author).
* Includes those parties, which participated in the national elections but could not obtain more than 10 percent of the national vote, such as the RP and the MHP in the 1987, the HADEP and MHP in the 1995, and the HADEP and CHP in the 1999 elections. Data for the table are based on the GNA election results 1950–2002. The figures in the columns indicate the extent to which national vote and parliamentary seat shares of political parties diverge. Large numbers indicate less proportionality and smaller numbers indicate more proportionality between vote and parliamentary seat distributions across political parties.

Source: Ersin Kalaycıoğlu, "Elections and Governance," in Sabri Sayarı and Yılmaz Esmer (eds.), *Politics, Parties, and Elections in Turkey* (Boulder, London: Lynne Rienner, 2002): 55–71. The figures of the table are calculated by the author from the data in chapter 5, table 1 of this book.

the role of the public sector (state economic enterprises), and the overall outcome of the overhaul in the economic policies, encourage small and middle scale private initiatives.[5] When the DP assumed power in 1950, they started to champion liberal domestic and international economic policies, free-trade practices, and assumed that if private initiative were given an upper hand, the economy would take off and sustain a high level of growth. The DP governments failed to see any wrongdoing from treating the public sector as the fount of emoluments to be allocated to patronage politics, while the private sector mushroomed. Consequently, the DP governments not only increased government spending, but also neglected to increase direct taxes, and even abolished some, such as the direct agricultural taxes, as a gesture for the peasant voters who helped them to ascend to power. As of 1952 Turkish budgets started to experience deficits.[6] The Military Committee of National

Unity (MBK) that was established with the coup of May 27, 1960, also stressed the need to guarantee that the macro economic tools are managed more professionally so that the economic crises of the 1950s would not be repeated again.[7]

The MBK was also sensitive about the erosion of the principles of the cultural revolution of the 1920s and the 1930s.[8] However, the young officers seemed to have been moved by injustice, especially income inequalities between the rich and the poor, and between the west and the east of the country.[9] They felt the need to establish a new economic regime and a democratic system that would diminish the economic disparities and bring about social justice.[10]

New Constitution: A Cure for Past Ailments

The new Constitution incorporated a bicameral legislature. The Turkish Grand National Assembly was to be composed of a lower chamber, the National Assembly (NA), and an upper chamber (Senate). The NA would hold 450 members, serving four-year terms. The Senate contained three different types of Senators. First, 150 members popularly elected, the MBK members would now become permanent, yet nonelected members of the Senate, finally, an additional 15 Senators appointed by the President.[11] The first group of 150 Senators would be popularly elected for a six-year term; and one-third of the Senate was to be renewed every two years.[12] The TGNA would then elect the President of the country for a seven-year term. The President served as the Head of State and the exercised the authority to appoint the Prime Minister (PM), and also act as the commander-in-chief of the armed forces. The essence of the parliamentary system with its Westminster model format was preserved in the 1961 Constitution.[13]

The 1961 Constitution contained several institutions independent or autonomous from the parties at the helm of government, the most important of which was the Constitutional Court, which the 1924 Constitution had not incorporated. Charged with the authority of constitutional oversight of the legislative procedure and the substance of the adopted bills, the Constitutional Court was installed as an effective judicial check upon the excesses of legislative majorities of the TGNA. The judiciary was made as fully independent from the influence of the government as possible in Turkey in 1961.[14]

The status of the state owned Turkish Radio and Television administration was also modified to insulate it from the interventions of the government.[15] The 1961 Constitution also tried to cure the problem of the management of the economy. The mismanagement of the macro economy in the 1950s was considered to be one of the main reasons for the deepening of the economic crisis of the mid to late 1950s. What the country needed was serious economic planning, through an autonomous agency of the state, which would help the government devise rigorous policies to realize rapid economic growth. The State Planning Organization (DPT) was established to forecast economic developments, measures, and design and propose five-year plans to the government and the TGNA.[16]

The 1961 Constitution provided a relatively liberal system for the establishment and management of voluntary associations, trade unions, and political parties. However, the ban on communist, fascist, and Islamic revivalist associations and parties were preserved.[17] The 1961 Constitution imposed no limits upon the establishment and running of associations and political parties, though legal stipulations to register them with the Ministry of Interior Affairs persisted, and so did ideological and other limitations foreseen by the Associations and Political Parties Acts, and the Criminal Code. However, the decision concerning the closure of associations and parties were to be solely made by the courts of law and in the case of political parties by the Constitutional Court.

The 1961 Constitution did not incorporate any references to the elections other than that voting will be based on the principles of freedom, equality, secret ballot, and public counting of votes (art. 55). However, the Election Act (*Seçim Kanunu*) to follow clearly stipulated that Proportional Representation (PR) would be used to convert votes to seats in the TGNA.[18] Consequently, the majoritarian election practices of the 1946–1960 era were dropped in favor of a PR formula in converting votes to seats for the first time in 1961.

The 1961 Constitution did little to amend the overwhelmingly centralist tendencies of the public administration of the country, yet it enabled the city administrations to become independent of the governors of provinces within which the cities are established (art. 116). The 1961 Constitution enabled the city administrations to be popularly elected. Hence, from the 1960s onward the city mayors and councils have been popularly elected. The previous system of electing a village council and its head (headman, *muhtar*) was preserved, unscathed. However, the traditionally heavy-handed practice of administrative tutelage of the central bureaucracy (Ankara) over the administrations and administrators of the provinces, cities, small towns, and villages continued throughout the 1960s and the 1970s.[19]

Finally, the 1961 Constitution integrated a new structure, called the National Security Council (Milli Güvenlik Kurulu, MGK) consisting of the prime minister and a number of ministers, the chief of general staff, the commanders of the army, navy, and the air force, and the President of the country, who presided over the Council (art. 111). The MGK was entrusted with the authority of "*notifying*" to the Council of Ministers the fundamental views necessary in taking decisions and coordinating efforts concerning national security" (art. 111). The relevant article of the 1961 Constitution was later amended in 1971, after a military intervention, to read as "*advising* the Council of Ministers concerning the fundamental views necessary in taking decisions and coordinating efforts concerning national security" (art. 111). Students of law in Turkey tended to stress that, from a legal point of view, the difference between the concepts of "notifying" (*bildirmek*) and "advising" (*tavsiye etmek*) is negligible.[20]

Thus in the "constitutional structure" the military was given a central role. The lack of confidence of the military in the capability of the civilian politicians in managing the public affairs of the country without endangering political stability and breaching national security thus became crystal clear. They would now monitor the activities of the politicians from within the Senate and through the MGK, and make sure that the game of "democracy as patronage politics" would not get out of hand and undermine the collective interest of the nation-state, endangering the stability and security of the realm. Such a deep sense of distrust would linger on for the next four decades, and only show signs of waning in the 2000s.[21]

TURKEY MEETS WITH COALITION GOVERNMENTS

The new Constitution came into effect after a popular referendum adopted it in 1961. The MBK moved swiftly to start the transition back to democracy. The first multiparty elections of the 1960s took place on October 15, 1961.[22] The defunct DP could not take part in the elections. However, several political parties emerged to fill in the vacuum created by the closing up of the DP. Two of those political parties, the New Turkey Party (YTP) and Justice Party (AP) emerged as the potential replacement of the DP as "the powerhouse" of the Periphery. The combined vote of AP and YTP in the 1961 National Assembly elections was almost exactly the same as that of the DP in 1957; however, the CHP had obtained almost 5 percent more of the vote in 1957 than it could obtain in 1961.[23] Nevertheless, the CHP still managed to get the plurality of the vote with only 36.7 percent, while the vote of the Periphery split between the AP (34.8 percent) and the YTP (13.7 percent) in the 1961 National Assembly elections (see table 4.2).

The new PR formula used in the conversion of votes to parliamentary seats resulted in the distribution of the seats in the NA in close proximity to the vote shares of the political parties (see table 4.2). Unanticipated or not, consequence of PR emerged to leave its indelible mark on Turkish politics as Turkey stepped into the uncharted terrain of coalition politics.

The electoral laws of Turkey had also changed before the October 15, 1961 National Assembly elections. Although the multimember districts and ballots consisting of party lists were inherited from the electoral practices of the previous decade, the conversion rules of votes to seats still rewarded the front-runner, allocating proportionally more parliamentary seats to the political party with the most votes.[24] In spite of all the election engineering, the distribution of the votes across the political party lists impeded the establishment of a majority party government.

The problem for the voters located in the Periphery was to identify the true successor of the DP. The leader of the YTP, Ekrem Alican was not a newcomer to Turkish politics. Alican had been a member of the DP for a while, though he fell apart with Menderes in 1955 and set up a separate, Freedom Party in the mid-1950s.[25] He also had a long career of being anti-CHP as well, and he had turned down an offer to establish a military-sponsored party after the military coup of May 27, 1960.[26] However, neither Alican's political personality, nor the front bench of the YTP seemed to give the impression to the Periphery that they were capable of shouldering the responsibility of being

Table 4.2   National Election Results (1961–1977)

Election Year	Vote and Seat Shares (%)	AP	CHP	CKMP	DemP	MP	GP CGP	MHP	MSP	TIP	TBP	YTP	Indep,**
1961	Votes	34,8	36,7	14,0	–	–	–	–	–	–	–	13,7	0,8
	Seats	35,1	38,5	12,0	–	–	–	–	–	–	–	14,4	0,0
1965	Votes	52,9	28,7	2,2	–	6,3	–	–	–	3,0	–	3,7	3,2
	Seats	53,3	29,8	2,5	–	6,9	–	–	–	3,3	–	4,2	0,0
1969	Votes	46,5	27,4	–	–	3,2	6,6	3,0	–	2,7	2,8	2,2	5,6
	Seats	56,9	31,8	–	–	1,3	3,3	0,2	–	0,5	1,8	1,3	2,9
1973	Votes	29,8	33,3	–	11,9	0,6	5,3	3,4	11,8	–	1,1	–	2,8
	Seats	33,1	41,1	–	10,0	0,0	2,9	0,7	10,7	–	0,2	–	1,3
1977	Votes	36,9	41,4	–	1,9	–	1,9	6,4	8,6	0,1	0,4	–	2,5
	Seats	42,0	47,3	–	0,2	–	0,7	3,6	5,3	0,0	0,0	–	0,9

Notes: In the table "Votes" refer to the percentage of the national vote the corresponding party obtained in the elections.

"Seats" refer to the percentage of the National Assembly seats the corresponding party received in the national elections.

"?" indicates missing values, there are no records of how many votes or what percentage of the vote any of the political parties that participated in the race obtained in the 1946 national elections.

"–" refers to non-existence of the corresponding party at the time of the elections, for example CKMP eventually became MHP.

* Political party names in the table are as follows: AP (Justice Party, *Adalet Partisi*), CHP (Republican People's Party, *Cumhuriyet Halk Partisi*), GP (Reliance Party, *Güven Partisi*, which later became CGP, Republicanist Reliance Party, *Cumhuriyetçi Güven Partisi*), CKMP (Republicanist Peasant Nation Party, *Cumhuriyetçi Köylü Millet Partisi*), DemP (Democratic Party, *Demokratik Parti*), MP (Nation Party, *Millet Partisi*), MHP (Nationalist Action Party, *Milliyetçi Hareket Partisi*), MSP (National Salvation Party, *Milli Selamet Partisi*) TBP (Turkish Union Party, *Türkiye Birlik Partisi*), TIP (Turkish Labor Party, *Türkiye İşçi Partisi*) YTP (New Turkey Party, *Yeni Türkiye Partisi*).

** Column consists of the vote share of the non-party or independent candidates. Only those political parties, which were able to win representation in the National Assembly, have been included in the table.

Source: Erol Tuncer, *Osmanlı'dan Günümüze Seçimler: 1877–1999* (Ankara: Toplumsal Ekonomik Siyasal Araştırmalar Vakfı (Tesav) Yayınları, 2002): 324–328.

the legitimate inheritor of the legacy of the DP. The founding leader of the AP, Ragıp Gümüşpala, was a retired general, who would by definition be considered as an agent of the Center. The AP elite had decided to adopt him as a titular leader to placate the MBK, and at the same time tried to signal to the Periphery that they were the genuine successors of the DP legacy. Unfortunately, the sophisticated subtlety of the cultural symbolisms failed to fully arrive at the target population.[27] In the confusion, the vote of the Periphery split among the two competing parties, which provided the CHP with the seat of the PM they had been so assiduously seeking to occupy, since the early 1950s. Nevertheless, the leader of the CHP, İnönü, and his associates now faced the tough task of cooperating with their archrivals in government.

Neither the CHP elite, nor the newly established AP and the YTP had any experience with coalition government. The elite political culture of the country failed to cultivate such values as compromise, cooperation, coordination, and tolerance for opposition.[28] It came as no surprise that the first İnönü government failed to survive long (see table 4.3). İnönü had to come up

Table 4.3 Government Tenure and Formation Difficulty by Government Type

	Government Type	Tenure (days)	Formation Difficulty (days)
1. Party:			
1950	Menderes I	317	7
	Menderes II	1164	0
1954	Menderes III	671	15
	Menderes IV	717	0
1957	Menderes V	908	29
1965	Demirel I	1467	17
1969	Demirel II	117	22
	Demirel III	20	0
1983	Özal I	1468	37
1987	Özal II	688	22
	Akbulut	563	0
	Yılmaz I	150	0
2002	Gül	117	8
2003	Erdoğan	–	0
	Average	643.6	12,1
2. Coalition:			
1961	İnönü VIII	212	36
	İnönü IX	183	0
	İnönü X	57	0
	Ürgüplü	249	0
1973	Ecevit I	295	104
	Irmak	134	(no confidence)*
	Demirel IV	812	134
1977	Ecevit II	30	(no confidence)*
	Demirel V	171	46
	Ecevit III	676	0
	Demirel VI	304	0
1991	Demirel VII	581	32
	Çiller I	467	0
	Çiller II	25	0
	Çiller III	127	0
1995	Yılmaz II	114	70
	Erbakan	367	0
	Yılmaz III	557	0
	Ecevit IV	135	0
1999	Ecevit V	1265	40
	Average	366,5**	22,2**
		338,1***	24,8***

Notes: * Government in question failed to obtain vote of confidence in the TGNA.

** The Irmak, and Ecevit II governments failed to win vote of confidence of the TGNA, and are excluded from this average.

*** All governments are included in the data.

Source: Ersin Kalaycıoğlu, "Elections and Governance," in Sabri Sayarı and Yılmaz Esmer (eds.), *Politics, Parties, and Elections in Turkey* (Boulder, London: Lynne Rienner, 2002): 66. Calculations for the governments established after 1999 were inserted in the table by the author from data provided at <www.tbmm.gov.tr/ambar/hukumet>.

with two other coalition governments, before he was toppled in the TGNA with the rejection of the proposed budget on February 20, 1965. Furthermore, a caretaker government was established by a senator, PM Suat Hayri Ürgüplü in February 1965, which survived until the new National Assembly elections of October 10, 1965 (see table 4.3). Shaky and short-lived governments gave the impression that coalitions undermine government stability, and fail to contribute to democratic governance.

THE COUP TO END ALL COUPS

The early 1960s was a period of turbulence in Turkish politics. The new Constitution enabled freedom of association and speech to flourish. However, the activism of young officers failed to calm down after the October 15, 1961 elections. The military cadets, who had been incorporated into the coup of May 27, 1960 by their commanding officers in Ankara were restive for two more years. As young vigilantes who self-designated themselves to be the guardians of the regime, they rose up in 1962 and once more in 1963 against the PM İnönü's coalition governments. Some colonels and their peers failed to be satisfied with the MBK and the civilian governments to follow. There emerged two irreconcilable tendencies in the ranks of the armed forces. One was to continue with the revolutionary zeal of the 1960 coup, and the other was to help consolidate parliamentary democracy.[29] The former seemed to be motivated by some socialist ideas intertwined with ardent ethnic nationalism, which seemed to be contributing to the development of an authoritarian tendency, which would eventually be represented by an ambitious colonel, Talat Aydemir.[30] It also seemed as if they had held beliefs that democracy needed to be postponed for an indefinite period of time.[31] What they attempted was to recapture government, ban all political parties, and rule the country, more or less along the lines that their counterparts did in Greece after 1967. The final attempt by ex-colonel Aydemir in May 1963 to capture the government again by the help of the military cadets led to his arrest, trial, and execution. What Hale calls "a reckless piece of adventurism by an impetuous ex-colonel" in May 1963 was the last instance of the political struggle in the shadow of the guns between the young officers and the military, on the one hand, and political establishment of Turkey, on the other.[32]

It was the personality of PM İnönü, as well as the differences of opinion among the branches of the military, which seemed to enable the government to suppress the uprisings and eventually eliminate all of those who had taken part in the military coup attempt.[33] Similarly, the military cadets were also dismissed from the War College to eradicate all tendencies of restiveness and reestablish military discipline. What followed was an assiduous and vigilant policy of the military avoiding the repetition of any other attempt at a "young officers' coup" in Turkey. The military establishment worked very hard to impose institutional norms, professionalism, and preserve the hierarchy intact from 1963 onward. Although, the military establishment has been highly successful at rendering the professional norms over the armed forces supreme, they failed to prevent a quasi coup by ultimatum in 1971, and an institutional coup in 1980 from occurring.

Various steps were taken soon after 1963 to insulate the military against the vicissitudes of the Turkish social and economic developments. The small savings of the officers were pooled in a savings and loans association called Armed Forces Mutual Assistance Fund (*Ordu Yardımlaşma Kurumu*, OYAK) to improve the welfare of the retired personnel of the armed forces. Military cooperatives (ORKO) were established to purchase large quantities of staple foods and other needs of the families of the officers and supply them with goods at relatively cheaper prices. The officer corps of the army, navy, and the air force started to establish special residences where the officers and their families could live at affordable rent. OYAK began to be managed professionally, and began various ventures with the French automobile company Renault, cement production, food canning industry, and other similar ventures started to take shape.[34] Eventually, OYAK grew strong enough to establish a bank (OYAK Bank) in the 2000s. Consequently, the economic deprivation of the soldiers, which had been considered as a factor contributing to their restiveness in late 1950s was eliminated.

FOREIGN POLICY ORDEAL: CYPRUS

If the restiveness of some colonels constituted one of the potentially catastrophic challenges to the coalition governments of the early 1960s, the dire and horrific developments in Cyprus presented another. The former Ottoman island had been a British dominion since 1914. Its population mainly consisted of the remaining members of the two former Ottoman millets of Greek Orthodox and Turkish Muslims. In the 1930s the Cypriots, especially the Greek community of the island, had started to show signs of eagerness to seek independence from Britain. World War II interrupted the process. However, in 1954 when the Greek Parliament in Athens asked the British government to acknowledge union of the island (*enosis*) with Greece, the Turkish government started to pay attention to the status of the ethnic Turks on the island. In the 1950s better organized Greek Cypriots started to toy with the idea of getting rid of the Turkish community on the island and unite with Greece. Turkey perceived this move as an attempt to revise the status of Eastern Mediterranean, and reacted diplomatically to prevent such a development. The British government eventually decided to alter its relations with the island, and started negotiations with both Greece and Turkey to settle the issue concerning the status of the island.[35]

The tripartite negotiations progressed successfully in 1959 and culminated in a compromise among the major parties of Britain, Greece, and Turkey in 1960. The parties agreed to the establishment of an independent Republic of Cyprus in that year. Britain kept two large military bases on the island, and in conjunction both Greece and Turkey became guarantors of the *status quo* of the new, unitary state of Republic of Cyprus. A democratic government that would be sensitive to ethnic and religious differences was established.

However, the complicated constitutional design of the island was never fully accepted by the Greek Cypriots, and the political regime of the country only worked for about three years. In 1963, the President of Cyprus, Archbishop Makarios and the Greek Cypriot political elite opted out of the constitutional design, and decided to lock their Turkish counterparts out of the government.[36] They simultaneously started to use their relative military prowess to rid the island off the Turkish community. The massacres of the Turks on the island precipitated military action by Turkey, as a guarantor of the political status quo on the island in full agreement with the Accords of Zurich and London. It was the intervention of the United States, which brought relative calm to the island for about a year.[37]

In 1964, when the Greek Cypriots started where they had left off a year earlier, Turkey reacted with greater vehemence, and this time, the Turkish government took a drastic step toward the Greeks living in Turkey, and cancelled their residence permits.[38] Nine thousand members of the Greek minority, who had been living as the contemporary populace representing the Roman past of the city and popularly called as *Rum* (Romans) in Turkey, yet never acquired Turkish citizenship, departed for Greece.[39] Hence, the final wave of migration of the Greco-Roman minority from Istanbul and the rest of the country to Greece occurred in 1964.[40] In the meantime, the Turkish navy and air force threatened to intervene on the island of Cyprus. It was at this juncture that the U.S. President Lyndon B. Johnson wrote a letter to PM İnönü reminding him that all of the Turkish army was assigned to NATO. The arms at the disposal of the Turkish troops were also provided by NATO, and thus, mostly by the United States. Hence, President Johnson argued that it was legally binding for Turkey to seek approval of the United States to use NATO troops and weapons in Cyprus or anywhere else.[41] The letter was written in a language not usually employed in diplomatic communications; for it was highly blunt, threatening, and at times rude.[42] Simultaneously, the United States started to exert pressure on Turkey and Greece to cool off. The Cyprus conflict was put on ice for another three years.

President Johnson's letter arrived as a wake-up call for Turkey. It triggered a major debate over the foreign policy that the country had been conducting since acquiring NATO membership in 1952, in 1964. In the meantime, it became clear that in the Cuban missile crisis of 1963, Turkey had been involved, without being alerted to the fact, in the nuclear negotiations between the United States and the USSR. The U.S. nuclear weapons in Turkey were withdrawn in return for the Soviet withdrawal of those in Cuba. The letter written by President Johnson had also precipitated doubts about whether the United States would be willing to help defend Turkey at all, in a major international crisis.[43] Waking up to the fact that Turkey had committed too much and showed blind loyalty to NATO and the United States, to the detriment of all other forms of bilateral and multilateral relations with her neighbors and neighboring regions led to modifications in the execution of Turkish foreign policy in the mid-1960s. Turkey started to act in two ways. One was to establish and improve bilateral and multilateral relations with neighbors, and neighboring regions of the Balkans, Middle East, and the USSR. The other was to start developing a Turkish arms industry and plan ahead to establish armed forces outside of the NATO command structure, which eventually led to the establishment of the Fourth Army Corps in the western, Aegean region of the country.

LIBERTY AND INSTABILITY

In 1964, the founding leader of the AP, the retired General Ragıp Gümüşpala passed away. The AP summoned an extraordinary convention to elect a new leader. A young bureaucrat, Süleyman Demirel, who was brought up as a civil engineer at the Istanbul Technical University (İTÜ), earned his masters degree in the United States, and served as the director of the State Water Works (DSI) under PM Menderes, won the support of the convention delegates and became the leader of AP. He was from an extremely humble background. Indeed, his life is a success story that the Republic could proudly boast about. He was born in a small village (Islamköy) in Atabey, Isparta, in central-south Anatolia. He started life as a shepherd boy. His wits and stamina enabled him to attend secondary school and İTÜ on full state scholarship. His political career lasted, with interruptions due to military coups, until 2000, when he finished a seven-year term as the President of the country.[44]

In the 1965 elections Demirel, a true son of the Periphery who had made it big in life, led his party to battle. His image was enough of a signal for the Periphery to choose a successor of the DP from the competing AP instead of supporting the YTP. The AP had a landslide victory during the National Assembly elections of 1965 (see table 4. 2), never to be repeated by any other political party. The CHP settled for being the main opposition party of the country again. In the process leading up to the election and in its aftermath, the leader of CHP İnönü declared that his party was "a left-of-center" precipitating a new ideological debate in the country. Eventually, the AP and other parties started to define their political positions on the left–right spectrum, yet with much less clarity than CHP. The AP seemed to suggest that it was a rightist party, but they never cared to indicate where on the right of the left–right spectrum they were to be placed.

In the meantime, yet another important development started to take place. The liberal 1961 Constitution provided a window of opportunity for political personalities, forces, and groups to the far left and far right of the ideological spectrum to emerge and gain representation under their own banners. They also managed to establish legal political parties and associations after winning some court battles in the 1960s. The socialist Turkish Workers' Party (TİP) was the first of those new political associations, and others followed suit soon. For example, the former MBK member *Alparslan Türkeş* and his Gray Wolves (Bozkurtlar) organization, officially known as the "Idealists" (*Ülkücüler*), established the ethnic Turkish nationalist anticommunist Nationalist Action Party (Milliyetçi Hareket Partisi, MHP) in 1969.[45]

Turkey began to experience a sudden flourishing of political and ideological debate in the country. The liberal 1961 Constitution converted Turkish politics to convert itself into a marketplace of socialist, social democratic, liberal, conservative, national-socialist, and religious ideas. The communists—still considered to be the stooges of the Soviet Union and perceived as constituting a grave danger—were seriously monitored, prosecuted, and banned. The official organ of the Comintern, the Turkish Communist Party (TKP) had to stay underground in the 1960s and the 1970s. Indeed, they could only surface and gain legal status in the process leading to the November 3, 2002 elections, that is, a full 11 years after the collapse of the Soviet Union.

The other missing link in the marketplace of political parties was the Islamic revivalists, and other sectarian religious parties. A party of political Islam, propagating the reestablishment of Şeriat, in place of the secular laws of the land finally emerged in 1969 led by Professor Necmettin Erbakan. He established the National Order Party (Milli Nizam Partisi, MNP) and prepared to enter the elections in 1970.[46] However, his party was considered in violation of the Political Parties Act and banned by the Constitutional Court. It was his second attempt with the National Salvation Party (Milli Selamet Partisi, MSP) four years later that propelled him to center stage of Turkish politics, as MSP gained more than 11 percent of the national vote in the 1973 elections.

In spite of the liberal nature of the 1961 Constitution and the political laws of the 1960s, the liberalization of the political spectrum was not an easy or smooth process. The electoral laws were amended before the 1965 National Assembly elections. The quota of the 1961 election law was abolished, and a pool of national remainder (*milli bakiye*) was established. Votes, non-allocated to any parliamentary seat in an electoral district after the application of the largest average (*d'Hondt*) formula in converting votes to seats, were pooled nationally and distributed among the political parties in terms of their share of the pooled surplus votes. Smaller parties such as TİP benefited from the new practice. Although their size was small in the NA, they demonstrated remarkable skills at opposition. The TİP not only targeted the AP government, but also what they considered to be the entire gamut of parties of the "capitalist establishment." They began to ask the thorniest questions about the Turkish–U.S. relations, the status of Turkey in NATO, the credibility of the U.S. nuclear umbrella, the fairness of income distribution, commercial policies, workplace safety, and so on. They also found themselves assiduously resisted, pressured, threatened, and even physically assaulted on the floor of the NA. The AP and the other right-wing political parties treated them as if they were the "fifth column" of the Soviet Union. Consequently, the floor of the TGNA was again converted from a forum of deliberation to an arena of gladiators.[47]

The relations between the government and the opposition further degenerated into war-like confrontation after the start of the student revolts of 1968. The liberalization of the political system in Turkey provided for the translation of major works of philosophy, Marxist, conservative, liberal, national socialist, and Islamic literature from various languages into Turkish. Socialist and social democratic ideas suddenly found many sympathizers.

The unanticipated declaration of the CHP itself as a left-of-center party also moved many youth to further examine socialist and social democratic ideas. Coincidentally, membership in associations and the number of voluntary associations increased dramatically with the liberalization of the legal system with the 1961 Constitution.[48]

STUDENT REVOLTS AND MORE INSTABILITY

In the meantime, social mobilization continued apace. The number of Turks living in Germany increased with leaps and bounds in the 1960s. As more Turks could experience what modernity was like in western Europe and hear about the developments elsewhere in the world, they seem to become less tolerant of the domestic status quo. Turkey became much more vulnerable to the vicissitudes of international developments. Frustration with politicians and with the performance of the economy (though economy grew by about 7 percent per annum in the late 1960s), which seemed to lag behind the expectations of the college students, began to emerge as unsettling factors breeding restiveness among the college youth. In 1967 issues involving oil explorations, finds, excavation, refining, and sales erupted in student protests. However, it was the news about the student uprisings at the University of California at Berkeley, and elsewhere in the United States, in Paris, France, Berlin, Federal Republic of Germany, and eventually Cairo, Egypt in 1968, which further seemed to have inspired the students to hop on to the wave of the diffusion of student protests around the globe. Ankara University students went on strike in late spring 1968, which was almost immediately followed by the occupation of the buildings of Istanbul University main campus in *Beyazit* by right-wing student organizations. Soon, the rightist students vacated the buildings and the leftists took over. The summer of 1968 started with a tough challenge for the AP government.

In the beginning the CHP opposition seemed not to create problems for the AP government over its handling of the student revolts. İnönü's immediate reaction to the students, who mainly demanded an overhaul of the educational system, which seemed to harbor many educational, administrative, and financial problems, was quite short of sympathy or even tolerance. İnönü referred to the striking students as "hoodlums" (*haytalar*). It is difficult to assess exactly what sort of a role such an attitude played in the radicalization of the student movement, but soon students started to show signs that they found CHP too meek or tepid for their taste. Within a year, and with some provocation, the student movements began to show signs of radicalization.

In the 1969 elections student revolts did not constitute a major campaign issue. AP won the 1969 elections without much difficulty. In the meantime, the AP-dominated TGNA had made the necessary amendments in the election laws to get rid of the national remainder system that enabled the TIP to win 14 seats in the 1965 elections. Indeed, without the aid of the national remainder the TIP failed to get enough votes to get back in the TGNA in the 1969 elections and pester the AP. The TIP failed to improve its performance in the 1969 elections and was marginalized and eventually became a more radical fringe left-wing party in the 1970s. The CHP, which had been self-declared as a left-of-center party also failed to convert into the party of workers, landless peasants, and of the downtrodden of Turkey. It seemed as if the image of the party as that of the symbol of the Center (or the State) continued with little alteration in the minds of the voters.

Winning the 1969 National Assembly elections failed to help the AP much. Student revolts did not to die down, but on the contrary, increased in frequency and radicalism. The frustration of the students with the callous attitude of the AP government, and the recalcitrant predisposition of the university administrations provided an excellent recipe for provocation and radicalization of the student movement. The students were able to observe that only one out of five students who graduated from the high schools could get high enough scores in the nationally administered university examinations to enroll in a college program.[49] It was only a matter of luck for most students to pursue degrees in the areas of the undergraduate programs of their choice. Then, the job market seemed to provide them little opportunities for employment. In 1970 the students, with some provocation, started to move protest rallies outside of the university campuses on to the streets of Ankara, and Istanbul. Some started to argue that unless the "political establishment" became more sensitized to their woes, and to the conditions of the "people," who the students considered to represent, the ills of the higher education and the job markets would persist. Consequently, some students started to organize for a revolution to oust the political and economic forces that rule the country. Clashes between the students and security forces started to turn nasty and eventually bloody. Such developments further radicalized the students, who started to view the educational issues as part of a larger picture of the political system. Different student groups armed with the ideas of Marx, Lenin, Mao, Hitler, and their Turkish proponents started to organize into various armed groups to fight each other, on the one hand, and the political establishment, on the other.

In the meantime, the trade union movement in Turkey gained a similar tendency of radicalization. The two major trade unions, the larger confederation of *Türk-İş* and the smaller but more radical Confederation of Revolutionary Trade Unions (DİSK) began to pressure the budding private sector and the larger State Economic Enterprises (KITs) with various demands, and when not met organize strikes, walkouts, boycotts, and the like. Civil unrest seemed to give the impression that the AP government was not doing a good job of managing the polity and the economy of Turkey.

Economy Slides into Crisis

In spite of the political problems of the early 1960s the economy seemed to do fairly well. The State Planning Organization (DPT) began to determine all public sector investments, and through the incentives it incorporated into the plans private investments also took off from 1963 onward.[50]

Turkey adopted import-substitution policies and textile, consumer durables, automotive, electrical engines, fertilizers, and chemical industries grew rapidly in the late 1960s.[51]

The main deficiency of the import substitution model was the performance of Turkish exports of goods and services. Foreign trade and current account deficits continued to grow throughout the 1960s, as exports stagnated. Dramatic devaluation of the TL vis-à-vis the U.S. dollar in 1970 failed to trigger any major growth in the exports of the country. It seemed like an irony of history that another dramatic devaluation of the TL had occurred in the heat of student revolts of the 1968 and 1971. The mix was again ominous for teh Turkish political system as the country veered toward another military intervention.

The social security net of Turkey grew more robust in the 1960s. Most important was extended by the labor legislation in the early 1960s, for which the Minister in charge Bülent Ecevit got a huge credit. His political career experienced a tremendous boost, which eventually carried him to the leadership of the CHP and the seat of the Prime Minister in 1973. Legislation on labor rights and unionization breathed life into the lethargic and subdued trade unions of the pre-1963 era and wages were boosted considerably throughout the period.[52] In the meantime, agricultural subsidies continued to cater to the interests of the farmers in the country vis-à-vis the practice of support and minimum prices for such critical commodities as tobacco, sugar beets, tea, sunflower seeds, hazelnuts, and so on. The scope and variety of agricultural produce included in the support pricing policies of the governments further led to the draining of the national budgets, as budget deficits continued to soar in late 1960s through 1980.[53]

However, we should hasten to mention that the economy grew by an average of 6.8 percent per annum throughout from 1962 to 1980.[54] The growth rate of the industry was even a higher 9.6 percent per annum, and agriculture also grew by a humble average of 3.9 percent per annum. The latter was far less than sufficient to keep the rapidly expanding rural population at home. The population growth rate reached a staggering 2.5 percent per annum and the rural migration to the cities began to increase in the 1960s and the 1970s.[55] Such a development caused the political parties and elites to pay increasing attention to the urban problems of the country, and the CHP, which gave the impression that it was dealing with urban issues more effectively gained support in the urban centers. The Turkish party system, legislature, and the entire political establishment started to experience new challenges and new developments.

THE ULTIMATUM OF MARCH 12, 1971

By 1970 group of deputies from the governing AP with close links with the budding industrial groups of the Anatolian heartland had been showing signs of dissatisfaction. In an unanticipated move they voted against PM Demirel during a parliamentary vote in February 1970, and forced his cabinet to resign. It became apparent that the AP could not continue to host the rebels, who were either purged as disciplinary measures or they resigned. In December 1970 those who split from the ranks of the AP created a new party, called the Democratic Party (DemP) group in the National Assembly.[56] The image of the AP government further suffered from the split. The AP still controlled the majority of the seats in the TGNA, and thus Demirel again returned to the helm of the government, yet Demirel and his cabinet seemed not to be fully capable of providing political stability, and improve economic welfare, which the country much needed. In the meantime, the government seemed to have lost the support of the military establishment.

On March 12, 1971 the Chief of Staff of the military and the commanders of Army, Navy, Air Force issued a communiqué addressed to the President of the country, in which they demanded that more stern steps be taken to deal with the civil unrest in the country. PM Demirel and his Cabinet handed in their resignations right away. A longtime frontbench member of the CHP, Nihat Erim was sworn in as the new PM, and established a cabinet of technocrats, popularly referred to as the "Brain Cabinet" received vote of confidence in the TGNA, and a new period of quasi-military government started. Martial law was imposed on the country, and civilian government was sidelined until October 1973, though the TGNA was not suspended. Erim's government failed to last long, however, government by technocratic cabinets continued as a practice until the October elections of 1973 and beyond.

In the meantime, the military dealt with the radical students, academics, journalists, and trade unionists through their own methods. Some of the former MBK members, such as Major General Cemal Madanoğlu, were also tried for seditious activities against the state. Another purge from within ranks of the military took place.[57] The 1961 Constitution was preserved but amended in ways not much different from what the PM Demirel and AP had advocated in the past[58] and never considered the 1961 Constitution legitimate; because they argued, they had not taken part in the Constitutional Assembly of 1961, and they had never been consulted in the designing of the Constitution. They contended that the Constitution was the reflection of the "image of good society" of the CHP elite, which had allotted too much power to the nonelected, bureaucratic institutions of Turkey, such as the Constitutional Court, the universities, DPT, and so on, and too little to the "elected" representatives of the people. The elected majority of the TGNA was unfairly harnessed. Demirel and colleagues tried hard to diminish the authority and independence of the courts, and reign unchecked by any institution or power, except for the ballots of the people. It was ironic to watch the military, so much in disagreement with the AP, to follow some of its suggestions during the 1971–1973 military *interregnum*, and many more of them in the early 1980s.

Eventually, Turkey reverted back to multiparty politics in 1973. In the same year, the seven-year tenure of President Cevdet Sunay ended.[59] A pattern of electing generals as President seemed to have been developing. In 1973, the Commander of the Army General Faruk Gürler resigned his job, and upon the resignation of a Senator was appointed to the Senate by President Sunay, with the clear intent of running for the imminent vacation in the job of the President. Indeed, he emerged as a candidate.

General Gürler was one of the signatories of the communiqué of March 12, 1971. Hence, the expectation was that he would be smoothly elected as the next President of the country. The military failed to demonstrate solidarity in supporting him, and not enough votes in the TGNA were cast to elect him as the next President of the country. After some negotiations between the AP and CHP leadership, a compromise candidate was found. Former Admiral Fahri Korutürk, who had also formerly served as the Turkish Ambassador in Moscow upon his retirement from the Navy, was elected as the new President of the country in 1973.[60]

The 1971 military coup, which had been carried out under the leadership of the commanders of the armed forces came to an end after 19 months. The military emerged with relatively little erosion of its institutional character and professionalism from its intervention in civilian politics. However, the coherence of the old Center, which had been built around the coalition of the public bureaucracy, universities and secularist intellectuals, and the military started to show signs of breaking apart. Many academics, intellectuals, journalists, student leaders, trade unionists with leftist reputations were arrested, some were tortured, and most were imprisoned by the military authorities. The CHP elite, rank-and-file members, and sympathizers, identified with the left-of-center were deeply influenced by the acts of the military authorities in the coup of 1971. The CHP leadership could do little to stop the excessive measures taken by the military. However, their image of the party also suffered from the performance of the Nihat Erim government, the callousness of its leadership to the anguish of their sympathizers in the hands of the military. It looked as if the military had taken a sharp turn to the right and acted with deep enmity against the left-of-center and CHP, in spite of the fact that their hand-picked PM was an old hand of the CHP.

The 1972 Convention of the CHP was a true milestone for the party. Its leader since 1938, İsmet İnönü failed to be reelected as the party leader. İnönü resigned his CHP membership and started to serve as a Senator, in the upper chamber of the TGNA, until his death in November 1973.[61] The former general secretary of the party, who ran on a relatively radical and antiestablishment platform, was elected as the leader of the party in 1972.

BACK TO DEMOCRACY

The 1973 National Assembly elections brought about some interesting developments. Surprisingly, the CHP managed to obtain the plurality of the national vote, and the AP seemed to have suffered dearly. The MSP of Necmettin Erbakan had a forceful entry into the TGNA, gaining more than 11 percent of the vote (see table 4.2).

In the 1973 elections the CHP propagated that land and water should belong to who till the land and use the water. The landless peasants and small farmers, who constituted a large plurality of the electorate, was their target audience. The CHP managed to project an image of seeking equality, justice and fairness as the pivotal principles. The CHP would now be the party of the downtrodden and stand up for the rights of those who were marginalized by rapid social mobilization. The millions who had been developing squatter settlements on the fringes of the big cities of the country would be served well by CHP government in Ankara and the CHP municipalities in the big cities. The CHP argued that the political establishment and the economic order were in need of fixing, and once in government they would seek to establish a "Fair Order." Ecevit's blue shirt and peasant cap became symbols of admiration and he started to gain some of the Periphery to the CHP.[62]

A new and curious political image of the old CHP began to emerge. It was still the party of the Center, with secularist, nationalist, revolutionary, and populist image combined with the added sensitivity to the plight of the downtrodden in Turkey. For a while almost a miracle seemed to be happening in Turkey, which of course, was a severe challenge for the AP, the powerhouse of the Periphery.

The AP not only lost votes to the new CHP, but also to the emerging revivalist MSP, ultranationalist anticommunist MHP, and even to its former faction turned into the Democratic Party. The attitude of the AP to the ultimatum of March 12, 1971 seemed to have undermined the party. Free market liberalism and political conservatism of the AP were not considered effective remedies for the ills of the country. In the outcome of the 1973 elections the distribution of the seats in the National Assembly disabled CHP from coming to power alone. Turkey reverted back to coalition politics.

The AP was in no position to seek a coalition with the religious revivalist MSP, the ultranationalist MHP, and the party that split from them earlier, the DemP. The AP leadership was anxious not to develop an image of veering toward radical anti-secularism, especially when the memories of the coup of March 12 were still fresh. The CHP broke the impasse by unexpectedly approaching the most avid anti-secularist party of the time, the MSP, and work out a compromise toward establishing a coalition government. A coalition government of the powerhouse of secularism and a party of ardent Islamic revivalists united their forces to undermine the "the corrupt order" of Turkey, and establish the reign of "fair order" supreme. Finally, as if those dire developments for the AP were not enough, a coup on the island of Cyprus and the Turkish military intervention as the guarantor of the status quo on the island, suddenly elevated CHP and its leader and PM Bülent Ecevit to new heights as a national hero.

THE CYPRUS CRISIS AND THE TURKISH QUAGMIRE

The Cyprus problem had flared up in 1967 when the Greek Cypriots again started to massacre the Muslim Turks on the island, precipitating the same progression of reactions and actions. Turkey started to flex its military muscle, which precipitated U.S. mediation and temporary termination of hostilities. In 1967 the AP government's policies were not much different from those of the İnönü's coalition government of 1964, but in the interim, a military coup in Greece established a junta of colonels to come to power.

Beginning in 1973 the economic and international relations of Greece had started to worsen. It seemed as if, in early 1974 the Greek junta plotted to unite the island with the Greek mainland (*enosis*) by means of a military coup, which would also eliminate their political headache President Archbishop Makarios of Cyprus as well.

The news of the coup and the widespread massacres of Turkish Cypriots hit the Turkish press and the media almost simultaneously in July 1974. It also happened at a time when the Turkish love affair with the black and white TV screens was just getting under way. The stark pictures of Turkish Cypriots pleading for help, and reports of massacres further pressured the coalition government to take urgent action in Turkey.

The government coalition consisted of odd bedfellows, and had been experiencing various strains and stresses. The CHP was the party and flag bearer of the secularizing revolution of the 1920s, while the MSP was the party of the Islamic revivalists, who had been the archenemies of the secularizing revolution. The "brain trust" of the CHP had come to the conclusion that both the "new CHP" and the MSP were united in opposing the "corrupt establishment." They had failed to see that what the two parties considered to be wrong about the establishment was not only completely different, but also diametrically opposite.

The party program of the CHP flirted with social democratic ideas and was based upon a criticism of landlordism in agriculture and the practices of monopolistic corporations and faulty market mechanisms in the developing industry of Turkey. The CHP was also critical of the foreign relations of Turkey, considered to be overdependent on NATO and the United States. Hence, the CHP of the 1970s was called for the development of a more independent foreign policy, which would distance Turkey from NATO and the United States.

The party program of the MSP called for the end of capitalism and establishment of heavy industry and "Islamic economics," and its anti-Americanism blended with anti-Jewish and anti-Israeli sentiments.[63] While both the CHP and MSP were anti-American, the former was more like a French socialist party, while the latter was more like an Arab national/socialist party. The partners in coalition had nothing in common over cultural, educational, economic policies. Therefore, it did not take long for the two coalition partners to lock horns in bitter internecine struggles. Such an image of the Turkish government may have even encouraged the Greek junta to make its move on the island of Cyprus.

The Greek junta was hard pressed by the opposition of the elected President of Cyprus, Archbishop Makarios, whose popularity seemed to be on the rise even in mainland Greece. The diminishing popularity of the junta may have led the Greek colonels in Athens to consider a move that would both eliminate Archbishop Makarios and create union (*enosis*) with Cyprus at the same time.[64] From early 1974 on an existential struggle seemed to be unfolding between Archbishop Makarios and the Greek junta in Cyprus. The climax of the power struggle came in the form of a military coup in July 1974. However, Archbishop Makarios managed to flee the island and renewed his political campaign against the coup in the United Nations and elsewhere. The Archbishop's political campaign abroad also encouraged the Turkish government to stress the dire circumstances of the political situation on the island, and the need to restore the *status quo ante* by any means possible.

It was under those circumstances that Turkish PM Ecevit started to test the waters with the British government, and the Ford Administration in the United States, for a combined military intervention with Britain on the island of Cyprus to reestablish the status quo before the coup.[65] The British seemed to favor diplomacy over military action. British lives were not at stake, while the Turkish community on the island was bleeding. Under the circumstances, the Turkish coalition government and the TGNA showed remarkable solidarity and determination to decide to land troops on the island, which in a sense, prolonged the cumbersome relationship of the two parties in government for a while longer.

The initial intervention of Turkey on the island in July 1974 was not in breach of its legal and moral commitments, or of international law. However, when Turkey decided to establish a safe haven for Turks in a northern enclave of the island in August 1974, and physically separate the two ethnic communities, which had failed to demonstrate the ability to live together, the legality of the Turkish moves were cast in doubt.[66] A complicated diplomatic and legal process started to unfold between Turkey, on the one hand, and Greece, Britain, United States, UN, and eventually the European Community and its successor European Union (EU), on the other. Turkey and Greece failed to show capability to efficiently deal with the Cyprus problem, forge a compromise, and negotiate their differences to settle the issue on the island.

The Turkish efforts at keeping the Cyprus problem within the confines of the tripartite format of the London and Zurich Accords of 1959–1960 failed. On the contrary, the Cyprus issue was internationalized. It became one of the problem areas, which the UN continued to mediate since 1963 and also after the Turkish military intervention of 1974, though with slight, if any success until the end of 2003. Greek foreign policy met with greater success both in the internationalization of the "Cyprus problem," and eventually establishing a quasi union (*enosis*) through the EU membership of both Greece and the southern, official Greek–Cypriot government of Cyprus. However, the island has been divided between the northern Turkish part, which declared its independent statehood in 1983, though recognized by no other state than Turkey, and the southern Greek part, which continued to be recognized as the official Republic of Cyprus in the international community, except for Turkey. Nevertheless, the de facto partition of the island failed to come to an end, through a peaceful, fair, and equitable settlement for the next 30 years. The conflict-ridden island has recently moved toward a more peaceful status quo, yet the divisive issues still plague the island, continued to jeopardize the stability of Eastern Mediterranean at the end of 2003.

The Turkish military intervention in Cyprus created considerable amount of internal friction within the coalition government in Turkey after the war was won, and the Turkish Cypriot community was put under the protection of the Turkish army in a northern safe haven. The coalition partners seemed to fall apart over the issue of who was to be credited for the victory. Mr. Erbakan, the deputy PM and the leader of the MSP argued that it was he who ordered the military to land troops on the island, and he who persuaded the government to decide to intervene on the island. However, the media and public opinion seemed to have given the most credit to PM Ecevit.

The coalition did not work as a partnership of the two parties, but more along the lines of partition of the turf of the state between them. Turkey seemed to have two parallel governments in charge at the same time. Worse, the two parties had no common understanding as to how to run the government or what policies to follow, and the ministries under each party veered toward different directions. The CHP leadership concluded that time had come to opt out of the coalition and call for early elections; and so they did. However, what the CHP frontbench could realize, their opponents could also visualize with utmost clarity. Hence, all of the other parties did what they could to avoid an early election. The CHP did not have the votes in the TGNA to produce a definitive decision on the matter. A period of uncertainty, coalition negotiations, extra-parliamentary or "technocratic" governments reigned in early 1975 (see table 4.3).

In the meantime, the Cyprus issue continued to poison Turkish–U.S. relations in the 1970s. The United States, after a protracted struggle between the Congress and the White House, imposed an arms embargo upon Turkey on February 5, 1975.[67] The Turkish army had used NATO and U.S. weapons in a way not authorized by the treaties that made the sales of those weapons to Turkey in the first place. Just like the letter of President Lyndon B. Johnson almost a decade earlier, Turkey was made to realize again that the U.S. resolve to defend Turkey was not as great as the Truman Doctrine had suggested. Turkey was further motivated to seek alternative markets and means to supply its armed forces. To make matters even worse, the Cyprus crisis coincided with the ill effects of the OPEC oil embargo, which had been precipitated by the Arab–Israeli War of October 1973. Turkey has never had enough oil reserves and production to supply its own energy hungry market. In 1975, when Turkey had to spend more than its entire export revenues to buy oil from international sources, and was simultaneously slapped with an arms embargo, Turkey encountered another severe foreign currency shortage.

It did not take long for Turkey to react to the developments. On February 13, 1975 the northern safe haven declared itself to be the Turkish Federated State of Cyprus of the Republic of Cyprus. The Air Force base in Incirlik (near *Adana*), Sinop and other bases and facilities in Turkey were closed down or taken out of the U.S. jurisdiction and returned to the NATO fold, and all bilateral treaties between Turkey and the United States concerning the bases were unilaterally abolished in Turkey by July 1975. Ironically, it was Qaddafi's Libya, which had earlier been supplied with similar U.S. weapons that came to Turkey's aid and provided Turkey not only with spare parts for warplanes, and other NATO grade U.S. weapons, but also oil. It looked as if, the U.S.-led arms embargo began to pressure Turkey to develop new alliances, and seek interesting foreign suppliers. However, no major step toward the settlement of the Cyprus issue was taken during the embargo. In the meantime, the U.S. government started to realize that the arms embargo was also breaching security of the Eastern Mediterranean, and proved to be considerably counterproductive to the United States itself. A few years later upon President Carter's appeal to the Congress the arms embargo ended in July 1978, and the Turkish–U.S. relations started to improve once again.[68] In the meantime, Turkey had taken the first timid steps toward establishing a national arms industry.

The events set into motion by the military coup in Cyprus brought about the demise of the reign of the Greek junta in Greece. It was ironic that the Greek junta was ousted from power by virtue of the Turkish intervention on the island of Cyprus. It is also ironic that the Turkish military intervention on the island of Cyprus that not only saved the lives of Turkish Cypriots, but also ended the internecine fratricide among the Greeks and Greek Cypriots; and finally, by toppling the Greek colonels from power, paved the way for democracy to be reinstalled in Greece, and on the island of Cyprus.

TURKEY IN THE GRIP OF INTERNATIONAL ETHNIC TERROR

Although a *modus vivendi* eventually emerged between Turkey and the United States over the Cyprus issue, another international difficulty, which began in 1973, continued to complicate Turkish–American relations ever since. The Consul General Mehmet Baydar and Consul Bahadır Demir, who were serving at the Turkish Consulate General in Los Angeles, California were lured to a motel in Santa Barbara and were shot dead,[69] allegedly by an elderly Armenian American who had acted under the influence of what had transpired in 1915. It was hard to believe that an octogenarian Armenian who had survived the atrocities of World War I could have acted alone (if he ever did act), to plan the murder of young diplomats and perpetrated the murders. Indeed, in a matter of two years, the foundation of ASALA (Armenian Secret Army for the Liberation of Armenia) was promulgated in Beirut, Lebanon. Until 1983 ASALA attacked many Turkish diplomats and killed 30 of them and wounded others. They also attacked what they considered to be other Turkish targets, such as the Turkish embassies, Turkish Airlines offices and bureaus in such places as the Orly Airport, Paris, France.[70] Interestingly enough, the ASALA seemed to operate not only in the Middle East, but also throughout the world, and eventually moved their offices into Cyprus in the 1980s.[71] The Greek Cypriot government and territory started to emerge as the Center of anti-Turkish activities for a while to come.

ASALA seemed to have been mainly operated and supported by the Armenian diaspora in France, United States, Lebanon, and elsewhere. ASALA and its supporters kept pressing the governments in question to recognize the bloodbath that took place in eastern Anatolia during World War I as genocide of the Armenians of the Ottoman Empire. Such efforts met considerable amount of success both in France and the United States, which, to say the least, complicated and cooled the relations between those countries and Turkey in the 1980s, and on and off since then.[72] Nevertheless, the ASALA terror campaign came to an abrupt end when the French government reacted vehemently against the ASALA organization after they bombed the Orly Airport in Paris in the early 1980s. However, a new wave of terror started almost as the ASALA and Armenian terror campaign against Turkey came to a halt. This time, it was Marxist–Leninist, Maoist Kurdish nationalists, who began to launch attacks on the eastern towns and settlements of Turkey from August 15, 1984 onward. In the 1990s and the early 2000s groups motivated by Islamic dogmas and ideologies, such as Wahhabism and other orthodoxies, started to launch attacks on communities, sites, and buildings of various Muslim, Jewish, American, and European entities in Turkey. In short, Turkey has become the target of various international terror groups since the 1970s, and continued to suffer from their aggresiveness in the early 2000s.

"NATIONAL FRONT" GOVERNMENT: ECONOMY AND DEMOCRACY AT RISK

The political and economic consequences of the oil and Cyprus crises, domestic and international terror, and the U.S. arms embargo were debilitating both for the Turkish economy and democracy. After lengthy negotiations, and even a government of technocrats under the leadership of a former professor of medicine, Sadi Irmak, which stayed in power for more than four months without a vote of confidence in the TGNA (where 99 percent of the deputies voted against it), former PM Demirel managed to establish a coalition of conservatives (AP), ultranationalists (MHP) and Islamic revivalists (MSP), which has been popularly known as the "National Front" government. What would have been extremely difficult in the 1960s had become politically feasible between 1973 and 1974 thanks to Ecevit's CHP, which extended the MSP political legitimacy by establishing a coalition and cohabiting with it for almost a year in government. Hence, the CHP was in no position to criticize the AP for coalescing with the Islamic revivalist party in government, for the CHP had already done so earlier. The AP–MHP–MSP barely scored the majority vote of confidence in 1975. The hopes of the CHP for a major electoral victory at a presumed early election were dashed once again.

The style of government of the new coalition government was no different from the CHP–MSP government. The political parties partitioned the Ministries in the Cabinet among themselves, and each became the full authority over the domain of the Ministry, which it came to control. The tripartite coalition now started to act as three parallel parties in government.

Each party considered itself committed to its own party programs, creed, and clientele. They did not bother to seek cooperation, let alone solidarity of government action. In cases where Ministries controlled by different political parties had to cooperate for a policy to be implemented, there was usually a full paralysis of the government. However, political parties continued to act as excellent popular patronage mechanisms, distributing largesse and emoluments from the state budget to their key supporters, as best and efficiently as they could. The easiest way to distribute largesse was to employ their supporters in their Ministries they occupied or the state enterprises (KIT) their Ministries had control over. The Islamic revivalists (Nakşibendi *Sufi* order) and the "gray wolves" (*ülkücüler*, ethnic Turkish nationalists) thus started to make inroads into the public bureaucracy in large numbers, where they were to stay for many years to come.

Turkey was ruled by the AP–MHP–MSP coalition from 1975 until the 1977 National Assembly elections. Under the dire economic conditions dictated by the high oil prices and the U.S. arms embargo, the performance of the government failed to help the partners win votes, and led to the reemergence of the student uprisings, which were eventually hijacked by extra-campus political forces. The territorial span of the armed political struggle started to climb to new heights. Almost all provinces of the country began to suffer from the armed struggle of the "left" versus the "right" ideological groups. The public bureaucracy of the system began to suffer from a similar divide to an extent that even the police began to split into "leftist" (POL-DER) and "rightist" (POL-BIR) associations, which seemed to participate in the struggle for control of the streets, towns, and cities of the country.[73]

The National Assembly elections of 1977 were again another early election, in which the governing coalition had hoped to win more votes (see table 4.2). However, the CHP increased its stand at the polls, yet still coming slightly short of controlling the majority of the seats in the TGNA. CHP failed to establish a coalition government after the 1977 elections, and another "national front" coalition was established. However, in a few months' time the CHP was able to allure 11 deputies of the AP to join its ranks in ousting the AP–MHP–MSP coalition of 1977, and form a new coalition government on January 1, 1978.

PM Bülent Ecevit's government acted more like a coalition of 12 parties, with each of the 11 former AP deputies, who now became Ministers of Ecevit's new cabinet, acting as if each was a leader of his own party. Ecevit failed to reign in on them and establish coordination and cooperation among the Ministries controlled by the 11. The largesse of the 11 in distributing patronage started to resemble a plunder of the resources of their Ministries. Accusations of corruption began to reverberate, as the government seemed to look like a rudderless vessel in the middle of an ocean.

The high hopes placed on the CHP-led coalition government in its ability to deal with the armed struggle of the ideological groups was dashed soon. In the city of Kahramanmaraş the Sunni majority under the guise of "suppressing the communists" attacked the *Alevi* minority in December 1978.[74] The government declared martial law and the army was, once again, called in to restore law and order. Soon the same scenario was staged in the provinces of Malatya, Çorum, Tokat, Erzincan, and elsewhere in the country. Most major cities of Turkey came under martial law by 1979. Bombings and assassination of celebrities, politicians, academics, journalists, and others began to occur as daily events.[75]

The performance of the economy continued to suffer. The CHP government rightfully diagnosed that it was the lack of manufactured goods produced in the country to export, which constituted a major bottleneck, and launched an "export drive." However, Turkish industry had been solidly based upon import-substitution practices since the 1960s, and the overall economic policy of the government remained solidly based upon the mixed economy, planned growth, and import-substitution policies.[76]

While it had been hoped that an import-substitution industry would solve the cyclical crises of foreign currency shortages through the contraction of imports,[77] what the politicians had not seemed to realize was that import-substitution industry still needed imports of raw materials and intermediary products.[78] For example, cars needed gas to run, and engine parts to be assembled, which were imported from the international markets. The demand for foreign goods and services did not diminish with import-substitution practices, but increased. The size of Turkish imports changed parallel to the demands of the developing domestic industry in Turkey from the 1950s to the 1970s (see table 4.4). When the bill for oil imports increased five folds between 1973 and 1975, Turkey had to pay an oil bill of $3 billions, while the Turkish exports hovered around $1.4–2.9 billions.[79] In the 1960s Turkey had converted from relatively expensive domestic coal to imported fuel oil to produce electrical energy, and to provide heat to corporate and residential buildings. The oil shortages brought about long lines of cars at the gas

Table 4.4   Trends in Turkish Foreign Trade (1945–1980)

Year	Imports Million $	Exports Million $	Balance of Foreign Trade Million $	Ratio of Exports to Imports %	Share of Exports in GNP %
1945	97	168	71	173,5	4,0
1950	286	263	−23	92,2	7,6
1955	498	313	−185	63,0	4,6
1960	468	321	−147	68,6	3,7
1965	572	464	−108	81,1	5,4
1970*	886	588	−360	62,1	3,2
1975	4,739	1,401	−3,338	29,6	3,0
1980**	7,909	2,910	−4,999	36,8	4,1

Notes: * Imports of goods without official allocation of foreign exchange are not included.
** The figures for 1980 based on the declarations received, included some 242 million dollars of crude petroleum imports which were actually made in 1979, but declarations were not received during the closing period of "1979 foreign trade statistics."

Source: T. C. Başbakanlık Devlet İstatistik Enstitüsü (State Institute of Statistics), Statistical Yearbook (Ankara, 1993): 541–542.

stations, and a black market for the fuel oil, for those who could afford to pay, or else could not put up with the cold of winter. The CHP-led coalition government seemed to have dismally failed to cope with the bloodshed in the country, on the one hand, and with the deteriorating conditions of the economy, on the other.

Five seats of the Senate were to be contested in the by-elections of November 1979. Those elections turned out to be a disaster for the ruling CHP and a new hope for AP, for the latter had another landslide victory. When the AP won all of the five Senate races with a large margin of electoral victory, PM Ecevit handed in his resignation to President Korutürk and stepped down. Korutürk appointed Demirel as the new PM once again. After some negotiations Demirel was able to form a minority AP government, as his former coalition partners, the MSP and MHP, agreed to support his Cabinet in the TGNA until the elections scheduled for June 1981.

In a daring move, PM Demirel ended the economic policies of the former governments, and announced the beginning of free market capitalism in Turkey on January 24, 1980. State permits and regulations over the production and distribution of goods and services were to be gradually lifted. The mixed economy of Turkey, which operated under the weight of the public sector, dominated by the state-owned banks and KIT's would be gradually phased out, and replaced by a private sector dominated market economy.[80]

Almost instantly the black market started to wither away. Scarcity of staple foods and consumer durables were over within a few months. However, the prices of commodities increased with leaps and bounds, as the demand for them soared, while the supply was sluggish due to foreign currency shortages. Turkey had begun to experience high rates of inflation of consumer prices in the late 1970s. The "January 24" economic decrees of the government were a cure for the scarcities, but they failed to halt the inflationary pressures of consumer prices. For the next 23 years Turkey experienced what could best be termed as "stable high inflation" of the general level of consumer prices.

HOW NOT TO ELECT A PRESIDENT

The tenure of President Korutürk ended in early 1980. In a parliamentary regime it is the job of the legislature to elect the next President. Traditionally the TGNA would meet and the leading party group leaders, who would be the PM and the leader of the main opposition party would test the waters. Their lieutenants would negotiate and reach a compromise over whom to elect as the new President of the country. However, in early 1980 the political situation of the country had become complicated.

Turkey was now governed by a minority government for the first time in its history. PM Demirel knew that he now had regained the support of the voters, and it was only a matter of time for the AP to win the next National Assembly elections, the AP preferred early elections, yet CHP and all of the other major parties preferred to delay the National Assembly elections until the very last minute, and hope that the AP mismanaged the economy and the political affairs of the country, in the meantime. Because largest parliamentary group belonged to the CHP with the support of the other parties and independent candidates it had enough votes to block early elections.

However, the CHP failed to command enough votes to get a new President elected. The Constitution stipulated that the legislative process stops until a new President is elected. Many candidates were put forward, but with no agreement between the major parliamentary groups in the TGNA none could get the necessary two-thirds majority to get elected. In the meantime, Demirel's Cabinet ruled the country by governmental decrees with the force of law. The TGNA in gridlock made life easier for the minority cabinet of PM Demirel. He did not have to deal with any legislative business, meet the challenges and the capricious demands of the smaller parties, could avoid oral and written questions, and other procedures of legislative control to be imposed upon the government by the abrasive CHP opposition in the TGNA.

Again, the country seemed to be immersed in severe political and economic crises. It was ruled by a party that paralyzed the legislative system and locked the opposition out of the legal channels of governance. Martial law was imposed on the country gradually since 1978, and in spite of the fact that the military went out of its barracks to the streets of the country the bloodshed seemed to be continuing unabated. In the summer of 1980 the official death toll from internecine ideological, ethnic, sectarian violence had reached 20 dead and many more wounded per day, and the total death toll for the entire period of 1975–1980 had reached 5,000.[81]

The AP government of PM Demirel, failed to do anything about the increased restiveness of the military, not withstanding ample lessons of the past.[82] It may even be argued that the AP preferred to hand over the helm of government to the military rather than seek a compromise with the CHP to elect a President. Indeed, on September 12, 1980 the military carried out a coup to topple the government, suspend the TGNA, and end all democratic forms of political interaction in the country. This time Turkey was in the grips of an "institutional coup." The new rulers of Turkey were the Chief of Staff General Kenan Evren, and the Commanders of the Army, Air Force, Navy, and the Gendarmerie. The military ruled the country until the November 6, 1983 National Assembly elections. They also undertook one of the most sweeping political regime changes that the country ever experienced in its Republican history since the 1920s.

THE CHALLENGE OF GOVERNANCE: STABILITY VERSUS LIBERAL DEMOCRACY

It became crystal clear by the early 1970s that the Center finally started to change. An enlarging spectrum of representatives of the Periphery has taken permanent residence in the decision-making processes of the national government. The Islamic revivalists who Atatürk and the revolutionary elite of the CHP had so assiduously worked to get rid of the Turkish politics, started to creep back into the system to take their place not only in the TGNA, but also in the entire gamut of the public bureaucracy of the national (central) government. The irony of the matter was that it was the CHP, the very party that Atatürk had founded himself and led until his death, which played a major role in the reestablishment of the Islamic revivalists in the Center of the Republic! The Center–Periphery relations changed from what they had used to be, once and for all after the 1970s. In the 1961–1980 era the cultural and the political (power) aspects of the Center completely diverged, and the latter began to be penetrated with increased effectiveness by the agents of the Periphery, and especially the Islamic revivalist National Viewpoint (*Milli Görüş*) and MSP, and ethnic nationalist Gray Wolves (*Ülkücü*) and the MHP organizations.

The cultural divide between those who believed in an "image of good society" built around secularism, science, rational thinking, and those who believed in the opposite "image of good society" built around tradition and Sunni Islam continued to influence lifestyles, attitudes, behavior, and political preferences of the citizens of Turkey. However, new political ideas, parties, and interest groups began to mushroom in the 1961–1980 era.[83] It was also a period of political openness, where liberties and especially freedom of expression was exercised by large swathes of the Turkish population. Expressions of opinions, ideas, and criticisms were considerably free and most citizens experienced it liberally in the country.[84] The transistor radios, which were cheap, light, and small enough to be versatile, were used extensively in the countryside in the 1960s. The black and white TV sets emerged as status symbols and eventually constituted a major means of mass communication in the 1970s. The increased access to mass media through the widespread use of transistor radios and the black and white TV sets enabled the least educated Turkish citizens to overcome their parochialism, and flared up their imaginations and expectations (table 4.5).

In the 1950s only those who dared and could move to the big cities, and/or to Germany, were able to have first hand information about modernity and urban styles of life. In the 1960s, but much more so in the 1970s it was the transistor radios and the TV sets that brought about images of modernity and urban lifestyles into the coffee and tea houses of rural Turkey, where men gathered to listen to the news, watch football and other sports events, and to discuss and debate the meaning of what they hear and see. Eventually, women were also able to watch TV programs at home, and often in company with their neighbors and relatives, especially toward the end of the 1970s when black and white TV sets became more affordable.

The entire gamut of social interactions between families changed for a while in the early 1970s. Those who owned the new status symbols suddenly discovered that they, or rather their TV sets, constituted a great attraction. Relatives, friends, and neighbors, who they had not had very close interactions, suddenly rushed to take their seats in front of the TV sets, in their now "beloved" relatives', friends', or neighbors' homes. This created a new chore for the ladies of the houses, who started to prepare for the gush of "TV visitors"

Table 4.5   Communications and Social Mobilization in Turkey (1950–1980)

Year	Radio Licenses	Black and White TV Sets (000)	Color TV Sets (000)	Postal Traffic		Telephone Subscribers (000)
				Letters (000)	Parcels (000)	
1950	320,853	–	–	130	976	58
1956	1,047,243	–	–	n.a.	n.a.	n.a.
1960*	1,426,462	–	–	234	1,353	180
1965	2,442,919	–	–	229	n.a.	242
1970**	3,855,913	133	–	305	n.a.	426
1976***	4,198,272	999	–	471	2,378	1,112
1980****	4,288,536	3,433	63,5	562	1,893	1,148

Notes: "n.a." stands for "not available."
"–" indicates inapplicability of the corresponding item.
* 1961 figures for radio licenses.
** 1971 figures for radio licenses, letters sent, and telephone subscribers, and 1972 figures for black and white TV sets.
*** The corresponding figure for black and white TV sets belong to 1975.
**** The corresponding figures are production figures for the color TV sets from the year 1982.
Source: Europa Yearbooks 1969 and 1975.

every evening. The dinner time and after dinner interactions of the families changed dramatically. Their private lives came under the invasion of "TV" friends, neighbors, and relatives. Families even discovered relatives long out of touch with them, and friends from the past, such as those who had served in the same company in the army once upon a time, suddenly emerged from the shadows to reserve their seats in the living rooms for the TV séances. If urbanization was the main force driving social mobilization in the 1950s, the transistor radio in the 1960s, and the black and white TV sets in the 1970s were the added influences, which fueled the process of social mobilization.

The pace of urbanization also picked up throughout the 1960s and the 1970s (see chapter 3, table 3.4), and so did the number of migrants who obtained jobs in Europe, and most specifically in Germany, and elsewhere, such as Libya, Saudi Arabia, and even Australia.[85] The growing size of the cities created severe problems of urbanization by the 1970s. The flux of population from the countryside overwhelmed the capacity of the cities to cope with the demands for housing, jobs, transportation, sanitation, and other municipal services. The centralized public administration of Turkey was ill equipped to deal with the problems. Hence, demands for decentralization and devolution of power began to be made with increased assertiveness. The first timid step in that direction was the creation of the elected office of mayors in the 1960s. A multitier administration started to gain credibility in Turkey.[86]

As the city populations soared the municipal administrations lacked the financial and human resources, and management capacities to cope with the increasing demands for municipal services. Consequently, the practice of establishing shantytowns emerged as the popularly invented, yet illegal solutions to the housing needs of the rural migrants of the cities. They confiscated public land, often owned by the state or the municipalities, and occasionally even private land by sheer force, and built the replicas of their peasant dwellings, almost overnight, which is why they were referred to as the *gecekondu* (which means "landed over the night" in Turkish). Whole new *mahalles* and even towns of *gecekondu* houses emerged around the suburbs of the major cities of Turkey. The people who settled there often moved in from certain villages as a group of relatives and neighbors. They continued to practice their village folklore in their new environment. The solidarity of the group rested upon blood-ties. However, people from the same province or even region of the country also managed to establish strong social bonds and networks through their territorial relations. They needed to establish some form of solidarity and interpersonal trust to establish their new *mahalles* (neighborhoods), get jobs, to obtain credit, and most critically to deal with the municipal and provincial authorities and politicians. They only had blood or soil ties to function as a strong cultural bond and support system to enable their survival in their new environment.[87]

As illegal settlements *gecekondu* have always been vulnerable. Their illegal dwellings could always be under the threat of being demolished by the authorities. However, if their solidarity was strong enough, they could stand against the encroachments of the authorities. Thus, survival depended upon their ability to pool their resources to resist, cajole, and influence the authorities. Hence, they almost always followed a pattern of settlement that shielded them against the wrath of the authorities. They tended to build a mosque and an elementary school building first, and their houses in between. Even when illegally built, no politician of the 1960s and the 1970s could consider demolishing a mosque or a school as good public relations. Furthermore, the squatter dwellers had a valuable political resource at their disposal, the sheer size of their population. They offered their votes *en bloc* for any politician who would be ready to provide them with protection against the encroachment of the authorities.[88] Immaculate patronage ties contributed to the smooth operation of populist patronage mechanisms, which latched on to local and national political parties and interest groups.[89]

Many found jobs as cleaning ladies, gardeners, door keepers, janitors, drivers, servants, and so on in the middle- and upper-middle-class homes of the bigger cities, which provided them the chance to experience a style of living, which was more immediate than the images of the movies or TV screens, yet so unattainable. The urbanization of the rural masses brought urban lifestyles and the rural values in sudden contact. The cultural shock is not an intense enough term to explain such an intimate contact of two separate and diametrically opposite lifestyles and values. The "little culture" of Anatolia and the "big culture" of capital or seat of power, and the like, have always been at odds with each other in Turkey, however they never had to share the same space or city before. They had lived their separate lives in geographically segregated parts of the country. Their contacts were few and undesirable. However, now the social mobilization and democratization of the country led to proximal living conditions and continuous interactions between them.

The great income gap in between, the differences of values, which are reflected upon the lifestyles, brandished by the middle and upper middle classes and envied by the *gecekondu* dwellers, and the impossibility of attaining such living standards by the latter led to envy, disappointment, and hatred of the well-to-do and the powerful by the have-nots. Some tried to emulate the urban middle classes in dress, manners, and lifestyles, which often resulted in increased friction within the squatter communities. In order to forestall any breakdown of solidarity the emulators were often quickly ostracized. Consequently, some tried to survive alone and began to take part in such illegal professions as prostitution, drug smuggling, and so on, to get rich quick, and go up the social ladder fast. Many failed and joined others, who had to grapple with even greater poverty and powerlessness in lonely lives.[90]

The shantytowns began to provide fertile ground for political mobilization not only for political parties, but also for the radical left- and right-wing associations bent on terror. All major cities started to host "emancipated areas" controlled by fringe left- and right-wing extremists, who fought their own political struggles with guns between 1975 and 1980. Maoism, Soviet, Albanian styles of communisms, fascism, ethnic nationalism, intertwined with Sunni or *Alevi* Islamic orders and communities started to vie for control of the rural migrants of the big cities. These political ideologies provided them with explanations as to why they were in such a pitiful state of existence, while the "happy few" in the urban middle classes did so well. They were also given a recipe for how to change their conditions by joining whichever association managed to control their area. The choice was often between joining, or moving out or being assassinated. The major political parties of the country tried to compete with or latch on to such organizations for the vote pool of the shantytowns, and did little to cope with the cauldron of illegal activism developing in their midst.[91]

Freedom of association and expression provided by the 1961 Constitution seemed to have paved the way for a downturn in conventional forms of political participation in Turkey.[92] Instead of mainly strengthening the legal and conventional channels of political participation, the democratic regime had given way to the development of a highly fragmented, polarized, and volatile electorate[93] at the mercy of a plurality of illegal, alegal, and semi-legal political organizations who often tended to wield bullets rather than ballots to get to the helm of government. The rapid social mobilization in the country created a culture of envy, hatred, and rulelessness in the urban areas of the country, which rendered peaceful competition of political parties and interest groups an exception by 1980.[94]

A paralyzed National Assembly, a style of rule by a minority government based on decrees with the force of law, and spiraling political violence and political instability seemed to have been pushing the country down the road of civil war. In the meantime, the military had been out of their barracks to protect the branches of banks, university buildings, and provide security in the streets of the cities since 1978. Although it was initially the CHP government, which had declared martial law in *Kahramanmaraş* and elsewhere, the AP government had little choice but continue the practice. The declaration of martial law has always been a risky step to take on the part of civilian governments. Martial law constitutes a clear sign of the lack of capability of the democratic civilian government to rule the country through peaceful means. It also entrusts the military with the establishment and maintenance of law and order. Ironically, the civilian, democratic government legitimizes the role of the military in running the domestic affairs of the country, and simultaneously, admits the shortcomings of the civilian government in managing the home affairs. The declaration of martial law provides the military with a clear and legitimate ground to meddle into politics to put the political house in order. That constitutes a short step to a full-scale coup. When frustrated with the civilian politicians bickering over the powers they demanded to put out the fire at home in 1980, the military seemed to have taken that short step and ousted PM Demirel's government, once again.[95]

This time Turkey was to experience an "institutional military coup," whereby the military chain of command (*emir komuta zinciri*) was kept intact. The military did not suffice by promulgating a communiqué, as they had done on March 12, 1971, but moved their troops to oust the government, and arrested all of the party leaders including PM Demirel. In almost every declaration of the new locus of power, the National Security Assembly (Milli Güvenlik Konseyi, MGKo) the intact nature of the military hierarchy was underscored with utmost care. The military declared that they were in charge to put an end to bloodshed, establish law and order, and redesign the democratic regime of the country, so that democracy can perform without undermining stability of the political system.[96]

CONCLUSION: LIBERAL CONSTITUTION AND ILLIBERAL POLITICAL ACTORS

Turkey experienced a liberal democratic regime at work in the 1961–1980 era. Such previously taboo subjects and ideas of the past as Marxism-Leninism, Socialism, Social Democracy, Fascism, and Political Islam and Revivalism (*Şeriatçılık*) came out of the closet. People had the chance to read, discuss, and deliberate various works from Karl Marx's *Das Capital* to Adolph Hitler's *Mein Kampf*, all of which were also translated into Turkish. Freedom of expression and association led to the establishment of many voluntary groups, which organized to propagate ideologies, which spanned a large spectrum from various shades of socialism to conservatism, racism, ethnic nationalism, and religious extremism. The party system of Turkey changed its character from the two-party or predominant party structure of the 1950s to multiparty format of the 1960s and the 1970s.

However, the country also experienced an increased tendency of fragmentation of the voting blocs along ideological, sectarian, and ethnic lines. The increased pace of social mobilization further led to the emergence of many, small, and relatively well-organized, disciplined yet illiberal groups. The squatters in and around the major cities provided fertile ground for such groups to gain control, establish patronage networks, and mobilize masses. The fragile Turkish democratic system came under the stresses and strains of illiberal groups, often propagating against democratic principles, procedures, and institutions. The established political parties were compelled to seek the support of such groups, which polarized the party system further, as the main powerhouses vied for the votes on the fringes of the ideological spectrum. The fragmented voters started to change sides from one election to the other, often opting for the highest bidder in getting better services and favors to their settlements. The volatility of the voters increased in the 1970s, which contributed to the development of unstable coalition governments, and the overall instability of the party system.[97]

The political regime of the 1961–1980 era also had to function with a constitution, which one of the leading parties of the system, the AP had never considered as legal and legitimate. The antimilitarist stand of the AP always considered the 1961 Constitution of Turkey as the product of a CHP-led military conspiracy against the DP government of the 1950s. It was another irony that the champion of the Periphery, the AP, defended the 1924 Constitution designed by Atatürk and close associates of the former Center, and ironically the party that Atatürk founded and led, the CHP, defended the 1961 Constitution and disowned the 1924 Constitution. However, the dilemma was that people continued to vote for the AP in the 1960s and the late 1970s, which placed the AP in government, which in turn necessitated that the AP implemented a constitution, that it failed to believe to be legitimate. Therefore, it was no surprise that Turkey slid into a political legitimacy crisis par excellence, when the country was ruled by AP governments that did not feel bound by the very constitution through which their very existence and claim to government were justified. Democracy degenerated into a game of voting arithmetic, and the distribution of the emoluments of the national budget and state jobs through patronage networks.

Leaders and their political parties who ruled Turkey in the 1961–1980 era propagated to reform the political system in many, usually contradictory, and disparate ways. They all seemed to be pitted against the political and/or the economic regime of the country, and all vied for power to change, what they had deemed to consider as illegitimate, some practice or structure of the political or economic regime of the country. CHP was against the economic regime (*Bozuk Düzen*), the AP was against the political regime (the 1961 Constitution); the MSP and MHP were pitted against both the economic and political regimes. It looked as if there was one common ground that all of the main political parties agreed upon: opposition to the "established order (*düzen*)." However, they fully disagreed over what to change and how to change it. It is great wonder that with no major political party to stand for both the economic and democratic regimes of the country, and with so much disagreement over the fundamentals, that some form of liberal democracy did survive until 1980.

While people seemed to have supported multipartyism, elections, and such institutions of representative democracy as the national legislature,[98] they also failed to support the laws of the land. In fact, at a time when all of the political parties, leaders and the political elites showed a disdainful predisposition toward the constitution or the laws of the land, why would or should people have any respect for the laws? Most wanted exemptions and favors contrary to law, such as land titles for the plundered state land of the squatters, conversion of forest areas to agricultural fields or grazing land for their animals, and the like. Neither democracy nor rule of law seemed to have much chance of survival between 1961 and 1980.

Now, the military government of September 12, 1980 was to grapple with all those anomalies in Turkish society, economy, and politics. The military set out, for the third time to devise a new political regime for Turkey that would cure all the socioeconomic and political ills of the country. In the next chapter of the book we examine the military at the helm of government and the transition back to democracy for the third and the last time in Turkey.

5

The Third Republic (1980–)

The Praetorian Guard at Work

The coup of September 12, 1980 was the last of the three coups that deeply influenced the substance and style of politics and governance in contemporary Turkey. Both the 1971 ultimatum and the 1980 institutional military coups were carried out by the military as "corrective measures" to remedy the ills of the coup of the young officers in 1960. The trial and sentencing to death of the Chief of General Staff of the Armed Forces, General Rüştü Erdelhun in 1961, and the purges of 4,500 officers in 1960–1961 left an indelible ominous mark in the minds of all officers who came to serve as the commanders of the Turkish military forces afterward[1] providing a model of action for the military command to follow after the coup.

The 1980–1983 military government was primarily concerned with establishing law and order and tried to put an end to sectarian, ideological, and ethnic violence ravaging the country. The military authorities immediately set out to suppress all left- and right-wing associations in Turkey. The excessive use of force, expedient, swift work of the courts, and stiff sentences and death penalties produced by the military tribunals brought the "reign of the terror associations" to an abrupt end. The military government was quite efficient at establishing law and order within a year of the coup of September 12, 1980.[2]

Second, they established a new form of government, which resembled the earlier example of the MBK and the Constituent Assembly of 1960–1961. The military commanders established a National Security Assembly (Milli Güvenlik Konseyi, MGKo), which consisted of the commanders of the Army, Air Force, Navy, and Gendarmerie, and presided by the General Chief of Staff General Kenan Evren, who also became the Head of State. The MGKo substituted the suspended Turkish Grand National Assembly (TGNA) as the supreme political decision-making body of the military regime.

The MGKo searched for a suitable candidate among the civilian politicians for the role of the Prime Minister (PM), but none was found. Hence, the MGKo opted for the recently retired Commander of the Navy, Admiral Bülend Ulusu as the PM of their new government, which consisted of a combination of technocrats of the previous era, retired bureaucrats, and generals. The economy of the country had become too industrialized and modernized to be managed by military fiat alone. Furthermore, the Turkish business community and their foreign partners needed to be assured of competence of the government. Hence, the MGKo decided to devolve most of its powers to civilian ministers in charge of the economy in a division of labor. The technocratic civilians managed the economy, while the military managed all other affairs of the state. The military government continued the economic policies of the previous civilian government, liberalizing the economy. The performance of the economy improved in the same period.

Third, the MGKo declared the former 1961 Constitution null and void. Eventually, the MGKo established a Consultative Assembly, which drew up a draft constitution,[3] which, after some modifications, was approved by the MGKo. The new Constitution was then subjected to a popular referendum in 1982, where an overwhelming 90 percent of the electorate participated, and the "yea vote" amounted to 92 percent of the valid ballots.[4] Hence, the military revised the constitution of the country once again, and Turkey

Table 5.1 National Election Results (1983–2002)

Election Year	Vote and Seat Shares (%)	Political Parties*										
		ANAP	HP SHP CHP	MDP	DSP	DYP	RP FP SP	MÇP MHP	AKP	HADEP DEHAP	GP	Indep.**
1983	Votes	45,1	30,5	23,3	–	–	–	–	–	–	–	1,1
	Seats	53,0	29,2	17,8	–	–	–	–	–	–	–	0,0
1987	Votes	36,3	24,8	–	8,5	19,1	7,2	2,9	–	–	–	0,4
	Seats	64,9	22,0	–	0,0	13,1	0,0	0,0	–	–	–	0,0
1991	Votes	24,0	20,8	–	10,8	27,0	16,9	***	–	–	–	0,1
	Seats	25,6	19,5	–	1,6	39,5	13,8	***	–	–	–	0,0
1995	Votes	19,6	10,7	–	14,6	19,2	21,4	8,2	–	4,2	–	0,5
	Seats	24,0	8,9	–	13,8	24,6	28,7	0,0	–	0,0	–	0,0
1999	Votes	13,2	8,7	–	22,2	12,0	15,4	18,0	–	4,7	–	0,9
	Seats	15,6	0,0	–	24,7	15,5	20,2	23,4	–	0,0	–	0,6
2002	Votes	5,1	19,4	–	1,2	9,5	2,5	8,4	34,3	6,2	7,3	1,0
	Seats	0,0	32,4	–	0,0	0,0	0,0	0,0	66,0	0,0	0,0	1,6

Notes: In the table "Votes" refer to the percentage of the national vote the corresponding party obtained in the elections. "Seats" refer to the percentage of the National Assembly seats the corresponding party received as a result of its vote share.
"–" refers to non-existence of the corresponding party at the time of the elections. For example CKMP eventually became MHP.
* Only those political parties which have coalition or blackmail potential (Sartori, 1976: 121–125) are included in the table. Political party names in the table are as follows: ANAP (Motherland Party, *Anavatan Partisi*), HP (Populist Party, *Halkçı Parti*, which merged with a social democratic party to form the SHP by 1985), MDP (Nationalist Democracy Party, *Milliyetçi Demokrasi Partisi*, merged with ANAP in 1986), SHP (Social Democrat Populist Party, *Sosyal Demokrat Halkçı Parti*, which merged with CHP after it became legal again in 1995), CHP (Republican People's Party, *Cumhuriyet Halk Partisi*), DSP (Democratic Left Party, *Demokratik Sol Parti*), DYP (True Path Party, *Doğru Yol Partisi*), RP (Welfare Party, *Refah Partisi*, banned by the Constitutional Court in 1998, participated in 1987, 1991, and 1995 elections), FP (Virtue Party, *Fazilet Partisi*, banned by the Constitutional Court in 2001, participated in the 1999 elections), SP (Felicity Party, *Saadet Partisi*, participated in the 2002 elections) MÇP (Nationalist Toil Party, *Milliyetçi Çalışma Partisi*, merged with MHP after it became legal again in 1995), MHP (Nationalist Action Party, *Milliyetçi Hareket Partisi*), AKP (Justice and Development Party, *Adalet ve Kalkınma Partisi*), HADEP (People's Democracy Party, *Halkın Demokrasi Partisi*, which participated in the 2002 elections in alliance with DEHAP), DEHAP (Democratic People Party, *Demokratik Halk Partisi*), GP (Young Party, *Genç Parti*). For the ideological characteristics of the parties see figure 5.2.
** Column consists of the vote share of the nonparty or independent candidates.
*** MÇP participated in the elections in alliance with the RP, and under the RP banner.
Source: Erol Tuncer, *Osmanlı'dan Günümüze Seçimler: 1877–1999* (Ankara: Toplumsal Ekonomik Siyasal Araştırmalar Vakfi (Tesav) Yayınları, 2002): 329–335, Official Gazette (Resmi Gazete) November 10, 2002, no.: 24932: 39.

adopted the third constitution and political regime of the country became operative as of 1982.

During the referendum the people also approved of the Presidency of General Kenan Evren. President Evren became the first and the last popularly elected Head of State of Turkey. Soon after the referendum, the military government scheduled the multiparty elections to take place on November 6, 1983. The 1983 National Assembly elections were more like the 1946 elections, which were neither fair, nor free. Only three political parties were permitted to take part in the 1983 elections. The military government played a major role in the establishment of the Populist Party (*Halkçı Parti*, HP) and the National Democracy Party (Milliyetçi Demokrasi Partisi, MDP). Turgut Özal established the Motherland Party (Anavatan Partisi, ANAP), which was reluctantly permitted to take part in the 1983 elections by the military authorities, and won the majority of the seats in the TGNA (see table 5.1).

The military government had screened the founding members and candidates of ANAP, and used their veto to impede some from participating in politics. The former powerful organizations of CHP, AP, MHP, MSP, and the like, were all banned. Their newly established "cousins" were also vetoed and failed to take part in the 1983 elections. Turkey went back to some form of multiparty politics in 1983. However, the new regime of Turkey had to perform under the constant pressure of legitimacy crises, fragmentation of the vote, and increasing potential for protest participation.

THE MULTIPARTY REGIME OF THE THIRD REPUBLIC

If the objective of the 1961 Constitution had been to enable liberal democracy to function in Turkey, the objective of the 1982 Constitution was a complete reversal. The main objective of General Evren and associates was to render the Turkish political system stable, while keeping a façade of democracy. They were of the opinion that Turkey was faced with yet another existential challenge by its Soviet neighbor in the 1970s and the early 1980s,[5] believing that the communists had been plotting to divide Turkey up from the middle of Anatolia into an "eastern" and a "western" Turkey. The east of Turkey would rise up against the central government and be ready to signal the Soviet Army to come to their help and "emancipate them." The leftist activism in Turkey was there to undermine the national solidarity of the country. The Kurdish nationalist activism was hiding behind the smokescreen of the socialists and the communists to divide the country into two.[6] Evren and his colleagues seemed to conclude that the cure for such an existential threat was to "strengthen the state," which had been rendered frail by the former, liberal political regime, coalition governments, and amoral politicians who mismanaged the economy to their benefits. The way forward was to create a regime in which the executive branch of government reigns supreme under the command of a President, who would act with full impunity and with a view of the collective interest of the realm as his objective, unfettered by judicial, legislative, or any other control or accountability.

The most distinctive feature of the 1982 constitution has been the institution of the Presidency. However, that should not mislead the reader that Turkey has a form of semi-presidentialism somewhere along the lines of *Gaullist* paternalism in France, or that of Putin's supremacy in Russia. Turkey still has a parliamentary regime, with a President who is elected for a single seven-year term by the TGNA.[7] All of that is so parliamentarian in nature, however, that should not deceive anyone. If the French Constitution of 1958 were designed for General de Gaulle to reign supreme in France, the 1982 Constitution was designed for General Evren to act likewise in Turkey. Turkey's President is devoid of any political and legal responsibility for his or her actions, except for treason, yet is entrusted with enormous authority to act in all matters political, legal, economic, and so on (art. 105).

The original design[8] of political regime of the "Turkish Third Republic" is designed to have a legislature subservient to the executive, that is only nominally controlled by the legislature, a judiciary strictly monitored and even harnessed by the Ministry of Justice (executive), an omnipotent, yet legally and politically irresponsible, and hence arbitrary Presidency, and a concomitant docile civil society, largely apathetic toward politics. It seems to constitute a hybrid of parliamentary and semi-presidential regimes, and thus best deserves to be called "semi-parliamentary." A prominent student of Turkish state and public bureaucracy Metin Heper argued that "the 1982 Constitution, not unlike the French Constitution of 1958, locates the sovereignty of the Turkish state in the Office of the President."[9] Hence, what differed the Turkish President of a semi-parliamentary regime, from the French President of a semi-presidential one is that the former has no political responsibility and accountability, while the latter is accountable to the voters, for the French Presidents are elected by popular vote, while the Turkish Presidents, except for General Kenan Evren, are elected by the TGNA, yet are not accountable to that institution or any other political body. Consequently, the Turkish Presidents seem to "have a cake and eat it too," and resemble "Greek Gods," rather than Head of State and top executive of a parliamentary regime.

If there was any principle underlying the pristine form of the 1982 political regime in Turkey, it might safely be called the legal norm of "executive supremacy as strong state." For a country that had started to build its political system under the dire circumstances of the War of Liberation of 1919–1922 on the legal norm of "national sovereignty" as embedded in the institution of the national legislature and upon the legal norm of "legislative supremacy," the 1982 regime constitutes quite an ironic development. It is also ironic that, though Turkey made sweeping amendments of its 1982 Constitution after 1995, the Presidency, with all of its arbitrary powers has been left unscathed.

THE POST–1982 PRESIDENCY

In the late 1980s, a pattern of electing party leaders as President emerged when PM Özal became President, and was repeated with his sudden death in

1993 by PM Demirel. The office of the Presidency thus became immersed in partisan political affairs, and even emerged as an alternative center of decision-making to the government. Such a tendency appeared under Özal's Presidency and the ANAP governments. Both as the PM and later the President, Özal was inclined to govern through bypassing what he regarded to be the laggard, conservative, and cantankerous bureaucratic environment of the "Ankara establishment." He did not stop short of establishing his own entourage of special advisers, who were neither elected nor formally appointed as bureaucrats, yet they designed and executed policies through bonds of fealty and loyalty established with Özal, until his death. The press popularly referred to them as the "princes" of Özal. Such a development looked strikingly close to the Hamidian style of rule of a century ago (1877–1908), and it might thus be properly referred to as the emergence of a neo-patrimonial style of rule called "neo-Hamidianism" in Turkish politics.[10] The election of a Constitutional Court judge as the President in 2000 reverted the country back to formalism and tilted the system much closer to a parliamentarian regime. However, the dangerous potential of political meddling and arbitrary rule through the Presidential authority still persists thanks to the constitutional design of the Office of the President.

THE 1982 CONSTITUTION: INSTITUTIONS OF A STABLE ORDER

A second striking feature of the 1982 Constitution was its complete reversal of the status of the formerly independent or autonomous institutions. The independence of the judiciary had been a continuous matter of complaint of the former democratically elected PM Demirel and the AP, who had considered the judiciary as the bastion of the CHP and leftist forces in Turkey. The AP had argued that the "national will" was compromised with the power of the judiciary, especially of the Constitutional, the High Administrative, and the High Appeals Courts. Mr. Demirel and other spokespersons of the AP argued that the program and policies of their governments rested upon the "National Will," demonstrated at the polls. However, once they start to execute their popularly supported policies, the opposition appealed to the courts, and the judges were quite ready to strike down the laws, regulations, and policies of the AP-dominated TGNA. Ironically, such criticism seemed to have eased the way for the military government to curtail the powers of the judiciary in the 1982 Constitution.

In the 1982 Constitution no great latitude was entrusted to the judiciary. The promotion of the judges and public prosecutors was also put under the authority of a council presided over by the Minister or Undersecretary of the Ministry of Justice.[11] The recruitment procedures of the members of the Constitutional Court were altered. The procedure of the 1961 Constitution was that High Courts elected most members of the Constitutional Court, whereas the 1982 Constitution changed the recruitment process to exclusive appointment by the President (art. 146). The power of the Constitutional

Court was also curtailed.[12] The deliberation of the Constitutional Court of a constitutional amendment from the perspective of its procedural propriety rather than the substance seemed to have severely undermined the powers of the Court. State security court system was also introduced as a constitutional institution (art. 143).

In spite of all those changes in the political regime of the country the office and role of the prime minister and his cabinet, as well as his role as the leader of the largest party group in the TGNA were fully preserved. Hence, under normal circumstances, the PM sets the political agenda, and determines top-level bureaucratic appointments, though with the approval of the President. The PM also has the last say in the substance of policies, laws, regulations, and statutes that make the executive branch of the government function. The de facto influence of the President's office increases at times of governmental crisis. Otherwise, the PM is still the most influential and critical political office of the land. Hence, the parliamentary nature of the political regime is preserved, yet with important intrusions of Presidential power.

Political organizations and parties were also put under strict control of the agencies of the state. In its original form the 1982 Constitution stipulated that the political parties were not allowed to form such auxiliary bodies as youth or women's branches, which formerly they could freely form under the 1961 Constitution. The political parties were to be free of any association with any trade unions, business groups, corporations, foundations, cooperatives, and voluntary associations; and would be prohibited from receiving donations from them (art. 69). The trade unions of the country were also treated in the 1982 Constitution at length, for they had such a major role to play in the 1970s. The 1982 Constitution stipulated that the trade unions shall not pursue any political cause, engage in political activity, receive support from political parties or give support to them, and shall not act jointly for these purposes with associations, public professional organizations, and/or foundations.[13]

The 1982 Constitution in its original form stipulated that anyone has the right to form associations without prior permission, and also that associations shall not pursue political aims, engage in political activities, receive support from or give support to political parties, or take joint action with labor unions, public professional associations and/or foundations (art. 33).

Finally, one of the most striking novelties of the 1982 Constitution was the addition of compulsory religious and moral education under the supervision and control of the State, in the elementary and secondary schools of the country (art. 24). For the first time ever in the Republican era religious and moral instruction at elementary and secondary schools were incorporated in the Constitution of the land, and made compulsory for all students. The 1982 Constitution introduced this "novel" idea as part of freedom of conscience. It sounds like a contradiction that freedom of conscience is to be achieved through compulsory education through a "State controlled" instruction. Such a formulation seems to be a product of the thinking that religious extremism and political Islam emerges out of ignorance and ill instruction of religious beliefs and dogma. If they could be instructed in an "enlightened manner," students will learn the "correct" content of religion and would never be prey to the propaganda of religious extremists and revivalists.[14] It is such an irony that it was under the regime of the 1982 Constitution that Islamic revivalist parties and politicians came to power since 1996, serving as PM and Cabinet Ministers, and the popular support of such parties showed a stellar increase at the polls since the 1991 national elections.

A new electoral law was adopted for the 1983 National Assembly elections, which though revised many times, preserved its essential features over time. The 1982 Constitution abolished the Senate, and thus the TGNA reverted back to the former unicameral form. Hence, the electoral laws were amended to exclude Senate elections and redraw new rules for the elections of the only and lower chamber of the TGNA. According to this new law, the metropolitan electoral districts of *Ankara, Istanbul, İzmir, Adana, Bursa,* and so on, are divided into several less populous electoral districts. The rural and sparsely populated provinces of the country have all been preserved as single electoral districts. The electoral formula slants the representation of the population in favor of the rural and agricultural interests of the country by assigning one seat per province irrespective of the size of its population,[15] which rewards less populous and rural provinces, then allocate the remaining seats of the National Assembly in proportion to size of the population in electoral districts. Hence, in the 1983 elections 67 seats of the TGNA were distributed to provinces irrespective of their size, and the remaining 333 seats of the 400 seats of the TGNA were allocated on the basis of the size of the voter population per electoral district in the country.[16]

The law aimed at implementing proportional representation (PR) in converting votes to seats per electoral district, yet in addition a 10 percent national threshold was stipulated, such that if a party fails to receive at least 10 percent of the national vote, it would not be seated in parliament. The basic tendency of the previous electoral formula used in the 1961–1977 elections, which rewarded the party with the most votes was also preserved, and the national threshold, which had previously been declared as unconstitutional by the Constitutional Court, was now reinstalled in the system. Curiously enough, the Constitutional Court of the 1980s failed to find the incredible national threshold of 10 percent a violation of the 1982 Constitution. No amendment of the election law struck down the degenerative 10 percent national threshold, which results in undermining the representativeness of the elections, and disenfranchises many voters, and in the 2002 elections it finally helped to exclude the choice of a staggering 45 percent voters out of the TGNA!

THE 1982 CONSTITUTION AT WORK

In 1983 Turkey reverted back to democratic elections and multiparty politics with a political regime in which civilian politicians had no say in the drawing up of its rules. Morally and politically the civilian and elected politicians of the country felt unattached to, and unbound by the 1982 Constitution. No single party emerged to defend, adopt, or identify with the 1982 Constitution. In fact, the two parties set up by the military government in 1983 failed to survive more than a couple of years after the 1983 elections. When President Evren declared his dislike for ANAP right before the November 6, 1983 elections, the electorate rejected his tutelary predisposition, and signaled that they desired a fast return to multiparty, civilian rule, with the Motherland Party (ANAP) of Özal winning the most votes (45 percent) and controlling the majority of the seats in the TGNA.

Soon after the 1983 elections new left- and right-wing parties emerged to participate in the local elections of 1984. The ANAP government under PM Özal took steps to further liberalize the Turkish economy and institutionalize free market capitalism. An important piece of legislation undertaken by the ANAP government was the establishment of the metropolitan municipalities (Act No. 3030), which established a new tier of government at the metropolitan centers of Turkey. They were officially called the Greater City Municipalities. They were endowed with enhanced powers to provide municipal services to rapidly growing city populations of Istanbul, Ankara, Izmir, and Adana. The central government devolved some of its powers on land development and construction, property and environmental tax collection, and partially on transport authority to the mayors' offices in those cities.[17] The metropolitan city mayors started to control large budgets, allocate large funds, and distribute large resources, such as land and rent across many interests in their cities.[18] Local politics became a major part of the power game in the country. New political figures made careers out of their service as mayors of cities, large and small. For example, Tayyip Erdoğan, the leader of the Justice and Development Party (AKP), who became the PM of Turkey since March 2003, had served as the mayor of the "Greater Municipality of Istanbul" between 1994 and 1998.

The banned parties of the *ancién regime*, such as the CHP, AP, MSP, and MHP, could not be reestablished under the same names until the constitutional amendments of summer 1995. In the meantime, they were all organized under different names and leaders, for their previous leaders were also banned from politics for ten years as of 1982. Hence, HP soon found itself surrounded by competitors for the hearts and votes of the left-of-center voters in Turkey. The Social Democrat Party (SODEP) was legally established in 1983 by the rank-and-file and some of the front bench of the former CHP. Concomitantly, Bülent Ecevit, the former leader of CHP, who felt deserted by his former CHP comrades, established his own Democratic Left Party (DSP) through a proxy, Rahşan Ecevit (Bülent Ecevit's wife), for he was banned from politics at the time. When it became clear that HP enjoyed little chance of survival, it merged with SODEP and a new party emerged: Social Democrat Populist Party (SHP) in 1985, which eventually merged with the reestablished CHP after 1995. However, Bülent Ecevit and followers continued to serve within the ranks of the DSP, which experienced a stellar rise to power in the 1990s, and a similar dramatic and fast fall from power in the early 2000s.

A similar trajectory of the rightist parties emerged as well. They were split between the newly established ANAP, which claimed to be a totally new party, combining the nationalist, conservative, liberal, and social democratic traditions in Turkish politics into one big movement and party, and the new party of Süleyman Demirel and his close followers, the True Path Party (DYP).[19] In spite of ANAP's claim to embrace all of the four major currents of ideological thought in Turkish politics, the voters increasingly perceived it as a right-of-center party.[20]

Consequently, both the left-of-center and the right-of-center each have been occupied by two competing parties, incessantly clashing with each other over the control of the same turf, while they competed with their opponents to their right and left. In the meantime, the former MSP had been reorganized as the Welfare Party (RP), though Necmettin Erbakan, the former party leader, could not lead the organization at its inception, due to the political ban imposed upon him. Similarly, the ethnic nationalists established the Nationalist Work Party (MÇP) in place of the MHP of the 1970s. Again, the former leader Alpaslan Türkeş failed to lead the party for he also was banned from political activity. A popular referendum on the political ban of the leaders of the *ancién regime* took place in 1986, and barely over 50 percent of the people voted in favor of lifting the ban. All of the former leaders could return to their previous posts in their new parties and run for public office in the 1987 elections.

The military government of 1980 had imposed the ban on party names and politicians to eliminate the cliques of the "old guard" of the Turkish political parties.[21] They had hoped that once the older generation of politicians was eliminated, younger and hopefully less corrupt politicians would emerge to replace them.[22] In part such a substitution of the old guard with the new elite occurred. However, the old guard turned out to be much more resilient than the military had anticipated in less than a decade. They came back with great success to reclaim their positions in Turkish politics. Both Süleyman Demirel and Bülent Ecevit returned to their former posts as party leaders, and eventually, as Prime Ministers. Necmettin Erbakan, who in the past could not even come remotely close to being the PM, became so in 1996. Only the late Alpaslan Türkeş failed to serve as a PM, though his party, the ultranationalist MHP eventually became the second largest party in Turkey for a while in the National Assembly elections of 1999, after his death.

The political ban on party names and politicians created many complications in Turkish politics. The ban disrupted the political socialization of the young voters in Turkey. Turkish population grew by about 2.5 percent per annum in the 1960s and 1970s, which meant that there were a large number of voters who were approaching age 21, the legal age for voting at the time, and vote for the very first time in the 1983 elections. Previously, parents, families, or even large lineage groups had been identified with the CHP and its main rivals DP or AP in the country, which used to share about 80–90 percent of the national vote among them.[23] However, in 1983 neither CHP nor any of its rivals were around. The HP and the MDP were identified as the stooges of the military, and the ANAP seemed to be somewhat civilian, yet hard to identify as a left-of-center party, or a simple continuation of the DP–AP tradition. Many of the first time voters failed to get any clear signal from their parents or peer groups.[24]

In the 1987 elections, the confusion further deepened. The pardoned old guard made a come back, but they established brand new parties, which failed to clarify the complicated picture of the party system in the eyes of the voters. Now at each strategic location of the left–right spectrum emerged two or more competing parties, which seemed to stand for the same ideas, values, and programs, and vied for the votes of the same bloc of voters. The competitor parties seemed to only differ with respect to leaders and their entourage. Under those circumstances it became increasingly difficult to develop any identification with political organizations, which failed to give a clear picture of what they stood for. Most young voters failed to develop any party identification, and the older voters started to lose theirs. Consequently, independent voters who drifted from political party to party, though not necessarily across the full extent of the left–right spectrum emerged in large numbers.[25] The volatility of the voters increased while party identification seemed to dip to new lows.[26]

In the meantime, the number of effective parties, that is, parties which could form the government alone or in coalition with other political parties, or that could influence the outcome of elections and change the distribution of the vote increased from four in the 1970s, to six in the 1970s and to seven in the 1990s.[27] This development also indicated that the national vote further fragmented into many voting blocs, thus causing fragmentation of the party system as well. The 10 percent national threshold, originally intended to encourage voters to rally around two or three major parties, and discourage them to vote for the radical, extreme right and left-wing small party organizations of the past, failed to work. The military rulers of Turkey who had implanted the 10 percent national threshold in the election law had failed to comprehend that such a legal constraint mattered only when highly institutionalized parties with large numbers of card-carrying members, followers, and sympathizers functioned in the party system. Even then, for such a legal constraint to have a desired psychological effect on the voters, other additional constraints, such as party identification would be needed. Party identification is an emotion that would normally inhibit the voters from altering their choices, abandon their parties and veer toward the other parties. Any good that had been expected of the high national threshold was pretty much cancelled out with noninstitutionalized parties with very few identifiers.[28] The voters seemed to focus their attention, hopes, fears, and expectations on the political leaders of the new parties. Personalities of the leaders began to loom larger than the political organizations they established or lead.[29]

The vacuum created by the withering away of the older patronage networks created new challenges. The former Center–Periphery *kulturkampfs* started to fragment into further religious and ethnic voting blocs, on the one hand, and various patronage networks established around blood-ties and regional bonds, on the other.[30] Cultural characteristics that had been ignored for many years or previously of diminishing importance reemerged to divide the voters into new blocs,[31] including divides between Turkish versus Kurdish ethnic nationalists, Turkish civic nationalists versus Turkish ethnic nationalists, *Alevi* versus Sunni brotherhoods, secular versus *Şeriatçı*[32] voting blocs (favoring Islamic law).[33]

The former (1961–1980) ideological cleavages of socialist and social democrat versus liberal-conservatives dissipated due to two main reasons, one of which was domestic, and the other international. The first reason mainly consisted of the dismal performance of the CHP at the helm of government. The CHP government of 1978–1979 had been severely criticized for cajoling 11 deputies from the ranks of the AP parliamentary group. The hopes of those who had thought that the CHP could deliver law and order, as well as economic growth were dashed by 1979.

In addition, the military government of 1980–1983 persecuted anyone who had been involved with any socialist or social democratic organization or party in the 1960s and the 1970s. Large numbers of intellectuals, students, artists, and politicians who had been involved in leftist politics were imprisoned for long periods of time, even when no charges could be pressed against them, or fled Turkey, and took refuge abroad, mainly in Germany. The military government effectively liquidated the left-of-center organizations, eradicated their patronage networks in the major *gecekondu* districts of the metropolitan areas and their rural tentacles, and thus rendered the left incapable of mobilizing the masses for a long time to come. Worst hit was the CHP, which lacked the political culture and readiness to cope with a ban imposed on it by the very "State" with which it had always cooperated and represented in the past. Its organization crumbled and fell. The party leaders and rank-and-file could never get over the shocks of 1978–1979, and of the ban and the mistreatment of the military government of the early 1980s.

Second, the international developments of the early 1980s further undermined the appeal of socialism and social democracy in Turkey. The Soviet Union and the Warsaw Pact countries started to show signs of trouble and even dissolution. The Solidarity Union had made a big impact on Polish politics and beyond. Soon after it emerged in Gdansk, General Jaruzelski came to power in Poland through a military coup in 1981. However, the more important developments were still to come with the introduction of *glasnost* and *perestroika* in the Soviet Union. The idea of reform clearly indicated that Marxism–Leninism was not what the Soviets purported it to be, that is, the perfect system on the road to the future emancipation of humanity from alienation. Otherwise, why would a "perfect system" need any reforms of openness (*glasnost*) and restructuring (*perestroika*)? However, worse news was still in the making. On December 31, 1991 the Soviet Union collapsed. What the Turkish Marxist–Leninists had so much sacrificed for turned out to be a corrupt and unsustainable system! All shades of leftist ideologies suffered dearly from persecution of the 1980s at home, which debilitated the leftist political organizations as patronage mechanisms, and the collapse of Marxist–Leninist states abroad.[34]

In the meantime, in Europe major changes toward liberal market economy and privatization began to take shape. In 1979 Margaret Thatcher led Tories to power in Britain. Almost a year later Ronald Reagan won the U.S. Presidential elections. The message was clear: Private Sector-dominated market economy was in, state enterprises and nationalized companies were out! Turkey was not too far off the mark, when on January 24, 1980 PM Demirel decided to veer toward market reforms and announce the end of price controls and import-substitution policies.

In short, the left-of-center parties were decimated by the early 1980s. The downfall of their organizations, networks, and erosion of their capability to mobilize the *gecekondu* dwellers created a vacuum. It did not take long for the religious revivalists, and ethnic nationalist Kurds and Turks to fill in the vacuum. The military authorities had calculated that they could use the revivalists to counter and suppress the "challenge of the communists." The irony was that, the "Kemalist" military government of the 1980–1983 seemed to have played a major role in undermining the "secular left" and implanting the "Islamic revivalist" and "ethnic Turkish nationalists" in their place among the downtrodden of Turkey by the 1980s. It is small wonder that the Islamic revivalists and the ethnic Turkish nationalists made their indelible imprint on the government of Turkey in the 1990s and beyond.

Whether by design or default, five voting blocs became discernable by the 1990s, which are carried over into the twenty-first century. One such bloc seems to consist of the Kurdish ethnic nationalists, which emerged in the 1980s and gained stability and visibility through both conventional and protest participation in domestic politics.

Another is the secular bloc, which often overlaps with Turkish civic nationalists, most of who are nominally Sunni Muslims, who consider Turkish identity as a "national identity" that transcends beyond and above ethnic identities that exist in Turkey. According to such a perspective on national identity, the gist of national bond between the Turkish citizen and the Turkish state is a legal–political bond, which is often self-defined by the free will of the citizen.

The third bloc consists of the sectarian voters of the religious community of the *Alevis*, who also overlap with the former secular bloc on most political issues. They had been around for a long time. In the past they had been assumed to be staunch supporters of the CHP, yet no reliable data exists to extend empirical proof to that such a claim is totally valid.

The fourth bloc consists of the pious Sunni Turks, who belong to the *Hanefi*, and pious Sunni Kurds who mainly belong to the *Shafi* School of Law. They constitute another sectarian, religious bloc. They seem to demand that religion and religious morals and law (*Şeriat*) play a dominant role in society and politics, but at the same time they also seem to stand for increased economic freedom, less taxation, and selective government subsidies to promote their businesses. Some students of Turkish politics have suggested that their understanding of "*Şeriat*" is probably no more than the moral principles of Sunni Islam and respect for the ceremonial practice of religion, with few legal or political connotations, if any.[35] However, it is very difficult to extend the same argument for those who pious Sunnis vote to represent them in the TGNA.

The fifth bloc consists of the ethnic Turkish nationalists, who consider Turkish identity as acquired through birth. Hence, for the ethnic nationalists "Turkish" identity is fully determined by blood-ties and lineage that travels back to the Central Asian origins of the "Kayı" and other Turkish tribes that migrated to Anatolia in the eleventh century.

More than a single party emerged per electoral bloc, while their political fortunes have been erratic over time. Consequently, the number of effective political parties, which impacted on the outcome of the competition for the hearts and minds of the voters oscillated over time.[36] So, what explains the changing fortunes of the political parties, governments, and intra and extra-parliamentary opposition to them in the Third Turkish Republic?

POLITICAL FORTUNES OF THE PARTIES IN GOVERNMENT

Weak institutionalization of the political party organizations, low party iden-tification, and the political bans and suppression at the hands of the military government of the 1980s have already been suggested as some of the factors accounting for the "musical chairs of parties" in government in Turkey. The political regime and the legal system of the country also constitute another destabilizing factor, contributing to the volatility of the vote in Turkey. Indeed, the Public Prosecutors sued many political parties since 1983, and the Constitutional Court found large numbers of them guilty of various breaches of the Political Parties Act or of the Constitution, banning them from political activity. Although 18 political parties have been banned by the Constitutional Court in the last two decades,[37] the most famous cases were the Islamist Welfare and Felicity Parties, the former of which was prosecuted while in government, and both of which were banned for their anti-secular activities, which the Constitutional Court decided to be a threat to the dem-ocratic regime in Turkey.[38] However, after each decision to ban a political party, new political organizations with very similar aims and personalities have been established. The Political Parties Act defines such action as illegal, and often the Public Prosecutor sued the new parties with ties to the formerly banned ones. In short, the legal regime has also been a factor that deter-mined the fortune of political parties. We should hasten to add that not all political parties have been equally influenced by the zeal of the Public Prosecutors as parties with Şeriatçı, Kurdish ethnic nationalist, Marxist–Leninist credentials have been much more at risk of suffering from a legal ban than the others.

Another factor that contributed to increases in volatility of the vote has been the inability of the governing political parties to manage the macro economy in Turkey. Whenever asked what they considered to be the most pressing problem of the country, the voters consistently declared that infla-tion, unemployment, and economic instability constitute the major problems of the country. Poll after poll revealed that no less than three fourths of the voting age population mentioned economic mismanagement as the most pressing problem of the country. However, no government managed to make any progress in harnessing the high inflation rate between 1983 and 2002.

After every election the TGNA members are inundated with voters, who line up to prove their credentials as supporters of the party that won the most votes in the elections.[39] Their foremost demand is for employment by the state,[40] since such jobs provide low salaries but immaculate job security and many fringe benefits. Under a very old legal regime dating back to Ottoman times, which defines the status of state employees, it is virtually impossible to fire a state official. Even when fired, they have the right to appeal to the Administrative Courts, which demand the firing authority to prove that their decision is not arbitrary or partisan. Most state employees, even when fired for inaptitude, economic recession, and so on, are often reinstituted at their old offices by the lenient Administrative Courts. The pitifully low salary levels could be complemented through various fringe benefits, from almost free housing to paid summer vacations in "educational facilities" of the state agencies. Additionally, opportunities for kickbacks, commissions, and gifts for services provided to interested company exist in most state enterprises and Ministries. PM Turgut Özal argued that the low salary rates of the state employees do not matter, for "my state officials know how to get by." Consequently, in the eyes of the voters landing a job in a state enterprise as a "state official" is a prime reward.

Political parties, especially when they participate in the government, control jobs for public employees and often provide additional job opportunities in local government offices under their control. They also control multibillion dollar budgets of state investments and bids. Those voters who make the right kind of calculation often rush to become card-carrying members of the political parties, which seem to enjoy the highest chance of winning the next election.[41] Patronage or expectation of pecuniary rewards for electoral support at the polls have often led to increased voter volatility, in a political milieu of weak party identification, that would normally inhibit such oscillations of the voters' choices.

However, the reader should not be led to think that vote has been subject to wild swings across the left–right spectrum (see figure 5.1). To the contrary, attitudes toward religiosity and identity often acted as the main parameters, and make vote swings rather limited to political parties that shared common cultural images across the left–right spectrum.[42] Most voters tended to shift their choices among competitors, such as the CHP and DSP on the left, and the ANAP, DYP, MHP-RP or FP, on the right for a while.

In recent times two electoral realignments occurred. One was in the 1970s, when the voting patterns drastically shifted in favor of the CHP.[43] A second major realignment of the vote in the mid-1990s, during the 1995 National Assembly elections, when for the first time in the Republican era a party with clear ties to religious orders with "Şeriatçı" credentials managed to get a plurality with 21 percent of the national vote (see table 5.1). The Turkish

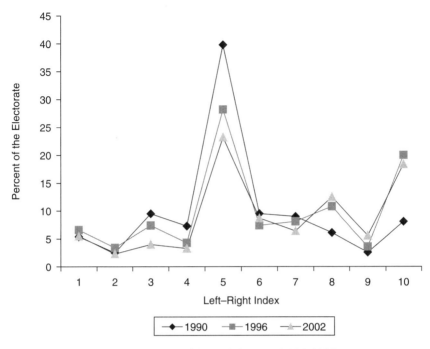

Figure 5.1   The Left–Right Spectrum of the Turkish Voters (1990–2002)

Note: The distributions of the Figure are constituted from the self-placement of the voters on the Ten-Point Left–Right Spectrum where "1" indicates extreme left, and "10" indicates extreme right.

Source: Ersin Kalaycıoğlu, "Elections and Party Preferences in Turkey: Changes and Continuities in the 1990s," *Comparative Political Studies*, vol. 27, no. 3 (October 1994): 415; Ersin Kalaycıoğlu, "The Shaping of Party Preferences in Turkey: Coping with the Post–Cold War Era," *New Perspectives on Turkey*, no. 20 (Spring 1999): 58; and Ersin Kalaycıoğlu, "Electoral Realignment or Protest Vote: November 2002 Elections in Turkey," (unpublished paper presented at the Annual Convention of the International Studies Association, Portland, Oregon, U.S.A., February 25–March 1, 2003): 3.

voters started to vacate the center of the left–right spectrum, which they had occupied for decades[44] moved sharply to the right.[45] Indeed, by the mid-1990s an unprecedented 20 percent of the electorate declared that they considered themselves on the extreme right (10 out of 10 on a left–right spectrum, where 1 stood for extreme left and 10 stood for extreme right) (see figure 5.2). The incapability of the left-of-center parties to manage the affairs of the country when in government, the suppression of the left by the military governments, and the downfall of Soviet Union and socialism in the world seems to have paved the way for the stellar rise of the "revivalist *kulturkampf*" in Turkish politics.

Consequently, political parties that had been occupying a marginal status in Turkish politics, below the national threshold of 10 percent enormously benefited from the shifting allegiances of the Turkish voters. Turkey also came to be dominated by a chauvinistic, xenophobic, ultranationalist ideological climate.[46]

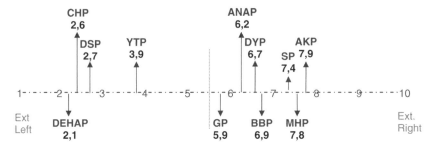

Figure 5.2   Political Parties in the Eyes of the Voters (October 2002) (The average score of each party assigned by the voters)

Note: The numbers that appear immediately below the party acronyms stand for the average response given by the voters during October 2002 to the question "On the following ten point scale where '1' stands as extreme left, and '10' stands for extreme right, please indicate where each of the following parties stand?" Therefore, it is not wrong to assume, where each party was perceived as standing on the left–right spectrum in the eyes of the Turkish voters right before the November 3, 2002 elections.

Source: Ersin Kalaycıoğlu, "Electoral Realignment or Protest Vote: November 2002 Elections in Turkey," (unpublished paper presented at the Annual Convention of the International Studies Association, Portland, Oregon, U.S.A., February 25–March 1, 2003): 4.

The voters seemed to have also gone over an additional ideological threshold by supporting ultranationalists, and "Islamic revivalist" parties, a shift that also seemed to have roots solidly entrenched in the international affairs of the end of the Cold War and the "New World Order."

A NEW WORLD ORDER: CLASH OF IDENTITIES

In the 1980s the bipolar international system started to experience severe crises, which eventually led to the collapse of the Warsaw Pact in Eastern Europe and to the implosion of the Soviet Union in 1991. In the meantime, Turkey experienced several crises emanating from its neighbors. In the mid-1980s The Bulgarian Communist leadership decided to impose a policy of Bulgarization over its Turkish minority, forcing Turks to change their family names from Turkish to Bulgarian or face persecution. Many Turks of Bulgaria were imprisoned, tortured, or killed, and many more suffered as Turkey started to protest the Bulgarization policy. Eventually, in 1989 the Turkish government declared its willingness to accept all Turks of Bulgaria wishing to take refuge in Turkey. Over the summer of 1989 the Bulgarian government forcefully evicted more than 300,000 of its one and a half million Turkish minority to Turkey.[47]

Turkey found itself confronted with a severe immigration problem. Those who could track down their relatives eventually set up camp in their houses, yet most others were initially settled at hastily established refugee camps in Thrace and elsewhere in the country. The Turkish refugees of Bulgaria were both a blessing and a curse for Turkey. The Turkish labor market experienced a sudden influx of relatively well-educated professionals from Bulgaria, though not all could find jobs. However, the Turks of Bulgaria were used to operating in a centrally planned economy. The challenge of adjusting to a market economy turned out to be too difficult to handle for most of them. A large plurality of the immigrants consisted of farmers. It seemed as if they had the anticipation of finding some farmland where they could be settled as farmers. They soon realized that such an abundance of vacant farmland does not exist in Turkey, and most had to settle in the cities. When Bulgarian communism collapsed soon after their arrival in Turkey, about half of the immigrants decided to go back to their old farms in Bulgaria. Those who stayed on in Turkey were able to establish links with their Bulgarian cousins and some started commercial ties between the two countries. Hence, at the end of the day, the outcome of the tragedy of the Turks of Bulgaria in the 1980s turned into mixed blessing for them, and for both Bulgaria and Turkey.[48]

The persisting problems of Greece and Turkey over the Aegean and Cyprus continued in the 1980s and the 1990s. The two countries had developed a completely opposite understanding of the status of the Aegean Sea, their continental shelves, territorial waters, and corresponding national air spaces. The presence of 120,000 Turks as Greek citizens in the western Thrace, which neighbors Turkey, also further complicated Greco-Turkish relationships. Excessive control and pressure exerted on the Turks of Greece by the Greek government (which considered them as Muslims without any ethnic identity), resulted in various malpractices, such as loss of Greek citizenship when they traveled to Turkey, or prohibition on the sale of their property to Turks, which precipitated Turkish governments to monitor the status of the Turks of Greece closely.[49]

The Treaty of *Lausanne* had earlier established three miles of territorial waters for both Greece and Turkey in the Aegean Sea. However, in the 1960s the two countries had negotiated a change in the extent of the territorial waters from three to six miles. Since 1960 Greece had been involved in oil explorations on the continental shelf of the Aegean Sea and early signs indicated that there could be some oil deposits there. The imminent find of oil precipitated an interest by Turkey, which is also an oil importing country, in the explorations of oil underneath the Aegean Seabed in the 1970s.[50] However, such a Turkish initiative presented a new problem for both countries.

The Greek government started to argue that the continental shelf of the Aegean belongs to Greece, while Turkey argued that it should be considered as international waters. The dispute was referred to the Security Council of the United Nations (UN), which decided in 1976 that the parties to the conflict should find a diplomatic solution to it through negotiations.[51] Dissatisfied with the UN resolution the Greek government appealed to the International Court of Justice, which decided that it has no jurisdiction over the matter. Eventually, the representatives of the two governments met in Switzerland and agreed not to make any attempts at drilling for oil while the dispute continues.[52] However, the conflict was not put on ice. In 1987, when the PASOK government of *Andreas Papandreou* calculated that the international circumstances were ripe, for Turkey was gearing up to apply for full membership in the European Union (EU), of which Greece was already a member, Greece restarted drilling for oil in the northern Aegean. Turkey warned the Greek government, and when rebuffed decided to flex its military muscle, and the two countries came very close to war.[53]

In the meantime, the Greek government assiduously worked to arm the Greek Islands of the Aegean Sea, which Turkey considers as a blatant violation of the Treaty of *Lausanne* (for that treaty stipulates that the Aegean Islands be demilitarized and disarmed), and Turkey established and beefed up its Fourth Army in western Anatolia in response.[54] Simultaneously, the Greek government stepped up its efforts to increase the Greek territorial waters to 12 miles, which with so many Greek islands on the Aegean would turn the sea to a Greek lake and convert almost all of the present international waters to Greek territorial waters.[55] Turkey not only resisted the Greek initiatives, but also declared that such a declaration would be *casus belli* (cause of war). In the meantime, Greece participated, signed, and ratified the new International Maritime Treaty of the United Nations in the 1990s, which honors 12 miles of territorial waters for the participants. However, Turkey is still not a party to that Treaty, and legally speaking, the Treaty does not bind Turkey. However, Greece considers the Turkish recalcitrance toward accepting the International Maritime Treaty of the United Nations as an indication of Turkish callousness toward international law.[56]

In the meantime, Greece has been following a revolutionary practice of "conic air space" since 1931 in the Aegean, which is not accepted by any other state, including Turkey.[57] Furthermore, Turkish and NATO warplanes, which patrol the Aegean Sea, continue to fly between six miles of "internationally recognized, legal Greek air and territorial space" and the ten miles of air space declared as "internationally unrecognized, yet Greek declared air space." We should also add that both air forces often engage in dogfights over the Aegean, and on at least two occasions Turkish and Greek jets crashed since the 1980s. Similarly air and naval forces have been modernized and beefed up to render Turkish deterrence toward a Greek *fait accompli* of revising its territorial waters in the Aegean Sea credible. Hence, the gist of Turkish foreign policy toward Greece has become containing and deterring revisionist Greece bent upon undermining the status quo, as Turkey perceives it, in the Aegean Sea.[58]

The southern and eastern neighbors of Turkey also presented her with various challenges. In the 1980s Iraq and Iran had been at war, while Syria and Israel were fighting over the control of Lebanon. The Iran–Iraq war was both a perilous development and an opportunity for improving commercial ties with both countries for Turkey, while preventing further encroachments of Iranian activities to export its form of Islamic government to Turkey. Both Iran and Iraq used Turkish companies to import their needs from abroad. In that process Turkey built the largest fleet of trucks in Europe, which at one time increased to beyond 40,000.[59] The roads, gas stations, lodging facilities, catering services on the road from Turkey to Iran and Iraq, in particular in the southeastern parts of the country improved with leaps and bounds. Trade with Iran, Iraq, and the rest of the Middle East also blossomed. Turkish exports to the Middle East increased to 23 percent of all of Turkish exports right before the Gulf War of 1990.[60] However, weapons of mass destruction at the disposal of Iraq became too dangerous for Iran to prolong the war. In 1988, Iran offered a ceasefire to Iraq, which had also grown weary of war after about eight years of fighting. A ceasefire was brokered soon after some negotiations, though both countries continued to import military and civilian goods through Turkey until Iraq's invasion of Kuwait in 1990.[61]

Turkey was one of the first countries to impose an embargo on Iraq when that country invaded Kuwait, and trade with Iraq came to a standstill. The service economy of the southeastern Turkey, which had blossomed due to increased trade with Iraq experienced a sudden shock. A few months after the imposition of the embargo, the Gulf War of 1991 occurred, and the coalition of forces led by the United States liberated Kuwait, and defeated the Iraqi army. Although Saddam Hussein's government had weapons of mass destruction, which had been wielded against the Iranian army and against the rebellious Kurdish communities in their own country in the recent past, Iraq did not resort to use of biological or chemical weapons during the Gulf War. However, a few Scud missiles with conventional payloads were fired at Israel and Saudi Arabia, yet none were wielded against any other neighbor, including Turkey. However, in the aftermath of the Gulf War of 1991 Iraq failed to implement the UN resolutions concerning the obliteration of weapons of mass destruction effectively and efficiently. Consequently, the embargo imposed upon Iraq continued, and so did its dysfunctional effects on the Turkish economy.

In the meantime, Saddam Hussein's government exacted a high price for those religious and ethnic communities, which showed their hatred for the dictatorial practices of the *Ba' athi* regime. The Shi'ite Muslims in the south and the Kurdish tribes in the north became targets of the wrath of Hussein in Iraq. The Iraqi army was deployed to punish the Kurds and large groups of Kurds fled northern Iraq and took refuge in Turkey and Iran. Close to half a million Kurdish men, women, children, and elderly appeared almost overnight at the southern borders of Turkey. They had fled with almost no food, and with whatever they could carry on their backs. It was not only a pitiful sign of human tragedy, but Turkey was faced with a severe challenge of providing shelter, food, and livelihood for half a million refugees.[62]

Refugee camps were set up almost instantly, yet the sheer number of refugees overwhelmed Turkey. The resources at the disposal of the country were not sufficient to deal with the gush of hungry, poor, and sick people who took refuge in Turkey. To make matters worse, Turkish police authorities discovered that members of a gang, which had been waging terror against Turkey since August 15, 1984 also infiltrated the migrating masses and penetrated the refugee camps and eventually established themselves in the countryside of southeastern Turkey in relatively large numbers. Sifting through the camps for terrorists created further problems. Nongovernmental organizations and the media, particularly the foreign media started to level severe criticisms of the Turkish government's handling of the refugee problems. Under mounting pressure the Turkish government requested the American led coalition forces to declare a "safe haven" for Kurds in the north and Shi'ites in the south of Iraq to facilitate the return of the Kurds and Shi'ites back to their homes under the protection of the coalition forces. The U.S. base near *Adana* at Incirlik, Turkey was allocated for patrolling the northern skies of Iraq by the United States, British, and French warplanes in 1991, from which the French pulled out shortly afterward. These "no fly zones" and the "safe havens" practices continued until the invasion of Iraq in April 2003 by the U.S. led coalition forces. A huge majority of Kurds eventually returned to their homes in the north of Iraq, yet a small number of them settled in southeastern Turkey. However, the *Partiye Karkeren Kurdistan* (Workers' Party of Kurdistan, PKK) terrorists stayed on in southeastern Turkey to fight the Turkish security forces.

The PPK was established as an illegal organization in Turkey, on November 27, 1978 to fight for an independent state for Kurds, and that is why it called itself as a "party of Kurdistan."[63] The leader of the party is a citizen of Turkey by the name of Abdullah Öcalan, who came from a very humble family background in the southeast of Turkey. His education was sponsored by the scholarships extended to him by the Turkish state. He was an undergraduate student at the Faculty of Political Science of Ankara University, when he established the PKK as a Marxist–Leninist party to fight for the "national liberation" of the Kurds. The PKK was involved in a rather parochial armed struggle against tribes and landlords of Siverek, Urfa area in southeastern Turkey between 1978 and 1980. Öcalan and associates fled Turkey after the military coup of 1980 and took refuge in the *Bekaa* valley of Lebanon, under the protection of Syria.[64] Owing to the close relations between Syria and the Soviet Union in the 1980s, the Turkish security establishment considered the PKK as a tool of the Soviet conspiracy to drive a wedge through Turkey.

The PKK made a strong comeback in 1984. A small band of PKK terrorists, trained and equipped in the Beka'a Valley, infiltrated Turkey and attacked the security forces in the small town of Eruh of the southeastern province of Siirt on August 15, 1984.[65] They stayed in control of the town for a while and pulled out and vanished soon after. The gendarmerie and the police forces that tried to pursue the PKK band failed to capture them all. Similar attacks continued to ravage the southeastern countryside. The PKK bands attacked several military outposts, police stations of small towns, and villages, which failed to cooperate with them. The PKK terror campaign resulted in 1,500 dead and many more injured between 1984 and 1991. Most of those who died seemed to be the terrorists perpetrating the attacks and the innocent civilians caught in the middle of armed struggle. However, in the aftermath of the Gulf War of 1991 the firepower and the influence of the PKK increased with leaps and bounds. The death toll between 1991 and 1999 increased by twenty folds to 30,000 and many more were injured or crippled.[66] It is obviously warranted to ponder about why such a development occurred.

THE CURSE OF THE GULF WAR

The Gulf War, collapse of the Soviet Union, and the end of the Cold War coincided in 1991. The joint impact of the post–Gulf War Iraq and the end of Cold War played a major role in the havoc the PKK wreaked on Turkey in the 1990s. The end of the Gulf War left an embittered *Ba'athi* regime in Iraq, while the policy of "safe havens," a product of the Turkish government, effectively curtailed the power and control of Hussein's government over the north and south of his country. The Iraqi lack of control on the north of Iraq enabled the PKK to deal with the Kurdish tribes headed by Jelal Talabani of Patriotic Union of Kurdistan (PUK) and Mesud Barzani of Party of Democratic Kurdistan (PDK), who were bent upon establishing their own territorial sovereignty, and thus, they could not or would not systematically resist another Kurdish independence movement. In the relative safety of the power vacuum created in the north of Iraq, the PKK effectively organized training camps and other facilities, obtained heavy weapons left over by the Iraqi army, which had hastily pulled south of the thirty-seventh parallel, and acquired new weapons from their Arab and European mentors, such as Iraq, Syria, Greece, and Germany. It became widely believed among the Turkish political elite that EU, led by Germany, was behind the PKK.[67] Soon after the Gulf War of 1991 the PKK and Greek generals as advisers started to use antipersonnel and antitank landmines from Iraq, Syria, Germany, and Italy,[68] shoulder mounted rocket propelled grenades, antitank and antiaircraft missiles, AK-47 rifles, and weapons specifically designed to perpetrate assassinations. Soon enough, the PKK had the means to attack not only military barracks and police stations in southeastern parts of Turkey, but wreak havoc all over Turkey and attack Turkish missions all over the world.

The post–Gulf War and post–Cold War international and domestic conditions provided the PKK with an excellent opportunity to recruit new members by the droves. The prolonged embargo on trade with Iraq had brought the burgeoning service economy of the southeastern parts of Turkey to a standstill. Alexis de Tocqueville first realized the potential danger from the sudden bust of a booming economy,[69] where expectations of sustained improvement of well-being are disappointed, leading to social upheavals, and even social revolution.[70] Indeed that seemed to have happened in the southeastern parts of Turkey, thanks to the Turkish eagerness to impose and assiduously implement an embargo on Iraq, created sudden downturn of a previously booming economy, which precipitated conditions for social upheaval in southeastern Turkey. Worst yet, the impact of the embargo was not fully felt across Turkey, for the rest of the country continued to experience steady economic growth of 6.4 percent in 1992 and 8.1 percent in 1993. Only belatedly the economy had a severe u-turn in January–February 1994, and the economy shrank by 6.1 percent.[71] However, in 1992–1993 as the rest of Turkey was developing with leaps and bounds, the southeast seemed to be dismally lagging behind and suffering in a deep recession and skyrocketing regional unemployment.[72]

In the meantime, the PKK emerged to provide anyone willing to take part in its activities a meaningful salary, a steady job, and pay the family of the individual recruited into the organization, and compensate their losses if the person in question become disabled or died. Ironically, the PKK emerged as a source of employment for an increasingly alienated population, who were developing a feeling of being discriminated by the government policies in Turkey.

Similarly, the Turkish authorities provided employment for those who would work as "village guards" and defend their territory against the encroachments of the PKK. The population of the southeast had three choices confronting them as of 1991–1992: cooperate with the PKK, work for the Turkish authorities battling the PKK, or pack-up and leave their homes for the western parts of Turkey or Germany. Indeed many left, yet some cooperated with the PKK and some with the Turkish security forces, and for the next eight years the southeastern region of Turkey was declared as an emergency area, and in practice turned into a battleground.

By the mid-1990s the PKK and their sympathizers declared all Turks, Turkish authorities, and all who worked for Turkey or served in the Turkish army, which is a conscript army where all Turkish men above the age of 19 must serve for a certain period of time of their life, were "legitimate targets!" Bombings and assassinations spread throughout the country. All major cities became target for attacks.[73] Teachers, who instructed elementary or secondary school children in Turkish, midwives, nurses, doctors, and even engineers, and architects, who worked in various projects from dam building to road construction were killed by tens and hundreds by the PKK.

EUROPE'S CHOICE: KEEPING TURKEY AT BAY

In 1987 Turkey had applied for full membership into the EU, and earlier Turkey and the Common Market countries had signed the Ankara Treaty in 1963, which had foreseen a Customs Union between Turkey and the Common Market countries in the early 1970s. However, the international developments of the 1960s through the 1980s failed to contribute to such a development, and by the late 1980s most European Union (EU) countries started to perceive Turkey as more of a threat than a partner. A major concern was the inundation of the European job markets by unskilled Turkish workers, and the EU imposed visas to avoid the automatic application of the clauses of the Ankara Treaty, which would have enabled free movement of Turks across the EU as of the late 1980s. It took the EU two years to reject the Turkish application, yet the response of the EU was less than a full rejection. It reiterated that if Turkey were to meet conditions, which all other applicants had met earlier, Turkish membership would be possible. Hence, Turkey was considered as an eligible member, yet not an imminent one in the short-run.

The EU powerhouses had their priorities altered by the late 1980s. Turkish strategic partnership against the Warsaw Pact was no longer on the agenda. The no-longer communist East European countries could become new EU members with greater ease, and their integration into the EU would constitute a stability dividend for the EU and NATO. However, Turkey was too big (about 60 million people in early 1990s), too poor (with a GNP/cap of $2,500 in late 1980s), too complicated (with a Muslim population, a sharp regional imbalance, Kurdish nationalism, and political Islam), and too close to the United States as a strategic partner. The EU seemed to have resorted to a policy of keeping Turkey at bay.

The EU strategy was to require Turkey to take various steps to establish a democratic political regime, as well as market capitalism and welfare state policies at par with the EU members. In the meantime, Turkish membership was held at as a possibility of potentiality. The Turkish struggle with the PKK seemed to have been ideal for the EU to show how poor the Turkish human rights record is, and how troublesome Turkey would be as a candidate country. The media and the press of the EU member countries turned their critical focus upon Turkey, as the struggle with the PKK terror increased its intensity. The PKK began to receive semiofficial recognition in Greece, Germany, France, Sweden, Belgium, Netherlands, and Italy, through its affiliates, which acted as "cultural non-governmental organizations (NGOs)," while the same countries argued that they recognized the PKK as a terror organization.

THE RISE OF TURKISH ETHNIC NATIONALISM

Hence, Turkey suddenly discovered a large front of the NATO allies from Europe aiding the PKK in one way or the other, while Turkey was grappling hard with differentiating between Kurds and Kurdish nationalists, fighting the Kurdish nationalists, while sparing the Kurds. In the 1990s, as Turkey took dramatic steps to confront a domestic and international challenge for its territorial integrity, it tried not to till seeds of hatred between its ethnic communities, and exacerbate the problem further. The PKK precipitated a challenge, which seemed to have ethnic and racial overtones. The Kurdish nationalists argued that "Turkish identity" was not a "national identity." It was just an ethnic identity, which could only be at par with any other ethnic identity in Turkey, such as being a Kurd, Laz, Çerkes, Abhaz, Gürcü, Türkmen, and so on. Kurds could thus only be citizens of Turkey, but could not accept to be called a Turk, Turkish, or even Turkish with a Kurdish origin. Once pressured to question the meaning of Turkish identity, the rest of the country soon found itself engulfed in the debate over "who are Turks?"[74] The debate extended into the meaning of Turkish citizenship, and the century old debates of identity once upon a time formulated by Akçuraoğlu Yusuf, Ziya Gökalp, and others. The gist of the Kurdish nationalist argument was obviously "ethnic nationalist," which traced the roots of Kurdish identity to tribal groups, blood-ties, and lineage groups that "presumably" went back to the ancient Meds. The PKK established a television station called the Med-TV in Europe and broadcasts its programs into Turkey.

Turkish nationalism seemed to have two responses to the challenge. One is the classical argument originally formulated by Gökalp, which had eventually become the core argument of Atatürk. "Turk" is a "super" identity, which does not belong to any ethnic community, tribe, or lineage group. Anyone who "feels like a Turk is a Turk!" It is a self-adopted identity, which instills one with feelings of belonging to a land (patriotism), and history of a people, who speaks Turkish and enjoys Turkish cultural norms, values, and practices. The second, answer was a mirror image of the Kurdish ethnic nationalist formulation. Turkish ethnic nationalists argued that one is born a Turk, with Turkish blood running through his/her veins. The origins of the Turks are located in parts of Central Asia. Kurds are no more than another Turkish tribe, though they do not know it!

As the death toll from the armed struggle increased the ethnic nationalists on both sides started to gain more supporters. The stellar rise of electoral support for the MHP as the leading party of the Turkish ethnic nationalists, and the steady support for the Kurdish ethnic nationalist parties of DEP, HEP, HADEP, and DEHAP indicate of the support that the two points of view gathered in Turkey. Unfortunately, the ethnic nationalist perspectives on identity constitute a recipe for armed struggle for power. The other "ethnic nationalist" bloc is perceived as traitors, and thus treated as such. The civic nationalists have been increasingly ignored as representing an old recipe. Instead, another perspective on national integration was formulated with considerable amount of allure in the country. This time a nonnationalist, indeed an antinationalist ideology, which considers nationalism as a sin, propounded by the Sunni revivalists started to attract support from both the Sunni majority among the Kurds and among the pious Sunni Turks.[75]

The Islamic revivalist Welfare Party (RP) spokespersons began to argue that the overwhelming majority of the Turkish society, Kurds included, consists of Muslims. Indeed, most Kurds are Sunni Muslims, yet they believe in the teachings of the Shafi School of law, whereas most Turks belong to the Hanefi School. The Sunni revivalists argued that since most Kurds are staunch believers in Sunni Islam and vigorously practice it, they should join the ranks of the Sunnis, and shun away from the sin of nationalism of ethnic nationalists. Hence, the integration of the Turkish society could now be forged through rallying around Sunni Islam, if only the secularism of the Republic is somehow eroded or pushed into the background. The RP spokespersons even went so far as suggesting the resurrection of the *millet* system of sorts by accepting separate laws, legal systems per faith or religious school of law. Indeed, the RP started to obtain vast amount of votes from the pious Sunni Kurds in the 1991 and the 1995 elections.[76] It was banned soon after, yet its successor Virtue Party (FP) was also able to garner similar support at the polls from the pious Sunni Kurds. Eventually, when FP was banned, its frontbench and followers split into two parties, the Felicity Party (SP), and the Justice and Development Party (AKP). Indeed, both SP and AKP seemed to have received similar support from pious Sunni Kurds in the 2002 elections, though the latter managed to do far better than the former at the polls.[77]

Secular, civic nationalist, and *Alevi* communities failed to rally around a single party as the left-of-center parties hardly managed to obtain more than one, third of the national vote in any of the national elections since 1983. The Turkish voters shifted their allegiance away from the moderate, civic nationalist, liberal, and even conservative political parties, toward ethnic nationalist and/or Sunni revivalist political parties and organizations. As we have earlier argued, the political mood of the country began to possess increasing amount of xenophobia, chauvinism, and patriotism. If the challenge leveled by the PKK was one factor, the developments of the "New World Order" constituted another major factor.

As of the early 1990s Turkey discovered itself in the hub of sweltering ethnic and religious conflicts of many shape and guises. The collapse of the Soviet Union resulted in the clashes between the Abkhaz and the Georgians, the Georgians and the Ossets, the Chechens and the Russians, the Armenians and the Azeris in the Caucasus to the immediate east of Turkey. All of those tribal groups had blood relations to pockets of voters and citizens of Turkey. The Abkhaz minority of Turkey started to pressure the Turkish governments to support their independence movement from Georgia. However, Turkish national interests seemed to require that Georgia be kept insulated against Russian meddling not least as Georgia constituted the gateway to the east, where another Turkish nation-state, Azerbaijan lay, but also the Turkish communities of the newly emerging Turkic states of Central Asia. The Russian attempts at slamming that door shut on the face of Turkey by supporting Abkhaz rebels was highly detrimental to cultural, economic, and political solidarity of the emerging Turkish world. As a result, Turkish national interests necessitated that Georgia maintain its territorial integrity, and independence from Russian influence. The Abkhaz rebellion constituted a severe danger to Georgian independence. Consequently, the Turkish government has been trekking a very narrow road with little latitude in its policy toward Georgia.[78]

Similarly, the Armenians and Azeris went to war over Nagorno-Karabakh, which had been a part of Azerbaijan in the twentieth century, and under Soviet rule, yet populated mostly by Armenians. As early as the 1980s the Armenians of the Nagorno-Karabakh demanded union with Armenia. Azerbaijan declined to accept any such loss of territory. The two countries became embroiled at war. Turkey had its own severe problems with the ethnic nationalist Armenians in the past, and would now rather establish peaceful relations with Armenia. However, in the Armenian–Azeri war, Armenian occupation of Azeri territory and a huge refugee problem suffered by the Azeris, with who Turks have mutual deep cultural ties, virtually rendered any rapprochement between the newly established independent Armenia and Turkey impossible. Turkey recognized the independence of the new Armenian state, yet stopped short of establishing diplomatic relations and regular contact through border gates on land.[79] In practice, Turkey continues to impose an economic embargo on Armenia, until a peace treaty is negotiated between that country and Azerbaijan.[80]

In the meantime, as relations with Bulgaria improved, the Yugoslav crisis erupted in 1991. The German and eventual EU recognition of the status of

Slovenia as a new independent state brought about the dismemberment of the federal state of Yugoslavia, and undermined the fundamental norm of the Helsinki Accord of 1975 that the borders in Europe are inviolable. This was a new and devastating development for Turkey. Turkey was a signatory of the Helsinki Accord of 1975. If the "inviolability of borders" in Europe is no longer to be recognized by the EU, what was Turkey to expect?

The impression that the Turkish public got was that the EU was recognizing the PKK as the legitimate "representative" of the Kurds in Turkey, and was thus supporting division of Turkey, more or less similar to the disintegration of Yugoslavia. The Turkish reaction to these developments was also deeply influenced by the images of cantankerousness and callousness of the European response to the "ethnic cleansing" campaigns of the Yugoslav and Serb armies in Bosnia-Herzegovina of the Muslim population as "Turks."

Indeed, the Bosniaks are Slavs, who converted to Islam under the reign of the Ottomans. They were the relatively well to do when the Ottomans invaded Bosnia in the fourteenth and fifteenth centuries. The landowner Slavs tended to convert to Islam to cultivate closer links with the Ottomans. The landless peasants continued to stick to their Orthodox religion. Over the centuries the Bosniaks were identified as the vestiges of the Ottoman past in Bosnia. Since Serb Orthodox had referred to Ottomans as Turks, they considered the Bosniaks as Turks, or the residue of Ottoman–Turks in the area.[81] Thus, when the Bosniaks were cleansed by the Serbs as "Turks" there was strong popular pressure in Turkey for the government to take effective action against the Serbs. The diplomatic initiatives of the Turkish governments were neither able to stop the bloodshed in Bosnia, nor were deemed strong enough for the taste of the Bosniaks and their supporters in Turkey.

Hence, by the mid-1990s it looked as if Turkey was coming under attack from Syria and Iraq by means of the PKK, by a revisionist Armenia demanding territory, and the EU through the support it provided for the PKK. Turkey began to develop a siege mentality by the mid-1990s. The political elites and the masses alike started to dig their heels into the ground and show their resolve to fend off all forms of revisionism directed at Turkey. Similarly, it was small wonder that an upsurge of patriotism, ethnic nationalism, chauvinism, and xenophobia occurred in the mid-1990s.[82]

THE FIGHT FOR SOLIDARITY

The clash of identities led to a showdown between the Kurdish and Turkish ethnic nationalists. The increased firepower of the PKK was met by the Turkish army, which started to use warplanes, tanks, and heavy artillery against the PKK hideouts in the countryside. Eventually, the Turkish army changed its tactics. Housing the soldiers in their barracks and garrisons unless they were to be involved in antiterror operations provided the PKK with targets to launch sudden raids. Now, the Turkish army, with the aid of the village guards recruited from among the local Kurds, started to become mobile, extend its operations throughout the eastern parts of the country, and deployed troops across the entire countryside around the clock. This tactic turned to be very effective. The army pursued the PKK bands wherever they went, constantly keeping them under pressure, while providing no obvious targets for the PKK to hit. Eventually, the Turkish army started to make "hot pursuits" beyond the southern borders of Turkey into Iraq, and established a "*cordon sanitaire*" inside Iraq to seal off the border with Iraq from the incursions of the PKK from the south in 1996,[83] which increased the pressure on the PKK bands in the countryside even further.

The PKK also changed tactics and organized protest rallies in the urban areas of Turkey. They were able to create more material for the media, and occasionally wield "*molotov* cocktails" (firebombs), and other weapons to burn establishments, and terrorize the inhabitants of urban centers in the western parts of the country as well. Occasionally, even the burgeoning tourist centers of Turkey were threatened by the PKK spokespersons. However, their urban campaigns met with little success.

In the meantime, the rural population of southeastern Turkey confronted a huge dilemma. The PKK demanded shelter, medicine, and food from them, and if refused they punished the villagers by burning their houses, killing them, or even bombing their villages. If they did provide the PKK with food, medicine, and other needs, then the Turkish authorities started to interrogate, arrest, and imprison them for their involvement in seditious activities and committing treason.[84] Finally, the Turkish authorities decided to evacuate the villages where the PKK could receive logistic supplies. The inhabitants of hundreds of villages were forcibly evicted from their settlements, and most found their ways to big cities of the southeast and other parts of the country.[85] When the countryside came under the effective control of the Turkish army, and the logistic lines of the PKK were severed, the PKK started to lose ground in the countryside. However, the last and the final step that ended the warlike conflict came in the summer of 1998.

General Atilla Ateş, the Commander of the Turkish Army, insinuated in a speech he delivered at Hatay that unless Syria stops harboring the leader of the PKK, Turkey should consider applying "all options" on Syria.[86] The same message, with a relatively more severe tone was reiterated by the PM Mesut Yılmaz, in which he argued that Turkey would consider going to war with Syria to capture the PKK's leader Abdullah Öcalan.[87] On October 1, 1998 President Demirel reinforced the message in his speech on the occasion of the opening of the annual session of the National Assembly.[88] It was at that time that the Turkish press started to announce that Greece had signed alliance accords with Syria and Armenia. In the Turkish press editorials started to appear, which argued that the Turkish armed forces should gear up for a two-and-a-half wars, that is simultaneously going to war with Syria, Greece, and the small state of Armenia, if necessary. Within the next two months the Turkish second army, with 250,000 troops started to redeploy about 10,000 troops toward the Syrian border. Syria, with no fortifications to the north, and with troop concentrations toward Israel in the south and about 35,000 elite troops in control of Lebanon, seemed to be in no shape to meet the Turkish challenge.

Syrian President Hafez Assad was in poor health at the time, yet he had to deal with the Turkish challenge. It looked as if Syria also had to deal with two-and-a-half conflicts, with Israel, Turkey, and Lebanon at the same time. According to the Syrians the Taurus mountain range and the Hatay (Antioch) province of Turkey should have been allocated to the historical territory of "Syria."[89] Damascus never accepted the plebiscite of 1938, which allotted Hatay to Turkey and in political maps of Syria, Hatay was always shown to be an integral part of Syria. In 1997 and 1998, although Kurds had never lived in Hatay, and Kurdish nationalists could not have made any historical claims to the area, the PKK had even started to attack construction sites, manufacturing plants and other "targets" in Hatay. It was in Hatay that the Turkish soldiers and PM made the declarations that Turkey is getting ready to go to war with Syria in late 1998.

One should not overlook the role of another burning issue between Turkey and Syria, which had been the waters of the river Euphrates.

Syria and Iraq had made the claim that the Euphrates and Tigris were "Arab rivers," and belonged to "Arab Mesopotamia" since the 1960s and objected to Turkey building 22 dams and several hydroelectric plants, and constructing pipelines to irrigate higher elevations, as part of a major agricultural and economic project called the "Southeastern Anatolian Project" (GAP). Syria seemed to have been trying to wield terrorism through the services of the PKK to halt Turkish efforts at GAP.[90]

Turkey, Syria, and Iraq had been negotiating the use of the waters of Euphrates and Tigris rivers since the 1970s, when Turkey started to build its first dam, Keban on the Euphrates. The issue at hand is the amount, and the quality of water that flows south from Turkey and Syria into Iraq. If Turkey only uses its dams to power hydroelectric generators, the water will flow to the south unhindered. However, if pipelines could be built from the dams to irrigate large swathes of land to be utilized for cash crops, then the quality of water flowing to the south may deteriorate. Syria and Iraq came to believe that, under those circumstances, insufficient amount of good quality drinking water could flow into their territories.

Obviously part of the problem arises from the very way the Syrian authorities themselves think and act, and assume all along that the same mentality and action plans would be followed by their Turkish counterparts. For example, the Orontes river originates in the mountains of Lebanon, then flows east and north, and eventually bends westward and flows, or we should say used to flow, into the Hatay province of Turkey and eventually into the Mediterranean. However, Syria built seven dams on the Orontes, which have, starting in the 1990s, blocked the waters of Orontes from flowing into Turkey during the summer months.[91] It is not too difficult to imagine whether the Syrians started to ponder what would Turkey do with the Euphrates?

Indeed, in the late 1980s Turkey seemed to be getting the chance. In 1987 Turkey notified Syria and Iraq that due to the construction of the

Atatürk dam built on the Euphrates, Turkey could halt the waters of Euphrates for three months to fill the lake of that dam. Turkey and Syria negotiated a protocol, which committed Turkey to providing no less than 500 cubic meters of water per second to Syria during those three months.[92] However, during January 13 and February 12, 1990 Turkey completely cut-off all water flow to the south.[93] The Syrian and Iraqi governments loudly protested, and so followed the Arab League.[94] Arab governments had been threatening to boycott any company doing business in the development of the GAP, and pressured international banks and other governments from lending credit to Turkey to build dams on the Euphrates and Tigris rivers. So much international activity and hostility toward Turkey seemed to have emerged from a deep-rooted lack of trust in the minds of the Syrian and Iraqi elites of their Turkish counterparts. This was, in part, a self-fulfilling prophecy. They seemed to have acted in sheer distrust, callousness, and even hostility, and they expected the same in return. A technical issue, such as how much clean water was to be allocated to Syria and Iraq in an environment of distrust got out of hand, and precipitated long periods of hostility and fostered an acrimonious environment, which even led to the speculations of war.

In short, in the 1990s Syria and to a lesser extent Iraq seemed to be following a policy of threatening Turkey with terror and Kurdish nationalist insurgency, in return for concessions on the development of GAP. Turkey declined to negotiate under those circumstances. The logic followed by Turkey was simple. If terror could be effectively wielded to wring certain concessions out of Turkey on the water issue, then all adversaries of Turkey would wield the same weapon of terror, whenever they needed to extract concessions out of Turkey. However, as soon as the Turkish threat of war led to the extradition of the PKK leader Abdullah Öcalan from Syria, Turkey started negotiations with Syria. In the Police Recreation Center at Seyhan, Adana a treaty was negotiated and signed, and eventually ratified by the two countries, which have put the two on the road to negotiations to settle their differences through diplomacy.[95]

The Turkish threat of war seemed to have paved the way for improved relations. Syria had always denied that PKK had camps in Syria or in the *Bekaa* Valley in Lebanon under Syrian control, and that the leader of the PKK was under Syrian protection. However, on October 12, 1998 the foreign minister of Egypt, who was sent to Turkey to negotiate a settlement with Syria announced that Abdullah Öcalan was no longer in Syria, and the PKK camps were all closed, and PKK activists are put on trial.[96] Syrians had finally admitted that they were culprits in the PKK action against Turkey, and that they were wielding the "weapon of terror" against Turkey.

The relations between the two countries took a u-turn, similarly as had the relations between Bulgaria and Turkey in the aftermath of the collapse of the Communist regime in Bulgaria. Currently, both Turkish–Syrian and Turkish–Bulgarian relations are conducted on similar friendly and neighborly manner. Hostilities between those two neighbors and Turkey seemed to have ceased to exist.

In the meantime, the PKK leader Öcalan sought refuge in a number of countries. He first showed up in Italy. Turkey asked for his extradition. The Italian government refused, on the grounds that Turkey still had the death penalty, while Italy had abolished the death penalty more than a previous decade. Turkish diplomatic pressures and domestic uproar against Italy started a civic movement to ban all sales of Italian goods in Turkey. This led to a new design for the shop windows for all Benetton shops in Turkey, which were covered with the Turkish flags and huge posters, claiming that all products on sale at the Benetton shops in Turkey were produced in Turkey. Italian–Turkish relations and economic ties were severely strained. Soon Öcalan was sent abroad to Russia, and eventually to Greece. However, neither country held on to him for long. Soon he surfaced in the Greek Embassy in Nairobi, Kenya. Turkey started to exert diplomatic pressure on Kenya for Öcalan's extradition to Turkey. On February 15, 1999 the international news agencies reported that Abdullah Öcalan was abducted by the Turkish authorities in Kenya and was on his way to Turkey. Within hours, Turkish PM Ecevit appeared on the media to confirm the news and that Öcalan would be incarcerated in a prison on the island of İmralı in the Sea of Marmara, until his trial. His capture almost instantaneously resulted in the collapse of the PKK organization in Turkey. Some armed groups took refuge in northern Iraq, where they still were when war erupted between the U.S led coalition forces and Iraqi government of Saddam Hussein in 2003, and in the aftermath of the war when the U.S. led coalition forces occupied Iraq. Sporadic fighting continued, however, with no more than a few clashes and casualties per year between 1999 and 2005. In the meantime the PKK changed its title to KADEK and eventually to Kongra-Gel and then back to PKK again. In June 2004 the Kongra-Gel organization declared that its self-declared armistice is over, and it restarted terrorist attacks in the southeastern parts of Turkey. However, so far such attacks have failed to attract any popular support from the Kurds in the eastern provinces of Turkey. Turkey now seems to be veering closer to begin negotiation for full membership with the EU, and the Kurds seem to know full well that Turkish membership in the EU will provide them with economic and democratic opportunities, which they cannot obtain otherwise. Occasional clashes and armed conflict continue with few casualties on both sides occurring since 2004.

In the meantime, the State Security Court (DGM) tried Öcalan in 1999. EU circles reacted adversely to the composition of the judges, for one of them was a military judge. The TGNA swiftly acted on the matter and amended the 1982 constitution, and the necessary changes in the laws were made to substitute the military judge with a civilian. During his trial Öcalan admitted to organizing his gang to commit terror activities in Turkey and to many atrocities of his organization since the 1970s.[97] As expected, he was sentenced to death by the judges of the State Security Court.[98] The lawyers of Öcalan immediately appealed the decision of the Court. The High Appeals Court met with a jury of nine judges, who approved of the decision of the State Security Court. Then, the lawyers of Öcalan appealed to the European

Court of Human Rights (ECHR), which overturned the decision. The Turkish state appealed Öcalan's case with the ECHR, and it was referred to its Grand Chamber. The Grand Chamber of the ECHR decided on May 12, 2005 that the trial of Öcalan was unfair. Now the Council of Europe will decide upon whether Turkey needs to retry Öcalan if the Council of Europe decides so, a very sensitive period of retrial will unfold in Turkey. No government in Turkey views such a prospect with any favor, for Öcalan's trial will fan hostile attitudes and it will be a major challenge to political stability in Turkey.

In the aftermath of the hostilities, a major political outcome has been the establishment of ethnic Kurdish political parties, under various names and guises. They have become fixtures of the Turkish political party system and elections. They have been able to garner 4 to 6 percent of the national vote, and almost exclusively from the southeastern parts of Turkey.[99] It is an interesting fact that those parties obtain almost no votes anywhere else in the country, in spite of the fact that most Kurds live in western parts of the country now. So far, they have been regional or local ethnic parties, with no national appeal. However, they do make a major impact on the outcome of the National Assembly elections. They do not gain any representation in the TGNA, for they fail to get 10 percent of national vote required to win parliamentary seats. However, once their votes are eliminated, the next big vote getter in the southeast has been the Islamic revivalist parties. Hence, the performance of the ethnic Kurdish parties has boosted the representation of the Islamic revivalists in the National Assembly.

Emergency rule over the southeast of Turkey came to an end in 2003. Turkish governments have taken some steps to increase investment in the southeastern parts of the country and start economic recovery of the region, overtook, the Turkish economy was rocked by two major financial crises in 1999 and 2001 and fell into a deep recession in the early 2000s. At the same time, there has been increased openness to Kurdish expressions of identity. PM Demirel declared in Diyarbakır, a major settlement of the Kurds in Turkey, that the Turkish government recognized the "Kurdish identity" in the early 1990s. Kurdish daily and monthly publications appeared, and Kurdish songs and movies started to be marketed in the 1990s as well. They have been meticulously screened, and some have been confiscated and destroyed by the authorities for the messages they carried. The mouthpiece of the PKK the Med-TV has been on the air, transmitting via satellite from Europe and received by dish antennas in Turkey by whoever wishes to watch it. However, it took Turkey until 2003 to take any action toward permitting TV and radio transmissions in Kurdish to take place in Turkey. These moves by Turkey were deeply influenced by the Turkish resolve to become a full member in the European Union.

THE HARD ROAD OF COALITION POLITICS

Turkey took some bold steps toward becoming a candidate for full membership in the EU after 1996, when the Customs Union Treaty between the EU and

Turkey came into effect. However, the first attempt at deepening the relations between Turkey and the EU came to an impasse in December 1997. The domestic developments of Turkey were partly to blame.

The 1995 elections had led to a governmental crisis, in the midst of which Turkey and Greece came close to fighting another war over the disputed status of some rocks in the Aegean. The elections failed to create a clear winner. The RP got the plurality of the vote with 21 percent of the national vote, however, ANAP and DYP even got about 19 percent of the national vote each. The latter two occupied the same ideological spot in the eyes of the electorate (see figure 5.2) but the ideological proximity of the two parties failed to help them to work together. Each tried to eliminate the other and each treated the other party as "fake." Nevertheless, they established a coalition government but it collapsed after 114 days when the RP moved against the leader of the DYP, Tansu Çiller and accusing her with perjury and corruption. The ANAP failed to extend her its support, and the government collapsed.

Amazingly, the RP and the DYP were able to forge a coalition quickly, although the RP had accused the DYP with corruption and Çiller with perjury. The coalition legitimated Erbakan, a politician with an immaculate anti-secular record, who had vowed to establish a "just order" (*adil düzen*) on the basis of his Sunni Islamic "image of Good Society." Less than three years earlier that a group of Sunni revivalists attacked and burnt 37 *Alevi* and leftist artists, novelists, poets, and journalists in the city of Sivas in Central Anatolia. Then in the hands of the RP, the RP mayor and some city councilors had been implicated with the crime. Some of the RP deputies in the National Assembly defended the Sunni radicals of the Sivas atrocities in the State Security Courts. In the new government one of them, Mr. Şevket Kazan was sworn in as the Minister of Justice. Obviously, the RP–DYP coalition government and the occupation Erbakan of the seat of the Prime Minister alarmed the *Alevi* community in Turkey.

A few months after the establishment of the RP–DYP government, in November 1996, a traffic accident in Susurluk, in the northwestern province of Balıkesir, began to cast a dark shadow on the Turkish political elite. A luxury Mercedes-Benz car traveling at a very high speed hit a truck pulling out of a gas station on to the intercity highway. A DYP deputy of the TGNA was injured, and the three other passengers traveling in the car died. One was a high-ranking police officer, another was a young woman in show business, and the third casualty was a renowned member of the ultranationalist Grey Wolves of the 1970s, who the press argued had been involved in the bloody political campaign of the 1970s. Awful odors seemed to be filling the Turkish political system. The accident raised suspicions that politicians, mafia bosses, and bureaucrats seemed to be working as bosom bodies. The reports in the press indicated that the trunk of the demolished car was full of special weapons and ammunition used in assassinations. The press further reported that the car was not traveling alone, but as part of a convoy of cars, which seemed to have fled the scene with some of the weapons. Inquiries into the

"Susurluk accident" started to reveal considerable amount of corruption. In the meantime, various civic associations started a protest campaign, accusing the government with dragging its feet. The campaign was called "one minute of darkness for enlightenment" and every evening at 9.00 p.m. people were requested to turn off the lights of their houses and apartments for one minute to protest the government's procrastination in launching an inquiry into political corruption.[100]

The Minister of Justice, Kazan, when asked about the protest movement, remarked that it was nothing more than a "candle blowing ceremony." This remark was directed at the *Alevis*, who the pious Sunni consider as heretics and view with contempt; for ages they had attempted to liquidate the *Alevi* communities. The Sunni radicals promote the idea that the *Alevis* congregate, dine and wine in candlelight, and eventually they blow out the candle and get involved in a sexual orgy (*mum söndü*)! Mr. Kazan's remarks bore out the worst fears of not only the *Alevis*, but also all of the secular voters that RP–DYP stood for discrimination and even suppression of the *Alevis* and the secular *Kulturkampf* of the Turkish society. The Justice Minister also gave the impression that the government was either belittling the "accident" or covering it up. The protest movement suddenly gained momentum and began to spread across all big towns of Turkey.

In early 1997 the media aired a theatrical performance at Sincan, a small town immediately to the west of the metropolitan city of Ankara. The RP mayor of Sincan greeted the Iranian Ambassador at a gathering organized by the municipality and delivered a speech, in which he argued that all would be converted to the path of "*Şeriat*." If they resisted, they would be "injected the vaccine of *Şeriat*" by force. Then, a play was put on the stage, where rock throwing "Muslim" heroes attacked the Israeli Defense Forces to save Jerusalem, and got shot and died in the process. Another play put on stage continued with a criticism of the Turkish army for being a secular force, and the main character calls for a boycott of conscription into the armed forces of Turkey. Almost simultaneously, the media reported the speech of the mayor of the Greater Municipality of Kayseri, where he called upon the "faithful" that they should never let revenge and hatred toward the secular Republic die in their hearts. The press started to report that the RP was purchasing shotguns to train a militia to combat the Turkish army.

These reports precipitated a wave of protests by the feminist and middle-class civic associations, who perceived that their lifestyle was in danger. Especially middle-class women started to show signs of alarm, wariness, and even panic under the threat of a "*şeriatçı*" takeover of the government. The DYP leader Ms. Çiller, a U.S. educated professor of economics, to placate the secular reactions, argued that as the minor partner of the coalition government she was a guarantee against the excesses of the government, which fell on deaf ears. The DYP and its leader Çiller were openly accused of being Machiavellian power mongers and too corrupt to act. The DYP deputies started to receive condemnation by voters at their constituencies, and some started to resign from their party by early 1997. In the meantime, for the first time in the

Republican era five major interest groups, representing the employees and employers of the Turkish Union of Chambers and Stock Exchanges (TOBB), Turkish Confederation of Small Business (TESK), Turkish Confederation of Business Associations (TISK), Turkish Workers' Unions (TÜRK-İŞ), Confederation of Revolutionary Workers' Unions (DISK) announced a common platform to battle the government. It was then that a battalion of tanks, on their way to their routine training exercises took a detour, and rolled through the town of Sincan. The mayor of Sincan was forced to resign by the RP leadership almost instantly.

However, the real showdown took place between the military establishment and the government during the National Security Council (MGK) meeting of February 28, 1997. The military commanders tabled serious accusations and questions concerning the activities of the illegal *sufi* orders (*tarikats*) in Turkey, whose heads had earlier been invited to the Prime Minister's residence for a fast-breaking dinner (*iftar*) during the holy month of Ramazan (Ramadan). The minutes of the MGK were secret and it constitutes a felony to publish them. However, leaks did occur, and the press was replete with how the government failed to answer questions leveled at them by the military commanders, and particularly by the commander of the Navy.[101]

The meeting of the MGK ended with an 18-point resolution, encompassing proposals for the Council of Ministers to act upon. The PM Erbakan, Deputy PM Çiller, and the other participating Ministers of the government signed and sealed the MGK resolution. Among the 18 points was a decision to extend compulsory elementary education from five to eight years. The Middle Schools would thus be abolished, and so would be the junior high school levels of the Imam-Hatip Schools, which have been breeding grounds for the RP organization in the eyes of the secular *kulturkampf*. Soon, the military announced that Islamic revivalism is the greatest national threat confronting Turkey and a "Western Study Group" was established in the armed forces to monitor the activities of the Islamic revivalists.[102] The *Alevis*, middle-class women, feminists, major business groups, trade unions, and finally the military seemed to have joined forces against the RP–DYP government by February 1997. The government limped on for another three and a half months and resigned on June 18, 1997.

However, as soon as PM Erbakan handed in his resignation to President Demirel, Mr. Erbakan and Mrs. Çiller appeared in public to argue that they had a coalition protocol. The protocol stipulated that in the midterm of their government Mr. Erbakan and Mrs. Çiller would alternate. They, and especially Çiller argued that the President must honor the protocol. She had served as the first woman Prime Minister of Turkey between June 1993 and December 1995. She seemed to have believed that unless she became the Prime Minister, her political career would be at risk due to formerly motioned corruption investigations in the TGNA, implicating her party, as well as herself, and her husband. However, she seemed to have overlooked the fact that the Turkish Constitution solely entrusts the President of the country with the task of the appointment of the Prime Minister.[103]

Indeed, appointment of the Prime Minister is the most critical and probably the only constitutional role that the Head of State should have in any parliamentary regime. Hence, there was no legal, constitutional, or political reason why the President should consider himself bound by the protocol of the former coalition government. He turned to the leader of ANAP Yılmaz as the head of the next largest party group in the TGNA after Erbakan's RP, in true spirit of the traditions of the Turkish political norms, and appointed him as the next Prime Minister. Çiller immediately reacted to the decision and argued that it was no less than a "Presidential coup." Yılmaz was able to establish a coalition with Ecevit's DSP and Deniz Baykal's CHP, though the latter asked to be kept out of the Prime Minister's Cabinet, yet promised his party group's support in the TGNA. When Yılmaz's coalition was able to obtain a vote of confidence, Çiller and Erbakan started to argue that they were now faced with a "military coup." The radical right and left wing members of the Turkish press started to adopt the same line. The press ignored the corruption charges, the plight of the *Alevis*, the reactions of the business community, the wariness of the middle-class women, the protests of the trade unions and civil society groups, and all of the other reactions to the RP–DYP coalition government. They also ignored the prerogative of the Head of State in a parliamentary regime in selecting a PM, and the stipulations of the 1982 Constitution. They singled out the rolling out of tanks through the streets of Sincan, and the MGK of February 28, 1997 as constituting the main "problem" of Turkish democracy. The press loved the drama precipitated by the fury and anguish of Çiller upon losing the office of the PM. The foreign press got contaminated with the same love affair with the picture of Turkey being run by the military. It also played well into the hands of the "rejection front" in the EU. What better evidence could they have unearthed of the "fact that Turkey was run by the military alone?"

THE QUAGMIRE OF THE EU

In the Luxembourg Summit of December 1997 the EU not only rebuffed Turkey, but also humiliated and insulted the Turkish government through the declarations of the PM of Luxembourg, who argued that Turkey was run by the military, which renders it unfit for the EU.[104] Immediately after the announcement of the declaration of the Luxembourg Summit, PM Yılmaz announced that political relations between EU and Turkey were put on ice. For the next two years EU and in particular German and Turkish authorities exchanged little more than political insults. However, in the aftermath of the capture of the PKK leader Abdullah Öcalan in Kenya while under the protective custody of Greece, the relations between the EU and Turkey started to go through a dramatic change. The Greek government seemed to play a major role in that regard. The hawkish Foreign Minister of Greece Mr. Pangalos resigned almost immediately after the Öcalan debacle. He was replaced with a dovish and sophisticated Foreign Minister Mr. George Papandreou in 1999.

The Greek foreign policy toward Turkey seemed to be based on the idea of keeping Turkey's hopes for full membership in the EU credible, while frustrating Turkey at every step of the way and wringing concessions in return for Greek lack of opposition. However, such a policy rested upon brinkmanship, that is, careful management of animosities and confrontation between the two countries, which could easily escalate to clashes and exchanges of fire between the troops confronting each other. For example, on the day of the December 25, 1995 National Assembly elections in Turkey, a Turkish vessel, "Figen Akat," ran aground at some rocks a few miles of the shores of Turkey.[105] The Greek Coast Guards responded to the S.O.S signals of the vessel first. Eventually, the Turkish Coast Guards responded, and in cooperation they floated the vessel and hauled it to a Turkish shipyard for repairs. However, this incident precipitated a debate over the identity of the rocks, which Greeks call Imia, and Turks call Kardak. In a few days' time the mayor of a city in the nearby Greek island of Kalimnos, in cooperation with the town vicar and football club players landed on the islet, in company of some goats, which were deposited on the rocks, and hoisted a Greek flag.[106] About a day or so later, a Turkish private TV network and daily newspapers discovered the incident in the Greek press. They leased a chopper and landed on the islet, took the Greek flag away, hoisted a Turkish flag instead, and televised the incident. Almost immediately after that incident Greece landed a team of commandoes on one of the rocks. The next day, Turkey landed a team of ten commandoes by stealth on a nearby rock. Hence, the rocks had by then become hot enough to start an exchange of fire between the two armies. The United States intervened once more and threatened each side that whoever fires the first shot will be fired upon by the U.S. army.[107] The diplomats started negotiations, which ended the simmering crisis through simultaneous pull back of the commandoes by Greece and Turkey. There is no report about the fate of the poor goats on the rocks with little water to survive on. However, the moral of the Imia/Kardak crisis of January 1996 is that even a shipwreck has the potential to escalate into an international crisis, and trigger a war in the Aegean.

From such incidents a lot of material emerges for the Greek government to prove to the world that Turkey threatened Greece. With the United States so eager to intervene whenever things seem to get out of hand, brinkmanship provided Greece with the necessary tools to prove Turkish hostilities to the EU and keep its "veto" against the Turkish rapprochement to the EU.

However, the new embroilment of the Greek Foreign Ministry in the case of PKK's leader signaled that something much worse than *Imia/Kardak* could crop up. The replacement of hawkish Pangalos with dovish Papandreou was an early signal from Greece that it was not ready for another period of escalating tension. Foreign Ministers of the two countries started to meet and discuss the issues separating the two countries. The Turkish Foreign Minister Ismail Cem seemed to have developed closer and more trusting rapport with Papandreou. The chemistry of the two Ministers in question seemed to have mixed well. Greece and Turkey started to deal with relatively easy and technical issues and sign some accords by May and June 1999. However, what seemed to have increased the momentum of rapprochement was natural disaster.

The north Anatolian fault line moved with an immense force that shifted Turkey five meters to the west on August 17, 1999, and again on November 12, 1999. A total of 450 km (280 miles) of the northern Anatolian fault line erupted, causing tremors measuring as much as 7.4 on the Richter scale. Two major towns of Turkey, İzmit, the hub of the Turkish manufacture industry, and Adapazarı were devastated. Istanbul was also deeply shaken, where some buildings to the south of the city collapsed or were damaged beyond repair. In the northwestern parts of the country more than 18,000 died and about 10,000 buildings crumbled into rubble. In between the Turkish quakes, a devastating earthquake demolished a few buildings and caused about 50 dead in Athens, Greece. Greece was one of the first countries to send aid to Turkey after the earthquakes of 1999, and Turkey reciprocated with similar urgency to the quake in Athens. The peoples of the two countries seemed to share the sorrows of each other. The popular mood made the already moving rapprochement between Greece and Turkey gain momentum. Later in that year was the Helsinki Summit of the EU. Greece announced before the Summit that it would support Turkish full membership to the EU. The traditional "Greek veto" to Turkish membership in the EU was lifted! Turkey started political contacts with the EU, and a negotiated settlement was worked out for the Turkish entry into the EU, when Turkey took some major steps to abolish the death penalty, show sensitivity to ethnic and religious rights, and improve its human rights record.

The Turkish political elite had started to tinker with the 1982 Constitution to liberalize the political regime of the country since the summer of 1995. The Helsinki Summit of the EU provided further motivation for taking more drastic steps to jettison the restrictions imposed on political and other rights in the 1982 Constitution. The end to the bloodshed after the capture and imprisonment of the PKK's leader Öcalan also helped to take some steps, such as designing legislation to enable language courses in Kurdish, and transmissions of radio and TV programs in Kurdish. The most dramatic of all were the steps taken by the TGNA on August 3, 2002, after it had agreed upon a date for early elections. The highly fragmented body of the National Assembly continued to meet and voted to amend the Constitution by more than two-thirds majority, to fulfill the Copenhagen Criteria[108] of the EU. This could only be interpreted as the strength of the resolve of the Turkish elite to go ahead with the membership procedure set by the EU. However, the process of rapprochement between Turkey and the EU has never been smooth or easy.

The Conservatives and Christian Democrats of Europe, led by the former French President V. Giscard d'Estaing of France started to campaign against Turkish full membership in the EU from November 2002 on. It came as another surprise to Turkey, almost two full years after the Helsinki Summit, that the European right would come up with such hypocrisy to argue that the

Turkish culture is Islamic and unfit for the EU. Europe, the Conservatives argued, is established on Christian or Judeo-Christian values, and a Muslim country, such as Turkey could and should never be a member. One would wonder where those people had been in the Helsinki Summit two years earlier when Turkey was declared as an eligible member, if and when Turkey meets the political and economic tests of the Copenhagen Criteria. There were no references to Christianity or Judeo-Christian "culture tests" that Turkey should meet in the Helsinki Summit decisions. The EU was gearing up for another summit in Copenhagen in December 2002, where the Conservatives and Christian Democratic rejection front emerged to form a new hurdle to Turkish entry into the EU. In the meantime, the early elections of November 3, 2002 brought about dramatic changes in Turkish politics.

Justice, Development, and the EU

Only two political parties and some independent candidates managed to win seats in the TGNA in the November 3, 2002 National Assembly elections. The fragmented party system, the financial crisis of 2001, and the 10 percent national threshold combined to create a two-party system in the TGNA.[109] A brand new political party established by the younger generation of politicians of the former National Viewpoint movement of Necmettin Erbakan came to power.

In 1997 the Constitutional Court had decided to close up the Welfare Party of Erbakan, and also impose a political ban on him and some of his deputies for violating the Political Parties Act and the Constitution of the country, on the grounds of perpetrating anti-secular activities. Erbakan's deputies, who were spared from the political ban imposed on the party, established the Virtue Party (FP), which took part in the 1999 National Assembly elections and received about 15 percent of the national vote. The day the TGNA met for the new deputies to take their oath, a new controversy broke out. One of the deputies elected on the FP ticket was a woman who wore a headscarf that covered her hair, neck, and shoulders. That style of covering the head is referred to as the "*türban*" and it had emerged as a main problem influencing the higher and secondary education, and the public sector employees since the 1980s, as the Constitutional Court decisions stipulated that the *türban* could not be worn in state premises. However, since the 1980s it had become a more important problem, for not only the sheer size of the women wearing the "*türban*" increased, but also the court cases involving such women students who would not remove their headscarves in operation theaters of the medical schools and nursing schools began to capture the headlines of major dailies. For the first time, Ms. Merve Kavakçı, the daughter of an *imam* (prayer leader in a mosque) living in Texas, and apparently an American citizen, appeared as a FP deputy in the TGNA wearing her *türban* to take the parliamentary oath, which was to stress that she would be faithful to the secular Republic. The leader of the DSP and PM to be, Mr. Bülent Ecevit took the floor and objected to the appearance of

Kavakçı in *türban*, which he argued, not only violated the Constitution, but also the Standing Orders (*İçtüzük*) of the TGNA. She was not permitted to take her oath that day. However, the controversy grew in intensity and precipitated another debate over whether "*türban*" was a sign of revivalist Islam, a sign of being traditional, or a sign of "modernity" for those who are trying to throw off their peasant culture, but could not go all the way due to pressures of social conformity. The members of the secular *kulturkampf* argued that the case for *türban* has always been presented as a religious obligation for women, and not even Muslim women, but also for all women who even visit a Muslim state, such as Iran. Hence, this was perceived as part of a project for converting Turkey into a form of theocracy.

Indeed, the issue of the "*türban*" had been on the political agenda before the 1999 National Assembly elections in Turkey. It was even exploited by other extreme right parties, such as MHP. Their election slogan "vote for the macho, not the timid" was directly relevant to the issue of the "*türban*."[110] The MHP seemed to be arguing that they had the credentials to change the relevant legislation to "solve" the *türban* problem and thus they should be supported at the polls. The MHP indeed was supported at the polls and received the second highest percentage of the national vote in the 1999 elections. They became a partner of the government coalition yet dismally failed to make any amends on the "*türban* issue." In 2000, the Public Prosecutor argued that the FP violated the Constitution and the Political Parties Act due to their anti-secular propaganda and activities, and asked the Constitutional Court to ban the FP, which the Court eventually did in 2001.

Among the elite of the FP emerged a debate about the role of the party in Turkish politics, the meaning of modernization and the relationship of the FP to modern society, and the role of religion in modern politics and economics. A relatively younger group of deputies and their followers, who had been referred to as "the progressives" in the FP, had started to argue for a change in party policies and image. They wanted the party to defend human rights rather than religious obligations, engage with capitalist and free market institutions, act more like a conservative party in a democratic party system, than a party after some kind of Islamic revolution through the ballot box. They even vied for power in the FP national convention.

The leader of that group, Recep Tayyip Erdoğan was also banned from politics for fomenting seditious conspiracy due to a speech he made in the eastern province of Siirt, when he was still the Mayor of the Greater City of Istanbul, to protest the ban of the Welfare Party on December 12, 1997. He quoted a poem from Gökalp, which incited protest against foreign occupation of the Ottoman lands in the aftermath of World War I. In the poem, the poet argued that the Muslims had nothing but their faith, yet their mosques would be turned into army barracks of the army of the faithful. The Public Prosecutor's Office claimed that this was no less than calling for people to rise up against the Republic and charged Erdoğan with seditious activity. Erdoğan was tried and found guilty, sent to prison, and was banned from all political activity for five years in 1998.

In the meantime, Abdullah Gül emerged as the candidate of the young "progressives" against the old guard represented by Recai Kutan, the official leader of the FP also a close associate of Erbakan (who was also banned from political activity by the Constitutional Court). Gül lost the contest to Kutan by a few votes. Soon after, there were rumors that the "progressives" considered splitting ranks with the FP, and establish their own political party. In the meantime the FP was tried and banned from political activity. That incident provided the opportunity the "progressives" were yearning for. On August 14, 2001 Tayyip Erdoğan, Abdullah Gül and other members of the "progressive" camp of the FP established the Justice and Development Party (AKP). Fifteen months later, and for the unprecedented first time in the Republican history, they rose to power by getting 34 percent and the national vote and 66 percent of the seats of the TGNA, thanks to the 10 percent national threshold that eliminated all other political parties but one, the CHP (see table 5.1). What made the performance of the AKP at the polls so unprecedented was that its founder and real leader, Tayyip Erdoğan was still banned from running for office, though he campaigned for his party as a citizen. The voters supported the AKP at the polls knowing full well that AKP would have a PM other than Tayyip Erdoğan, due to his political ban, he could not even participate in the November 3, 2002 elections as a candidate. Indeed, Mr. Erdoğan had a large number of court cases implicating him with serious violations of the law while he served as the Mayor of the Greater City of Istanbul. However, the voters still supported him and his AKP, and the plurality of the voters seemed to have considered the court cases against him as plots concocted up by the "corrupt Ankara establishment."

During the 2002 national elections the voters seemed to be motivated with an antiestablishment, anti-Ankara mood. They voted for the newly established, untried AKP, which could not be implicated with the financial meltdowns of 1999 and 2001 (which in turn, caused a severe recession in the Turkish economy), or the "Susurluk style" corruption of the DYP, ANAP, MHP, and others of the 1999 parliament. The people seemed also to support the extra-parliamentary opposition of CHP, which they had not supported much in the 1999 elections (see table 5.1).

Those who had been considered as having played some role in managing the political affairs of the country between 1999 and 2002 were ousted from the TGNA. Yılmaz of ANAP, and Çiller of DYP resigned their posts and bowed out of politics and Bülent Ecevit of the DSP followed suit two years later. The 2002 elections seemed to be a milestone in Turkish politics, whereby some leading members of the old guard of Turkish politics have thus been eliminated, and others have received serious and even lethal blows to their political careers.

Now, it was the turn of the former members of the Welfare and Virtue party, who had spent long careers representing Islamic revivalism, political Islam, creating a "Just Order" or "rule of Şeriat," to deal with the European Union. In fact, Tayyip Erdoğan could not enter the TGNA until March 2003, due to his political ban; the decision of the election commission in

2002 to renew the elections in the province of Siirt in southeastern Turkey, provided him with an opportunity to run for office. Coincidentally, Siirt is the province where Erdoğan's wife was born, and where his famous speech had caused him to be banned from politics for a while.

In the meantime, the AKP government had Abdullah Gül as the PM for a couple of months, whose government had to represent Turkey in the Copenhagen Summit of the EU, and in the negotiations with the United States before the War in Iraq in Spring 2003. The unelected leader of the AKP, Tayyip Erdoğan, with no official title, also accompanied Gül to Europe and the United States. It is ironic sight that formerly staunch anti-European deputies of the RP and FP, who had lectured for years that EU was no more than a "Christian Club," which "Muslim" Turkey should not even have applied for membership, let alone be a member, propagated, defended and promoted Turkey's membership. It was PM Gül and his government who were given the "green light" of eligibility by the Conservatives and Christian Democrats of Europe. It was PM Gül's government, which also got a "date for a date" from the EU. It was decided in the Copenhagen Summit of the EU in December 2002 that the start of Turkish accession talks for full membership in the EU might be determined as early as December 2004 by the EU. It was also ironic that the Turkish press reported by 2003 that Mr. Erdoğan was testing waters to apply for membership in the Conservative and Christian Democratic club of People's Parties of Europe, and that AKP was gearing up to join ranks with the Christian Democratic parties of Europe.[111]

It was also quite a sight to observe the "unelected" yet popular AKP leader Erdoğan sit side by side with President George W. Bush in the White House, as if he were a representative of the Turkish State. It was even more interesting to watch Mr. Erdoğan talk of solidarity with the United States, as he had formerly represented a political movement that had often portrayed the United States as the "Evil Force behind Zionist Israel" set to undermine the Muslim world. The metamorphosis of Erdoğan was remarkable by any standard. Could he be involved in a form of "double-talk" or "*takiyye*" as it is well known in the Turkish culture? *Takiyye* is to act in a way completely contrary to one's beliefs, values, and faith under the pressing conditions and out of expediency of the circumstance, without changing one's beliefs or values. Various Islamic revivalists had acted so in the past in Turkey. Could someone such as Erdoğan, who had spent all of his adult life and even served in prison for his beliefs, who had argued that "democracy was no different than a tramcar, and when the car arrives at the right station, one would get off and walk in the direction one deemed correct," change so much as to be a staunch supporter of democratic and secular government? More critically, would he be able to convince his political opponents and the opposing "*kulturkampf*" of Turkey of his new image, new credentials, and new role in Turkish politics?

It is too early to judge Erdoğan, his close associates, such as Gül, and his party, the AKP. However, it is a matter of fact that the AKP is not a doctrinaire party. It is not another one of those National Viewpoint parties.

Erdoğan and friends split from the National Viewpoint movement arguing that its doctrinaire image undermines rather than enhances their chances for government. They wanted to draw up a different image of being at peace with modernity, tolerant to diversity, and be pragmatic, yet conservative in their outlook. The AKP deputies have a hardcore of former RP–FP members, who constitute most of the frontbench of their parliamentary party group. However, they also have large numbers of former ANAP, DYP, MHP, and even some DSP or CHP members among them. The parliamentary group of the AKP is composed of anything but an ideologically compact community of disciplined deputies. In fact, in some thorny issues, such as sending Turkish and U.S. troops into Iraq through southeastern Turkey, cracks in the ranks of the AKP parliamentary group suddenly appear. It is plausible to refer to AKP as a coalition of moderate and extreme rightwing politicians, who had been sidelined by the former party establishments of similar colors. Therefore, another question that needs to be addressed is whether the AKP leaders could manage their parliamentary political party group, their extra-parliamentary party organization, as they effectively satisfy the demands of the voters who had supported them at the polls, or not. Similarly, it is also a matter of debate and speculation to what extent the AKP elites could manage the affairs of the state, establish their credentials as the masters of the public bureaucracy, and manage the affairs of the Turkish society and economy, while preventing political instability and resort to authoritarianism? In the following and final chapter of this book, we examine the governance, democratization, and stability of Turkey under the current political regime and government of the country.

6

Governance, Change, and Risk

The historical, geographic, and cultural characteristics of Turkey have shaped political, economic, and social developments. Historical and cultural ties haunt and challenge Turkey. Beginning in the eighteenth century, the decomposition of a medieval, patrimonial empire reaching its climax with the legal collapse of the Ottoman Empire in 1922, still reverberates. There is hardly a contemporary conflict, whether in the Balkans, the Black Sea and the Caspian Sea basins, Central Asia, Caucasus, and the Middle East, that does not somehow involve, influence, and even threaten Turkey. Hence, governing Turkey first and foremost involves simultaneously managing multiple international, regional, and domestic challenges, which often interact and influence each other.

Engrossed and embedded in such an environment filled with such turbulence and volatility, it is no wonder that the Turkish society, economy, and polity constantly vibrate with dynamism, challenges, and struggle. The agricultural society of the Ottoman system is long gone, yet its cultural heritage still lingers on. In the meantime, Turkey has been trying hard to modernize its society and polity, and develop its economy. This is not only because the founding father of the Republic, Mustafa Kemal Atatürk and his followers proposed so. There is a societal drive to become modern, industrialize, and urbanize. The debate is not so much about whether Turkey should or should not modernize, but more about how much and fast to do so. Modernization involves change, yet various societal and ethnic groups, and social classes have been at odds with each other about the substance of change. What are those values, beliefs, styles of life that need to be preserved and considered as constituting the gist of the cultural existence of the Turkish society? What are dispensable habits, mores, traditions that have no longer utility for Turkish society, culture, and people?

The Ottoman, and later on, the Turkish societies, just like many others that have experienced change and modernization, have been grappling with those and other similar questions. Many recipes have been suggested on how to deal with socioeconomic change, socioeconomic and political challenges, and about conducting foreign relations of Turkey. Most of those recipes or prescriptions fall into two broad categories; one of preservation and even going back to some golden age in the past, and the other of severing all ties with the past and forging ahead with progress. Interestingly enough, the conservatives and the radical modernizers kept changing their list of values over time; and hence, intriguing combinations emerged. Some wanted to preserve social habits, such as kissing the hands of the elderly, or visiting their relatives during religious holidays, yet were ready to take the most dramatic steps in economic modernization, such as in adopting the latest electronic technology for their enterprises. Others, who would not touch the buttons of a computer keyboard, often considered all traditional social habits and customs as cumbersome impediments to social development. Irrespective of the way people reacted to change, economic and sociopolitical changes kept fast occurring around them.

Economic necessities pushed millions out of the countryside to the fringes of the big cities. State-initiated industrialization, eventually led to a burgeoning private sector investing in manufacturing and other industries. Ease and affordability of transportation by intercity buses, and media exposure increased social mobility and social mobilization with leaps and bounds. Urban residents experimented with new lifestyles, fashions, fads, and behavior. In its own peculiar, wobbly fashion Turkey started to trek down a road of modernity.

MODERN OR NOT TO BE MODERN?

Modernity created new lifestyles, social structures, work ethic, which necessitated that one adapted one's habits, attitudes, and behavior to a new work environment, novel settlement patterns, and emerging social interactions. The task involved required to seek higher standards of education, learn new skills and be trained in modern methods of learning and education, learn a foreign language or two, get a professional job, and lead the life of a professional middle-class family in a developing urban, industrialized, and eventually free market economy.

However, most failed to part with their earlier adopted parochial, rural values, and the vestiges of the Ottoman medieval norms and habits they grew up with. The outcome has been a painful psychological process for the individual involved, and his or her loved ones, especially parents and extended family. Different, interesting, tragic, and even funny developments occurred.

Occasionally, a balcony full of chicken, couple of cows on the roof terrace of a six-story high building, a sheep or a goat in the bathroom of an apartment unit are discovered by the press and the media of the big cities. The "Istanbul Turkish"[1] is gone, and probably forever, and so are the ladies and gentlemen who talked that dialect. The "Istanbul *beyefendisi*" (gentlemen of Istanbul)[2] have also long migrated to Europe or the United States, and most are by now deceased. The rural migrants that gushed into the city were so many, and they came in so short a time that there was no way they could be acculturated to the lifestyle of a metropolis such as Istanbul (population 10.5 million). The old Ottoman cosmopolitanism of the seat of the Empire is lost. A new form of cosmopolitanism is gradually developing, yet it is too early to say what sort of a metropolitan culture will eventually gain stability and respect in the city of Istanbul. Other major cities of the country are not that different from Istanbul. The urban sprawl is a cauldron of many cultures, habits, values, and beliefs, which have not yet settled to create a distinct urban culture characterizing the metropolitan cities of the country. The mix of cultures demonstrates Turkey's complexity and diversity in many ways. Probably, the dresses of women and men are the most visible of those cultural signs one would immediately spot in any sojourn in the downtown of any big city in Turkey.

A huge variety of attires have become visible in the major metropolitan centers of the country. The latest fashions of mini skirts, tight jeans, short shirts that leave the belly button of women exposed, mingle with women donning headscarves covering their hair, parts of their foreheads, cheeks, necks, and all the way down to their shoulders. Some women wear long overcoats even in summer to cover their entire body, in a way that the shape of their body would not be visible. Others just suffice with wearing long sleeved shirts and long skirts with dark stockings, yet wearing high-heeled shoes, or even gym shoes. It is not only the shapes of the attire that differ, but the quality of the fabrics used also differ widely. Some of the headscarves are pure silk or pure wool, and some dresses are products of famous international brands.

Even among men one can observe similar differences of attires worn. The differences in the quality of textiles is indicative of wealth or influence of the person donning the dress, though gives little clue about the other cultural characteristics of the individual in question. For example, the leader and founder of the National Salvation and Welfare Parties, and a symbol of radical Sunni/Islamic political activism in Turkey, former Islamist PM Erbakan has a habit of wearing *Versace* ties since the 1990s. A keen foreign observer, who is not well versed in the intricacies of Turkish politics, could easily mistake Erbakan for a businessman. However, for an average Turkish voter, there is little doubt about what Erbakan stands for.

Dress codes have always been an integral part of one's cultural identity and even political outlook in Turkey. The peasants, both men and women often wear functional clothes, which cover up their bodies. They have never been the concern of cultural reformers and they were always treated as part of the Anatolian and Thracian folklores of the country. However, with rural migrants appearing in the urban centers of Turkey, and demanding a place in every walk of life, interesting to peculiar styles of dresses started to appear, and so has political conflict surrounding those who don them.

Some wear the traditional black "*çarşaf*," which is no more than a black piece of material that covers the whole body, except the face of the women who wear them. Some of the women even cover their faces in veils (*peçe*) when they wear the "*çarşaf*." There are traditional and religious symbolisms attached to such behavior. Still, some women don their humble rural dresses in the cities, which also come with a headscarf, but it is not so meticulously applied to cover the head all the way to the shoulders. Such a dress would reveal rural roots of the person involved, though gives no more hints about cultural or political orientations of the individual in question. Headscarves worn in a way to cover the head and the shoulders, yet not the face of women often indicate Sunni religiosity, though political orientations may be harder to guess. However, women belonging to certain religious orders (*tarikats*) wear a certain color and style of scarves and overcoats, which not only indicate their cultural and religious identity, but also their specific political choice as well. Men are hardly any different. Some don religious garbs, even though it is illegal to wear them in public. From time to time governments show tolerance to such ostentatious demonstration of self-declared religious identity or even religious learnedness, and at other times they do not. The pious Sunnis usually do not wear ties, although others have been brandishing their colorful ties for years. Most rural migrants have started to wear ties, with a jacket, yet the color harmony of their attire often times look bizarre. Often they wear white socks that do not match the rest of the outfit, while the shoes are often unpolished. The beards and moustaches of men often signal their cultural identity, and at times, even their political orientations. Especially in the 1970s it was possible to identify some men from the way they stylized their moustaches whether they belonged to the ethnic nationalist "gray wolves" or to some leftwing organization. In the same years it was also fashionable for leftist men to don military parkas.

TRADITIONAL MODERNISM OR MODERNIST TRADITIONALISM

In general, the style of attire and how one brandishes it constitute a sign of social class, one's orientation to tradition and modernity, and even political affiliation. In the case of a woman, it may also be a sign of how her extended family, which often includes in-laws, brothers, grandparents, uncles, and the like, reacts to modernity as well. For most the issue in question is how to become modern, while maintaining one's traditional values and norms, and most specifically a family's pride. The parents often demand from their children that they seek college diplomas, and have professional middle-class jobs, and earn well, but respect and even practice the values and lifestyles of their parents. At the least, the young are expected not to look down upon their parents, parental families, and social milieu of their origin, when they become successful professionals. Modernity is perceived as a process that decomposes and undermines families, communities, and the values of the society. Such a perspective on modernity almost equates it with moral decadence and sociopolitical corruption. Hence, the problem becomes one of socialization of the children. How could the children be "educated" so that they could be both "modern" and yet possess or share the same "values" as their "traditional" parents do? The answer to the demand of creating this "modern-traditional (wo)man" seems to have precipitated one of the most controversial and burning issues of Turkish politics.[3]

One of the most important cultural reforms Turkey undertook was the closing down of all institutions of religious instruction in 1924, and introduction of a policy of "unity of education" (*tevhid-i tedrisat*). This policy entrusted the Ministry of National Education with establishing, running, and monitoring all instruction in all educational facilities in the country. It also obligated the same Ministry with establishing a "national curriculum," which all schools would follow. Religious instruction would not be a part of that curriculum, and that would be carried at the privacy of the homes, where parents would teach religion to their children. Only schools of theology of the universities were given the freedom to do research on religion and teach theology. This policy was followed until 1948 when the government established secondary schools to educate *imams* (prayer leaders) and their assistants (Imam-Hatip Schools). Many more were established over the years as the more traditional Periphery gained political clout. There was a remarkable increase in the number of students, especially girls, who could not become *Imams*, for that is a job exclusively for men. The traditional *kulturkampf* approached the peasant and small town families and offered them a formula for educating their children into "traditional-modern" individuals. They were subject to the propaganda that, if they enrolled their children in the Imam-Hatip schools, the children would preserve their "traditional morality" through instruction of religion, while they would be instructed in math, Turkish, science, and other subjects, and get the educational credentials to land well-paying professional jobs.[4]

It is ironic that the Turkish educational system managed to reconstruct the dualist structure of education, which had been an Ottoman practice, where religious and secular education inculcated two different and even antagonistic value systems in the minds of their graduates. A similar, though not identical, dualism has now been established in Turkey, where graduates of the secular schools and Imam-Hatip schools often tend not to share the same "Image of Good Society."

As the numbers of the graduates of the Imam-Hatip Schools increased, they started to make an impact on all walks of life in Turkey, including politics. Indeed, the Imam-Hatip Schools delivered what they have been promising all along: Graduates who are educated in natural and social sciences, and thus possess the credentials to become professionals, yet maintaining the traditional moral values of an "image of good society" built around religion.

Until 1997, the Imam-Hatip and other vocational schools were treated as if they were no different than other high schools of the country. The university system of Turkey ranks and places all high school graduates according to the grades they receive in the nationally, and even internationally administered Student Selection and Placement Examination (ÖSYS). The secondary school performance of the students only played a minor role in the calculation of their ÖSYS scores, and the colleges had no say as to who would be enrolled in their programs. In 1997 the Higher Educational Council (YÖK) adopted a new rule and treat the vocational schools as qualitatively different from the other *lyceé* (high schools) of Turkey, which prevented them from being included, disabled them from being placed in the rankings to be enrolled in any science or social science undergraduate program of the Turkish universities, with all other vocational secondary school graduates.

Consequently, it has become impossible for the Imam-Hatip schools to deliver their earlier promises any longer.

However, the graduates of the Imam-Hatip schools are well organized, and they had climbed up the social and political ladder rapidly. Finally, they even had a graduate of an Imam-Hatip school, Tayyip Erdoğan elected as the Prime Minister of Turkey as of March 2003. The national legislature (TGNA) has a plurality of members who have had their secondary education at Imam-Hatip schools. Consequently, the new policy of the YÖK and PM Erdoğan's government started to clash. The school curricula, the status of the Imam-Hatip schools, the "*türban*" have become some of the most critical political issues reinforcing the division between the *kulturkampfs* of the country.[5]

The *türban* issue also relates to the status, role, and perception of women in Turkish society. Sunni revivalists argue that it is an obligation for all women to cover up. They propagate that it is the strict command of Allah, a religious obligation, which all faithful should abide by. They argue that women who would prefer to live their religion should be permitted to cover up. The *raison d'être* is that women who do not cover their hair constitute objects of sexual attraction for men. This perspective defines women as "sex objects," and assumes that men are ready to be aroused by any sign of women, that the two genders need to be segregated, or at best, the women should cover up.

The secular *kulturkampf* considers such a perspective as a gross violation of *laicist* (secular) principles of the Republic. Consequently, the full integration of women, as female members of the society, with equal rights as male members should be the goal of the Republican governments. The secularists tend to define gender discrimination and segregation as violation of secular principles of Cultural Revolution of the 1920s and the 1930s.

However, some secular feminists and some social scientists argue that those women who cover up do so for the sake of participation in public life.[6] The alternative for those women is to stay at home and be fully isolated from public life, or even be killed by some family member for undermining the honor and pride of the family (*namus*). Hence, the argument now becomes one of emancipation. They escape the imprisonment in their home environment, as slaves of their husbands or other paternal elders, thanks to their "*türban*" or "*çarşaf*," and some argue that women who cover up should be encouraged to take greater part in public life rather than be banned from participation in education and other public activities.

Some pundits and students of sociology, politics, and culture also argue that the "*türban*" is a sign of transformation, a transient state for women who are trying to adapt to a modern environment and sever their ties with their traditional and even peasant roots. The *türban* thus becomes a sign of modernity, not traditionalism or reactionary action against the secular state. It constitutes a new form of dress for those who aspire to be "urban women" but could not take the "plunge into modern" style of living. They dress up, use makeup, mingle with women who themselves are not covered up, and even work with men. Some eventually shed their turban and convert into "modern, urban" women in looks.[7]

Finally, it is also argued that covering up gives the "right" kind of message to the other gender. Those women who cover up signal that they are "ladies" (*hanım*), as opposed to others who look "easy or frivolous" to men, and most specifically to lower middle class, proletarian, and lumpenproletarian men. In a sense, then the "*türban*" is a class issue.[8] The women who wear the "*türban*" and their families come from a peasant, proletarian, or lower-middle-class background. Some have climbed up the social ladder to become wives of prominent businessmen, bankers, professionals, technocrats, cabinet ministers, and even Prime Ministers. However, covering up is extremely rare among women from middle class, upper middle class, and upper-class families, and urban *Alevi* women.[9]

Consequently, a cultural, religious fault line sharply divides the Turkish society into the radical orthodoxy (Sunni) versus the secular Sunnis and the *Alevi* on the issue of the "*türban*," the dress code, and role of women in public life. Notwithstanding the sociocultural cleavages of the Turkish society where the courts stand on this issue is crystal clear in Turkey. When appeals to the courts were made by women wearing the "*türban*," who have been prevented from attending universities or obtaining jobs in the state sector, overwhelmingly the decisions of the courts have been against *türban* in public life.[10] The courts have tended to argue that *türban* and *tesettür* amount to an upheaval or challenge against the secular regime of Turkey, and thus they constitute violation of the articles of the 1982 Constitution that are pertinent to secularism.[11] The Constitutional Court argued that no link can be established between the dress codes and religious beliefs, except for those who serve as the clergy, and they can only don their religious garb in their offices, office buildings, and during the execution of their religious duties.[12] The decision of the Constitutional Court in Turkey exhausted all chances of repeal of the ban against the *türban*, but now appeals have been made at the Human Rights Commission and Court of the Council of Europe.

The European Human Rights Commission turned down the students, and argued that if the schools have rules, which the students accept at enrolment, they should abide by those rules and act accordingly. The Human Rights Commission proposed that the schools have the right to impose secular principles, if they so wish. As a result, some celebrities, such as the wife of Turkish Foreign Minister and former PM Gül have decided to pull back their cases from the European Court of Human Rights (ECHR). Domestically, there is no legal way that Turkish political system can bring any solutions to this issue, so long as the decision of the Constitutional Court stands.

The cultural fault lines in Turkey have now converted a religious and educational issue, which only affects a very small minority of women into a political hot potato.[13] Every right wing political party and coalition that comes to power feels great pressure from their constituents to "solve" the "*türban* issue," that is, to enable the girls in *türban* to act as they wish in the colleges of the country. The AKP government is no exception, and in the Spring and Summer of 2003 it initiated legal procedures to trim the powers of the President in appointing the judges of the Constitutional Court, on the one hand, and bring about a "University Reform" bill, which will enable the government to purge most of the current university administrators and implant their own rectors and other administrators instead, on the other,[14] yet with no success.

POPULAR WILL VERSUS RULE OF LAW

This move brings us back to one of the perennial paradoxes of Turkish democracy: Elected governments are met with popular demands, which contradict the constitution, laws, regulations, and court decisions. The governments are in no place to alter those legal constraints, but, their supporters at the polls pressure them to deliver what they had been promised during the campaign, which are in contradiction of the law. What is to be done? The typical act of Turkish governments has been to pander to populist patronage, and undermine the authority of the courts and the law of the land. The overwhelming popular demand in Turkey has been for favoritism, cronyism, and free riding.[15] The more respect and effectiveness democratic government develops through distributing favors, the more erosion occurs in the rule of law in the country.[16] Consequently, a severe problem of "good governance" has become institutionalized.

One major example of the governance problem in Turkey is the economic bottlenecks Turkish governments have failed to eliminate. Although economic development has been a high priority for the Republican governments, how to balance investment, consumption, and debt has been perennial. After 1923 the devastated agricultural resources of the country were hardly up to the job of generating enough national income to finance the necessary investments to rebuild the country, and Turkey had accepted the burden of the Ottoman debts as part of the settlement at Lausanne. Such dire constraints left little room for populism and popular grand projects the economic feasibility of which could at best be dubious. Industry was insulated against foreign competition by means of high customs taxes, duties, and tariffs,[17] and industrialization occurred through state-owned and-run companies (KIT).[18]

Dramatic changes in the economic objectives and policies started to occur in the 1950s influenced by two main developments. One is the image of democracy as "amoral populism," in which the game of politics functions through political parties and interest groups that acted as "populist patronage" mechanisms.[19] The second driving force behind the new economic policies of the governments was the rapid social mobilization, which precipitated a major jump in popular demand for public spending in Turkey. These two factors combined, when in the 1950s, new attempt at industrialization through private enterprise, as well as state sponsored investments and state guaranteed foreign loans precipitated the emergence of new patronage networks of private land developers, construction companies, textile firms, and so on, which latched themselves onto the central government bureaucracy and the political elites. The allocation of the state owned and guaranteed funds to various patronage networks contributed to the development of new clientelistic relations between the government and the "new business class" of Turkey. A well-oiled machine emerged to distribute and share the emoluments of the state budget and newly acquired loans between the political elites, public bureaucracy, and the new Turkish middle class. Developing industry attracted many to move to the cities of the country to work for better pay and benefits. Urbanization and the demand for skilled labor began to increase.

The transformation from agricultural to industrial economy, with all its sociopsychological ramifications, has led Turkish society to demand more variety and better quality of services from the government, often far exceeding the financial, human, and other resources at its disposal.[20] Of course, such a tendency has been universally experienced around the globe, and hence the Turkish efforts at economic growth constituted nothing special. However, what seems to be more peculiar to Turkey has been the perception of Turkish citizens of "Papa State."

In part, this tradition is inherited from the Ottoman Empire.[21] The essence of the tradition consists of a marked statist orientation (*étatism*), which stresses community over its members, uniformity rather than diversity, an understanding of law that stresses collective reason instead of the will of membership.[22]

The state is paramount mechanism of control, and traditionally the awe of the state is such that no group dares to challenge its control or even hegemony over the society. Coexistence or conformity with the "Papa State" has been much more beneficial than to challenge it.[23] The image of the state as an "omnipotent hegemon," controlling every social process and suffocating any freedom of social, economic, or cultural action, yet possessing vast resources to deliver an infinite amount of largesse (*ihsan*) to who it deems as loyal and supportive has popular acceptance.

If the Turkish state tradition has suffocated civic initiative, voluntary associability, and civil society, it also precipitated a strategy for survival among its citizens. In the absence of an image of "public good" to the production of which the individual member of the political community feels as if s/he contributes, people revert back to two strategies for survival. One strategy is exemplified in the acts of the pure form of the rational actor.[24] The survival strategy of the individual consists of seeking to maximize one's immediately short-term individual and/or household benefits. This yields a strategy that anthropologist Edward Banfield unearthed in southern Italy of the 1950s and called "amoral individualism," or "amoral householdism."[25] The individual feels no moral obligation to the public, or common weal, exploitation of public realm for personal or family benefit becomes the norm. The outcome of this strategy creates highly rational individuals, who seek to steer their households to prosperity, acting as free riders, through the plunder of the public realm as far as they can.[26]

Another strategy of survival depends upon primordial relations, such as lineage, blood ties, tribalism, and the like, which are simple extensions of the household structure to co-opt a larger gathering of one's family, clan, and even community for both protection and advancement. Three characteristics seem to emerge as the pivotal properties around which solidarity could be established in Turkish society: blood, territory (soil), and religion. Families, and lineage-groups, which may be extensive enough to coagulate thousands of members, and may reach even tribal proportions, often help to promote careers in business or politics. Similarly, being from the same town (*hemşehri*) also functions to establish solidarity among members of the Turkish society. Business partners, political party delegates, and cultural organizations are often established around *hemşehri* bonds. Finally, the religious or *Sufi* orders or brotherhoods (*tarikat*) constitute a very strong coagulation function among the pious members of the Turkish society. Although *tarikats* have been rendered illegal since the 1920s, they could easily establish legal window-dressing structures, such as Mosque Building Societies, or Endowments for Qur'an Recitation, and so on, which would be quite legal.

Belonging to any one of those communities often provides a modest young individual with vast opportunities, such as a thriving business, a spouse, a middle-class lifestyle, which s/he could not otherwise even dream of acquiring alone. However, blood-ties and territorial affinities are ascriptive properties, which one would or would not acquire at birth. Religious affiliation is only partly ascriptive. The family environment one is born into and grows up in often determines one's religious sect and piety in Turkey. Some do change their ideology and lifestyle later on in life, yet many do not, or cannot. Such a step often entails being ostracized from a community, which in turn may mean losing one's credibility, business, customers, job, and so on.

There are other social bonds, which are also relevant yet not as important in Turkey. For example, Turkey has a conscript army, and thus all male members of the Turkish society must serve in the armed forces for a certain period of their youth, unless they have a health reason, which disqualifies them. Solidarities may also be established among comrades in arms (*askerlik arkadaşı*). They are often not extremely durable, and very few comrades in arms meet and establish partnerships, such as corporations, nongovernmental organizations, and the like, later in life.

The primordial solidarity groups extend protection and patronage opportunities to their members. Often one has to compromise one's individualism and free-rider activities with membership in such patronage networks. Large gatherings can muster a lot of financial and human resources in and outside of Turkey, which often lead to further political influence, deference, and prosperity. Some networks extend their webs into Germany and elsewhere in Europe, Asia, Australia, and the United States. They can mobilize huge resources globally. The most famous and probably influential of them are the Nurcus, currently under the guidance of Fethullah Gülen, who possess such a network, build schools all over the world, which instruct students in English and Turkish, and funding various cultural and commercial activities in and out of Turkey.[27]

The political influence of such interest groups is often very difficult to monitor and check. The levels of institutionalization of such interest groups are much more advanced than the level of institutionalization of the Turkish political parties. Consequently, such factions can be extremely effective in establishing their moles in the public bureaucracy, and extract emoluments from the state budget.[28]

Operating under the influence of such patronage networks and the callous attitudes of the free-riding voters to rules and regulations governments experienced great difficulty to establish or maintain budgetary discipline and balanced budgets. The provincial and municipal administrations have also been effectively penetrated and manipulated by the same patronage groups and networks. Once such patronage networks were given a free hand to mushroom, in no time, most national and local governments started to run huge deficits, which undermine any chance of managing the macro economic tools and policies of the country.

A vicious cycle seems to have been unfolding since the 1950s. Political parties often promise far beyond their capabilities to win elections. They are hard pressed to deliver their promises. They try to cater to the demands of the patronage groups, who had supported them at the polls. The budgetary discipline is undermined in no time. Public spending and often money supply increase dangerously, the value of the Turkish Lira plunges to new lows, and inflation of consumer prices begins to hurt vast swathes of people. Simultaneously, large sums of foreign currency deposits are used up to sustain the demand for imported luxury goods, raw materials and intermediary goods, which have been in increasing demand as the Turkish industry develops. Turkish export goods become more affordable as the TL loses value, yet they are not as much in demand as the imports. The foreign trade deficit of the country increases. Eventually, foreign currency becomes scarce enough hampering the necessary demand for raw materials and intermediary goods. The industrial production of the country suffers, and high prices or commodity shortages and black market operations flourish and take their toll from the lifestyles of the middle, lower middle, and lower classes.[29]

It is not much of a surprise that social unrest starts to occur under such circumstances, which precipitates the government to clamp down on the opposition, which further contributes to the widening of the scope and number of protests and protestors. The country slides into mayhem, and it looks as if the government steers away from democracy and toward authoritarianism. A military coup becomes quite an attractive alternative, and often emerges as the only means to get rid of a corrupt government, takes place. The military junta draws up a new constitution, and Turkey reverts back to some form of pluralist multipartyism. The same cycle of events start to unfold.

POLITICAL MISMANAGEMENT AND POLITICAL ECONOMY OF CRISIS

The deficiencies of the rule of law often contributed to the further deterioration of the economic situation. Courts failed to act effectively and efficiently in resolving economic conflicts. Bad checks, unpaid loans, bad credits extended from the state banks to patronage networks, and the like could not be adjudicated effectively. Consequently, some turned to various thugs, popularly referred to as the "mafia," as bad loan collection agents to benefit from their services. Even banks and corporations seemed to have used the services of such "*Mafiosi.*" Ironically, Turkey seemed to be privatizing by default what absolutely needed to be public, such as the judiciary function of government, and failing to privatize what needed to be privatized by design, such as the state banks.

One main reason has been the popular understanding of democracy as a mechanism that enabled people to gain access to the emoluments of the "economic resources of the State" with the help of such populist patronage mechanisms as political parties.[30] Operating under the free rider rationality of the voters, elections provided opportunities for the masses to swap votes with services. Multiparty politics also provided the masses to swap one group of patrons with others, when the procurement of services, by a party or coalition of parties runs into various difficulties.[31] The democratic game is supported by the masses so long as they are able to receive tangible and specific benefits from the government through the rituals of democracy. Indeed, the findings of the Turkish Values Surveys indicate that Turkey does not seem to possess various values, such as social tolerance, interpersonal support, associability, which are often assumed to constitute the core values of a burgeoning civil society, which in turn provides for the cultural context for a democratic regime to function.[32]

Under those circumstances the problem becomes one of keeping the flow of benefits going for the duration of a government in power, at the very least for the patronage networks that supported the party or parties in government. However, "for patronage to work, authorities must distribute favors to their clientele, which is very hard if bids, recruitment, promotion, hiring, and firing are solely based on meritocratic values and through transparent procedures. Unless rules and laws are relaxed, favoritism does not work."[33] Such a practice does not only jeopardize rule of law, but it also undermines tax collection and other economic good governance practices. There is no evidence that indicate that the rational, free riding voters of Turkey have the slightest intent of becoming meticulous taxpayers, either.

In a newspaper column a student of public finance announced that there were about two million taxpayers in Turkey, who are legally obliged to file income tax in 2003.[34] There are 2,250,000 state employees and around 2.5 million or so blue and white-collar labor whose income taxes are withheld at the time of the payment and they do not file any taxes. These figures bring the total number of taxpayers who pay income tax to around the ballpark figure of six to seven million in Turkey. The population of the country is around 70 million in 2003 and the numbers of eligible voters are around 41.5 million! Obviously, many more people pay the Value Added Tax (KDV),[35] whether they are cognizant of it or not, whenever they purchase a bus ticket, gasoline, natural gas, football ticket, consumer goods of any sort, and so on. However, consumers also tend to negotiate with the retailers over cash payments and dodge the KDV, and hence get a discount, which may be as high as 18 percent on some consumer durables. In short, there seems to be a relatively large gap between those who demand services from the central government, and who vote to elect representatives to the Grand National Assembly. There seems to be an imbalance between taxation and representation in Turkey, which constitutes a significant constraint on the smooth operation of representative democracy. Those who are not eager to pay taxes are not necessarily eager to pressure their representatives to give an account of their public service, either. Such lax accountability also bodes ill with the practice of economic good governance. The large communities of free riders demand services without necessarily paying taxes that are crucial to make the production of public services and goods. They apparently believe in no deposit but big return, a recipe to break the back of the state finances.

The patronage mechanisms also discourage the voters to become meticulous taxpayers, for they seem to have no trust in the government that the taxes they pay will be spent for their needs rather than to the clientele or patrons of the politicians in power. The financial or banking sector crisis of 2001 revealed that approximately $40 billion USD disappeared from the accounts of more than 20 banks and financial institutions, quite a few of which are primarily owned by people related to former PM and President Demirel, who cannot be held accountable for the constitution exonerated the President from all legal and political responsibility. Hence, the taxpayers seem to ponder, why contribute to the state budget to bail out or nationalize banks and financial institutions mismanaged by the cronies of politicians in the guise of bankers? It is no wonder that the Turkish public finances have been experiencing recurring crises and repetitive breakdowns.

Given the difficulties in collecting taxes and high demands for expenditures a major discovery to placate the large community of free riders of the country has been to finance public spending by borrowing nationally and internationally. The gist of the matter was not to increase the tax burden or the tax base (i.e., the number of tax payers), while the government borrows from domestic and international markets to finance the gaping deficit between measly revenues and spectacular public spending. It amounts to payments of debt with new debt obtained at higher interest rates. This may be considered nothing more than a "pyramid scheme" by most, yet to the amazement of many, the scheme worked for a long while. One side effect of that policy was the spiraling consumer price inflation, which seemed to bother the have-nots and fixed income earners (i. e., labor, state employees, etc.), but not those who could use hard currencies in their businesses and daily transactions. Indeed, the decisions to relax the rules through a government decree (no. 32) in 1989 and render the Turkish Lira (TL) convertible enabled many to write up their contracts in D-Marks, eventually euros, or U.S. dollars.

However, a major financial tremor occurred in 1994 and signaled what was to be expected in the years to come. People deserted the TL in droves and rushed to convert their TL savings into the hard currencies of USD and the D-Mark. This move led to a huge drop in the value of the TL from $1 = 14,000 TL on December 31, 1993 to $1 = 42,000 in February 1994. The intervention of the Central Bank eventually pulled the value of the TL up to $1 = 33,000 TL. However, the damage was done. Some private banks collapsed while the government decided to insure all deposits in the Turkish banks immediately. Turkish economy entered a vortex of economic crises, from which it could only emerge ten years later.

Since 1995, many amendments of the 1982 Constitution and the related laws, regulations, and statutes have taken place, in part spurred by Turkey's determination to join the EU. The government has repeatedly announced that Turkey will erect the democratic standards demanded of her by the EU, and fulfill all of the Copenhagen Criteria of democratic standards. Hence, Turkey seems to be set to trek down the road to consolidating democracy. Paradoxically, there is scant evidence that there is any change in the popular proclivity of laxness toward rules, laws, and regulations, let alone any evidence that the people are demanding "rule of law" or strict imposition of laws, regulations, status in their daily interactions with the public bureaucracy. The overall demand for "favoritism" and patronage seems to continue. The press has been replete with stories of new attempts at erecting buildings (*gecekondus*) on state forests, where building is banned. The size of the parallel or black market still seems to be no less than about half of the legal market in Turkey. Tax collection, social security, and tax payments are still as lax as ever. The courts do not seem to have gained any more effectiveness or efficiency. Decisions of the High Administrative Court (*Danıştay*) that contradict government policies and ministerial action are still criticized vigorously by such Ministers as the Minister of National Education. There seems to be little change in the contempt that the top political and bureaucratic elite felt toward the court decisions. The High Court judges still appear in public requesting respect for the decisions of their courts from the government and the executive branch of the central government and local administrations alike.[36] Consequently, the democratic standards of the country have improved by constitutional amendments and legal reforms, while the demand and practice of rule of law stays quite modest.

In Turkey democracy and rule of law still seem to be inversely related. The overall perception is that laws and regulations are impediments holding back people from advancing in life. They are perceived in almost the Marxist sense of the term as superstructures or machinations established to protect the privileges of the few rich, and frustrate all others from having what they deserve as birthrights.[37]

FEBRUARY 2001: "MOTHER OF ALL ECONOMIC CRISES"

The gist of popular demands, other than the mainstream demand for favoritism, concentrated on economic policies. Especially important is the elimination of Turkish exceptionalism: stable high consumer price inflation of

60–80 percent price hikes per annum. It was the collapse of 21 out of 89 banks in Turkey since February 2001 that brought the country to the brink of economic bankruptcy.

The "pyramid scheme," which had been unfolding since the 1980s, had given ominous signals of financial collapse before, yet the Turkish political elites had not demonstrated the strength of taking the necessary decisions to end the practice of funding lavish public spending with loans obtained at exorbitant interest rates from the domestic and foreign markets. Turkey needed sensible tax reform, including extending the tax base in direct taxation to all voting age population. Similarly, existing steeply progressive tax rates needed to be readjusted to make income taxes non-punishing. Concomitantly, tax loopholes and tax evasion needed to be diminished for a more effective system of taxation. Of course, a reform of that nature is highly unpopular. There was one attempt at tax reform by PM Ecevit's coalition government in the early 2000s; all that accomplished was major capital flight out of the country. The government immediately reverted back to its former policies and postponed various measures.

In the meantime, the ratio of public sector borrowing requirements (PSBR) to the gross national product (GNP) of the country continued to increase dangerously. The government continued debt led economic growth policies. The increased need to borrow from the domestic markets also increased the real interest rates, which in turn increased the burden of interest payments and increased the budget deficits—debts used to pay interest on previous borrowing instead of investment.[38] Private banks moved away from direct loan extensions to the government, and borrowed from foreign markets and then used those loans to purchase government securities. Such a strategy increased the foreign exchange and interest rate risks of the banks. In short, Turkish economic growth came to depend upon highly volatile short-term capital inflows.[39] One of the most prominent students of Turkish economy concludes that it was the "populist nature of the Turkish party system that failed to provide an appropriate environment for capitalizing on the benefits and minimizing the losses associated with financial globalization."[40]

Although the IMF brokered and monitored the Turkish austerity package since 1999, the initial steep drop in interest rates simply fueled consumer spending and led to a major surge in imports.[41] The trade and current account deficits of Turkey slide from bad to worse.

The financial crisis of February 2001 came on top of a minor political crisis. The PM and the President of the country seemed to have gotten involved in a passionate exchange during a meeting of the National Security Council. PM Ecevit's announcement that the country was in a severe political crisis undermined the confidence of the markets in the government. The rapid erosion of confidence in the government tipped off a public sector banking crisis, which led to the total collapse of the austerity program, while the reputation of the IMF also suffered dearly. The TL was devalued again, from $1 = 680,000 T.L. in February to $1 = 1,200,000 T.L. in May 2001. However, this time the coalition government managed to move rapidly.

PM Ecevit appointed Kemal Derviş of the World Bank as the State Minister in Charge of the Economy. Derviş managed to instill confidence in the minds and hearts of the Turkish business community and their foreign creditors within a year.

The economy started to grow rapidly again in 2002, after a huge downturn in 2001, which also precipitated widespread unemployment of blue and white-collar labor. It seems as if the economic package put together by Derviş and the IMF has finally begun to work.

In the meantime, the confidence of the voters in the coalition government had completely waned. As the health of PM Ecevit deteriorated from bad to worse, and a shuffle in the cabinet looked possible, another government crisis broke out. In the mayhem, MHP leadership seemed to have calculated that they could go for early election, play on the feelings of nationalism, and garner enough votes to win some seats in the TGNA. The MHP called for early elections on November 3, 2002. Their calculations failed, and they performed so poorly in the national elections, and so did the other two coalition partners that they were unable to win any seats in the TGNA.

The AKP came to power in November 2002. The AKP governments of PM Gül, and later on, PM Erdoğan have essentially stuck to the same basic economic policies with success. However, the long-term performance of the Turkish economic recovery will depend upon the stability, reliability, and thus predictability of the Turkish political and economic systems. The critical conditions, which would determine that outcome, are the simultaneous consolidation of democracy and the rule of law in Turkey. Can Turkey manage to get out of the paradoxical relationship between democracy and rule of law?

AKP AT THE HELM OF GOVERNMENT

Survey research indicated that the AKP was supported at the polls by the pious Sunni, economically downtrodden, and anti-EU young voters.[42] The AKP government coincided with difficult times in Turkish politics. The first AKP government of PM Gül participated in the negotiations with the EU in the Copenhagen Summit of the EU in December 2002. Quite unexpectedly, the AKP government, and the then banned leader of AKP Erdoğan showed great enthusiasm to defend Turkish secularism against the criticisms of the Christian Democrats in the EU.

The AKP governments also had to deal with the dilemma created by the accession of Greek Cypriot government as the government of the Republic of Cyprus to the EU on May 1, 2004. The initial expressions of Erdoğan seemed to indicate that he was gearing up to give large concessions to settle the differences over a plan proposed by Kofi Annan, the General Secretary of the United Nations, known as the "Annan Plan," which proposed to establish a new federal state of Greek and Turkish political entities tied together with a loose bond. However, the AKP seemed to dither soon and returned to the traditional position of the former governments on the issue.[43] In the meantime, the U.S. plans for a preemptive strike in Iraq became a crucial development. Specifically, the government was faced with a request to use Turkish territory to attack Iraq.

The AKP government of PM Gül negotiated a plan of action with the Bush administration, and accordingly the National Assembly voted in favor of modernization of the infrastructure in Turkey for the passage and temporary deployment of the U.S. troops. However, as the U.S. action in Iraq approached the negotiations began to show signs of trouble. The AKP parliamentary group, which hosts many deputies from different political backgrounds, seemed to show signs of rupture. Some argued that the U.S. troops could not be supported against "Muslims." Others objected to the deployment of 60,000 U.S troops in Turkey for an indefinite time and status. In the meantime, Erdoğan's ban was over, and he began to organize a campaign to run for a seat of the National Assembly from the southeastern town of Siirt. He tried not to risk his election and gave no clues until the very last moment as to how he expected the AKP deputies to vote. Eventually, on March 1, 2003, the government's bill to send Turkish and U.S. troops into Iraq through Turkey failed to get enough votes in the TGNA. Technically, that would mean a no confidence vote for the government. Indeed, on March 9 Erdoğan got elected, and soon took over the prime ministership from Gül. A new era had started with PM Erdoğan at the helm of the AKP government. The Turkish army stayed out of Iraq, except for the northern enclave that the Turkish troops had been controlling for a long time to counter the potential infiltration of the PKK, which was still stationed in northern Iraq. Turkey opened up its air space to U.S. flights into Iraq, and provided logistic and humanitarian supplies to the U.S. troops and the Iraqis during 2003.

The Turkish anxiety over the threatening posture of the PKK in northern Iraq continued throughout. Although the United States considered the PKK as a terror group, and the U.S. army mopped up every terror group in Iraq, the PKK was not eliminated. The Kurdish tribes to the north of Iraq had fully cooperated with the U.S. troops in Iraq, and the terrorists they were harboring went without any notice. So, one may argue that the war on terror started to show signs of double standards in Iraq. Terrorists threatening Turkey were once more getting a "most favored" treatment, this time by the Bush administration. In international relations following principles have always been difficult. Where national interests dictated, principles could be bent, and so goes the "special relations" between PKK and the Bush administration in northern Iraq.

The AKP governments failed to do anything on the matter. Instead, Turkey was put under considerable pressure by the Bush administration to provide attractive amnesty measures to enable the PKK rank—and—file to surrender. The AKP government and the TGNA promulgated an amnesty law, yet in vain. Following such a policy, the AKP can suddenly found itself in dire contradiction with the voters of the provinces, where many had lost dear ones to PKK terror over the years. Hence, there does not seem to be much room for maneuver for the AKP government. In the meantime, Turkey seems to be marginalized over the developments of Iraq, which can have a deep running influence on Turkish society and politics.

In the midst of such international challenges, the AKP government was pressured to deal with the economic crisis, and hence, quickly decided to adopt the package offered by the IMF, and work for its success. In the meantime, the AKP was also pressured hard by the EU to adopt a series of democratic reforms, which they carried out with efficiency. However, with movement by the AKP into such difficult territory as religious education, higher education reform, religious instruction in and out of the school system, adultery, and the like, which created considerable anxiety among the ranks of the secular *kulturkampf*. While the AKP government did not follow a confrontational strategy and refrained from creating mounting tensions, it occasionally became more assertive on such conservative issues as adultery and women's rights, after the major victories at the local elections of March 28, 2004, and probably more so after the start of negotiations for full membership in the EU of October 3, 2005, Turkey can easily slide back to the 1950s, and re-live the war of the *kulturkampfs*. Whatever awaits Turkish politics, the central question that looms still pertains to democracy. How could Turkey consolidate democracy, so that democracy becomes a cherished style of life? And, how is it possible for Turkey to survive as a democracy in the midst of the most volatile regions of the world?

DEMOCRATIC VALUES AS A STYLE OF LIFE

The country has experienced dramatic changes in its settlement patterns. Two thirds of the Turkish population are now city dwellers, though most were born and raised in the villages, hamlets, and small towns, and thus possess rural— nomadic values. Production activities changed from production of agricultural products to manufactured products. Consumption patterns also adapted to such changes. The products of the Turkish textile industry are widely consumed, and so are the products of the other manufacturing industries.

Consequently, Turkey is now steadily moving toward an industrial society in which businesses that are involved in global trade are on the rise. Indeed, the waves of economic crises have led to two forms of behavior among the corporations of Turkey. One has been to become export-oriented and thus diminish full dependence upon the Turkish economy and avoid the oscillations of the Turkish market. Services, such as construction and transport have also moved part or most of their operations near abroad, such as Russia, Balkans, and Central Asia. Second has been foreign investment, which since the end of the Cold War increasingly meant investing in Eastern and Central Europe, Russia, Central Asia, Azerbaijan, and less so in Georgia. Globalization in communication, liberalization of export–import regimes of Turkey, free market capitalism at home, and Customs Union practice with the EU abroad have all contributed to the emergence of "globalization of economic practices" of Turkish companies, big and small alike since the 1990s.

The overall outcome of that process has been the gradual emergence of an entrepreneurial middle class in Turkey, whose livelihood do not fully depend upon their performance in the Turkish market. They follow, adapt, and react to changes in the global market and international trade. They depend upon professional input from Turkish and other experts, and their operations require punctuality, performance, and quality standards dictated by global demand for their products, whether they are textiles, automotive parts, processed food, or electrical and other machinery. Their demand for well-educated professional, white-collar labor has precipitated the widening of a professional middle class in Turkey. However, the changes in the labor market have been slow enough not to make a big difference in the Turkish society yet. The majority of working age population in Turkey consists of the self-employed farmers, and small shop owners and street peddlers, who are producing mainly for the domestic Turkish market. If the current trend continues into the future, in half a century or so, Turkey can have a solidly established and a large professional and entrepreneurial middle class, and a relatively large blue-collar labor as well.

If students of politics since Aristotle have been correct in arguing that democracy can only thrive in a society dominated by the middle-class and a concomitant cultural milieu, which are highly influenced by middle-class values, expectations, and priorities,[44] then Turkey has been gradually moving toward such a sociocultural environment since the 1970s.[45] However, the current society of peasants, farmers, petty shop owners, street peddlers, and their housewives, which constitute about two-thirds of the voting age population in Turkey, does not necessarily promote such a cultural milieu, that coheres with democratic values. Indeed, studies of Turkish values conducted in the last decade give clear indications that a combustible mix of values exists in the Turkish society.[46] The studies conducted on Turkish values indicate that Turkey seems to be short on social tolerance, interpersonal trust, associability, partnership, and confidence in political institutions and public authorities.[47] Using the terminology of political science, it is safe to argue that Turkish "social capital" is relatively shallow. Turkey seems to share the characteristics of southern Italy, such Latin American countries as Argentina and Colombia, and the Balkan societies in terms of the level of social capital invested in the country. Such a social milieu fails to invigorate civic action, initiatives, and citizen participation in the political affairs of the country. Such a frail picture of civil society seems to give the impression of a strong state, though that seems to be quite misleading.

As some analyses and assessments indicate, the state is quite weak in terms of its capability to regulate the behavior of its citizens, extract human and economic resources from the Turkish society, and distribute resources and values equitably and effectively.[48] The weakness of the Turkish state often leads to harsh executive action, which after the adoption of the 1982 Constitution may even be justified on constitutional grounds, for the 1982 Constitution legitimizes "executive supremacy" as the penultimate principle of organization of the political regime of Turkey. Under those circumstances, arbitrary and unaccountable executive action leads to infringement of human rights and liberties, and undermines the credentials of the democratic regime and the rule of law in Turkey.

Table 6.1 Direct Foreign Investment in Selected Countries and Regions (billion U.S. Dollars)

	1991	1995	1999	2001
World	160,2	330,5	1088,3	735,2
Developed Countries	113,1	203,3	837,8	503,1
EU Member Countries	77,7	114,4	487,9	323,0
Industrializing Countries	44,4	112,5	225,2	204,8
TURKEY	0,8	0,9	0,8	3,3
Malaysia	4,1	5,8	3,9	0,6
China	4,4	35,9	40,3	46,9
Mexico	5,7	9,6	12,5	24,7
Brazil	1,1	4,4	28,6	22,5
Argentina	2,4	5,6	24,1	3,2

Source: T.C. Başbakanlık, *Kamu Yönetiminde Yeniden Yapılanma: 1, Değişimin Yönetimi için Yönetimde Değişim* (Ankara: T.C. Başbakanlık, October 2003): 55.

The emerging middle class may demand the consolidation of democracy and rule of law, for the success of Turkish business ventures in global trade cannot be sustained without full establishment of rule of law in Turkey. Similarly, high credentials of rule of law would also trigger further interest of foreign investors in the Turkish market, which is the eighteenth largest market on earth, and Turkey is a member of G-20 countries. However, in terms of foreign investment Turkey obtains about $1 billion or less while, for example, Mexico receives approximately $5–10 billions and China obtains about $30–40 billions per annum (see table 6.1).

The slow pace of changes that would uphold democracy and fully establish rule of law eventually seem to be too slow for the taste and comfort of the burgeoning middle class of Turkey. How could the pace of those reforms be hastened?

THE EUROPEAN UNION MEMBERSHIP: POTENTIALS AND RISKS

The only plausible means of hastening the full consolidation of rule of law in Turkey seems to be associated with the Turkish efforts at becoming a member of the European Union (EU). The EU has stipulated that all candidates, and Turkey has already been declared as a candidate and eligible for full membership in the EU, should be in conformity with the criteria of the Copenhagen Summit of 1993 including "stability of institutions guaranteeing democracy, the rule of law, human rights and respect for and protection of minorities; the existence of a functioning market economy as well as the capacity to cope with competitive pressure and market forces within the Union; and the ability to take on the obligations of membership including adherence to the aims of political, economic and monetary union."[49] Given the desire of Turkey to join the EU it has to take serious strides toward rule of law.

During the accession negotiations Turkey and the EU will establish how administrative structures of the Turkish political system will be adjusted so that the European Community legislation gets "transposed into national legislations implemented effectively through appropriate administrative and judicial processes."[50] The negotiation process also involves financial support to be extended to Turkey for measures to be taken during the adjustment operations. The negotiations often take long, and for a country with the credentials of Turkey would not be surprising for the negotiations to take a minimum five to six years or more. They will on October 3, 2005 with a survey process, which will end in April 2006. Only after the latter date the negotiations will start on how Turkey is to internalize the *acquis communataire* of the EU, which are expected to last no earlier than 2013 or 2014.

As Turkey takes the steps to erect the necessary administrative structures and good governance practices to implement the *acquis*, within a decade democracy, free market capitalism, and the rule of law can be established on the infrastructure of rapidly developing modern industrial society in Turkey. In comparison to the timetable involved in the EU membership, spontaneous development of democracy, free market capitalism, and the rule of law in Turkey seem to be a snails pace process, which may materialize over some generations. What the EU accession process does is to make the demands of the emerging business community, professional and entrepreneurial middle class in Turkey more specific, pointing to concrete steps of adopting and implementing EU legislation, rules, regulations, and court decisions. Thus added to their domestic interests in the rule of law is the broader interest of joining the EU.

It is thus ironic that European ambivalence about Turkey joining the EU weakens the process of consolidating democracy and the rule of law in Turkey. For example, in October 2003, the leader of the Christian Democratic party (CDU) in Germany made it very clear that the size of Turkey and the relative poverty of the country are intimidating factors, explaining that Germany has spent all its resources in eastern Germany and eastern Europe and could not sponsor Turkish membership in the EU.

Domestically, Turkey does not seem to have a clearer picture vis-à-vis its EU orientation. The pious Sunni Muslims have grave doubts about the Roman Catholics and other Christian communities of Europe. The Turkish nationalists are also apprehensive about the idea of relaxing national sovereignty. Some have been acting with what some students of political science have been calling "*Sévres* Syndrome." It is false to assume that the European victorious powers of World War I who negotiated the draconian Treaty of *Sévres* with the Ottoman Empire are no different than the political leaders of the EU today. It is no less absurd that the political leaders of the EU today or their bureaucrats know anything about the Turkish War of Liberation, the Treaties of *Sévres* and *Lausanne*. Nevertheless, ethnic nationalists and pious Sunnis seem to unite to oppose the Turkish orientation to the EU. They seem to have an uphill battle to fight. In the 2002 elections the parties that clearly campaigned against the EU, such as the MHP and the SP got 7 percent and 2 percent of the national vote respectively. Most polls indicate that anywhere between two-thirds to three-fourths of the population are for the EU membership. Nevertheless, it is unlikely that the anti-EU camps will resign to that fact, but likely they will bitterly fight to the very end.

A failure in getting increasingly involved with the EU and an eventual membership will have unpredictable developments in Turkey. It is difficult, though not impossible, for Turkey to change its current course of increased industrialization and democratization. It is not too difficult to envision a relatively slow and tormenting pace of democratization under those circumstances. The establishment of the rule of law will also become a much more laggard process. Turkey, which perceives blatantly unfair treatment by the EU, will become much more nationalist and hostile toward the EU in the Mediterranean and the Balkans.[51] The frictions, conflict, and the risks of war will be heightened to new levels in the Aegean and over Cyprus. Turkish cooperation with the United States and Israel will probably intensify and increase in magnitude in the Middle East, Caucasus, and Central Asia, most probably to the detriment of the EU. The end of Turkish anticipation of EU membership would mean that the EU would lose all its influence over Turkey. What has been motivating Turkish governments to cooperate with the EU member countries has been the credibility and commitment to eventual EU membership. With such an objective thrashed, EU would lose all of its credibility in the eyes of the Turkish elite.

A collapse of the EU–Turkey relations at this point would not be a simple phenomenon, but one that would contribute to the development of a more nationalist Turkey in the midst of the area of "Triangle of Terror." Turkish welfare should be expected to suffer dearly from such developments, as Turkey would heavily invest in defense and much less so in education, health, and social welfare. One hopes that both parties are cognizant of what is at stake in the relations between the EU and Turkey, and employ the required tact and style to handle the negotiation process with the required tact and style.

Conclusion: Making a Bridge Functional

The odyssey of the Turkish Republic started under extremely hard conditions of the 1920s. The Turkish state was built through a war of liberation, fought on the remains of a society and country, the human and material resources of which had been decimated by a series of wars fought between 1912 and 1918. Anatolia had mostly been spared from being a battle zone in that period, except in the east, where large refugee movements had been undermining its frail economy and shallow resources before the War of Liberation. However, the War of Liberation turned almost all of Anatolia into a battle zone. The ethnic nationalist armies viciously attacked each other killing, destroying, plundering, and decimating the landscape to the best of their ability. Not only lives were lost, but also whole city blocks, towns, even cities, such as Van in the east, or Salihli in the west were wiped off the earth. When the Greek army pulled out of the western parts of Anatolia in 1922 the fertile plains of the Aegean region lay in waste. The soldiers of the Turkish cavalry that rode through the wasteland of west Anatolia to İzmir (Smyrna) almost suffocated with the terrible smell of burnt flesh of the Muslim inhabitants of the villages and towns from Afyon to the coast. The "scorched earth" policies of the defeated nationalist armies of Greece in the west and Armenia in the east almost depleted all agricultural resources of vast regions of Anatolia at the end of the War of Liberation.

The performance of the Turkish economy under the leadership of Atatürk and the Republican People's Party governments of the single-party regime in the 1920s and the 1930s was remarkable, though it failed to last under the weight of the World War in the 1940s. Turkey moved toward multiparty democracy and industrialization through state initiated private entrepreneurship. These developments unleashed a rapid process of social mobilization, when large swathes of rural populations engulfed the urban centers of the country.

A comparative look at Turkish socioeconomic and political characteristics indicates that the performance of the government, economy, and social institutions fail to be impressive (see table 7.1). For example, the Turkish army participated in the United Nations Force in the Korean War, which also left that country and its economy in shatters in the early 1950s. However, when you compare the socioeconomic performance of Turkish society with that of South Korea since the 1950s, there seems to be an impressive gap between the two countries to the detriment of Turkey (table 7.1).

Table 7.1 Turkey, Neighbors, the European Union, the United States, and other Regional and Global Actors

Countries	Gross National Income per capita PPP* (U.S. Dollars) 2003	Gini Index	Life Expectancy at Birth 2002	Under-5 Mortality Rate per 1000 people 2002	Adult Illiteracy Rate (% people 15 and above) 2002	Electrical Power Consumption per captia kilowatt-hours** 1997	Internet Hosts per 10,000 people** 2000	Scientists and Engineers in R&D per million people** 1987–1997	Mobile Phones per 1000 people** 1998	TV Sets per 1000 people** 1998	High Technology Exports as % of manufacturing Exports** 1998
United States	37610	40.8	77	8		11822	1939.97	3676	256	847	33
Japan	28620	24.9	82	5		7241	208.06	4909	374	707	26
Germany	27460	28.3	78	5		5626	207.62	2831	170	580	14
France	27460	32.7	79	6		6060	131.47	2659	188	601	23
United Kingdom	27650	36	77	7		5241	321.39	2448	252	645	28
Italy	26760	36	78	6	1	4315	114.42	1318	355	486	8
Israel	19200	35.5	79	6	5	5069	225.1		359	318	20
Korea,Rep.	17930	31.6	74	5		4847	60.03	2193	302	346	27
Greece	19920	35.4	78	5	3	3493	73.84	773	194	466	7
Portugal	17980	38.5	76	6	7	3206	90.67	1182	309	542	4
Hungary	13780	24.4	72	9	1	2840	113.38	1099	105	437	21
Argentina	10920	52.2	74	19	3	1634	38.48	660	78	289	5
Poland	11450	31.6	74	9		2451	47.26	1358	50	413	3
Russian Federation	8920	45.6	66	21	0	3981	14.69	3587	5	420	12
Brazil	7480	59.1	69	37	14	1743	26.22	168	47	316	9
Romania	7140	30.3	70	21	3	1704	11.02	1387	29	233	2
Turkey	6690	40	70	41	13	1275	13.92	291	53	286	2
Iran	7190	43	69	41	23	1163	0.09	560	6	157	
Colombia	6520	57.6	72	23	8	885	9.59		49	217	9
Bulgaria	7610	31.9	72	16	1	3203	14.5	1747	15	398	4
China	4990	44.7	71	38	9	714	162.82		19	272	15
Syria	3430		70	28	17	776	0	30	0	70	
Azerbaijan	3380	36.5	65	96		1631	0.16	2791	8	254	
Armenia	3770	37.9	75	35	1	1141	2.11	1485	2	218	
Georgia	2540	36.9	73	29		1142	1.7		11	473	5

Source: World Development Report, 2005: 256-264.

Notes: * PPP stands for Purchasing Power Parity. ** The corresponding column is from the World Development Report, 2002: 308-311.

The same conclusions can be reached with ease in similar comparisons with Greece, Israel, and Poland (table 7.1). The overall standing of Turkey in international comparisons of economic and human development places her somewhere between Brazil, Colombia, Romania, and Bulgaria. The education, health, science and engineering research and development performances of Turkey seem to be quite dismal. The child mortality rates of Turkey have been appallingly high. Health care and education have failed to improve. There seems to be one main factor culpable for the poor human development record of the country, and that seems to concentrate over the issue of women's rights and empowerment. For example, the 15 percent illiterate among those who are above the age of 15 are overwhelmingly women (table 7.1).

Indeed, Republican Turkey was one of the first political systems of the world to extend socioeconomic and political rights to women in the 1930s. However, the chronic rule of law problems of Turkey emerged as a major hurdle before the girls of the country. The patriarchal patrons of their families (i.e., father, brother, uncle, husband, etc.), inhibit women from enjoying what the laws have provided for them. The political authorities have been lax in implementing the laws of the land to provide women with their legal rights. One reason seems to be the overall laxness of the rule of law practices in the country. Second, most political authorities in Turkey seem to act with the assumption that a problem gets solved when a law gets promulgated on the matter. There is no evidence that they pay much attention to whether the laws of the land get implemented. Third, politics has been a "male game" in Turkey (where currently less than 4 percent of the deputies of the National Assembly are women), and hence women have not been able to wield much influence to make political structures work to their advantage.

Governmental mismanagement of the socioeconomic and political affairs of the country accounts for Turkey's comparatively poor performance. Turkish politics has been replete with long periods of political instability, some of which were married also with government instability.[1] Its political culture fosters a form of democracy as populism and emphasizes the "awe of the state," lack of tolerance with dissent and pluralism, and promotes a vision of the political competition as taking place between the forces of "good" and "evil." Therefore relations between elected governments and oppositions are hard to manage. The image of the state as an omnipotent economic actor with infinite resources seemed to have precipitated the voters and the political elites alike, to act without any discretion, but as "free-riders," who jointly spoiled the emoluments of the state budget and other public resources. Huge budgetary and balance of foreign trade deficits were fueled through complicity of the voters and their representatives. Turkish political elite possesses a proclivity to act as if they have a rentier state, without possessing vast deposits of any strategic natural resource, such as oil, though political geography of the country provides a form of strategic "rent" that Turkey often manages to exploit.

There are also several properties of the country that provide for a lot of potential. Turkey has about 70 million population; its total Gross National

Product represents a large market, and it has a relatively large young population. The Internet, and information technology use has made strides into the remotest corners of the country. Mobile, standard, and cellular phones have become an integral part of Turkish social life in the early 2000s (see table 7.1). The ostentatious use of the cellular phones in every part of the country is one indication of the potential for the future of the information technologies in Turkey. The innovations made by the Turkish cellular phone companies in software applications are another. High technology product manufacturing has also been on the rise, with Beko, Goldstar, and Vestel as such corporations, producing fruits of digital technologies for the European and the world markets. The question now is: How far and effective can Turkey be in coping with the challenges of overcoming sociopolitical instability, uncertainty, and political bickering, and rise above them?

Being placed in the hub of the Balkans, Caucasus, and the Middle East, that is, the three most volatile regions of the world, and connected to all of them through history, ethnicity, religion, and socioeconomic ties renders Turkey a valuable asset in managing the conflicts of those areas, or a potential liability for world peace. Turkish foreign policy had been based on upholding the status quo provided by the Treaty of *Lausanne*. Having sharply deviated from the Ottoman foreign policy of revisionism Turkey refrained from irredentist policies. Turkey did not cause a war in its neighboring regions. Instead, the country played a major role in peacekeeping in the Balkans, Middle East, and the Transcaucasus. Indeed, Turkey seemed to have provided a scarce asset, that of following a status quoist foreign policy in the most volatile regions surrounding it.

Such a service became to function as "rent" or "strategic asset" for Turkey, which NATO, and in particular the United States valued in the past. Hence, the Turkish governments were able to get away with mismanagement of their own economic house. They found a safety net provided by the United States and some other NATO member countries, or through their intervention with the International Monetary Fund (IMF) or the IBRD (World Bank). Ironically, being cognizant of such a "safety net" seemed to have led Turkish governments to act with much laxness, more than they otherwise could afford. In fact, it is not very clear whether being a strategic asset was a curse or blessing for Turkey. So far, it seems as if it also contributed to the governmental mismanagement of the Turkish economy with full complicity of the Turkish voters.

TURKISH MODEL: ISLAMIC REVIVAL VERSUS SECULAR DEMOCRACY?

Turkey has been coping with the challenges of its foreign environment, and its domestic woes through a *sui generis* secular and democratic political practice. History and culture have endowed Turkey with a plethora of ethnic groups, religious communities, Islamic sects, and religious (*Sufi*) orders. Those ethno-religious communities are not only peculiar to Turkey, and they spread over a vast territory spanning from Bosnia, Albania, and Serbia (and since the 1960s Germany), in the west to Iraq, Syria, Jordan, Israel, Egypt, Tunisia, Algeria in the south, and to Tatarstan, and Yakutsk in Siberia in the north, through the Caucasus, Iran, and Central Asia to Xingiang, China in the east. Ethno-religious politics seems to be where the tribal meets the regional, and even, the international politics of the day. For example, when the Chechens in northern Caucasus are bombed by the Russian army, or when the Abkhaz are attacked by the Georgians, or when the Kurdish irregulars of north of Iraq clash with the Turkomen in Kirkuk, Iraq, or when the Serbs start to massacre the Bosniaks in Bosnia-Herzegovina, their relatives, compatriots, and brethren in Turkey, as Turkish citizens, start to pressure the Turkish government to take action. It is not uncommon to listen to the pleas of the Uzbeks of Afghanistan, or Uygur of China, or the Gagauz of Moldova, on the Turkish media for political and humanitarian relief. The weight of history is a heavy burden on the shoulders on Turkish society and on every Turkish government.

It is also a matter of fact that most nation-states, which have been established on the former Ottoman lands, continue to view the Turkish Republic as the new version of that, now defunct Ottoman political heartland. There has been considerable amount of interest in socioeconomic and political developments of Turkey around the Mediterranean, Black Sea, and Caspian Basins. It is quite common for Turkish academics to be approached by colleagues from these regions in international conferences with queries about the vicissitudes of Turkish politics, economics, and culture. Such practices and perceptions sometimes lead international and specifically U.S. commentators and pundits of international politics to speculate about a "Turkish Model." Some even toyed with the idea of making Turkey an example, or setting up a Turkish precedent to be replicated by the Middle Eastern, Trancaucasian, and Central Asian countries, which are assumed to share similar characteristics with Turkey. So, is there a "Turkish Model" that can be replicated elsewhere?

Turkish nation-state has specific cultural characteristics. Its cultural pattern is shaped by such forces and traits as patrimonial style of Imperial rule, Sunni versus *Alevi* Islam, secularization, modernization, nationalism, war of liberation, economic development, rapid social mobilization, and democratization. Since its establishment the Turkish Republic has gone through various challenges and developments all of which have left their indelible marks on the current political system and the regime of the country, and the "political self" of its citizens. Its birthmarks include an arduous existential national struggle of resistance to occupation.

The Turkish nation-state and citizens suffered a period of occupation, yet they were never colonized. The resistance to occupation was carried out against enormous odds and the nationalist forces won a victory. On the one hand, the image of the "West" that lingered on in the minds and hearts of the Turkish people was at best ambivalent. On the other, the image of the "West and the Westerners" in Turkish eyes may best be depicted as sly and slick businessmen, conniving politicians, cunning diplomats, and professional soldiers, who should be guarded against and great care taken when making deals, and signing treaties. However, the Turkish War of Liberation resulted in the development of a sense of parity with the European nation-states to develop among the Turkish citizens.

In the political consciousness of the Turkish citizens the War of Liberation still looms large. Consequently, it often surprises many foreign observers that there is so much affection for the founding leader and the first President of the Turkish nation-state, Mustafa Kemal Atatürk. He has been the symbol of resistance to foreign occupation and domination, and signifies national pride of Turkey.

Although one may discover many references to "Kemalism" or "Atatürkism," there is no evidence that Mustafa Kemal Atatürk tried to establish any form of "official ideology" for the republican regime. There are some indications to the contrary, that he warned his followers that they should only act with reason based on science, or act "reasonably" rather than through some kind of ideological rigidity based on what he had done or preached in his lifetime. However, under the rule of İsmet İnönü as the President of the country (1938–1950), and later, and most specifically again in the early 1980s there were efforts at establishing an ideology of "Kemalism" or "Atatürkism." There is no evidence that there was any mass appeal of such efforts, and though we have no study at hand, there are some unobtrusive measures, such as widely shared jokes, cartoons, ridicule, and the like, which indicate that such efforts have, in part, been quite counterproductive. Crass methods used in producing an ideology out of Atatürk's sayings and doings failed to erect an "official ideology," but the overdose of propaganda efforts, which created an industry of propagandists, on the one hand, and a reaction of callousness to such propaganda by the men and women in the street, on the other. There also seems to be some evidence that such efforts were popularly perceived as an attempt by corrupt governments to sanctify their otherwise unacceptable style of rule, and suppress opposition directed at their policies in the post-1980 politics of Turkey.

Nevertheless, there is hardly any doubt that Atatürk's dream of placing Turkey among the modern nation-states of a civilized world are taken to heart by a vast majority of the citizens of the country. His method, policies, and means to achieve modernity are still hotly debated, and the voters of Turkey are far from resolving their differences over how to develop and become modern. However, there is hardly any doubt that a huge majority of the people of Anatolia and eastern Thrace are keen on becoming modern and live in a developed economy.

The Turkish perception of the "West" also encompasses success in science, enhanced welfare, power, security, and civilized lifestyle. Atatürk's efforts of pointing to the fact that the Ottoman collapse had much to do with lack of industrialization, lack of attention paid to science education, and use of scientific knowledge in life have received widespread acceptance in Turkey. His depiction of "civilization" as advanced scientific enterprise, industrial development, and modern society has received popular acceptance from large swathes of the Turkish society. The image of the "ugly" European that other former Ottoman subjects, such as the Arabs have come to develop due to Western colonization, never took serious root in Turkey. Turkish nationalists of the 1920s seemed to believe that to become powerful, secure, and rich Turkey had to trek down the road of science and industrialization, and erect a secular sociopolitical order. Hence, European society and politics were not ignominious machinations to be avoided, but continued to be precedents to be emulated in the Turkish eyes. It has not been uncommon to read and hear references made to Japan on how to become modern, as a model on how to be successful by adopting, emulating and excelling at producing science and technology of the "West" yet preserve the "moral norms" of one's native culture.

There is still no political party that propagates to reinstall the Caliphate or the Ottoman monarchy. There have been some examples of political parties that have come close to suggesting some form of going back to the "golden past," yet they failed to convince more than one fifth of the voters, and were soon marginalized in Turkish politics. Overwhelming majorities of no less than two thirds of the voting age Turkish voters seem to be most committed to the idea of becoming a member of the European Union, rather than go forward to a "golden past."

Over the last 80 years Turkey developed a national economy, a more integrated society and culture, where habits, customs, foods, music, and other art forms have become accepted in parts of the country and the places of society in which they had never been experienced before. Someone growing up in Istanbul or Ankara in the 1950s hardly had a chance to eat "*lahmacun*" (originally Arabic *lehm-i ajun*, or bread with hamburger), which is a different version of pizza, and a product of the southeastern cuisine of Turkey, at a "*kebapçı*" (a restaurant that caters various styles of grilled hamburger, meat and poultry chops known as *kebab*). There were hardly any *kebap* restaurants in the major western parts of Turkey until the 1960s. Now, there is hardly any child who does not know a *kebap* restaurant in Istanbul or Ankara. At least two generations of Turks have been dancing to the styles tunes of Anatolian folk songs (such as *gazel*), in the most popular discotheques and dance clubs of the country, which even in the 1960s would have been considered as "absurd" or even "uncivilized."

It also took a lot of horizontal social mobility, whereby millions departed from their homes in search of new opportunities in the big cities of the country and abroad (Germany), which often started as a temporary search and eventually becoming a permanent change of lifestyle. Rapid urbanization sustained a labor market for a burgeoning industry. However, urbanization also provided fertile grounds for new social ills. Homeless children take their sojourns in the streets of the Turkish cities, shantytowns built on plundered public land exist in the gray zone of alegality often act as breeding ground for crime, as well as political extremism. Marxism–Leninism, ethnic nationalisms, religious eccentricity, political Islam, racism, and so on, find impeccable conditions to develop and persist.

Democratization has enabled the underground religious orders (*tarikats*), such as the Nurcu, Nakşibendi, Süleymancı, and so on, to surface, and to participate in politics through legal "front" associations, corporations, as well as clandestine factions in political parties. They soon were able to proselytize, though in violation of the laws of the land, large swathes of the rural population. Eventually, with the added success at the polls of the political parties that harbored such Islamic revivalist groups and communities, they were able to gain representation in the National Assembly, Cabinet Ministries, and the public bureaucracy. Gradually, the former cultural fault lines of the Ottoman Empire and the *kulturkampfs* strategically located at the opposite sides of such cultural cleavages reemerged in Turkey.

Nevertheless, the domestic and international experiences and developments reinforced democracy, and secularization in Turkey. Some would regret that the pristine form of Atatürkist secularism no longer exists. Sociopolitical conflict over specific issues that range from *tesettür* (covering up of some Muslim women in public) to teaching of creationism versus Darwinism at high schools and universities to *takiyye* (i.e., compelled to act with false pretenses while sticking to a hidden agenda until an expedient time arrives), of parties with religious credentials have been going on for the last two decades. In the 1950s such confrontations degenerated into a "no-holds-barred-war,"[2] and eventually precipitated a military takeover of civilian government. However, now the same debates have not degenerated into a clash of forces of Atatürkist revolution versus counterrevolution. Tolerance for political opposition seems to be increasing, and a terminology of "good governance" seems to be slowly creeping into the legal framework, although social tolerance still seems to be considerably shallow.[3] However, what seems to be a more important development has been the lack of success of political parties that overtly use Islam as a banner at the polls. The last of such political parties to experience some success at the polls were the Welfare (RP) and Virtue Parties (FP). They suffered severe difficulties in government or in the National Assembly. They developed an image of making trouble for the secular Republic, yet were unable to change it or manage the government.

Currently, the Justice and Development Party (AKP) was established by a group of younger members of the RP-FP elite, and had a stellar success at the latest elections of November 3, 2002, carefully distanced themselves from their past Islamic revivalist records, and have been systematically arguing that politics and religion should be kept apart. The leader of the party and the PM Erdoğan unambiguously stated at an international conference that political practice through and by means of religious propaganda is detrimental to democracy.[4] He further maintained that religion and politics should be kept apart to guarantee the smooth operation of democracy, and went on to argue repeatedly that his party is a "democratic conservative" party. It has already been mentioned that AKP has been vying for membership in the People's Parties (Christian Democratic parties) network of Europe.

In the meantime the legal framework of secularism is still preserved, mostly unscathed from all of the above-mentioned political bickering and conflict. However, we should not conclude that Turkey has solved all of its problems with secularism and religiosity in public life. There are still many small and well-organized groups in the country, which can easily be mobilized to attack what they consider to be evil symbols. In December 2003 Istanbul suffered four such attacks, which killed more than 60 people and injured hundreds, and caused havoc in the city, while destroying ancient Jewish temples, on the one hand, houses and businesses of Muslims, on the other. Some evidence was unearthed, which incriminated the al-Qaeda with those attacks. Turkey has been suffering from internationally funded and supported ethnic and religious terror since the early 1970s. Such a lengthy history of struggle with political, ideological, ethnic, and religious terror has left a lingering distaste for extremism among the Turkish public, on the one hand, and a search for stability and security, on the other. One outcome of such a proclivity has been the very high confidence in the institution of the armed forces that is often registered by mass surveys and national polls. Simultaneously, a tendency not to support political parties at the polls that seek confrontation and conflict with the major political forces of the country as business community and the army exists. Thus, former PM Erbakan, who depicted such a confrontational picture lost in the 1999 and 2002 general elections, while a much more soft-speaking and less confrontational PM Erdoğan and his Justice and Development Party (AKP) won in the 2002 elections.

A final characteristic of the Turkish political practice has been a drive toward democratic consolidation. Turkey was one of the earlier nation-states that vied for multiparty pluralist democracy. The start of the Turkish democratic odyssey cannot be dated any later than 1946, which should place Turkey in the same group of democratic states as Italy, Germany, India, Japan, Israel, and Greece. However, most students of democracy tend to ignore the Turkish case. Obviously, we can suspect of a deep-rooted sense of "orientalism" or "ethnocentricism" toward Turkey among some European scholars. However, it is also true that the Turkish record of democracy has been erratic. There were periods of democratic governance, such as 1950–1959, 1963–1971, 1973–1980, 1987–2004, and there were periods of one-partyism in disguise during 1946–1950, 1959–1960, military interregna, intervention and heavy-handed meddling into civilian, democratically elected governments during 1961–1963, 1971–1973, 1980–1987.

Indeed, Turkish political regime should be defined as a parliamentary form of democracy. Currently it may best be termed something like a "semi-parliamentary" practice of democracy, where a politically and legally irresponsible President elected by the National Assembly (NA) functions with a popularly elected NA and a Prime Minister (PM), who has both legal and political responsibility for his own, of his Cabinet's, and of the President's actions. The President is more than a titular head of state, yet his mandate is at best vague and at worst problematic. Coalition governments have been ruling Turkey for a long time, and they have been much more cantankerous, slow, and incoherent, often creating criticism for poor performance. However, a recent study seems to indicate that the current record of the AKP not withstanding, there was hardly any difference in their economic and human development performance of coalition or party governments in Turkey between 1946 and 1999.[5]

Finally, the Regular Report of the EU Commission on October 6, 2004 about Turkey's progress toward accession concluded that Turkey has met the Copenhagen Criteria for being a political democracy with a modern economy.[6] The European Council showed Turkey the green light on starting accession negotiation with the European Union on October 3, 2005 in the EU Summit on December 17, 2004. It is an interesting process to watch a PM, who had started his political career as a militant among the ranks of the National Viewpoint (*Milli Görüş*) movement, served as a RP mayor of Greater City of Istanbul, and spent time in prison for anti-secular seditious activity, to lead Turkey to negotiations with the EU. In the meantime, the main opposition party of CHP, which has been the powerhouse of secular modernism in Turkey, demonstrates great skepticism toward the pro-EU perspective of the AKP. However, the CHP and its leaders are ardent nationalists, while Erdoğan and the AKP frontbench members have spent long years as staunch believers of political Islam, which considers nationalism as a relic of the pre-Islamic society and a sin (*qavmiyyet*). Hence, what better party to negotiate with the EU than one with distinct nonnationalist proclivities to orient Turkey toward a regional integration project like the EU, which requires that some compromises be made of nationalism as economies and polities merge?

So, what is the moral of the story on the Turkish model? Although the answer to that is affirmative, it is a model not very different from any other agricultural society trying to modernize and industrialize through secularization and democratization, in a society sharply divided through cultural and social fault lines. The Turkish record of secularization has been quite *sui generis*, and very hard to export anywhere else. Turkish history had a determining role in the development of secular practices in the country. Had the forces of the Caliphate won the War of Liberation, it would have been immensely difficult or even impossible for Turkey to become secular.

It is totally off the point to refer to Turkey as an "Islamic democracy," "moderate Islamic society," or "moderate Islam," whatever those may mean. Turkey is a secular democracy operating in a society and culture deeply divided into profane/mundane versus sacred/spritual, into *Alevi* and Sunni sectarian communities, into anticlerical and clerical groups, into Kurdish and Turkish ethnic nationalists, into ethnic versus civic nationalists, and into leftists versus the rightists, and so on. Such cultural variety cannot simply be reduced to "Islamic society," and the political practice into a "moderate Islamic democracy." Turkey has so far managed to keep a track record of preserving a secular legal system, a distinct tendency toward multiparty parliamentary democracy, demonstrate a capability to co-opt and ameliorate the challenges of radical Islamic revivalist parties, preserve its national and territorial integrity, and still continue with the experiment of co-opting and de-radicalizing ethnic nationalist parties and forces. Could such a track record be replicated?

Secularism, just like any other political practice or idea, requires believers to be implemented. The stronger and the more populous its supporters, the stronger will become the practice of secularism. In Turkey urban middle class, intellectuals, most of the press and the media, middle-class women, most labor unions, the *Alevi* community, the legal establishment, the armed forces, and so on, are solidly lined up to defend secularism. It is very unlikely that one can find a similar line up in other Muslim countries now or in the foreseeable future.

Turkey also managed to sustain the same coalition of forces to engage in the game of democracy long enough with tangible dividends, that authoritarianism only becomes an alternative when the civilian, democratically elected politicians mismanage the political system, and drive it to the brink of collapse. And, even then authoritarianism had only been temporarily tolerated. Any attempt by the military to conspicuously establish themselves in the game of democracy, such as through their own political parties, has backfired. Most recently, the voters rebuffed the parties of the military government at the polls in 1983. NATO membership, and the EU vocation have also seemed to have helped Turkey to solidify its democracy.

CONSPIRACY VERSUS MAGNANIMITY

One fundamental factor that seems to be holding Turkey back from reaching her potential seems to be established in the deep sense of distrust the people and their leaders feel toward their neighbors, and toward the major international actors. One may refer to it as a sort of siege mentality. The Turkish elites as well as the masses are more inclined to view the world as a hostile place ready to take a bite out of Turkey, whenever Turkey slips. That Turks are alone in the world, have no friends and many foes often find their way into political slogans and clichés. Using such propaganda to win votes is one thing, believing in it is another.

Most recently Turkey found another Super or even Hyper Power next door. The longtime "strategic ally" of Turkey, the United States, armed with the ideology of "neoconservatism" married with the ideology of "clash of civilizations" invaded Iraq in 2003, and Turkey became neighbor to another powerful state to its south. The way the United States seemed to be handling Iraq again causes a lot of concern and even consternation among Turkish political pundits and authorities. Turkish authorities perceive that a break-up of Iraq along ethnic lines will function as another cause for rekindling hostilities between Kurdish nationalists and Turkey. Turkish authorities have started to argue since January 2004 that the U.S. authorities in Iraq have been following double standards on terrorism by sparing the PKK from the treatment exacted for Ansar-e Islam and other terror groups on Iraqi soil. The visit of the Turkish PM to Washington, DC in late January 2004 seemed to make some dent in the U.S. policies toward the PKK, though that may just be no more than a temporary "goodwill gesture" than a change of policy toward international terror threatening Turkey. In fact, such gestures failed to prevent the PKK, under the new name of Kongra-Gel to launch a new terror campaign against Turkey in June 2004. More recent visits by the commander of the U.S. troops in Iraq, General Abizade to Ankara in January 2005 led to another series of goodwill gestures, but made it very clear that the United States will do nothing about the PKK in Iraq.

Turkey has a large population, a rapidly modernizing and experienced army, and a comparatively large gross national product vis-à-vis its neighboring regions and states. The continued rapprochement with the EU would further reinforce the position of Turkey in the three regions she belongs in. Consequently, with EU membership self-confidence of Turkey would be ripe for a boost. Under those circumstances, foreign threats for territorial integrity of Turkey will become much more difficult to voice. Consequently, Turkey can act as a big brother for its neighbors, and provide them an opportunity to integrate with the European markets and the West. That, in and of itself, should function as a source of attraction for Turkey. Feeling more secure and self-confident Turkey can start to act with magnanimity toward her neighbors, neighboring communities and contribute to their stability, while reinforcing her own. The EU perspective of Turkey would also be expected to function as a greater impetus for stability in Turkey, as well as for the Caucasus, Middle East, and the Balkans. Interestingly enough, EU membership may indeed be no less than reinforcement of a role for Turkey that may best be defined as a bridge or as dynamic mechanism that hinges Eurasia with the Middle East and Africa. Such a role has mostly been a political or military strategic function for Turkey. Now, a multifarious economic, cultural, and diplomatic role of extending Europe's values and norms into the "Greater Middle East" and Eurasia seems to be developing for Turkey. It seems as if the current Turkish society and government seemed to have grasped the importance of the new role, and have now been gearing up for it for a change. Turkish government thus started 2004 with various initiatives, which not only demonstrate Turkey's resolve to live up to her self-image as a bridge over troubled lands, connecting cultures, but also show that Turkey can be part of the solution of such problems as Cyprus or Iraq abroad, and consolidating a democracy sensitive to ethnic and religious differences at home. How Turkey, EU, and the United States will manage this new Turkish resolve will have deep running influences over the future of Turkish polity and economy, and the regions that surround Turkey and beyond. If Turkey fails to live up to her new role now, the Turkish government and the Turkish voters will not be the only ones to blame.

NOTES

INTRODUCTION: CHANGE AND STABILITY

1. IBRD, World Development Report 2005, *A Better Investment Climate for Everyone* (New York: World Bank and Oxford University Press, 2004): 257.
2. Cem Behar et. al., *Turkey's Window of Opportunity: Demographic Transition Process and Its Consequences* (Istanbul: TÜSİAD Publication No-T/99-3-254, 1999): 32.
3. IBRD, World Development Report 2001/2002, *Building Institutions for Markets* (Oxford, England: Oxford University Press, 2001): 279.
4. Behar et. al., *Turkey's Windows of Opportunity*, 32.
5. Ibid., 34.
6. IBRD, World Development Report 2005, *A Better Investment*, 257. The figure reported in that publication is based upon purchasing power parity conversion of the actual figure for the Turkish national gross income.
7. TÜSİAD, *Türkiye Ekonomisi 2004* (İstanbul: TÜSİAD Publications, 2004): 91. The same publication reports on page 91 that the 2003 Gross National Product (GNP) was 356,981 million T.L., the 2004 GNP was 424,129 million T.L., and the 2005 estimate is 480,963 million T.L. In U.S. dollar terms those figures are $258 billions for 2003, $295 billions for 2004.
8. Ibid., 257.
9. Undersecretariat of the Prime Ministry for Foreign Trade <www.dtm.gov.tr/ead/english/indicators/indc.htm>, 2004: Table ecoindicators.
10. IBRD, World Development Report 2005, *Building Institutions*, 257.
11. Patrimonial rule constitutes a style of rule that functions as "an extension of the ruler's household in which the relation between the ruler and his officials remains on the basis of paternal authority and filial dependence," Reinhard Bendix, *Max Weber: An Intellectual Portrait* (Garden City, N.Y.: Doubleday, 1962): 360.
12. M. E. Yapp, *The Making of the Modern Middle East: 1792–1923* (London and New York: Longman, 1987): 63.

1 FROM COLLAPSE TO LIBERATION

1. Standford J. Shaw and Ezer Kural Shaw, *History of the Ottoman Empire and Modern Turkey: Volume II: Reform, Revolution and the Republic: The Rise of Modern Turkey, 1808–1975* (Cambridge, London, New York, Melbourne: Cambridge University Press, 1977): 182.
2. Ibid., 187.
3. This form of government may best be referred to as neo-patrimonialism as proposed by C. Clapham, *Third World Politics: An Introduction* (Madison, Wisconsin: University of Wisconsin Press, 1988): 44–50.

4. Niyazi Berkes, *The Development of Secularism in Turkey* (Montreal: McGill University Press, 1964).
5. Ibid., 256.
6. Ibid., 256.
7. Ibid., 256.
8. Tarık Zafer Tunaya, *Türkiye'de Siyasal Partiler: İttihat ve Terakki: Bir Çağın, Bir Kuşağın, Bir Partinin Tarihi*, vol. III (Istanbul: Hürriyet Vakfı Yayınları, 1989): 7.
9. Bernard Lewis, *Islam in History: Ideas, People, and Events in the Middle East* (New Edition, revised and expanded) (Chicago and La Salle, Illinois:Open Court Publishing Co., 1993): 327–328.
10. Y. Hakan Erdem, "The Wise Old Man, Propagandist and Ideologist: Koca Sekbanbaşi on the Janissaries, 1807," in Kirsi Virtanen (ed.), *Individual, Ideologies and Society: Tracing the Mosaic of Mediterranean History* (Tampere, Finland: Tampere Peace Research Institute, 2000): 153–177.
11. Bernard Lewis, *Islam in History*, 284, 339.
12. Ibid., 322.
13. Ibid., 322.
14. Stephen Fischer-Galati (1992), "Eastern Europe in the Twentieth Century: 'Old Wine in New Bottles,'" in Joseph Held (ed.), *The Columbia History of Eastern Europe in the Twentieth Century* (New York: Columbia University Press, 1992): 3.
15. Shaw and Shaw, *History of the Ottoman Empire*, 108, 137.
16. Tahir Taner, "Ceza Hukuku," in Komisyon (ed.), *Tanzimat 1* (Ankara: Milli Eğitim Bakanlığı Yayınları: no. 3273, 1999): 224; and Gülnihal Bozkurt, "Tanzimat and Law," in *Atatürk Kültür, Dil ve Tarih Yüksek Kurumu* (ed.), *Tanzimat'ın 150. Yıldönümü Uluslararası Sempozyumu* (Ankara: Türk Tarih Kurumu Basımevi, 1994): 280.
17. Hıfzı Veldet, "Kanunlaştırma Hareketleri ve Tanzimat," in Komisyon (ed.), *Tanzimat 1* (Ankara: Milli Eğitim Bakanlığı Yayınları: no. 3273, 1999): 175–202.
18. Sadrettin Celal Antel, "Tanzimat Maarifi," in Komisyon (ed.), *Tanzimat 1*, (Ankara: Milli Eğitim Bakanlığı Yayınları: no. 3273, 1999): 459.
19. Ibid., 458–460.
20. Ahmet Mumcu, *Osmanlı Devletinde Siyaseten Katl* (Ankara: Sevinç Matbaası, 1985): 58–67.
21. Ibid., 60–62.
22. Ibid., 65–67.
23. Veldet, "Kanunlaştırma," 140.
24. Nur Yalman, "Some Observations on Secularism in Islam: The Cultural Revolution in Turkey," *Daedalus*, 102 (1973): 152.
25. Berkes, *The Development of Secularism in Turkey*, 337–346.
26. Ibid., 346–366.
27. Kemal H. Karpat, *Ottoman Population 1830–1914: Demographic and Social Characteristics* (Madison, Wisconsin: The University of Wisconsin Press, 1985): 72.
28. Ibid., 74.
29. Ilter Turan, *Cumhuriyet Tarihimiz: Temeller, Kuruluş, Milli Devrimler* (Istanbul: Çağlayan Kitabevi, 1969): 29–30.
30. Ibid., 30.

31. David Kushner, *The Rise of Turkish Nationalism 1876–1908* (London: Frank Cass, 1977): 9.
32. Turan, *Cumhuriyet Tarihimiz*, 23.
33. Kushner, *The Rise of Turkish Nationalism*, 9.
34. Ibid., 10.
35. Ibid., 10.
36. Ibid., 11.
37. Ibid., 11.
38. Enver Ziya Karal, *"Preface,"* in *Yusuf Akçura, Üç Tarz-ı Siyaset* (Ankara: Türk Tarih Kurumu Basımevi, 1976): 4.
39. Kushner, *The Rise of Turkish Nationalism*, 13–14.
40. Karal, "Preface," 2; Kushner, *The Rise of Turkish Nationalism*, 13–14.
41. Karal, "Preface," 2.
42. Yusuf Akçura, *Üç Tarz-ı Siyaset* (Ankara: Türk Tarih Kurumu Basımevi, 1976): 19.
43. Ibid., 21.
44. Ibid., 23.
45. Ibid., 23.
46. Ibid., 34.
47. Ibid., 34–35.
48. Mehmet Kaplan, "Ziya Gökalp'in Hayatı ve Eserleri Hakkında Birkaç Söz," in *Ziya Gökalp, Türkçülüğün Esasları (Türk Klasikleri)* (prepared for publication by Mehmet Kaplan) (Istanbul: Milli Eğitim Bakanlığı Yayınları, 1990): I.
49. See also Niyazi Berkes, *Turkish Nationalism and Western Civilization: Selected Essays of Ziya Gökalp* (New York: Columbia University Press, 1959): 18, 20.
50. Ibid., 22.
51. Kaplan, "Ziya Gökalp'in Hayatı ve Eserleri Hakkında Birkaç Söz," IV.
52. Ibid., IV.
53. Ibid., V.
54. Berkes, *Turkish Nationalism*, 20.
55. Ibid., 65.
56. Ibid., 67.
57. Ibid., 74.
58. Ibid., 74.
59. Ibid., 75–76.
60. Ibid., 104.
61. Ibid., 108.
62. Ibid., 76.
63. Tunaya, *Türkiye'de Siyasal Partiler*, 15.
64. For more details see ibid., 7–10, 16–18.
65. "Rumeli" literally stands for "Roman lands." The Ottomans referred to their territorial possessions in and beyond the Balkan Peninsula in Europe as "Rumeli."
66. Tunaya, *Türkiye'de Siyasal Partiler*, 19.
67. Ibid., 23.
68. Ibid., 8.
69. Ibid., 8.
70. Ibid., 21.
71. Ibid., 28.
72. Ibid., 280.
73. Shaw and Shaw, *History of the Ottoman Empire*, 280.

74. Mevlanazâde Rıfat, *31 Mart: Bir İhtilâl'in Hikayesi* (simplified by Berire Ürgenci) (Istanbul: Pınar Yayınları, 1996): 44–45.
75. Joseph S. Joseph, *Cyprus: Ethnic Conflict and International Politics* (second ed.) (London: Macmillan Press, 1997): 16.
76. Ibid., 16–19.
77. Albert Hourani, *A History of the Arab Peoples* (New York, N.Y.: Warner Books, 1991): 285.
78. M. E. Yapp, *The Making of the Modern Middle East: 1792–1923* (London and New York: Longman, 1987): 245.
79. Ibid., 66–68.
80. Şevket Süreyya Aydemir, *Tek Adam: Mustafa Kemal, 1881–1919* (Istanbul: Remzi Kitabevi, 1966): 191.
81. Ibid., 181–191.
82. Ibid., 191.
83. Hâzim Âtıf Kuyucak, *Para ve Banka: Bankacılık*, vol. II (Istanbul: İsmail Akgün Matbaası, 1948): 157.
84. Ibid., 159.
85. Ibid., 157–159.
86. Donald Quataert, *The Ottoman Empire: 1700–1922* (Cambridge, England: Cambridge University Press, 2001): 174.
87. Ibid., 178.
88. Aydemir, *Tek Adam*, 196
89. Ibid., 196–197.
90. Enver had not only a stellar, but also a venturesome and a disastrous military career, which ended with his tragic death in pursuit of the establishment of Grand Turkistan (*Turan*), in a battle with the Red Army in Central Asia. His almost infinite ambitions and courage seemed to be no comparison to his political judgment and military acumen. For example, it was his "brilliant idea" to lead 95,000 of the best-trained troops of the Ottoman Army to their death over the mountains of *Sarıkamış* (now in the province of *Kars*, Turkey) in another daring but ill-equipped and ill-planned military campaign, in the middle of winter. The troops froze to death almost to their last man without firing a shot at the Russian troops they were supposed to engage in battle. The performance of the Ottoman Army in the eastern front in 1915 turned from bad to worse. If it were not for the Russian Revolution, the Ottomans would probably have been defeated by 1917, and a completely different picture of the Middle East and the Caucasus would have emerged at the end of World War I.
91. Aydemir, *Tek Adam*, 193.
92. Ibid., 199.
93. Ibid., 191.
94. Ibid., 199.
95. Ibid., 199–200.
96. Kemal Kirişçi, *Justice and Home Affairs: Issues in Turkish–EU Relations* (Istanbul: TESEV Publications, 2002): 11–17.
97. Cemal (Paşa), *Hatıralar: Ittihat ve Terakki, I. Dünya Savaşı Anıları* (Prepared for publication by Alpay Kabacalı) (Istanbul: Türkiye İş Bankası Kültür Yayınları, 2001): 152–153.
98. Ibid., 152–165.
99. Bernard Lewis, *The Middle East: 2000 Years of History from the Rise of Christianity to the Present Day* (London, G. Britain: Phoenix Giant, 1995): 339.

100. Ibid., 339.
101. Members of the Armenian millet living in Izmir (Smyrna), Bursa, Kocaeli, and Istanbul were not subjected to the same treatment as the members of the Armenian millet residing in eastern Anatolia. Some intellectuals among the Armenians who were suspected of their nationalist activism were also deported from Istanbul and vicinity to Syria, and perished on the road, while the rest of the Armenian communities continued to live in the same quarters as before in the western parts of the Empire during and after 1915. See Erik J. Zürcher, *Turkey: A Modern History* (London, New York: I. B. Tauris, 2001): 120 for additional details.
102. Zürcher, *Turkey*, 120.
103. Quataert, *The Ottoman Empire*, 185.
104. Lewis, *The Middle East*, 340.
105. Justin McCarthy, *The Ottoman People's and the End of Empire* (London: Arnold, 2001): 145.
106. Zürcher, *Turkey*, 120.
107. Lewis, *The Middle East*, 340.
108. Zürcher, *Turkey*, 120.
109. Lewis, *The Middle East*, 340.
110. Quataert, *The Ottoman Empire*, 185.
111. Ibid., Zürcher, *Turkey*, 121.
112. Zürcher, *Turkey*, 121.
113. Quataert, *The Ottoman Empire*, 185.
114. Zürcher argues that the German sources and archives indicate some complicity of the government in the atrocities perpetrated against the Armenians. However, he discards the British and American reports on the matters as propaganda material (121). He does not mention of either the need to search the Russian or the Armenian archives, and of the need to examine the *Dahsnakzutioun* or the *Hinchak* (the Armenian nationalist organizations) archives on the matter of similar atrocities carried out against the Muslims, and mostly the local Kurds, by the Armenian nationalists in or out of the Russian, French, Armenian army uniforms. When all documents and other archival material come out into the open then a proper, balanced and valid picture of the bloodbaths of both the Armenian and the Muslim *millets* will be available. Only then will we know whether there were any Muslim massacres by the Armenians in Russian, French, Armenian army uniform, who were also after solving their "Muslim problem"s through methods now exclusively alluded to the Ottomans, and even to Turks, or not.
115. McCarthy, *The Ottoman People's*, 184.
116. *Dashnakzutioun* is one of the two major organizations of the Armenian nationalists; and the other is the *Hinchak* organization. *Hinchak* was established in Europe and was less effective in eastern Anatolia, and mainly functioned in Russia and Europe. *Dahsnaks* were established in *Tiflis/Tbilisi*, Georgia to pursue the objectives of the Armenian nationalists in the Ottoman Empire (Zürcher, *Turkey*, 87).
117. Lewis, *The Middle East*, 341.
118. Shaw and Shaw, *History of the Ottoman Empire*, 356.
119. Ibid., 356.
120. Sabahattin Selek, *Anadolu İhtilali: Milli Mücadele II* (second ed.) (Istanbul: Istanbul Matbaası, 1965): 212–224.

121. Ibid., 324–336.

122. Nurdoğan Taçalan, *Ege'de Kurtuluş Savaşı Başlarken* (Istanbul: Milliyet Yayınları, 1970): 127–142.

123. Tarık Zafer Tunaya, *Türkiye'de Siyasi Partiler 1859–1952* (Istanbul: Doğan Kardeş Basımevi, 1952): 481–483.

124. Selek, *Anadolu İhtilali*, 225–312.

125. The deputies who were interned in Malta were also tried for the "war crimes" of the Ottoman Empire, including the Armenian atrocities. In 1922 the British prosecutor, after more than two years of research and preparation could not find enough evidence to press charges against the deputies and ex-Ministers of the Ottoman government, and the case was dropped, and Malta exiles were permitted to go back to Turkey, and eventually some were exchanged with the British officers and citizens interned by the Ankara government. See, Tarık Zafer Tunaya, *Türkiye'de Siyasal Partiler: Mütareke Dönemi 1918–1922*, vol. II (Istanbul: Hürriyet Vakfı Yayınları, 1986): 21–25.

126. Selek, *Anadolu İhtilali*, 329–336.

127. Zürcher, Turkey, 138.

128. See McCarthy, *The Ottoman Peoples*, 144, and Zürcher, *Turkey*, 160 for more details.

129. McCarthy, *The Ottoman Peoples*, 144.

130. Zürcher, Turkey, 213.

131. The Syrian nationalists have been objecting to the change of status of the *Sancak* of Alexandretta since 1939. In fact, the Syrian governments insisted on showing the *Hatay* province of Turkey as an integral part of Syria in the official maps of their country. Although Syrians questioned the legitimacy of the agreement between the French Mandate and the Turkish governments in 1939, the legal status of *Hatay* has never been in doubt, and legally it is a Turkish province. Incidentally, as relations between Syria and Turkey recently improved, some of the official maps published by the Syrian government in 2003 do not include *Hatay* any longer. Some treaties were signed during the Syrian President *Beshar Esad*'s visit to Turkey in January 2004. These documents seem to imply that the current border between Turkey and Syria is considered as not only legal, but also "legitimate" by the Syrian government. However, the Turkish press continued to publish weather maps of Syria, and TV news of the Syrian Television since late January 2004, which still included *Hatay* into Syria "proper."

132. Selek, *Anadolu İhtilali*, 308–320.

133. Ibid., 315–323.

134. Ibid., 323.

135. Tunaya, *Türkiye'de Siyasi Partiler*, 30–31.

136. Feroz Ahmad, *The Young Turks: The Committee of Union and Progress in Turkish Politics 1908–1914* (Oxford: The Clarendon Press, 1969): 168–169.

137. Mehmet Gönlübol and Cem Sar, "1919–1938 Yılları arasında Türk Dış Politikası," in Mehmet Gönlübol et al., *Olaylarla Türk Dış Politikası (1919–1973)* (enlarged third ed.), (Ankara: Ankara Üniversitesi Siyasal Bilgiler Fakültesi Yayını, 1974): 75.

138. Ibid., 81.

139. Ibid., 88.

140. Ibid., 88.

2   Founding the Republic

1. Patrick Kinross, *Atatürk: The Birth of a Nation* (London: Phoenix Press, 1964): 354–374.

2. Andrew Mango, *Atatürk* (London: John Murray: 1999): 433–438, 461, 463–467.

3. Selek Sabahattin Selek, *Anadolu İhtilali: Milli Mücadele I* (second ed.) (Istanbul: Istanbul Matbaası, 1965): 412–427.

4. Justin McCarthy, *The Ottoman Peoples and the End of Empire* (London: Arnold, 2001): 193.

5. Mango, *Atatürk*, 528.

6. Clement H. Dodd, *Democracy and Development in Turkey* (Walkington, England: The Eothen Press, 1979): 51.

7. Erik Jan Zürcher, *Political Opposition in the Early Turkish Republic: The Progressive Republican Party 1924–1925* (Leiden, New York, København, Köln: E. J. Brill, 1991): 113–116.

8. Mango, *Atatürk*, 384–387.

9. James A. Bill and Robert Springborg, *Politics in the Middle East* (fifth ed.) (New York: Longman, 2000): 139.

10. Mümtaz Soysal, *Dinamik Anayasa Anlayışı: Anayasa Diyalektiği Üzerine bir Deneme* (Ankara: Ankara Üniversitesi Siyasal Bilgiler Fakültesi Yayını, 1969): 11.

11. Zürcher, *Political Opposition*, 114–116.

12. Mango, *Atatürk*, 501.

13. Şerif Mardin, "Yenileşme Dinamiğinin Temelleri ve Atatürk," in (no editor), *Çağdaş Düşüncenin Işığında Atatürk* (Istanbul: Dr. Nejat Eczacıbaşı Vakfı Yayınları, 1983): 27–29; Dodd, *Democracy and Development*, 34–52; and Frank Tachau, *Turkey: The Politics of Authority, Democracy, and Development* (New York, Philadelphia, Eastbourne, Toronto, Sydney, Hong Kong: Praeger, 1984): 13–17.

14. Ibid.

15. Standford J. Shaw and Ezer Kural Shaw, *History of the Ottoman Empire and Modern Turkey: Volume II: Reform, Revolution and the Republic: The Rise of Modern Turkey, 1808–1975* (Cambridge, London, New York, Melbourne: Cambridge University Press, 1977): 368.

16. Atatürk, cf. Shaw and Shaw, "History of the Ottoman Empire," 368–369.

17. The Muslim communities of the world were in no shape to react to the decision of *Kemal Atatürk* and his nationalist colleagues and followers in 1924. In Central, South, and East Asia they were mainly under the colonial rule of the Soviet Union, and the British Empire, as well as the Dutch, Portuguese, and other European states. The picture was not much different in the Middle East or Africa. Hence, the priority of the Asian, Middle Eastern, and African Muslims was to rid themselves off colonial rule, rather than protest against the decision of the Turkish Grand National Assembly. Nevertheless, the Caliphate was abolished without much international reaction, let alone protest or mayhem in 1924.

18. Metin Toker, *Şeyh Sait ve İsyanı* (İkinci Basım) (Ankara: Bilgi Yayınevi, 1994): 42.

19. Ibid., 42; and Uğur Mumcu, *Kürt—Islam Ayaklanması: 1919–1925* (Istanbul: Tekin Yayınevi, 1991): 64.

20. David McDowall, *The Modern History of the Kurds* (London, New York: I. B. Tauris, 2000): 198.

21. Mumcu, *Kürt*, 63–68.

22. Mumcu, *Kürt*, 67–68.
23. Tarık Zafer Tunaya, *Türkiye'de Siyasal Partiler: İttihat ve Terakki: Bir Çağın, Bir Kuşağın, Bir Partinin Tarihi, vol. II* (Istanbul: Hürriyet Vakfı Yayınları, 1989): 187–204; and Mumcu, *Kürt*, 65.
24. Tunaya, *Türkiye'de Siyasal Partiler*, 195–196.
25. Ibid., 198–199.
26. (French Foreign Ministry secret documents, East Levant, 1918–1929 Kurdish Cause Series, cf. Mumcu, *Kürt*, 97).
27. Ibid., 97.
28. Toker, *Şeyh Sait ve İsyanı*, 92–99; and Mumcu, *Kürt* 93–95.
29. Zürcher, 1991, *Political Opposition*, 84.
30. Nur Yalman, "Some Observations on Secularism in Islam: The Cultural Revolution in Turkey," *Daedalus*, 102: (1973): 152.
31. Şerif Mardin, "Ideology and Religion in the Turkish Revolution," *Middle East Studies*, 2: (1971): 201–206, and Şerif Mardin, "Center-Periphery Relations: A Key to Turkish Politics?" in Engin D. Akarlı and Gabriel Ben-Dor (eds.), *Political Participation in Turkey: Historical Background and Present Problems* (Istanbul: Boğaziçi University Press, 1975): 7–19.
32. Mardin, 1983, "Yenileşme Dinamiğinin," 25–29.
33. Ibid., 39–45.
34. Niyazi Berkes, *The Development of Secularism in Turkey* (Montreal: McGill University Press, 1964): 281–288.
35. Sabri Ülgener, *İktisadi Çözülmenin Ahlak ve Zihniyet Dünyası* (Istanbul: Der Yayınları, 1981): 26.
36. Ibid., 26.
37. Ibid., 28.
38. Andrew Davison, *Secularism and Revivalism in Turkey: A Hermeneutic Reconsideration* (New Haven and London: Yale University Press, 1998): 18–50.
39. Ülgener, *İktisadi Çözülmenin*, 132–176.
40. Mardin, 1983, "Yenileşme Dinamiğinin," 25–27.
41. Halil Inalcık, *Osmanlı'da Devlet, Hukuk, Adalet* (Istanbul: Eren Yayıncılık, 2000): 106.
42. Ibid., 106–120.
43. Ilter Turan, *Cumhuriyet Tarihimiz: Temeller, Kuruluş, Milli Devrimler* (Istanbul: Çağlayan Kitabevi, 1969): 79.
44. Mango, *Atatürk*, 437.
45. For more details on the *Alevis* and their Turkish politial system see Paul J. White and Joost Jongerden (eds.), *Turkey's Alevi Enigma: A Comprehensive Overview* (Leiden, Boston: E. J. Brill, 2003): passim.
46. Turan, *Cumhuriyet Tarihimiz*, 80–81.
47. Ibid., 81; and Mango, *Atatürk*, 433–434.
48. Shaw and Shaw, *History of the Ottaman Empire*, 385.
49. Mango, *Atatürk*, 438.
50. Turan, *Cumhuriyet Tarihimiz*, 83.
51. Shaw and Shaw, *History of the Ottaman Empire*, 386–388.
52. Engin Tonguç, *Devrim Açısından Köy Enstitüleri ve Tonguç* (Istanbul: Ant Yayınları, 1970): 161–229.
53. Ibid. 178–208.
54. Turan, *Cumhuriyet Tarihimiz*, 91.

55. T. C. Başbakanlık Devlet İstatistik Enstitüsü (State Institute of Statistics), 2000 Genel Nüfus Sayımı: Nüfusun Sosyal ve Ekonomik Nitelikleri: Türkiye (Ankara: Devlet İstatistik Enstitüsü Matbaası, 2003): 33.
56. Kinross, *The Birth of a Nation*, 467.
57. Mango, *Atatürk*, 497.
58. Kinross, *The Birth of a Nation*, 468–469.
59. Mango, *Atatürk*, 495.
60. Ibid., 496–497.
61. Soysal, *Dinamik Anayasa Anlayışı*, 11.
62. Uğur Mumcu, *Kazım Karabekir Anlatıyor* (second ed.) (Istanbul: Tekin Yayınevi, 1990): 124.
63. Zürcher, 1991, *Political Opposition*, 58–61.
64. Uğur Mumcu, *Gazi Paşaya Suikast* (eleventh ed.) (Istanbul: Tekin Yayınevi, 1994): 57–62, 103–108.
65. Mango, *Atatürk*, 471.
66. Ahmet Ağaoğlu, *Serbest Fırka Hatıraları* (third ed.) (Istanbul: İletişim Yayınları, 1994): 81–101.
67. Ibid. 101–105, and Mango, *Atatürk*, 473.
68. Mango, *Atatürk*, 475.
69. Cemil Koçak, *Türkiye'de Milli Şef Dönemi (1938–1945)* (vol. 2) (Istanbul: İletişim Yayınları, 1996): 568–570.
70. Korkut Boratav, *Türkiye İktisat Tarihi: 1908–2002* (seventh ed.) (Ankara: Imge Yayınevi, 2003): 45.
71. Ibid., 45.
72. McCarthy, *The Ottoman Peoples*, 201.
73. Ibid., 201–202.
74. Ibid., 201.
75. For more data on the matter see ibid., 201.
76. For a recent analysis of the subject see Renée Hirschon (ed.), *Crossing the Aegean: An Appraisal of the 1923 Compulsory Population Exchange between Greece and Turkey* (New York, Oxford: Berghahn Books, 2003): passim.
77. Tevfik Çavdar, *Türkiye Ekonomisinin Tarihi (1900–1960): Yirminci Yüzyıl Türkiye İktisat Tarihi* (Ankara: Imge Kitabevi, 2003): 198–220.
78. Mango, *Atatürk*, 468–80.
79. Boratav, *Türkiye İktisat Tarihi*, 73–79.
80. Çavdar, *Turkiye Ekonomisinin Tarihi*, 310–372.
81. Kinross, *The Birth of a Nation*, 242–245; and Mehmet Gönlübol and Cem Sar, "1919–1938 Yılları arasında Türk Dış Politikası" in Mehmet Gönlübol et al. (eds.), *Olaylarla Türk Dış Politikası (1919–1973)* (enlarged third ed.) (Ankara: Ankara Üniversitesi Siyasal Bilgiler Fakültesi Yayını, 1974): 28–31.
82. Gönlübol and Sar, "1919–1938 Yılları arasında," 3–144.
83. For a more detailed analysis see Ahmet Şükrü Esmer and Oral Sander, "İkinci Dünya Savaşında Türk Dış Politikası" in Mehmet Gönlübol et al. (eds.), *Olaylarla Türk Dış Politikası (1919–1973)* (enlarged third ed.) (Ankara: Ankara Üniversitesi Siyasal Bilgiler Fakültesi Yayını, 1974): 177–196.
84. Boratav, *Türkiye'de Milli*, 81–91.
85. Ibid., 88.
86. Ibid., 88.
87. Ibid., 88.

88. Çavdar, *Türkiye Ekonomisinin Tarihi*, 297–298.
89. Ibid., 297–372.
90. Cemal Tukin, *Boğazlar Meselesi* (Istanbul: Pan Yayıncılık, 1999): 75–449.
91. Ibid., 448–449.
92. Philip Robins, *Suits and Uniforms: Turkish Foreign Policy since the Cold War* (Seattle: University of Washington Press, 2003): 126.
93. Ibid., 162.

3   DEMOCRACY AT WORK

1. M. E. Yapp, *The Near East since the First World War: A History to 1995* (second ed.) (Harlow, London, New York: Longman, 1996): 182.
2. Selim Deringil, *The Turkish Foreign Policy during the Second World War: An Active Neutrality* (New York, New Rochelle, Melbourne, Sydney: Cambridge University Press, 1989): 180.
3. William Hale, *Turkish Foreign Policy: 1774–2000* (London, Portland, OR: Frank Cass, 2000): 112.
4. Deringil, *An Active Neutrality*, 179–180; and Hale, *Turkish Foreign Policy*, 111–112.
5. Hale, *Turkish Foreign Policy*, 112–114.
6. Ibid., 109.
7. Deringil, *An Active Neutrality*, 180.
8. Hale, *Turkish Foreign Policy*, 112.
9. Ibid. 114.
10. Ibid. 115.
11. Kemal Karpat, *Turkey's Politics: The Transition to a Multiparty System* (Princeton, New Jersey: Princeton University Press, 1959): 144–146.
12. Ibid., 145.
13. Ibid., 146–147.
14. Ibid., 147.
15. Ibid., 144–145.
16. William Hale, *The Political and Economic Development of Modern Turkey* (London: Croom Helm, 1981): 76–77; and Yapp, *The Near East*, 164.
17. Karpat, *Turkey's Politics*, 114, Ayhan Aktar, "Varlık Vergisi ve Istanbul," *Toplum ve Bilim*, vol. 71 (1996): 101–104; and Tevfik Çavdar, *Türkiye Ekonomisinin Tarihi (1900–1960): Yirminci Yüzyıl Türkiye İktisat Tarihi* (Ankara: Imge Kitabevi, 2003): 318–328.
18. Aktar, "Varlık Vergisi ve Istanbul," 103–109.
19. Karpat, *Turkey's Politics*, 115; and Çavdar, *Türkiye Ekonomisinin Tarihi*, 318.
20. Ayhan Aktar, *Varlık Vergisi ve "Türkleştirme Politikaları,"* (fifth print) (Istanbul: İletişim, 2001): 113–126.
21. Aktar, 1996, "Varlık Vergisi ve Istanbul," 140.
22. As a high level Ministry of Finance official who was heavily involved in collecting the "tax on wealth" Mr. Faik Ökte published a book titled "*Varlık Vergisi Faciası*" (Tax on Wealth Disaster) in 1951.
23. Aktar, 1996, "Varlık Vergisi ve Istanbul," 144.
24. Aktar, 2001, "*Türkleştir Politikaları,*" 204.
25. Karpat, *Turkey's Politics*, 151.
26. Faruk Loğoğlu, *İsmet İnönü and the Making of Modern Turkey* (Ankara: İnönü Vakfi, 1997): 121–122.

27. Ibid., 130–135.
28. Ibid., 41–59 and 122–126.
29. Ibid., 145.
30. Ibid., 145.
31. Ibid., 145, 147.
32. Metin Toker, *Tek Partiden Çok Partiye* (Istanbul: Milliyet Yayınları, 1970): 141–142.
33. Tarık Zafer Tunaya, *İslamcılık Akımı* (Istanbul: Simavi Yayınları, 1991): 202.
34. Loğoğlu, *Making of Modern Turkey*, 147.
35. Tunaya, *İslamcilik Akımı*, 201.
36. Ibid., 201.
37. Ibid., 202.
38. Loğoğlu, *Making of Modern Turkey*, 147.
39. Tunaya, *İslamchılık Akımı*, 203.
40. Loğoğlu, *Making of Modern Turkey*, 148.
41. Cemil Koçak, *Türkiye'de Milli Şef Dönemi (1938–1945)* (vol. 2) (İstanbul: İletişim Yayınları, 1996): 568–570.
42. Toker, *Tek Partiden Çok Partiye*, 182.
43. Michael Keating, *The Politics of Modern Europe* (Hants, England, Vermont: Edward Elgar, 1993): 59–61.
44. Jorgen S. Rasmussen and Joel G. Moses, *Major European Governments* (Belmont, California: Wadsworth, 1995): 60–71.
45. Frederick W. Frey, "Patterns of Elite Politics in Turkey" in George Lenczowski (ed.), *Political Elites in the Middle East* (Washington, DC: American Enterprise Institute for Public Policy Research, 1975): 65–67.
46. Erol Tuncer, *Osmanlı'dan Günümüze Seçimler (1877–1999)* (Ankara: TESAV, 2002): 23.
47. TBMM (TGNA), *Secim, Seçim Sistemleri ve Türkiye'deki Uygulamalar* (Ankara: TBMM Basımevi, 1982): 92.
48. Ibid., 92.
49. Ibid., 92.
50. Hale, 1981, *Political and Economic Development*, 86.
51. Şerif Mardin, "Center-Periphery Relations: A Key to Turkish Politics?" in Engin D. Akarlı and Gabriel Ben-Dor (eds.), *Political Participation in Turkey: Historical Background and Present Problems* (Istanbul: Boğaziçi University Press, 1975): 29–32.
52. Ersin Kalaycıoğlu, "Constitutional Viability and Political Institutions in Turkish Democracy" in Abdo I. Baaklini and Helen Desfosses (eds.), *Designs for Democratic Stability: Studies in Viable Constitutionalism* (Armonk, New York, London, England: M. E. Sharpe, 1997): 181.
53. TBMM, *Secim, Seçim Sistemleri*, 93.
54. Hale, 2000, *Turkish Foreign Policy*, 117–118.
55. Mehmet Gönlübol and Haluk Ulman, "İkinci Dünya Savaşından Sonra Türk Dış Politikası," in Mehmet Gönlübol et al. (eds.), *Olaylarla Türk Dış Politikası (1919–1973)* (enlarged third ed.) (Ankara: Ankara Üniversitesi Siyasal Bilgiler Fakültesi Yayını, 1974): 244–245.
56. William Hale, *Turkish Politics and the Military* (London and New York: Routledge, 1994): 96.
57. Ibid., 246–260; and Hale, 2000, *Turkish Foreign Policy*, 119.
58. İsmail Soysal, *Soğuk Savaş Dönemi ve Türkiye: Olaylar Kronolojisi (1945–1975)* (Istanbul: ISIS, 1997): 245.

59. Gönlübol and Ulman, *İkinci Dünya*, 335–346.
60. William Hale, 1981, *Political and Economic Development*, 194.
61. Ibid., 95.
62. Ibid.,100.
63. Daniel Lerner, *The Passing of Traditional Society* (New York, N.Y.: The Free Press, 1958): 60–65.
64. Kemal Karpat, *The Gecekondu: Rural Migration and Urbanization* (Cambridge, England: Cambridge University Press, 1976): 59.
65. Frank Tachau, *Turkey: The Politics of Authority, Democracy, and Development* (New York, Philadelphia, Eastbourne, Toronto, Sydney, Hong Kong: Praeger, 1984): 148–149.
66. Nermin Abadan-Unat, *Bitmeyen Göç: Konuk İşçilikten Ulus-Ötesi Yurttaşlığa* (Istanbul: Bilgi Üniversitesi Yayınları, 2002): 37.
67. Ibid., 37.
68. Ibid., 42–43.
69. For more details see Donald J. McCrone and Charles F. Cnudde, "Towards a Communications Theory of Political Development," *American Political Science Review*, vol. 61: (1971): 72–80.
70. Lerner, *The Passing of Traditional Society*, 60.
71. Ibid., 60.
72. Ibid., 60.
73. Hale, 1981, *Political and Economic Development*, 104.
74. Hale, 1994, *Turkish Politics and the Military*, 94.
75. Karpat, 1959, *Turkey's Politics*, 429, and see also table 3.1.
76. Hale, 1981, *Political and Economic Development*, 106.
77. Hale, 1994, *Turkish Politics and the Military*, 94.
78. Ibid., 95.
79. Frey, "Patterns of Elite Politics in Turkey," 65.
80. Şevket Süreyya Aydemir, *İhtilalin Mantığı* (fifth print) (Istanbul: Remzi Kitabevi: 1993): 280.
81. Ibid., 281.
82. Ibid., 281.
83. Hale, 1994, *Turkish Politics and the Military*, 95.
84. Suna Kili, "Değerlendirmeler" in Suna Kili (ed.), *27 Mayıs 1960 Devrimi, Kurucu Meclis ve 1961 Anayasası* (Istanbul: Boyut Kitapları, 1998): 118.
85. Aydemir, *İhtilalin Mantığı*, 286.
86. Ibid., 286–287.
87. Walter F. Weiker, *The Turkish Revolution 1960–1961: Aspects of Military Politics* (Washington, D.C.: The Brookings Institute, 1963): 11.
88. Tunaya, *İslamcılık Akımı* 222.
89. Abdi İpekçi and Ömer Sami Coşar, *İhtilalin İçyüzü* (Istanbul: Uygun Yayınevi, 1965): 179.
90. Hale, 1994, *Turkish Politics and the Military*, 110.
91. İpekçi and Coşar, *İhtilalin İçyüzü*, 30–33; and Suphi Karaman, "Written Responses" in Suna Kili (ed.), *27 Mayıs 1960 Devrimi, Kurucu Meclis ve 1961 Anayasası* (Istanbul: Boyut Kitapları, 1998): 176.
92. İpekçi and Coşar, *İhtilalin İçyüzü*, 100–103.
93. Ibid., 74–90.
94. Ibid., 90–100.
95. Ibid., 105–109.

96. Ibid., 151–159; and Hale, 1994, *Turkish Politics and the Military*, 108.
97. Hale, 1994, *Turkish Politics and the Military*, 169.
98. Ibid., 169.
99. Hale, 1994, *Turkish Politics and the Military*, 143.
100. Ibid., 143.
101. Weiker, *Aspects of Military Politics*, 33.
102. Ibid., 32–43.
103. Ömer Faruk Gençkaya, "Türk Siyasal Sisteminde Kurucu Meclis: 1961 ve 1982 Deneyimlerinin Karşılaştırılması," in Suna Kili (ed.), *27 Mayıs 1960 Devrimi, Kurucu Meclis ve 1961 Anayasası* (Istanbul: Boyut Kitapları, 1998): 24.
104. Ibid., 23–24.
105. Weiker, *Aspects of Military Politics*, 72.
106. Frey, "Patterns of Elite Politics in Turkey," 65–67.
107. Zekai Baloğlu, *Türkiye'de Eğitim* (Istanbul: TÜSİAD Yayınları, 1990): 136.
108. Ibid., 136.
109. Ibid., 133–134.
110. Ibid., 133.
111. Ibid., 133.
112. Üstün Ergüder, Yılmaz Esmer, and Ersin Kalaycıoğlu, *Türk Toplumunun Değerleri* (Istanbul: TÜSİAD Yayınları, 1991): 22; and Yılmaz Esmer, *Devrim, Evrim, Statüko: Türkiye'de Sosyal, Siyasal ve Ekonomik Değerler* (Istanbul: TESEV Yayınları 1999): 45.

4 The Second Republic

1. Ahmet Yıldız, *İhtilalin İçinden: Anılar, Değerlendirmeler* (Istanbul: Alan, 2001): 177.
2. Frank Tachau, *Turkey: The Politics of Authority, Democracy, and Development* (New York, Philadelphia, Eastbourne, Toronto, Sydney, Hong Kong: Praeger, 1984): 45.
3. Frederick W. Frey, "Patterns of Elite Politics in Turkey," in George Lenczowski (ed.), *Political Elites in the Middle East* (Washington, D.C.: American Enterprise Institute for Public Policy Research, 1975): 50.
4. Yakup Kepenek and Nurhan Yentürk, *Türkiye Ekonomisi* (expanded and revised tenth ed.) (Istanbul: Remzi Kitabevi, 2002): 93.
5. Ibid., 93–95.
6. Ibid., 98.
7. Suna Kili, "Değerlendirmeler," in Suna Kili (ed.), *27 Mayıs 1960 Devrimi, Kurucu Meclis ve 1961 Anayasası* (Istanbul: Boyut Kitapları, 1998): 137, 151–157.
8. Ibid., 137–138.
9. Ibid., 126.
10. Ibid., 126.
11. TBMM, *Secim, Seçim Sistemleri ve Türkiye'deki Uygulamalar* (Ankara: TBMM Basımevi, 1982): 99.
12. Ibid., 99.
13. Mümtaz Soysal, *Dinamik Anayasa Anlayışı: Anayasa Diyalektiği Üzerine bir Deneme* (Ankara: Ankara Üniversitesi Siyasal Bilgiler Fakültesi Yayını, 1969): 31–50; and Ergun Özbudun, *Türk Anayasa Hukuku* (Ankara: Yetkin Yayınları, 1986): 143–148.

14. Soysal, *Dinamik Anayasa Anlayışı*, 87–106; and Özbudun, 351–356.
15. Özbudun, *Türk Anayasa Hukuku*, 27.
16. Turkish Constitution (1961), art. 129.
17. Although Marxist–Leninist, Racist, Fascist, Nazi, Islamist-revivalist (*şeriatçı*), and ethnic nationalist (particularly Kurdish) political parties were deemed too inimical to the smooth functioning of the democratic political system and were banned; in practice, under various guises, most managed to emerge and functioned freely in the 1961–1980 era. Their programs never made any clear references to the "buzz words" included in the Political Parties Act, the Criminal Code, and the Associations Act. However, the voters and especially those who participated in the activities of those organizations and who voted for their candidates in the elections seemed to be quite clear about what those political parties stood for. The authorities, including the judges, preferred to look in the other direction and thus enabled them to function within the democratic system. (For more information see Turkish Constitution (1961), art. 57.)
18. TBMM, *Secim*, 101.
19. Ersin Kalaycıoğlu, "Decentralization of Government," in Metin Heper and Ahmet Evin (eds.), *Politics in the Third Turkish Republic* (Boulder, San Francisco, Oxford: Westview Press, 1994): 88–90.
20. Rona Aybay, "Milli Güvenlik Kavramı ve Milli Güvenlik Kurulu," *Ankara Üniversitesi Siyasal Bilgiler Fakültesi Dergisi*, vol. XXXIII, nos. 1–2 (March–June 1978): 77–78.
21. Metin Heper, "The Consolidation of Democracy versus Democratization in Turkey," in Barry Rubin and Metin Heper (eds.), *Political Parties in Turkey* (London, Portland, OR: Frank Cass, 2002): 139–142.
22. Erol Tuncer, *Osmanlı'dan Günümüze Seçimler: 1877–1999* (Ankara: Toplumsal Ekonomik Siyasal Araştırmalar Vakfı (Tesav) Yayınları, 2002): 324.
23. Ibid., 323.
24. TBMM, *Secim*, 101.
25. William Hale, *Turkish Politics and the Military* (London and New York: Routledge, 1994): 133.
26. Ibid., 137.
27. Ibid., 137.
28. George Harris, "The Cause of the 1960 Revolution in Turkey," *Middle East Journal*, vol. 24, no. 3 (1970): 438–439; Frey, "Patterns of Elite Politics in Turkey," 64–73.
29. Feroz Ahmad, *The Turkish Experiment in Democracy, 1950–1975* (London: Hurst, 1977): 180.
30. Hale, *Turkish Politics and the Military*, 158–161.
31. Ibid., 155–156.
32. Ibid., 168.
33. Ibid., 160–168.
34. Ibid., 174.
35. See also for more information Yılmaz Altuğ, "Turkish Involvement in Some International Disputes," *Belleten*, vol. LIII, no. 206 (1989): 281–343; Joseph S. Joseph, *Cyprus: Ethnic Conflict and International Politics* (second ed.) (London: Macmillan Press, 1997): 35–126; and Faruk Sönmezoğlu, *Türkiye—Yunanistan İlişkileri ve Büyük Güçler: Kıbrıs, Ege ve Diğer Sorunlar* (Istanbul: Der Yayınları, 2000): 89–292.
36. Altuğ, "Turkish Involvement," 294–309.
37. Joseph, *Cyprus*, 42–48.

38. Sönmezoğlu, *Türkiye*, 185.

39. Ibid., 185.

40. Ibid., 186.

41. Ibid., 88–89.

42. Ibid., 88.

43. Ibid., 90.

44. For more information on Süleyman Demirel see <www.mfa.gov.tr/grupe/ea/ea009.htm>.

45. Erik J. Zürcher, *Turkey: A Modern History* (London, New York: I. B. Tauris, 2001): 266–276; and Tuncer, *Osmanlı'dan*, 414.

46. Zürcher, *A Modern History*, 270.

47. Ersin Kalaycıoğlu, "The 1983 Parliament in Turkey: Changes and Continuities," in Metin Heper and Ahmet Evin (eds.), *State, Democracy and the Military: Turkey in the 1980s* (Berlin, New York: Walter de Gruyter, 1988): 51–58.

48. Robert Bianchi, *Interest Groups and Political Development in Turkey* (Princeton, New Jersey: Princeton University Press, 1984): 162–164.

49. Zürcher, *A Modern History*, 276.

50. Korkut Boratav, *Türkiye İktisat Tarihi: 1908–2002* (seventh ed.) (Ankara: Imge Yayınevi, 2003): 118.

51. Ibid., 118–120.

52. Ibid., 124–125.

53. Ibid., 125–126.

54. Ibid., 130.

55. IBRD, *World 1997 Development Report* (New York: Oxford University Press, 1997): 146–167.

56. Zürcher, *A Modern History*, 265.

57. Celil Gürkan, *12 Mart'a Beş Kala* (Istanbul: Tekin Yayınları, 1986): 15–39.

58. For example, PM Demirel and associates have been calling for the curtailing of the powers of the autonomous institutions throughout the 1960s (see Hale, 1994: 198). A total of 44 articles of the 1961 Constitution were amended, and most of those amendments seemed to coincide with what PM Demirel and AP had demanded earlier. The establishment of a State Security Courts (*Devlet Güvenlik Mahkemeleri*) also dates back to those amendments, though they were abolished in 1976, and reintroduced with the 1982 Constitution (art. 143), and for more information see Zürcher, *A Modern History*, 273.

59. The titular leader of the MBK, General *Cemal Gürsel* was elected the President of the country in 1961. However, he could not complete his seven-year tenure due to a stroke he suffered in 1965. When he passed away, General Cevdet Sunay, who had been the General Chief of Staff of the Armed Forces at the time resigned his office, appointed as a Senator, and was elected by the TGNA as the President of the country in 1966.

60. See also Hale, *Turkish Politics and the Military*, 203–208.

61. The 1961 Constitution enabled the ex-Prime Ministers to serve as Senators. İnönü continued to occupy a seat in the TGNA in the capacity of an "Independent Senator" until his death in 1973.

62. For more details see Hale, *Turkish Politics and the Military,* 121–123.

63. William Hale, *The Political and Economic Development of Modern Turkey* (London: Croom Helm, 1981): 124–125.

64. Kemal Karpat, "War on Cyprus: The Tragedy of Enosis," in Kemal Karpat (ed.), *Turkish Foreign Policy in Transition: 1950–1975* (Leiden: E. J. Brill, 1975): 194.

65. Sönmezoğlu, *Türkiye*, 120, 202.

66. Ibid., 121–122, 203–209.
67. Ibid., 214–215.
68. Ibid., 227–229.
69. <www.mfa.gov.tr/turkce/grupg/ge/001.htm>.
70. Zürcher, *A Modern History*, 291.
71. Ibid., 291.
72. Ibid., 291; and Fahir Armaoğlu, "Yarım Yüzyılın Türk-Amerikan İlişkileri, 1947–1997" in Ismail Soysal (ed.), *Çağdaş Türk Diplomasisi: 200 Yıllık Süreç* (Ankara: Türk Tarih Kurumu Basımevi, 1999): 427.
73. For more details see Zürcher, *A Modern History*, 276–277.
74. Ersin Kalaycıoğlu, "The Turkish Political System in Transition: Multi-Party Politics in the 1980s," *Current Turkish Thought*, vol. 56 (Fall 1985): 15.
75. Ibid., 15.
76. Kepenek and Yentürk, *Türkiye Ekonomisi*, 289.
77. Ibid., 289–291.
78. Bilsay Kuruç, "Economic Growth and Political Stability," in Metin Heper and Ahmet Evin (eds.), *Politics in the Third Turkish Republic* (Boulder, San Francisco, Oxford: Westview Press, 1994): 142–143.
79. Kepenek and Yentürk, 289–290 and see also table 4.4.
80. Ibid., 291–196.
81. Zürcher, *A Modern History*, 15.
82. Kenan Evren, *Kenan Evren'in Anıları 1* (Istanbul: Milliyet Yayınları, 1990): 341.
83. Bianchi, *Interest Groups*, 149–201.
84. The environment in which thoughts were expressed deteriorated in the latter half of the 1970s. It was a period where terror seemed to have reigned. Armed militias of the communists, socialists, and ethnic nationalists fought each other, while they wreaked havoc in Turkey between 1975 and 1980. In a political milieu where legal institutions had shown considerable amount of tolerance for dissenting opinions, interest groups, civic associations, and political parties failed to show much tolerance. Many young people, and old celebrities, and politically active individuals were killed for what they had said or for the lifestyle or the attires they brandished. The press reported that in the city of Çorum, deeply divided between Sunni and *Alevi* sects of Islam, some were killed because of their looks. The mobs "decided" that a certain man was a "communist" for he had no beard or moustache and wore glasses! He was executed on the spot.
85. Nermin Abadan-Unat, *Bitmeyen Göç: Konuk İşçilikten Ulus-Ötesi Yurttaşlığa* (Istanbul: Bilgi Üniversitesi Yayınları, 2002): 48–91.
86. Michael N. Danielson and Rusen Keles, *Politics of Rapid Urbanization: Government and Growth in Turkey* (New York, NY: Holmes and Meier, 1985): passim; and Metin Heper and Ahmet Evin (eds.), *Democracy and Local Government: Istanbul in the 1980s* (Beverley, North Humberside: Eothen Press, 1987): passim.
87. Ayşe Güneş-Ayata, "Roots and Trends of Clientelism in Turkey," in Luis Roniger and Ayşe Güneş-Ayata (eds.), *Democracy, Clientelism and Civil Society* (Boulder, London: Lynne Rienner, 1994): 55–58.
88. Turkey has a well-established tradition of patronage politics wielded and oiled by the local notables, in the form of landlords, şeyh (sheik, religious leader), kadı (Muslim judge), and so on, who demanded the support of the peasants and nomads, and provided protection, jobs, livelihood, and other services for them. The gecekondu dwellers did not have to invent patronage ties from scratch. They

only seemed to have changed one set of masters in the countryside with another in the city suburbs.

89. Ilkay Sunar, *State and Society in the Politics of Turkey's Development* (Ankara: Ankara Üniversitesi Siyasal Bilgiler Fakültesi Yayını, 1975): 114–121.

90. Ersin Kalaycıoğlu, "1960 Sonrası Türk Siyasal Hayatına Bakış: Demokrasi, Neo-Patrimonyalizm ve İstikrar," in Üniversite Öğretim Üyeleri Derneği (ed.), *Tarih ve Demokrasi: Tarık Zafer Tunaya'ya Armağan* (Istanbul: Cem Yayınevi, 1992): 94–98.

91. Ibid., 98–104.

92. Ergun Özbudun, *Social Change and Political Participation in Turkey* (Princeton, New Jersey: Princeton University Press, 1976): 60–96.

93. Ergun Özbudun, "Turkish Party System: Institutionalization, Polarization, and Fragmentation," *Middle Eastern Studies*, vol. 17, no. 2 (1981): 228–238.

94. Kalaycıoğlu, 1992, "1960 Sonrası Türk," 110–111.

95. Evren, *Kenan Evren'in Anılarl 1*, 328–341, 355–356.

96. Ibid., 545–555.

97. Özbudun, 1981, "*Turkish Party System*," 238–239.

98. Ersin Kalaycıoğlu, "Why Legislatures Persist in Developing Countries: The Case of Turkey," *Legislative Studies Quarterly*, V, 1 (February 1980): 129–130.

5 THE THIRD REPUBLIC

1. Numan Esin, "13 Kasım 1960 Ogusu Üzerine Birkaç Söz," in Suna Kili (ed.), *27 Mayıs 1960 Devrimi, Kurucu Meclis ve 1961 Anayasası* (Istanbul: Boyut Kitapları, 1988): 265–269.

2. Ersin Kalaycıoğlu, "The Turkish Political System in Transition: Multi-Party Politics in the 1980s," *Current Turkish Thought*, vol. 56 (Fall, 1985): 16.

3. Ergun Özbudun, *Contemporary Turkish Politics: Challenges to Democratic Consolidation* (Boulder, London: Lynne Rienner, 2000): 58.

4. Kenan Evren, *Kenan Evren'in Anıları 3* (Istanbul: Milliyet Yayınları, 1991): 362.

5. Kenan Evren, *Kenan Evren'in Anıları 2* (Istanbul: Milliyet Yayınları, 1991): 119, 338–390.

6. Ibid. 400.

7. Özbudun, *Contemporary Turkish Politics*, 59–60.

8. The Turkish 1982 Constitution has been thoroughly amended several times since it was put into effect. Therefore, the current constitution and political regime in Turkey is substantially different from the original text of the 1982 constitution. My remarks here only pertain to the original text and the intent of its founding fathers.

9. Metin Heper, "Politics of Transition in the Third Turkish Republic," (occasional paper) (Boğaziçi University, Department of Public Administration, 1985): 3.

10. Ersin Kalaycıoğlu, "1960 Sonrası Türk Siyasal Hayatına Bir Bakış: Demokrasi, Neo-Patrimonyalizm ve Istikrar," in Üniversite Öğretim Üyeleri Derneği (ed.), *Tarih ve Demokrasi: Tarık Zafer Tunaya'ya Armağan* (Istanbul: Cem Yayınevi, 1992): 98–110.

11. Kalaycıoğlu, 1985, "*The Turkish Political System*," 21.

12. Ibid., 21.

13. Ibid., 22.

14. In practice many problems emerged. First of all, there is no State agency that can effectively control the curriculum of the elementary and secondary schools other

than the Ministry of National Education, which is part of the government. Governments are popularly elected. The voters, from time to time extend enough support to the religious revivalists to come to power as members of various political parties. Once in government, the revivalists could have quite a bit of influence on the Ministry of National Education, and through it, on the curriculum. Consequently, in practice compulsory religious and moral education have become compulsory "Sunni Islam and Morals" instructed to *Alevi*, Christian, and Jewish students in Turkey. Occasionally, non-Sunni students and their families protested the situation. However, their numbers and votes are so small as not to matter to the politicians, and their calls fall on deaf ears. Nevertheless, "compulsory religious instruction" still persists as a peculiar and strange practice in the "secular" Republic, which will continue to create a variety of concerns over the role of religion in education for many years to come (see İbrahim Kaboğlu, "Zorunlu Din Dersi Anayasaya Aykırı," interview reported in *Milliyet* daily) (Istanbul, 2003): 16.

15. Ali Çarkoğlu and Emre Erdoğan, "Fairness in the Apportionment of Seats in the Turkish Legislature: Is There Room for Improvement?" *New Perspectives on Turkey*, no. 19 (Fall 1998): 102.
16. Erol Tuncer, *Osmanlı'dan Günümüze Seçimler: 1877–1999* (Ankara: Toplumsal Ekonomik Siyasal Araştırmalar Vakfı (Tesav) Yayınları, 2002): 105.
17. Metin Heper, "Introduction," in Metin Heper (ed.), *Local Government in Turkey: Governing Greater Istanbul* (London: Routledge, 1989): 1–11.
18. Ersin Kalaycıoğlu, "Decentralization of Government," in Metin Heper and Ahmet Evin (eds.), *Politics in the Third Turkish Republic* (Boulder, San Francisco, Oxford: Westview Press, 1994): 87–100.
19. The name of the party is picked such that many connotations could be possible. At the inception of the party the political ban was still in effect, so Süleyman Demirel could not act as its legal founding father and become its leader. Hence, to avoid any confusion over the identity of the party the acronyms DYP were also referred to as "*Demirel'in Yeni Partisi*" (which may best be translated into English as "The New Party of *Demirel*"). Second, "Doğru Yol" in Turkish may mean the same as "*sirat-al mustakeem*" in Arabic, which appears as a phrase in the Holy Qur'an, may better be translated into English as "straight path." It definitely connotes the stipulation of the Holy Qur'an that Muslim's should trek the straight path of Islam. The saying "*Allah kimseyi doğru yoldan ayırmasın!*" in Turkish, which may be translated into English as, "Let Allah not stray anyone away from the straight path!" has been used routinely in daily conversations. If "Straight Path Party" were used as its English translation it would have given a better understanding of its political, folkloric, and religious identity. However, students of Turkish politics have been referring to it as the "True Path Party" since its inception, and hence not to create any confusion on the matter, the same translation has been employed in this book.
20. Ersin Kalaycıoğlu, "The Motherland Party: The Challenge of Institutionalization in a Charismatic Leader Party," in Barry Rubin and Metin Heper (eds.), *Political Parties in Turkey* (London, Portland, OR: Frank Cass, 2002): 54–55.
21. Evren, *Anılar 2*, 419–422.
22. Ibid., 420–422.
23. Üstün Ergüder, "Changing Patterns of Electoral Behavior in Turkey," *Boğaziçi University Journal*, nos. 8–9 (1980–1981): 45–47.
24. Ersin Kalaycıoğlu and Ali Yaşar Sarıbay, "İlkokul Çocuklarının Parti Tutmasını Belirleyen Etkenler," *Toplum ve Ekonomi*, no. 1 (March 1991): 148–149.

25. Ersin Kalaycıoğlu, "The Shaping of Party Preferences in Turkey: Coping with the Post–Cold War Era," *New Perspectives on Turkey*, no. 20 (1999): 74; and Özbudun, *Contemporary Turkish Politics*, 76.

26. Ali Çarkoğlu, "The Turkish Party System in Transition: Party Performance and Agenda Transformation," *Political Studies*, XLVI (1998): 544–571; and Özbudun, *Contemporary Turkish Politics*, 77.

27. Ersin Kalaycıoğlu, "Elections and Party Preferences in Turkey: Changes and Continuities in the 1990s," *Comparative Political Studies*, vol. 27, no. 3 (October 1994): 415; Kalaycıoğlu, 1999, "The Shaping of Party Preferences," 57–59.

28. Barry Rubin and Metin Heper (eds.), *Political Parties in Turkey* (London, Portland, OR: Frank Cass, 2002): passim; and Sabri Sayarı and Yılmaz Esmer (eds.), *Politics, Parties and Elections in Turkey* (Boulder and London: Lynne Rienner Publishers, 2002): passim.

29. Kalaycıoğlu, October 1994, "Elections and Party Preferences," 407; and Özbudun, *Contemporary Turkish Politics*, 81–82.

30. Kalaycıoğlu, 1999, "The Shaping of Party Preferences," 71–73. Hale argued along the same lines that, ". . . fissiparous tendencies are enhanced by the dominant role played by clientelism, rather than ideological or policy alignments, in constructing and preserving party structures," in William Hale, "Democracy and the Party System in Turkey," in Brian Beeley (ed.), *The Turkish Transformation: New Century—New Challenges* (Walkington, England: The Eothen Press, 2002): 183.

31. Özbudun, *Contemporary Turkish Politics*, 81.

32. The term "*şeriatçı*" stands for those who organize and act with the objective of establishing a state that enforces Sunni Islamic *Şeriat* (religious teachings, rules, and laws) as the law of the land. In concrete terms it is a political ideology that purports to establish the functional equivalent of the Iranian political system (which is based on implementing the *Caferi* understanding of Shi'ite law), in Turkey, where the majority of the people belong to Sunni Islam. Although, the Islamic heritage of Turkey is based upon the Sunni-*Hanefi* school of theology and law, most vocal "*Şeriatçı*" movements in Turkey tended to emerge from the ranks of Kurdish, Sunni-*Shafi* school of theology, *Said-i Kurdi* and later *Said-i Nursi* had founded and led that *Nurcu* order and movement during his lifetime. The Sunni-*Hanbali* school, which had not been present among the Turks, Kurds, and others in Anatolia during the reign of Ottoman Empire, but prominent in Saudi Arabia also gained ground in the late twentieth century in the political economy of the country. Thanks to the lavishly spent petrodollars Turks who were instructed in the *medreses* (schools) of Saudi Arabia, Egypt, and elsewhere in the Middle East, and Europe, and in particular Germany, returned to Turkey, fully socialized into *Wahhabism*, and Arabism as "true Islam." Many among them emerged as members of the "*Şeriatçı*" movements in Turkey, and propagated for the establishment of a state respectful of "*Şeriat*," and in enmity with the Jews and the "Zionist" state of Israel.

33. Kalaycıoğlu, 1999, "The Shaping of Party Preferences," 71–73.

34. Özbudun, *Contemporary Turkish Politics*, 89.

35. Ali Çarkoğlu ve Binnaz Toprak, *Türkiye'de Din, Toplum ve Siyaset* (Istanbul: TESEV Yayınları, 2000): 17.

36. Kalaycıoğlu, October 1994, "Elections and Party Preferences," 407; Kalaycıoğlu, 1999, "The Shaping of Party Preferences," 71–75.

37. Tuncer, *Osmanlı'dan Günümüze Seçimler*, 428–429.

38. The Welfare Party (RP) appealed the decision of the Constitutional Court to the European Human Rights Court (EHRC), which decided against the RP in its

first decision in the Summer of 2000. However, the RP appealed the decision of the European Human Rights Court and the final decision of the EHRC has not yet been made on the RP case.

39. See *Bülent Arınç*, "Interview with the Speaker of the TGNA," Milliyet daily (March 9, 2003): 12. This has been an ongoing phenomenon, which had been found to exist even in the 1930s. For a broader discussion of that phenomenon see Ersin Kalaycıoğlu, "The Turkish Grand National Assembly: A Brief Inquiry into the Politics of Representation in Turkey," in C. Balım et al. (eds.), *Turkey: Political, Social and Economic Challenges in the 1990s* (Leiden, New York, Köln: E. J. Brill, 1995): 42–60.

40. Kalaycıoğlu, "The Turkish Grand National Assembly," 48–52.

41. Incidentally, Mr. Necmettin Erbakan, who led his Welfare Party (RP) to government in the aftermath of the 1995 national elections, had his leg pulled by the media and the press for his gross miscalculations of his party's performance at the polls in that election. He had argued prior to the 1995 election that his party would obtain, at least half of the national vote in the election. However, the RP received about 21 percent of the national vote. Later, the spokespersons for the RP explained that previously they had obtained three votes per card-carrying member of their party. With the anticipation of their imminent success at the polls there was a sudden gush of demand for membership in the RP. The leader of the RP simply assumed that they would also get the usual three times as many votes as their members came up with a ballpark figure of about 45 percent and slightly exaggerated the results in his announcements. However, in the 1995 elections the RP failed to get the usual treatment. Almost half of its card-carrying members seemed to have failed to vote for that party at the polls. However, many card-carrying members later brandished their cards and argued that not only they voted for the party, but also did their entire extended family, and asked for benefits, jobs, projects, bid rigging, and so on, from the RP as usual.

42. Kalaycıoğlu, 1999, "The Shaping of Party Preferences," passim.

43. Ergun Özbudun, *Social Change and Political Participation in Turkey* (Princeton, New Jersey: Princeton University Press, 1976): 129–209; Ergüder, "Changing Patterns," 45–81.

44. Ergüder, "Changing Patterns," 45–81; Kalaycıoğlu, October 1994, "Elections and Party Preferences," 415.

45. Kalaycıoğlu, 1999, "The Shaping of Party Preferences," 58; Çarkoğlu and Toprak, *Türkiye'de Din*, 199; and Ersin Kalaycıoğlu, "Electoral Realignment or Protest Vote: November 2002 Elections in Turkey," (unpublished paper presented at the Annual Convention of the International Studies Association, Portland, Oregon, U.S.A., February 25–March 1, 2003): 3.

46. Yılmaz Esmer, *Devrim, Evrim, Statüko: Türkiye'de Sosyal, Siyasal, Ekonomik Değerler* (Istanbul: TESEV Yayınları, 1999): 85–94.

47. Şule Kut, "Soğuk Savaş Sonrasında Türkiye'nin Balkan Ülkeleriyle İlişkileri," in Ismail Soysal (ed.), *Çağdaş Türk Diplomasisi: 200 Yıllık Süreç* (Ankara: Türk Tarih Kurumu Basımevi, 1999): 390.

48. Ibid., 391–393.

49. Nazmi Akıman, "Türk-Yunan İlişkilerinin Değerlendirilmesi," in Ismail Soysal (ed.), *Çağdaş Türk Diplomasisi: 200 Yıllık Süreç* (Ankara: Türk Tarih Kurumu Basımevi, 1999): 582.

50. Ibid., 584.

51. Ibid., 584.

52. Ibid., 584.

53. The Turkish government accused Greece with violating the Bern Declaration of 1976, while the Greek government argued that the Declaration was only in effect so long as negotiations were actively and effectively continuing. However, the Greek government argued that, the negotiations were not moving ahead, so the Declaration could not be binding Greece, and in any case, the northern Aegean Sea was Greek territory. In reaction, Turkey sent its *Sismik* I exploration vessel to the area, and Greece threatened to sink *Sismik* I. The United States and the NATO allies of both Greece and Turkey intervened as the waters of the Aegean started to heat up again. The two countries stopped explorations for a while, and a new rapprochement started between PM Özal of Turkey and PM Papandreou of Greece in the *Davos* meetings of 1988. For more details on the matter see Şule Kut, "The Aegean Continental Shelf Dispute between Turkey and Greece," *Balkan Forum*, vol. 3, no. 1 (1995): 179–206; and Angelos M. Syrigos, *The Status of the Aegean Sea According to International Law* (Athens: Sakkoulas/ Bruylant, no date): passim; and Faruk Sönmezoğlu, *Türkiye—Yunanistan İlişkileri ve Büyük Güçler: Kıbrıs, Ege ve Diğer Sorunlar* (Istanbul: Der Yayınları, 2000): 248–249.

54. Akıman, "Türk-Yunan," 584.

55. Current 6 miles of territorial waters accords approximately 44 percent of the Aegean Sea as Greek territorial waters, and 8 percent as Turkish, and the rest, 48 percent of the sea constitutes the international waters of the Aegean. If the territorial waters of Greece are extended to 12 miles, the Greek territorial waters will cover 72 percent of the Aegean Sea, with Turkish waters consisting of only 9 percent, whereas only 19 percent of the waters of the Aegean would then still be designated international waters. Turkish access to the Mediterranean Sea routes would then be severely restricted, which Turkey finds unacceptable. For more information see Nazmi Akıman, "Bir Diplomat Gözüyle Türk-Yunan İlişkileri," in (no editor) *Balkanlar* (Istanbul: Orta Doğu ve Balkan İncelemeleri Vakfı Yayınları, 1993): 245–246.

56. Akıman, "Bir Diplomat Gözüyle Türk," 247.

57. Greece has six miles of territorial waters. The Greek governments since 1931 argue that they have 10 miles of national air space, which creates a unique "conic air space," whereby at its base it is six miles over the sea and ten miles over it in the atmosphere above the sea. Therefore, any sea going vessel that is seven miles from Greek land is in international waters, however any aeroplane that flies over that vessel at seven miles from the Greek land "violates Greek air space," according to the Greek government.

58. Sönmezoğlu, *Yunanistan İlişkileri*, 333–335.

59. Kemal Kirişçi, "The Future of Turkish Policy Toward the Middle East," in Barry Rubin and Kemal Kirişçi (eds.), *Turkey in World Politics: An Emerging Multiregional Power* (Boulder, London: Lynne Rienner Publishers, 2002): 97.

60. Ibid., 97.

61. Ibid., 97–98.

62. Ibid., 100.

63. Hasan Cemal, *Kürtler* (Istanbul: Milliyet Yayınları, 2003): 72.

64. Ibid., 72.

65. Ibid., 72.

66. Kirişçi, "The Future of Turkish Policy," 94.

67. Cemal, *Kürtler*, 309.

68. Ibid., 310–311.
69. James C. Davies, "Toward Theory of Revolution," *American Sociological Review*, vol. 27, no. 1 (February 1962): 5–6.
70. Ibid. 6–8.
71. Korkut Boratav, *Türkiye İktisat Tarihi 1908–2002* (seventh ed.) (Ankara, İmge Yayıncılık, 2003): 189.
72. Cemal, *Kürtler*, 76–80.
73. Michael M. Gunter, *The Kurds and the Future of Turkey* (Hampshire: Macmillan Press, 1997): 60; and David McDowall, *A Modern History of the Kurds* (London, New York, I. B. Tauris, 2000): 444.
74. Kemal Kirişçi and Gareth Winrow, *The Kurdish Question and Turkey: An Example of Trans-State Ethnic Conflict* (London, Portland, Oregon: Frank Cass, 1997): 91–103.
75. Kalaycıoğlu, 1999, "The Shaping of Party Preferences," 60.
76. Ibid., 60.
77. Ibid., 60; Kalaycıoğlu, 2003, "Electoral Realignment," 19.
78. Gareth Winrow, "Turkey and the Newly Independent States of Central Asia and the Transcaucasus," in Barry Rubin and Kemal Kirişçi (eds.), *Turkey in World Politics: An Emerging Multiregional Power* (Boulder, London: Lynne Rienner Publishers, 2002): 173–188.
79. Hakan Bingün, "Türkiye ve Güney Kafkasya İlişkileri," in Ismail Soysal (ed.), *Çağdaş Türk Diplomasisi: 200 Yıllık Süreç* (Ankara: Türk Tarih Kurumu Basımevi, 1999): 599–600.
80. Ibid., 600.
81. For more information see Richard V. Weekes et al., *Muslim Peoples: A World Ethnographic Survey* (Westport, Conn., London: Greenwood Press, 1978): 111–114.
82. Ersin Kalaycıoğlu, "Türkiye'de Siyasal Kültür ve Demokrasi," in Ergun Özbudun, Ersin Kalaycıoğlu, and Levent Köker (eds.), *Türkiye'de Demokratik Siyasal Kültür* (Ankara: Türk Demokrasi Vakfı Yayınları, 1995): 65–66.
83. Cemal, *Kürtler*, 316–317.
84. Ibid., 80–83 and 232–235.
85. Ibid., 287–289 and 482.
86. Ibid., 445.
87. Ibid., 445.
88. Ibid., 447.
89. Patrick Seale, *The Struggle for Syria: A Study of Post-War Arab Politics 1945–1958* (New Haven, London: Yale University Press, 1986): 11–15.
90. İlter Turan, "Sunuş" in Sabahattin Şen (ed.), *Su Sorunu, Türkiye ve Ortadoğu*, (Istanbul: Bağlam Yayınları, 1993): 14.
91. Aydın G. Alacakaptan, "Sınır Aşan Akarsularımız Dicle ve Fırat'ın Arap Komşularımızla Büyük Sürtüşmelere Neden Olmaları Beklentileri Abartılıdır," in Sabahattin Şen (ed.), *Su Sorunu, Türkiye ve Ortadoğu* (Istanbul: Bağlam Yayınları, 1993): 460.
92. Çağrı Erhan, "Türk-Suriye İlişkilerinde Fırat Suyunun Paylaşımı Sorunu," *Mülkiyeliler Birliği Dergisi*, XXI, no. 199 (May 1999): 43.
93. Ibid., 43.
94. Ibid., 44.
95. Cemal, *Kürtler*, 449–450.
96. Ibid., 449.

97. Ibid., 490–491.
98. Ibid., 492.
99. Tuncer, *Osmanlı'dan Günümüze Seçimler*, 356; and Kalaycıoğlu, 2003, "Electoral Realignment," 16.
100. Gürel Tüzün and Sibel Sezer (eds.), *World Summit on Sustainable Development Johannesburg 2002, National Report: Turkey* (Ankara: The Ministry of Environment and the United Nations Development Programme, 2002): 109.
101. Taner Baytok, *Bir Asker Bir Diplomat: Güven Erkaya—Taner Baytok Söyleşisi* (Istanbul: Doğan Kitapçılık, 2001): 248–258.
102. Ibid., 259–264.
103. For more details see ibid. 257–258.
104. Turkish Daily News (daily), December 16 and December 17, 1997.
105. Sönmezoğlu, *Yunanistan İlişkileri*, 340.
106. Ibid., 340.
107. Ibid., 340.
108. The EU had agreed upon a set of criteria during the Copenhagen Summit of 1993, which defines the democratic and economic standards a country should have to be eligible to full membership in the EU. They have been referred to as the "Copenhagen Criteria ever since, and they are listed in the following:

    1. *Europeanness*: The applicant country has to be a member of the European family of states.
    2. *Political criteria*: The political system must be characterized by democracy and the rule of law, respect human rights, and protection of minorities.
    3. *Economic criteria*: The country must have a strong market economy that encompasses the free movement of goods, capital, services, and people.
    4. *Other obligations*
       a. The aims of political, economic, and monetary union.
       b. Adoption of the *acquis communautaire*, the rights and obligations derived from EU treaties, laws, and regulations over the years."

    For more details see Birol Yeşilada, "The Copenhagen Criteria and the Challenge of Democratization in Turkey," (unpublished paper presented at the 2003 Annual Convention of the International Studies Association in Portland, Oregon, February 25–March 1, 2003): 4.
109. Kalaycıoğlu, 2003, "Electoral Realignment," passim.
110. Kalaycıoğlu, 1999, "The Shaping of Party Preferences," 73.
111. Milliyet (daily), August 31, 2003: 17.

6   Governance, Change, and Risk

1. "Istanbul Turkish" refers to a dialect used by those who were close to the palace, which also signified one's intellectual and political credentials.
2. A gentleman born and raised in Istanbul, who demonstrated a style of life by his elegant attire, manners, and upper-middle-class looks.
3. Yeşim Arat, *Political Islam in Turkey and Women's Organizations* (Istanbul: TESEV Publications, 1999): 35–36. For an early example of the tension between preserving the traditional society and yet seek modernity in Turkish countryside see J. Hinderink and Mübeccel Kıray, *Social Stratification as an Obstacle to Development % A Study of Four Turkish Villages* (New York, London, Washington: Praeger, 1970): passim.

4. Hinderink and Kıray, *Social Stratification*, chapters 2 and 3.
5. Ersin Kalaycıoğlu, "State and Civil Society in Turkey: Democracy, Development and Protest," in Amyn B. Sajoo (ed.), *Civil Society in the Muslim World: Contemporary Perspectives* (London, New York: I. B: Tauris Publishers, 2002): 263–268.
6. Nilüfer Göle, "Authoritarian Secularism and Islamist Politics: The Case of Turkey," in Augustus Richard Norton (ed.), *Civil Society in the Middle East* (Leiden, New York, Köln, E. J. Brill, 1996): 38–39.
7. Ersin Kalaycıoğlu, "The Mystery of the *'Türban'*: Participation or Revolt?" Turkish Studies vol. 6, no. 2 (June 2005): 239–240.
8. Arat, *Political Islam in Turkey*, 35–36.
9. Kalaycıoğlu, 2005, "The Mystery," 239–240. On lack of segregation between men and women among the *Alevis* see David Shankland, *Islam and Society in Turkey* (Hundington, Cambridgeshire, England: The Eothen Press, 1999): 157–164; and Elise Massicard, "Alevism as a Productive Misunderstanding: The Hacıbektaş Festival," in Paul J. White and Joost Jongerden (eds.), *Turkey's Alevi Enigma: A Comprehensive Overview* (Leiden, Boston: Brill, 2003): 132–133.
10. Vakur Alperen, *Başörtüsü Yasağı'nın Hukuki Açıdan Değerlendirilmesi* (Istanbul: İnsan Hak ve Hürriyetleri Vakfı Yayını, 1998): 4 and 13.
11. Ibid., 20–41.
12. Ibid., 22.
13. Ersin Kalaycıoğlu and Binnaz Toprak, *İş Yaşamı, Üst Yönetim ve Siyasette KADIN* (Istanbul: TESEV Yayınları, 2004): 42–48.
14. Milliyet (daily) (September 3, 2003): 17.
15. Ersin Kalaycıoğlu, "Turkish Democracy: Patronage versus Governance," *Turkish Studies*, vol. 2, no. 1 (Spring 2001): 54–70.
16. Ibid., 65–66.
17. Korkut Boratav, *Türkiye İktisat Tarihi 1908–2002* (seventh ed.) (Ankara, İmge Yayıncılık, 2003): 59–79.
18. Tevfik Çavdar, *Türkiye Ekonomisinin Tarihi (1900–1960): Yirminci Yüzyıl Türkiye İktisat Tarihi* (Ankara: Imge Kitabevi, 2003): 261–264.
19. Ilkay Sunar, *State and Society in the Politics of Turkey's Development* (Ankara: Ankara Universitesi Siyasal Bilgiler Fakültesi Yayını, 1975): 96.
20. Ibid., 96–97; and Ergun Özbudun, *Social Change and Political Participation in Turkey* (Princeton, New Jersey: Princeton University Press, 1976): 41–59.
21. Şerif Mardin, "Center-Periphery Relations: A Key to Turkish Politics?" in Engin Akarlı and Gabriel Ben-Dor (eds.), *Political Participation in Turkey: Historical Background and Present Problems* (Istanbul: Boğaziçi University Press, 1975): 7–32; Engin Akarlı, "The State as a Socio-Cultural Phenomenon and Political Participation in Turkey," in Engin Akarlı and Gabriel Ben-Dor (eds.), *Political Participation in Turkey: Historical Background and Present Problems* (Istanbul: Boğaziçi University Publications, 1975): 135–155; and Metin Heper, *The State Tradition in Turkey* (Walkington, England: Eothen Press, 1985): 67–97.
22. Heper, *The State Tradition*, 8, 50–66.
23. Ibid., 103.
24. Mancur Olson, Jr., *The Logic of Collective Action: Public Goods and the Theory of Groups* (New York: Schoken Books, 1971): 5–65 explains why and how it is economically rational for an individual member of a community, organization, or nation to act as a free-rider.
25. Edward Banfield, *The Moral Basis of a Backward Society* (New York: The Free Press, 1958): 83ff.

26. Kalaycıoğlu 2001, "Patronage versus Governance," 64–65.

27. Shankland, *Islam and Society in Turkey*, 84.

28. Ayşe Güneş-Ayata, "Roots and Trends of Clientelism in Turkey," in Luis Roniger and Ayşe Güneş-Ayata (eds.), *Democracy, Clientelism and Civil Society* (Boulder, London: Lynne Rienner, 1994): 55–60.

29. Ibid. 54–62.

30. Kalaycıoğlu, 2001, "Patronage versus Governance," 62.

31. Ibid. 63.

32. Yılmaz Esmer, *Devrim, Evrim, Statüko: Türkiye'de Sosyal, Siyasal, Ekonomik Değerler* (Istanbul: TESEV Yayınları, 1999): 78–80; and Ersin Kalaycıoğlu, "Civil Society in Turkey: Continuity or Change?" in Brian W. Beeley (ed.), *Turkish Transformation: New Century—New Challenges* (Walkington, England: The Eothen Press, 2002): 62–75.

33. Kalaycıoğlu, 2001, "Patronage versus Governance," 63.

34. For more information see OECD, *Tax Administration in OECD Countries: Comparative Information Series* (Paris, 2004): 32; and also N. Semih Öz, "Karşılaştırmalı Vergi İstatistikleri ve Uluslararası Vergilendirmede Geleceğe Yönelik Eğilimler," *Vergi Sorunları*, no. 196 (January 2005): 11–22; and Eser Karakaş, "Mali Krizin Bir Başka Boyutu" (August 29, 2003) <www.finansalforum.com>.

35. Value Added Tax (KDV) is a production and sales tax that is collected at each stage of production and sale of a commodity. It is levied on the surplus value added on to the value of a raw or intermediary product during its production, which is collected at the time of its sale. In the final stage the consumers end up paying it whenever they purchase a service or good.

36. Milliyet (daily) (December 23, 2003): 8; and Milliyet (daily) (September 7, 2004): 1.

37. Kalaycıoğlu, 2001, "Patronage versus Governance," 62–66.

38. Ziya Öniş, "Domestic Politics versus Global Dynamics: Towards a Political Economy of the 2000 and 2001 Financial Crisis in Turkey," *Turkish Studies*, vol. 4, no. 2 (Summer 2003): 7.

39. Ibid., 7–8.

40. Ibid., 8.

41. Ibid., 11.

42. Ersin Kalaycıoğlu, "Electoral Realignment or Protest Vote: November 2002 Elections in Turkey," (unpublished paper presented at the Annual Convention of the International Studies Association, Portland, Oregon, U.S.A., February 25–March 1, 2003): 16–18.

43. After a few months of indecision over the issue of the Cyprus, and once the Iraqi war of 2003 was over with, the AKP government took determined steps to negotiate the Annan Plan. In early 2004 it became clear that the AKP government would be supportive of a loose federation of two partner states of Turkish and Greek Cypriots on the island. From then on the Turkish government encouraged the Turkish State of Northern Cyprus (TRNC) to accept a settlement of the Cyprus issue within the confines of the Annan Plan. The elections in the TRNC also paved the way for a coalition government that accepted a settlement according to the Annan Plan, instead of prolongation of the divided status quo. Eventually, the UN General Secretary was able to present the Greek and Turkish communities on the island with a plan, which they will adopt or reject through a referendum on April 24, 2004. The Greek Cypriot government launched an emotional and nationalist campaign against the Annan Plan, and the Greeks

voted overwhelmingly against it, while the Turkish Cypriots voted overwhelmingly for the plan. The Greek rejection of the plan did not forestall the Greek Cypriot government from becoming a full member of the European Union (EU) on May 1, 2004 as "the government" of Cyprus, while they fully failed to represent the Turkish community living in the north. The division of the island between two communities and their states continued, while the Turkish Cypriots who voted for a settlement through the "Annan Plan" were once again marginalized, and left in a state of isolation. Ironically, the Greek Cypriots who championed nationalism and non-conciliation became EU members. The EU had assumed that the Turkish government was the main obstacle to the settlement of the Cyprus conflict. They had followed a policy of pressuring Turkey and the Turkish Cypriot governments. However, when the EU realized that Turkey was not the only obstacle to peace on Cyprus, it was too late for them to change their ill-conceived policy. Hence, the EU had to welcome the Greek Cypriots as a new member on May 1, 2004, yet fail to resolve the conflict on the island of Cyprus. Instead, the EU was able to import the Cypriot mess into its own organization. The EU still lacks a policy of solving the quagmire of Cyprus, except for pressuring Turkey to accept the Greek demands on the island, which the Turkish governments continue to resist. Currently, the EU has offered Turkey to start accession negotiations with the EU on October 3, 2005 and still pressures Turkey to extend the Customs Union agreement to cover the ten new members including Greek Cyprus. The Turkish government continues to argue that Turkey will not recognize the Greek government of Cyprus as the "legitimate government of the Republic of Cyprus," for it does not represent the Turks, and it is solely responsible for undermining the London and Zurich Accords and the constitution of the Republic of Cyprus in 1963 by evicting the Turkish Cypriots out of their constitutional roles in the government. Consequently, Turkish government argues that it will only recognize the Cypriot government when the Annan Plan or some other constitutional design integrates Turkish Cypriots into the government and state of Cyprus, and not before. However, Turkey has until October 3, 2005 to help solve the Cyprus quagmire, and otherwise risk starting EU negotiations with an organization, a member of which Turkey does not recognize, and also risk a veto by the Greek Cypriot member of the EU, which will stop accession negotiations before they start. Ironically, the nationalist Greek Cypriot government, now a member of the EU can afford to do nothing, and the mess is set to prolong as a marvelous EU debacle.

44. Seymour Martin Lipset, *Political Man: The Social Bases of Politics* (Garden City, New York: Anchor Books, 1963): 27–63.
45. Özbudun, 1976, *Social Change*, 221–222.
46. Esmer, 1999, *Devrim, Evrim, Statüko*, 83–92.
47. Kalaycıoğlu, "Civil Society in Turkey," 2002: 62–69.
48. Ibid., 69–70; and Cemil Oktay, *Yükselen İstemler Karşısında Türk Siyasal Sistemi ve Kamu Bürokrasisi* (Istanbul: Istanbul Üniversitesi Siyasal Bilimler Fakültesi Yayınları, 1983): 183–222.
49. <europa.eu.int/comm/enlargement/intro.criteria>: 1.
50. Ibid., 1.
51. Ersin Kalaycıoğlu, "Turkey's Choice: The Road Away from the European Union," in Bertil Dunér (ed.), *Turkey: The Road Ahead?* (Stockholm: The Swedish Institute of International Affairs, 2002): 123–130.

7 CONCLUSION: MAKING A BRIDGE FUNCTIONAL

1. Ersin Kalaycıoğlu, "Elections and Governance," in Sabri Sayarı and Yılmaz Esmer (eds.), *Politics, Parties, and Elections in Turkey* (Boulder, London: Lynne Rienner, 2002): 67–69.
2. Frederick W. Frey, "Patterns of Elite Politics in Turkey," in George Lenczowski (ed.), *Political Elites in the Middle East* (Washington, D.C.: American Enterprise Institute for Public Policy Research, 1975): 65–67.
3. Yılmaz Esmer, *Devrim, Evrim, Statüko: Türkiye'de Sosyal, Siyasal, Ekonomik Değerler* (Istanbul: TESEV Yayınları, 1999): 78–80.
4. Milliyet (daily) (January 8, 2004): 1.
5. Kalaycıoğlu, "Elections and Governance," 67–69.
6. Commission of the European Communities, *2004 Regular Report on Turkey's Progress Towards Accession* (Brussels, 6.10.2004 SEC (2004) 1201): 2–55.

BIBLIOGRAPHY

Abadan-Unat, Nermin, *Bitmeyen Göç: Konuk İşçilikten Ulus-Ötesi Yurttaşlığa* (Istanbul: Bilgi Üniversitesi Yayınları, 2002).

Adaman, Fikret, Ali Çarkoğlu, and Burhan Şenatalar, *Household View on the Cause of Corruption in Turkey and Suggested Preventive Measures* (Istanbul: Tesev Publications, 2002).

Ağaoğlu, Ahmet, *Serbest Fırka Hatıraları* (third ed.) (Istanbul: İletişim Yayınları, 1994).

Ahmad, Feroz, *The Young Turks: The Committee of Union and Progress in Turkish Politics 1908–1914* (Oxford: The Clarendon Press, 1969).

———, *The Turkish Experiment in Democracy, 1950–1975* (London: Hurst, 1977).

Akarlı, Engin, "The State as a Socio-Cultural Phenomenon and Political Participation in Turkey," in Engin Akarlı and Gabriel Ben-Dor (eds.), *Political Participation in Turkey: Historical Background and Present Problems* (Istanbul: Boğaziçi University Publications, 1975): 135–155.

Akçura, Yusuf, *Üç Tarz-ı Siyaset* (Ankara: Türk Tarih Kurumu Basımevi, 1976): 19–36.

Akıman, Nazmi, "Bir Diplomat Gözüyle Türk-Yunan İlişkileri" in (no editor) *Balkanlar* (Istanbul: Orta Doğu ve Balkan İncelemeleri Vakfı Yayınları, 1993): 241–250.

———, "Türk-Yunan İlişkilerinin Değerlendirilmesi" in Ismail Soysal (ed.), *Çağdaş Türk Diplomasisi: 200 Yıllık Süreç* (Ankara: Türk Tarih Kurumu Basımevi, 1999): 579–586.

Aktar, Ayhan, "Varlık Vergisi ve Istanbul," *Toplum ve Bilim*, vol. 71 (1996): 97–147.

———, *Varlık Vergisi ve "Türkleştirme Politikaları"* (fifth print) (Istanbul: İletişim, 2001).

Alacakaptan, Aydın G., "Sınır Aşan Akarsularımız Dicle ve Fırat'ın Arap Komşularımızla Büyük Sürtüşmelere Neden Olmaları Beklentileri Abartılıdır" in Sabahattin Şen (ed.), *Su Sorunu, Türkiye ve Ortadoğu* (Istanbul: Bağlam Yayınları, 1993): 455–471.

Alperen, Vakur, *Başörtüsü Yasağı'nın Hukuki Açıdan Değerlendirilmesi* (Istanbul: İnsan Hak ve Hürriyetleri Vakfı Yayını, 1998).

Altuğ, Yılmaz, "Turkish Involvement in Some International Disputes," *Belleten*, vol. LIII, no. 206 (1989): 259–360.

Akşin, Sina, "Siyasal Tarih (1789–1908)" in Sina Akşin, Metin Kunt, Ayla Ödekan, Zafer Toprak, Hüseyin G. Yurdaydın, (ed.) *Türkiye Tarihi 3: Osmanlı Devleti 1600–1908*, (Istanbul: Cem Yayınevi): 73–188.

Antel, Sadrettin Celal, "Tanzimat Maarifi" in Komisyon (ed.), *Tanzimat 1* (Ankara: Milli Eğitim Bakanlığı Yayınları: no. 3273, 1999): 441–462.

Arat, Yeşim, *Political Islam in Turkey and Women's Organizations* (Istanbul: TESEV Publications, 1999).

Armaoğlu, Fahir, "Yarım Yüzyılın Türk-Amerikan İlişkileri, 1947–1997" in Ismail Soysal (ed.), *Çağdaş Türk Diplomasisi: 200 Yıllık Süreç* (Ankara: Türk Tarih Kurumu Basımevi, 1999): 421–440.

Aybay, Rona, "Milli Güvenlik Kavramı ve Milli Güvenlik Kurulu," *Ankara Üniversitesi Siyasal Bilgiler Fakültesi Dergisi*, vol. XXXIII, nos. 1–2 (March–June 1978): 59–82.

Aydemir, Şevket Süreyya, *Tek Adam: Mustafa Kemal, 1881–1919* (Istanbul: Remzi Kitabevi, 1966).

———, *İhtilalin Mantığı* (fifth print) (Istanbul: Remzi Kitabevi: 1993).

Banfield, Edward, *The Moral Basis of a Backward Society* (New York: The Free Press, 1958).

Baloğlu, Zekai, *Türkiye'de Eğitim* (Istanbul: TÜSİAD Yayınları, 1990).

Baytok, Taner, *Bir Asker Bir Diplomat: Güven Erkaya — Taner Baytok Söyleşisi*, (Istanbul: Doğan Kitapçılık, 2001).

Behar, Cem, Hakan Ercam Sema Erder, Murat Güven, Oğçuz Isik, *Turkey's Window of Opportunity: Demographic Transition Process and Its Consequences* (Istanbul: TÜSİAD Publication No-T/99–3-254, 1999).

Bendix, Reinhard, *Max Weber: An Intellectual Portrait* (Garden City, New York: Doubleday, 1962).

Berkes, Niyazi, "Ziya Gökalp: His Contribution to Turkish Nationalism," *The Middle East Journal*, 8, no. 4 (Autumn 1954): 375–390.

———, *Turkish Nationalism and Western Civilization: Selected Essays of Ziya Gökalp* (New York: Columbia University Press, 1959).

———, *The Development of Secularism in Turkey* (Montreal: McGill University Press, 1964).

Bianchi, Robert, *Interest Groups and Political Development in Turkey* (Princeton, New Jersey: Princeton University Press, 1984).

Bill, James A. and Robert Springborg, *Politics in the Middle East* (fifth edition) (New York: Longman, 2000).

Bingün, Hakan, "Türkiye ve Güney Kafkasya İlişkileri," in Ismail Soysal (ed.), *Çağdaş Türk Diplomasisi: 200 Yıllık Süreç* (Ankara: Türk Tarih Kurumu Basımevi, 1999): 597–604.

Boratav, Korkut, *Türkiye İktisat Tarihi: 1908–2002* (seventh ed.) (Ankara: Imge Yayınevi, 2003).

Bozkurt, Gülnihal, "Tanzimat and Law" in Atatürk Kültür, Dil ve Tarih Yüksek Kurumu (eds.), *Tanzimat'ın 150. Yıldönümü Uluslararası Sempozyumu* (Ankara: Türk Tarih Kurumu Basımevi, 1994): 279–286.

Cemal (Paşa), *Hatıralar: Ittihat ve Terakki, I. Dünya Savaşı Anıları* (prepared for publication by Alpay Kabacalı) (Istanbul: Türkiye İş Bankası Kültür Yayınları, 2001).

Cemal, Hasan, *Kürtler* (Istanbul: Milliyet Yayınları, 2003).

Clapham, C., *Third World Politics: An Introduction* (Madison, Wisconsin: University of Wisconsin Press, 1988).

Commission of the European Communities, *2004 Regular Report on Turkey's Progress Towards Accession*, Brussels, 6.10.2004 SEC (2004) 1201.

Coşkun, Abdullah, "Mercümek'in Son Umudu" (2000) <www.aksam.com.tr/2000/05/14/guncel/ guncel8.html>.

Çarkoğlu, Ali, "The Turkish Party System in Transition: Party Performance and Agenda Transformation," *Political Studies*, XLVI (1998): 544–571.

Çarkoğlu, Ali and Emre Erdoğan, "Fairness in the Apportionment of Seats in the Turkish Legislature: Is There Room for Improvement?" *New Perspectives on Turkey* (Fall 1998), 19: 97–124.

Çarkoğlu, Ali and Binnaz Toprak, *Türkiye'de Din, Toplum ve Siyaset* (Istanbul: TESEV Yayınları, 2000).

Çavdar, Tevfik, *Türkiye Ekonomisinin Tarihi (1900–1960): Yirminci Yüzyıl Türkiye İktisat Tarihi* (Ankara: Imge Kitabevi, 2003).

Danielson, Michael N. and Rusen Keles, *Politics of Rapid Urbanization: Government and Growth in Turkey* (New York: Holmes and Meier, 1985).

Davison, Andrew, *Secularism and Revivalism in Turkey: A Hermeneutic Reconsideration* (New Haven and London: Yale University Press, 1998).

Davies, James C., "Toward Theory of Revolution," *American Sociological Review*, vol. 27, no. 1 (February 1962): 5–19.

Deringil, Selim, *The Turkish Foreign Policy during the Second World War: An Active Neutrality* (New York, New Rochelle, Melbourne, Sydney: Cambridge University Press, 1989).

Dodd, Clement H., *Democracy and Development in Turkey* (Walkington, England: The Eothen Press, 1979).

Drysdale, Alasdair and Gerald H. Blake, *The Middle East and North Africa: A Political Geography* (New York, Oxford: Oxford University Press, 1985).

Erdem, Y. Hakan, "The Wise Old Man, Propagandist and Ideologist: Koca Sekbanbaşi on the Janissaries, 1807," in Kirsi Virtanen (ed.), *Individual, Ideologies and Society: Tracing the Mosaic of Mediterranean History* (Tampere, Finland: Tampere Peace Research Institute, 2000): 153–177.

Ergüder, Üstün, "Changing Patterns of Electoral Behavior in Turkey," *Boğaziçi University Journal*, 8–9 (1980–1981): 45–81.

Erhan, Çağrı, "Türk-Suriye İlişkilerinde Fırat Suyunun Paylaşımı Sorunu," *Mülkiyeliler Birliği Dergisi*, XXI, no. 199 (May 1999): 42–45.

Esin, Numan, "13 Kasım 1960 Ogusu Üzerine Birkaç Söz," in Suna Kili (ed.), *27 Mayıs 1960 Devrimi, Kurucu Meclis ve 1961 Anayasası* (Istanbul: Boyut Kitapları, 1998): 265–269.

Ergüder, Üstün, Yılmaz Esmer, and Ersin Kalaycıoğlu, *Türk Toplumunun Değerleri* (Istanbul: TÜSİAD Yayınları, 1991).

Esmer, Ahmet Şükrü and Oral Sander, "İkinci Dünya Savaşında Türk Dış Politikası," in Mehmet Gönlübol et al. (eds.), *Olaylarla Türk Dış Politikası (1919–1973)*, (enlarged third ed.) (Ankara: Ankara Üniversitesi Siyasal Bilgiler Fakültesi Yayını, 1974): 147–200.

Esmer, Yılmaz, *Devrim, Evrim, Statüko: Türkiye'de Sosyal, Siyasal ve Ekonomik Değerler* (Istanbul: TESEV Yayınları, 1999)<europa.eu.int/comm/enlargement/intro.criteria>.

Evren, Kenan, *Kenan Evren'in Anıları 1* (Istanbul: Milliyet Yayınları, 1990).

———, *Kenan Evren'in Anıları 2* (Istanbul: Milliyet Yayınları, 1991).

———, *Kenan Evren'in Anıları 3* (Istanbul: Milliyet Yayınları, 1991).

Fischer-Galati, Stephen, "Eastern Europe in the Twentieth Century: 'Old Wine in New Bottles,' " in Joseph Held (ed.), *The Columbia History of Eastern Europe in the Twentieth Century* (New York: Columbia University Press, 1992): 1–16.

Frey, Frederick W., "Patterns of Elite Politics in Turkey," in George Lenczowski (ed.), *Political Elites in the Middle East* (Washington, D.C.: American Enterprise Institute for Public Policy Research, 1975): 41–82.

Gençkaya, Ömer Faruk, "Türk Siyasal Sisteminde Kurucu Meclis: 1961 ve 1982 Deneyimlerinin Karşılaştırılması," in Suna Kili (ed.), *27 Mayıs 1960 Devrimi, Kurucu Meclis ve 1961 Anayasası* (Istanbul: Boyut Kitapları, 1998): 15–31.

Gökalp, Ziya, *Türkçülüğün Esasları (Türk Klasikleri)* (prepared for publication by Mehmet Kaplan) (Istanbul: Milli Eğitim Bakanlığı Yayınları, 1990).

Göle, Nilüfer, "Authoritarian Secularism and Islamist Politics: The Case of Turkey," in Augustus Richard Norton (ed.), *Civil Society in the Middle East* (Leiden, New York, Köln, E. J. Brill, 1996, 1996): pp. 17–43.

Gönlübol, Mehmet and Cem Sar (1974). "1919–1938 Yılları arasında Türk Dış Politikası," in Mehmet Gönlübol et al., *Olaylarla Türk Dış Politikası (1919–1973)* (enlarged third ed.) (Ankara: Ankara Üniversitesi Siyasal Bilgiler Fakültesi Yayını, 1974): 3–144.

Gönlübol, Mehmet and Haluk Ulman, "İkinci Dünya Savaşından Sonra Türk Dış Politikası," in Mehmet Gönlübol et al. (eds.), *Olaylarla Türk Dış Politikası (1919–1973)* (enlarged third ed.) (Ankara: Ankara Üniversitesi Siyasal Bilgiler Fakültesi Yayını, 1974): 287–529.

Gunter, Michael M., *The Kurds and the Future of Turkey* (Hampshire: Macmillan Press, 1997).

Güneş-Ayata, Ayşe, "Roots and Trends of Clientelism in Turkey," in Luis Roniger and Ayşe Güneş-Ayata (eds.), *Democracy, Clientelism and Civil Society* (Boulder, London: Lynne Rienner, 1994): 49–63.

Gürkan, Celil, *12 Mart'a Beş Kala* (Istanbul: Tekin Yayınları, 1986).

Hale, William, *The Political and Economic Development of Modern Turkey* (London: Croom Helm, 1981).

———, *Turkish Politics and the Military* (London and New York: Routledge, 1994).

———, *Turkish Foreign Policy: 1774–2000* (London, Portland, OR: Frank Cass, 2000).

———, "Democracy and the Party System in Turkey," in Brian Beeley (ed.), *The Turkish Transformation: New Century—New Challenges* (Walkington, England: The Eothen Press, 2002): 165–197.

Harris, George, "The Cause of the 1960 Revolution in Turkey," *Middle East Journal* vol. 24, no. 3 (1970): 438–439.

Held, Colbert C., *Middle East Patterns: Places, Peoples, and Politics* (Boulder, Colorado: Westview Press, 2000).

Heper, Metin, "Politics of Transition in the Third Turkish Republic," (occasional paper) (Boğaziçi University, Department of Public Administration, 1985).

———, *The State Tradition in Turkey* (Walkington, England: Eothen Press, 1985).

———, "Conclusion," in Metin Heper and Ahmet Evin (eds.), *State, Democracy and the Military: Turkey in the 1980s* (Berlin, New York: Walter de Gruyter, 1988).

———, "Introduction," in Metin Heper (ed.), *Local Government in Turkey: Governing Greater Istanbul* (London: Routledge, 1989): 1–11.

———, "The Consolidation of Democracy versus Democratization in Turkey," in Barry Rubin and Metin Heper (eds.), *Political Parties in Turkey* (London, Portland, OR: Frank Cass, 2002): 138–146.

Heper, Metin and Ahmet Evin (eds.), *Democracy and Local Government: Istanbul in the 1980s* (Beverley, North Humberside: Eothen Press, 1987).

Hinderink, J. and Mübeccel Kıray, *Social Stratification as an Obstacle to Development: A Study of Four Turkish Villages* (New York, London, Washington: Praeger, 1970).

Hirschon, Renée (ed.), *Crossing the Aegean: An Appraisal of the 1923 Compulsory Population Exchange between Greece and Turkey* (New York, Oxford: Berghahn Books, 2003).

Hourani, Albert, *A History of the Arab Peoples* (New York Warner Books, 1991).

İpekçİ, Abdi and Ömer Sami Coşar, *İhtilalin İçyüzü* (Istanbul: Uygun Yayınevi, 1965).

IBRD, *World 1997 Development Report* (New York: Oxford University Press, 1997).

IBRD, World Development Report 2001/2002, *Building Institutions for Markets* (Oxford, England: Oxford University Press, 2002).

IBRD, World Development Report 2005, *A Better Investment Climate for Everyone* (New York: World Bank and Oxford University Press, 2004).

Inalcık, Halil, *Osmanlı'da Devlet, Hukuk, Adalet* (Istanbul: Eren Yayıncılık, 2000).

Joseph, Joseph S., *Cyprus: Ethnic Conflict and International Politics* (New York, St. Martin's Press, 1997).

Kaboğlu, İbrahim, "Zorunlu Din Dersi Anayasaya Aykırı" (interview reported in *Milliyet* daily) (Istanbul, 2003): 16.

Kalaycıoğlu, Ersin, "Why Legislatures Persist in Developing Countries: The Case of Turkey," *Legislative Studies Quarterly*, V, 1 (February 1980): 123–140.

———, "The Turkish Political System in Transition: Multi-Party Politics in the 1980s," *Current Turkish Thought*, vol. 56 (Fall 1985): 1–38.

———, "The 1983 Parliament in Turkey: Changes and Continuities," in Metin Heper and Ahmet Evin (eds.), *State, Democracy and the Military: Turkey in the 1980s* (Berlin, New York: Walter de Gruyter, 1988): 47–62.

———, "1960 Sonrası Türk Siyasal Hayatına Bakış: Demokrasi, Neo-Patrimonyalizm ve İstikrar," in Üniversite Öğretim Üyeleri Derneği (ed.), *Tarih ve Demokrasi: Tarık Zafer Tunaya'ya Armağan* (Istanbul: Cem Yayınevi, 1992): 87–126.

———, "Decentralization of Government," in Metin Heper and Ahmet Evin (eds.), *Politics in the Third Turkish Republic* (Boulder, San Francisco, Oxford: Westview Press, 1994): 87–100.

———, "Elections and Party Preferences in Turkey: Changes and Continuities in the 1990s," *Comparative Political Studies*, vol. 27, no. 3 (October 1994): 402–424.

———, "The Turkish Grand National Assembly: A Brief Inquiry into the Politics of Representation in Turkey," in C. Balım et al. (eds.), *Turkey: Political, Social and Economic Challenges in the 1990s* (Leiden, New York, Köln: E. J. Brill, 1995): 42–60.

———, "Türkiye'de Siyasal Kültür ve Demokrasi," in Ergun Özbudun, Ersin Kalaycıoğlu, and Levent Köker (eds.), *Türkiye'de Demokratik Siyasal Kültür* (Ankara: Türk Demokrasi Vakfı Yayınları, 1995): 43–69.

———, "Constitutional Viability and Political Institutions in Turkish Democracy," in Abdo I. Baaklini and Helen Desfosses (eds.), *Designs for Democratic Stability: Studies in Viable Constitutionalism* (Armonk, New York, London, England: M. E. Sharpe, 1997): 179–210.

———, "The Shaping of Party Preferences in Turkey: Coping with the Post-Cold War Era," *New Perspectives on Turkey*, no. 20 (Spring 1999): 47–76.

———, "Turkish Democracy: Patronage versus Governance," *Turkish Studies*, 2, no. 1 (Spring 2001): 54–70.

———, "The Motherland Party: The Challenge of Institutionalization in a Charismatic Leader Party," in Barry Rubin and Metin Heper (eds.), *Political Parties in Turkey* (London, Portland, OR: Frank Cass, 2002): 41–61.

———, "State and Civil Society in Turkey: Democracy, Development and Protest," in Amyn B. Sajoo (ed.), *Civil Society in the Muslim World: Contemporary Perspectives* (London, New York: I. B: Tauris Publishers, 2002): 247–272.

———, "Civil Society in Turkey: Continuity or Change?" in Brian W. Beeley (ed.), *Turkish Transformation: New Century—New Challenges* (Walkington, England: The Eothen Press, 2002): 59–78.

Kalaycıoğlu, Ersin, "Turkey's Choice: The Road Away from the European Union," in Bertil Dunér (ed.), *Turkey: The Road Ahead?* (Stockholm: The Swedish Institute of International Affairs, 2002): 119–133.

———, "Elections and Governance" in Sabri Sayarı and Yılmaz Esmer (eds.), *Politics, Parties, and Elections in Turkey* (Boulder, London: Lynne Rienner, 2002): 55–71.

———, "Electoral Realignment or Protest Vote: November 2002 Elections in Turkey," (unpublished paper presented at the annual Convention of the International Studies Association, Portland, Oregon, USA, February 25–March 1, 2003).

———, "The Mystery of the '*Türban*': Participation or Revolt?" *Turkish Studies,* vol. 6, no. 2 (June 2005): 233–251.

Kalaycıoğlu, Ersin and Ali Yaşar Sarıbay, "İlkokul Çocuklarının Parti Tutmasını Belirleyen Etkenler," *Toplum ve Ekonomi*, 1 (March 1991): 137–149.

Kalaycıoğlu, Ersin and Binnaz Toprak, *İş Yaşamı, Üst Yönetim ve Siyasette KADIN* (Istanbul: TESEV Yayınları, 2004).

Kaplan, Mehmet, "Ziya Gökalp'in Hayatı ve Eserleri Hakkında Birkaç Söz," in Ziya Gökalp (ed.), *Türkçülüğün Esasları (Türk Klasikleri)* (prepared for publication by Mehmet Kaplan) (Istanbul: Milli Eğitim Bakanlığı Yayınları, 1990): I–VII.

Karakaş, Eser, "Mali Krizin Bir Başka Boyutu," (August 29, 2003) <www.finansalforum. com>.

Karal, Enver Ziya, "*Preface*," in Yusuf Akçura (ed.), *Üç Tarz-ı Siyaset* (Ankara: Türk Tarih Kurumu Basımevi, 1976): 1–18.

Karaman, Suphi, "Written Responses," in Suna Kili (ed.), *27 Mayıs 1960 Devrimi, Kurucu Meclis ve 1961 Anayasası* (Istanbul: Boyut Kitapları, 1998): 173–189.

Karpat, Kemal, *Turkey's Politics: The Transition to a Multiparty System* (Princeton, New Jersey: Princeton University Press, 1959).

———, "War on Cyprus: The Tragedy of Enosis," in Kemal Karpat (ed.), *Turkish Foreign Policy in Transition: 1950–1975* (Leiden: E. J. Brill, 1975): 186–205.

———, *The Gecekondu: Rural Migration and Urbanization* (Cambridge, England: Cambridge University Press, 1976).

———, *Political and Social Thought in the Contemporary Middle East* (New York, Washington, London: Praeger, 1970).

———, *Ottoman Population 1830–1914: Demographic and Social Characteristics* (Madison, Wisconnsin: The University of Wisconsin Press, 1985).

Keating, Michael, *The Politics of Modern Europe* (Hants, England, Vermont: Edward Elgar, 1993).

Kirişçi, Kemal, "The Future of Turkish Policy Toward the Middle East," in Barry Rubin and Kemal Kirişçi (eds.), *Turkey in World Politics: An Emerging Multiregional Power* (Boulder, London: Lynne Rienner Publishers, 2002): 93–113.

Kirişçi, Kemal and Gareth Winrow, *The Kurdish Question and Turkey: An Example of Trans-State Ethnic Conflict* (London, Portland, Oregon: Frank Cass, 1997).

Kepenek, Yakup and Nurhan Yentürk, *Türkiye Ekonomisi* (expanded and revised tenth ed.) (Istanbul: Remzi Kitabevi, 2002).

Kili, Suna, "Değerlendirmeler," in Suna Kili (ed.), *27 Mayıs 1960 Devrimi, Kurucu Meclis ve 1961 Anayasası* (Istanbul: Boyut Kitapları, 1998): 109–269.

Kinross, Patrick, *Atatürk: The Birth of a Nation* (London: Phoenix Press, 1964).

Kirişçi, Kemal, *Justice and Home Affairs: Issues in Turkish—EU Relations* (Istanbul: TESEV Publications, 2002).

Koçak, Cemil, *Türkiye'de Milli Şef Dönemi (1938–1945)* (vol. 2) (İstanbul: İletişim Yayınları, 1996).

Kuruç, Bilsay, "Economic Growth and Political Stability," in Metin Heper and Ahmet Evin (eds.), *Politics in the Third Turkish Republic* (Boulder, San Francisco, Oxford: Westview Press, 1994): 135–159.

Kushner, David, *The Rise of Turkish Nationalism 1876–1908* (London: Frank Cass, 1977).

Kuyucak, Hâzim Âtıf, *Para ve Banka: Bankacılık, vol. II* (Istanbul: İsmail Akgün Matbaası, 1948).

Koçak, Cemil, *Türkiye'de Milli Şef Dönemi (1938–1945)* (vol. 2) (Istanbul: İletişim Yayınları, 1996).

Köprülü, Fuat, *Türk Edebiyatında İlk Mutasavvıflar* (Ankara: Diyanet İşleri Başkanlığı Yayınları, 1966).

Kut, Şule, "The Aegean Continental Shelf Dispute between Turkey and Greece," *Balkan Forum*, vol. 3, no. 1 (1995): 179–206.

———, "Soğuk Savaş Sonrasında Türkiye'nin Balkan Ülkeleriyle İlişkileri," in Ismail Soysal (ed.), *Çağdaş Türk Diplomasisi. 200 Yıllık Süreç* (Ankara: Türk Tarih Kurumu Basımevi, 1999): 387–408.

Küçük, Hülya, *The Role of the Bektaşis in Turkey's National Struggle: A Historical and Critical Study* (Leiden, Boston, Köln: Brill, 2002).

Lerner, Daniel, *The Passing of Traditional Society* (New York, The Free Press, 1958).

Lewis, Bernard, *The Emergence of Modern Turkey* (London, Oxford, Toronto: Oxford University Press, 1961).

———, *Islam in History: Ideas, People, and Events in the Middle East* (new edition, revised and expanded) (Chicago and La Salle, Illinois: Open Court Publishing Co., 1993).

———, *The Middle East: 2000 Years of History from the Rise of Christianity to the Present Day* (London: Phoenix, 1995).

Lipset, Seymour Martin, *Political Man: The Social Bases of Politics* (Garden City, New York: Anchor Books, 1963).

Loğoğlu, Faruk, *İsmet İnönü and the Making of Modern Turkey* (Ankara: İnönü Vakfı, 1997).

Maarif Vekaleti (Ministry of Education), *Tarih III* (Istanbul: Devlet Basımevi, 1931).

Mango, Andrew, *Atatürk* (London: John Murray, 1999).

Mardin, Şerif, "Ideology and Religion in the Turkish Revolution," *Middle East Studies*, 2: (1971): 197–211.

———, "Center-Periphery Relations: A Key to Turkish Politics?" in Engin D. Akarlı and Gabriel Ben-Dor (eds.), *Political Participation in Turkey: Historical Background and Present Problems* (Istanbul: Boğaziçi University Press, 1975): 7–32.

———, "Yenileşme Dinamiğinin Temelleri ve Atatürk," in (no editor), *Çağdaş Düşüncenin Işığında Atatürk* (Istanbul: Dr. Nejat Eczacıbaşı Vakfı Yayınları, 1983).

McCarthy, Justin, *The Ottoman People's and the End of Empire* (London: Arnold, 2001).

McCrone, Donald J. and Charles F. Cnudde, "Towards a Communications Theory of Political Development," *American Political Science Review*, vol. 61 (1971): 72–80.

McDowall, David, *The Modern History of the Kurds* (London, New York: I. B. Tauris, 2000).

Massicard, Elise, "Alevism as a Productive Misunderstanding: The Hacıbektaş Festival," in Paul J. White and Joost Jongerden (eds.), *Turkey's Alevi Enigma: A Comprehensive Overview* (Leiden, Boston: Brill, 2003).

Milliyet (daily) (August 31, 2003).

Milliyet (daily) (January 8, 2004): 1.

Mumcu, Ahmet, *Osmanlı Devletinde Siyaseten Katl* (Ankara: Sevinç Matbaası, 1985).

Mumcu, Uğur, *Kazım Karabekir Anlatıyor* (second ed.) (Istanbul: Tekin Yayınevi, 1990).

———, *Kürt–İslam Ayaklanması: 1919–1925* (Istanbul: Tekin Yayınevi, 1991).

———, *Gazi Paşaya Suikast* (eleventh ed.) (Istanbul: Tekin Yayınevi, 1994).

OECD, *Tax Administration in OECD Countries: Comparative Information Series* (Paris, 2004).

Official Gazette (Resmi Gazete) November 10, 2002, no.: 24932: 39.

Oktay, Ali, "Erbakan 3.7 milyon Doların Peşinde," (2003) <www.aksam.com.tr/2003/08/05/ozel/ozel1.html. >

Oktay, Cemil, *Yükselen İstemler Karşısında Türk Siyasal Sistemi ve Kamu Bürokrasisi* (Istanbul: Istanbul Üniversitesi Siyasal Bilimler Fakültesi Yayınları, 1983).

Olson, Mancur Jr., *The Logic of Collective Action: Public Goods and the Theory of Groups* (New York: Schoken Books, 1971).

Öniş, Ziya, "Domestic Politics versus Global Dynamics: Towards a Political Economy of the 2000 and 2001 Financial Crisis in Turkey," *Turkish Studies*, vol. 4, no. 2 (Summer 2003): 1–30.

Öz, Baki, *Bektaşilik Nedir? Bektaşilik Tarihi* (Istanbul: Der Yayınları, 1997).

Öz, N. Semih, "Karşılaştırmalı Vergi İstatistikleri ve Uluslararası Vergilendirmede Geleceğe Yönelik Eğilimler," *Vergi Sorunları*, no. 196 (January 2005): 11–22.

Özbudun, Ergun, *Social Change and Political Participation in Turkey* (Princeton, New Jersey: Princeton University Press, 1976).

———, "Turkish Party System: Institutionalization, Polarization, and Fragmentation," *Middle Eastern Studies*, vol. 17, no. 2 (1981): 228–240.

———, *Türk Anayasa Hukuku* (Ankara: Yetkin Yayınları, 1986).

———, *1921 Anayasası* (Ankara: Atatürk Kültür, Dil ve Tarih Yüksek Kurumu, Atatürk Araştırma Merkezi Yayınları, 1992).

———, *Contemporary Turkish Politics: Challenges to Democratic Consolidation* (Boulder, London: Lynne Rienner, 2000).

Peretz, Don, *The Middle East Today* (fifth ed.) (New York, Westport, London: Praeger, 1988).

Quataert, Donald, *The Ottoman Empire: 1700–1922* (Cambridge, England: Cambridge University Press, 2001).

Rasmussen, Jorgen S. and Joel G. Moses, *Major European Governments* (Belmont, California: Wadsworth, 1995).

Rıfat, Mevlanazâde, *31 Mart: Bir İhtilâl'in Hikayesi* (simplified by Berire Ürgenci) (Istanbul: Pınar Yayınları, 1996).

Robins, Philip, *Suits and Uniforms: Turkish Foreign Policy since the Cold War* (Seattle: University of Washington Press, 2003).

Rubin, Barry and Metin Heper (eds.), *Political Parties in Turkey* (London, Portland, OR: Frank Cass, 2002).

Rustow, Dankwart, *Turkey: America's Forgotten Ally* (New York: Council of Foreign Relations, 1987).

Sartori Giovanni, *Parties and Party Systems: A Framework for Analysis* (Cambridge, London, New York, Melbourne: Cambridge University Press, 1976).

Sayarı, Sabri and Yılmaz Esmer (eds.), *Politics, Parties and Elections in Turkey* (Boulder and London: Lynne Rienner Publishers, 2002).

Seale, Patrick, *The Struggle for Syria: A Study of Post-War Arab Politics 1945–1958* (New Haven, London: Yale University Press, 1986).

Selek, Sabahattin, *Anadolu İhtilali: Milli Mücadele I* (second ed.) (Istanbul: Istanbul Matbaası, 1965).

Shaw, Standford J. and Ezer Kural Shaw, *History of the Ottoman Empire and Modern Turkey: Volume II: Reform, Revolution and the Republic: The Rise of Modern Turkey, 1808–1975* (Cambridge, London, New York, Melbourne: Cambridge University Press, 1977).

Soysal, İsmail, *Soğuk Savaş Dönemi ve Türkiye: Olaylar Kronolojisi (1945–1975)* (Istanbul: ISIS, 1997).

Soysal, Mümtaz, *Dinamik Anayasa Anlayışı: Anayasa Diyalektiği Üzerine bir Deneme* (Ankara: Ankara Üniversitesi Siyasal Bilgiler Fakültesi Yayını, 1969).

Sönmezoğlu, Faruk, *Türkiye—Yunanistan İlişkileri ve Büyük Güçler: Kıbrıs, Ege ve Diğer Sorunlar* (Istanbul: Der Yayınları, 2000).

State Institute of Statistics (DIE), *Statistical Yearbook of Turkey* (Ankara, DIE Publications, 1993).

Shankland, David, *Islam and Society in Turkey* (Hundington, Cambridgeshire, England: The Eothen Press, 1999).

Sunar, Ilkay, *State and Society in the Politics of Turkey's Development* (Ankara: Ankara Universitesi Siyasal Bilgiler Fakültesi Yayını, 1975).

———, "Populism and Patronage: The Demokrat Party and Its Legacy in Turkey," *Il Politico*, vol. LV, no. 4 (October–December 1990).

Syrigos, Angelos M., *The Status of the Aegean Sea According to International Law* (Athens: Sakkoulas/Bruylant, 2000).

Tachau, Frank, *Turkey: The Politics of Authority, Democracy, and Development* (New York, Philadelphia, Eastbourne, Toronto, Sydney, Hong Kong: Praeger, 1984).

Taçalan, Nurdoğan, *Ege'de Kurtuluş Savaşı Başlarken* (Istanbul: Milliyet Yayınları, 1970).

Taner, Tahir, "Ceza Hukuku," in Komisyon (ed.), *Tanzimat 1* (Ankara: Milli Eğitim Bakanlığı Yayınları: no. 3273, 1999): 221–232.

T. C. Başbakanlık Devlet İstatistik Enstitüsü (State Institute of Statistics), *2000 Genel Nüfus Sayımı: Nüfusun Sosyal ve Ekonomik Nitelikleri: Türkiye* (Ankara: Devlet İstatistik Enstitüsü Matbaası, 2003).

Tekeli, İlhan and Selim Ilkin, "Türkiye'de Ulaştırmanın Gelişimi," in (no editor) *Cumhuriyet Dönemi Türkiye Ansiklopedisi* (Istanbul: Iletişim Yayınları, 1983): 2758–2768.

Toker, Metin, *Tek Partiden Çok Partiye* (Istanbul: Milliyet Yayınları, 1970).

———, *Şeyh Sait ve İsyanı* (İkinci Basım) (Ankara: Bilgi Yayınevi, 1994).

Tonguç, Engin, *Devrim Açısından Köy Enstitüleri ve Tonguç* (Istanbul: Ant Yayınları, 1970).

Tunaya, Tarık Zafer, *Türkiye'de Siyasi Partiler 1859–1952* (Istanbul: Doğan Kardeş Basımevi, 1952).

———, *Türkiye'de Siyasal Partiler: Mütareke Dönemi 1918–1922, vol. II* (Istanbul: Hürriyet Vakfı Yayınları, 1986).

———, *Türkiye'de Siyasal Partiler: İttihat ve Terakki: Bir Çağın, Bir Kuşağın, Bir Partinin Tarihi, vol. III* (Istanbul: Hürriyet Vakfı Yayınları, 1989).

———, *İslamcılık Akımı* (Istanbul: Simavi Yayınları, 1991).

Tuncer, Erol, *Osmanlı'dan Günümüze Seçimler: 1877–1999* (Ankara: Toplumsal Ekonomik Siyasal Araştırmalar Vakfı (Tesav) Yayınları, 2002).

Turan, Ilter, *Cumhuriyet Tarihimiz: Temeller, Kuruluş, Milli Devrimler* (Istanbul: Çağlayan Kitabevi, 1969)

———, "Sunuş," in Sabahattin Şen (ed.), *Su Sorunu, Türkiye ve Ortadoğu* (Istanbul: Bağlam Yayınları, 1993): 9–15.

Tüzün, Gürel and Sibel Sezer (eds.), *World Summit on Sustainable Development Johannesburg 2002, National Report: Turkey* (Ankara: The Ministry of Environment and the United Nations Development Programme, 2002).

TBMM (TGNA) (1982), *Secim, Seçim Sistemleri ve Türkiye'deki Uygulamalar* (Ankara: TBMM Basımevi, 1982).

Tukin, Cemal, *Boğazlar Meselesi* (Istanbul: Pan Yayıncılık, 1999).

Turkish Daily News (December 14 and 15, 1997).

TÜSİAD, *Türkiye Ekonomisi 2004* (İstanbul: TÜSİAD Publications, 2004).

The Under Secretariat of Treasury, *Treasury Statistics 1980–2002* (Ankara: General Directorate of Economic Research of the Under Secretariat of the Treasury, 2003).

Undersecretariat of the Prime Ministry for Foreign Trade <www.dtm.gov.tr/ead/english/indicators/indc.htm>, 2004: Table ecoindicators.

Ülgener, Sabri, *İktisadi Çözülmenin Ahlak ve Zihniyet Dünyası* (Istanbul: Der Yayınları, 1981).

Veldet, Hıfzı, "Kanunlaştırma Hareketleri ve Tanzimat," in Komisyon (ed.), *Tanzimat 1* (Ankara: Milli Eğitim Bakanlığı Yayınları: no. 3273, 1999): 139–209.

Weekes, Richard V. (editor-in-chief), *Muslim Peoples: A World Ethnographic Survey* (Westport, Conn., London: Greenwood Press, 1978).

Weiker, Walter F., *The Turkish Revolution 1960–1961: Aspects of Military Politics*, (Washington, D.C.: The Brookings Institute, 1963).

White, Paul J. and Joost Jongerden (eds.), *Turkey's Alevi Enigma: A Comprehensive Overview* (Leiden, Boston: E. J. Brill, 2003).

Winrow, Gareth, "Turkey and the Newly Independent States of Central Asia and the Transcaucasus," in Barry Rubin and Kemal Kirişçi (eds.), *Turkey in World Politics: An Emerging Multiregional Power* (Boulder, London: Lynne Rienner Publishers, 2002): 173–188.

<www.mfa.gov.tr/grupe/ea/ea009.htm>.

<www.mfa.gov.tr/turkce/grupg/ge/001.htm>.

Yalman, Nur, "Some Observations on Secularism in Islam: The Cultural Revolution in Turkey," *Daedalus*, no. 102 (1973): 139–167.

Yapp, M. E., *The Making of the Modern Middle East: 1792–1923* (London and New York: Longman, 1987).

———, *The Near East Since the First World War: A History to 1995* (second ed.) (Harlow, London, New York: Longman, 1996).

Yenal, Oktay, *Cumhuriyet'in İktisat Tarihi* (Istanbul: Türkiye Sınai Kalkınma Bankası, 2001).

Yeşilada, Birol, "The Copenhagen Criteria and the Challenge of Democratization in Turkey," (unpublished paper presented at the 2003 Annual Convention of the International Studies Association in Portland, Oregon, February 25–March 1, 2003).

Yıldız, Ahmet, *İhtilalin İçinden: Anılar, Değerlendirmeler* (Istanbul: Alan, 2001)

Zürcher, Erik Jan, *The Unionist Factor: The Role of the Committee of Union and Progress in the Turkish National Movement 1905–1926* (Leiden: E. J. Brill, 1984).

———, *Political Opposition in the Early Turkish Republic: The Progressive Republican Party 1924–1925* (Leiden, New York, København, Köln: E. J. Brill, 1991).

———, *Turkey: A Modern History* (London, New York: I. B. Tauris, 2001).

INDEX